IN THE BORDERLAND BETWEEN SONG AND SPEECH

LUND UNIVERSITY PRESS

In the borderland between song and speech

Vocal expressions in oral cultures

EDITED BY

HÅKAN LUNDSTRÖM AND JAN-OLOF SVANTESSON

Lund University Press

Copyright © Manchester University Press 2022

While copyright in the volume as a whole is vested in Lund University Press, copyright in individual chapters belongs to their respective authors.

Lund University Press
The Joint Faculties of Humanities and Theology

LUND
UNIVERSITY
PRESS

P.O. Box 192
SE-221 00 LUND
Sweden
http://lunduniversitypress.lu.se

Lund University Press books are published in collaboration with Manchester University Press.

British Library Cataloguing-in-Publication Data
A catalogue record for this book is available from the British Library

ISBN   978-91-985577-6-3   hardback

First published 2022

An electronic version of this book is also available under a Creative Commons (CC-BY-NC-ND) licence, thanks to the support of Lund University, which permits non-commercial use, distribution and reproduction provided the author(s) and Lund University Press are fully cited and no modifications or adaptations are made. Details of the licence can be viewed at https://creativecommons.org/licenses/by-nc-nd/4.0/

The publisher has no responsibility for the persistence or accuracy of URLs for any external or third-party internet websites referred to in this book, and does not guarantee that any content on such websites is, or will remain, accurate or appropriate.

Lund University Press gratefully acknowledges publication assistance from the Thora Ohlsson Foundation (*Thora Ohlssons stiftelse*)

Typeset
by Cheshire Typesetting Ltd, Cuddington, Cheshire

Contents

List of illustrations	page ix
Audio recordings	xii
List of contributors	xiii
Acknowledgements	xv

1 The borderland: singing or speaking or both?   1
Håkan Lundström and Jan-Olof Svantesson

Background	2
The borderland between song and speech	4
The performance template	9
The collaboration	10
The layout of the book	12
The source material	14
The transcriptions	16

2 Kammu vocal genres (Laos)   20
Anastasia Karlsson, Håkan Lundström, and Jan-Olof Svantesson

Kammu language and vocal expressions	23
ANALYSIS 1	
Lɔ̀ɔŋ, narrative style	31
ANALYSIS 2	
Kàm à-thí-tháan, prayer	43
ANALYSIS 3	
Ɔ̀ɔc, 'Begging' at New Year	49
ANALYSIS 4	
The vocal genre hrlii̵	55
ANALYSIS 5	
The vocal genre hrwə̀	64

ANALYSIS 6	
The vocal genre *húuwə̀*	68
ANALYSIS 7	
The vocal genre *yàam*	73
ANALYSIS 8	
The vocal genre *yùun tìiŋ*	77
ANALYSIS 9	
The vocal genre *tə́əm*	84
ANALYSIS 10	
Krùu, 'spells'	97
Kammu summary	118

3 Athabascan vocal genres in Interior Alaska   123
Siri G. Tuttle and Håkan Lundström

Alaskan Athabascan language and vocal expressions	125
ANALYSIS 11	
Raven song	135
ANALYSIS 12	
Caribou song (Tanana)	137
Dratakh ch'elik	140
ANALYSIS 13	
Dolo k'adi, 'Missing Dolo'	142
ANALYSIS 14	
Segoya (Bettis, Nenana)	147
ANALYSIS 15	
Segoya (Titus John)	152
Structural framework of *drathak ch'elik*	157
Ch'edzes ch'elik	160
ANALYSIS 16	
Joni ło'o, 'Here it is!' (Tanana)	164
ANALYSIS 17	
Christmas tree	167
Athabascan leadership and composing	170
ANALYSIS 18	
Caribou people version 2 by Norman Carlo	177
The *ch'edzes ch'elik* performance template	187

4 Seediq canonic imitation (Taiwan)   189
Arthur Holmer and Håkan Lundström

The Seediq language and vocal expressions	190

	ANALYSIS 19	
	Uuyas obio, 'The *obio* song'	192
	ANALYSIS 20	
	Meeting and working in the fields	195
	Poetry, metre, and rhythm	200
	The Seediq imitation performance template	202

5 An Akha shaman performance (Thailand) — 204
Inga-Lill Hansson and Håkan Lundström

	Akha language and the shaman's vocal expression	206
	General starting points	207
	The performance	208
	ANALYSIS 21	
	Realization of lexical tones in identical lines	210
	ANALYSIS 22	
	Performance of line-pairs	215
	ANALYSIS 23	
	Performance of the final part	218
	ANALYSIS 24	
	Variation	221
	The Akha shaman performance template	224

6 *Waka* and *ryūka* performances (Japan/Ryukyu) — 226
Yasuko Nagano-Madsen and Håkan Lundström

	Waka and *ryūka*	228
	ANALYSIS 25	
	Two *waka* performances	229
	The *waka* performance template	235
	ANALYSIS 26	
	Three *ryūka* performances	237
	The *ryūka* performance template	244
	Speech and vocal expression	244
	Waka and *ryūka* summary	246

7 Performance templates: method, results, and implications — 248
Håkan Lundström and Jan-Olof Svantesson

	Performance template as method	249
	Parameters in performance templates	252
	Implications	272

Appendix 1: Software used 290
Appendix 2: Number notation 300
Appendix 3: Terminology used 302

References 307
Index 319

Illustrations

Figures

1 Kàm Ràw performing a perception test with another Kammu speaker in the village of Thapen, close to Luang Prabang in Laos, 1996 (Photo: Håkan Lundström) — page 21
2 Kàm Ràw demonstrating the simultaneous playing of gong and cymbals when singing the song Kʔə́əy kɔ́ɔn mɔ́ɔ, 'Calling the shaman spirits', of the shaman seance (Photo: Håkan Lundström) — 99
3 Elders listen to, and comment on, archival recordings at Neal and Geraldine Charlie's house in Minto, August 2010 (Photo: Siri G. Tuttle) — 126
4 Norman Carlo dancing at the *Alaska Federation of Natives Convention* in Anchorage, in the autumn of 2015 (Photo used with permission from Norman Carlo) — 175
5 Wet-fields in the Seediq village of Gluban, central Taiwan, in August 2006 (Photo: Arthur Holmer) — 199
6 The swing festival in the Akha village of Saensuk, northwestern Thailand (Photo: Inga-Lill Hansson) — 206
7 A scene from the movie about Onna Nabii, showing the recitation of *Ryūka Unnadaki* and a transliteration with Japanese characters (Photo: Onna Village Chamber of Commerce and Industry) — 237

Maps

1 The geographical location of the languages and cultures included in the study (Courtesy of Jakob Cederblad) — 14

2 Map of Laos. The arrow shows the approximate location of the Yùan Kammu area (Courtesy of Jakob Cederblad) 22
3 Map of Alaska, including places and rivers occurring in the text (Courtesy of Jakob Cederblad) 124
4 Map of Taiwan with the approximate location of Seediq and other ethnic groups mentioned in the text (Courtesy of Jakob Cederblad) 190
5 Map of northern Thailand, with the approximate location of the Akha population and the village of Saensuk (Courtesy of Jakob Cederblad) 205
6 Map of the Ryukyu Islands, with the village Onna on the main island of Okinawa (Courtesy of Jakob Cederblad) 227

Tables

1 Vocal genres in the speech–song continuum with regard to the poetic techniques used in this study 30
2 Rice-narrative topics compared to the main agricultural seasons of the Kammu farming year 36
3 Number notation limited to the signs used in the examples 51
4 Characteristics of different Kammu genres of vocal expressions 119
5 Vocal expressions and native vocabulary in Minto (Lower Tanana) 132
6 Structural outline of *dratakh ch'elik* 158
7 Metres and their realization in the sections of the two performances 201
8 Summary of comparison between *waka* and *ryūka* performances 246
9 The *melody* parameter summarized from all performance templates (Analyses 1–26) 253
10 The *rhythm* parameter summarized from all performance templates (Analyses 1–26) 255
11 The *form* parameter summarized from all performance templates (Analyses 1–26) 257
12 The *phrasing* parameter summarized from all performance templates (Analyses 1–26) 259
13 The *initial/final formulae* parameter summarized from all performance templates (Analyses 1–26) 262

14 The *word variations* parameter summarized from all
   performance templates (Analyses 1–26)   265
15 The *lexical tones* parameter summarized from all
   performance templates (Analyses 1–26)   268
16 Kammu vocal genres in the speech–song continuum with
   regard to poetic techniques, word variations, rhythm,
   and melody   274

Audio recordings

These recordings are available on Manchester Open Hive, www.manchesteropenhive.com/borderland/sound

- 01 Rice narrative — Examples 5, 8
- 02 *Lɔ̀ɔŋ ŋɔ̀ɔr* — Examples 14–15
- 03 *Ɔ̀ɔc* — Examples 22–23
- 04 *Nàaŋ mɛ̀ɛn, hrlïi* — Examples 26–27
- 05 *Nàaŋ mɛ̀ɛn, hrwɔ̀* — Examples 32, 35
- 06 *Nàaŋ mɛ̀ɛn, húuwɔ̀* — Example 36
- 07 *Nàaŋ mɛ̀ɛn, yàam* — Examples 42–43
- 08 *Yùun tìiŋ* — Example 45
- 09 *Nàaŋ mɛ̀ɛn, tɔ́əm* — Examples 49–50
- 10 *Pàh mòŋ*, B1a — Example 52
- 11 *Táa píc*, Last phrase — Example 60
- 12 *Krùu ɔ̀ɔy róoy* — Example 61
- 13 *Krùu ptú róoy rwàay ɔ̀ɔk*, C–D — Example 63C–D
- 14 Raven song — Examples 70, 135–139, 141
- 15 Caribou song, Neal — Example 72
- 16 *Dolo k'adi* — Example 74
- 17 *Segoya*, Bettis — Example 77
- 18 Caribou people, v1 1st phrase a and b — Example 87a–b
- 19 Caribou people, v2 1st phrase — Example 87c
- 20 Caribou people v2 2nd phrase — Example 88
- 21 *Obio* — Example 98
- 22 Working in the fields — Example 99
- 23 *Sjhá-gàw* 166:6 — Example 100, 106
- 24 *Sjhá-gàw* 166:8 — Example 101a
- 25 *Sjhá-gàw* 167:8a — Example 101b
- 26 *Sjhá-gàw* 166:7 — Example 107
- 27 *Sjhá-gàw* 169:6 — Example 108
- 28 *Waka Naniwazu* 1 — Example 117
- 29 *Ryûka Unnamachi* — Example 130

Contributors

Inga-Lill Hansson, Associate Professor Emerita, Department of East Asian Studies, Lund University, specializes in Akha/Hani language and culture. She conducted fieldwork among the Akha in northern Thailand in several periods: two years 1977–78, about two months per year 1981–91 and shorter visits more or less annually until 2013, when one of her main informants passed away. She is currently working with digitization and archiving of her extensive fieldwork material.

Arthur Holmer, Associate Professor, Centre of Languages and Literature, Lund University, received his PhD in 1996 for a thesis dealing with the Austronesian language Seediq, spoken in Taiwan. He has also worked with an analysis of the syntax in the Mon-Khmer language Kammu, spoken in Laos, as well as with Basque. His research interests include syntactic typology and the mapping of semantics to syntax. He is currently engaged in investigating various aspects of word-order variation in Formosan languages.

Anastasia Karlsson, Affiliated Professor of Phonetics, Centre for Languages and Literature, Lund University, conducts research in phonetics with a main focus on typological prosody, with empirical studies of a number of typologically different languages, such as Kammu, Formosan languages (Bunun, Puyuma, and Seediq), and Khalkha Mongolian. Her thesis from 2005 is on the prosody of Khalkha Mongolian. She has described underlying differences between prosodic systems of tonal and non-tonal languages on the basis of Kammu speech data.

Håkan Lundström, Professor Emeritus, Inter Arts Center, Malmö Faculty of Fine and Performing Arts, Lund University, has been a member of the Kammu research project in Lund for a long time; his

PhD thesis in Musicology deals with a Kammu singing tradition. He has also studied Japanese and Alaskan Native American musics. As Dean of the Malmö Faculty of Fine and Performing Arts, he was involved in a long-term exchange and development programme between Malmö and Hanoi, which included research on the music of ethnic minorities in Vietnam.

Yasuko Nagano-Madsen, Professor Emerita of Japanese, University of Gothenburg, is a phonetician and linguist specialized in prosody (rhythm, accent, tone, and intonation), who has worked with Japanese, Ryukyuan, and Greenlandic (Eskimo). Her PhD thesis in phonetics (1992) deals with a comparison of syllable structure and related prosodic features in Japanese, Eskimo, and Yoruba. Recently, she has conducted intensive fieldwork in Okinawa in order to study the prosody of Ryukyuan dialects.

Jan-Olof Svantesson, Professor Emeritus, Centre for Languages and Literature, Lund University, is an expert on Yùan Kammu and the long-term coordinator of linguistic research on Kammu. He was awarded his PhD in General Linguistics in 1983 for a dissertation on Kammu phonology and morphology. He has subsequently worked on different aspects of the Kammu language, including a dictionary of Yùan Kammu. His other research interests include Mongolian phonology.

Siri G. Tuttle, Professor of Linguistics, Alaska Native Language Center, University of Alaska Fairbanks, is an Athabascan-languages specialist with a special interest in prosody (tone, stress, and intonation). Her dissertation was on the Tanana language. She has been involved in community-based linguistic research, including a Tanana learners' dictionary, 'bridge' materials to assist language-revitalization efforts, and continued study of Athabascan prosody and grammar. Her linguistic interests include the dissemination of archived language information in formats useful to communities.

Acknowledgements

The present volume is the outcome of many years of research conducted at Lund University, some of it within the framework of the so-called 'Kammu Project'. As editors, we wish to express our profound gratitude to all those, scholars and informants, who have taken part in this research over the years. From 2011 to 2014, the Swedish Research Council generously supported the research project after which this book was named, 'In the Borderland between Song and Speech: Vocal Expressions in Oral Cultures'. For this, too, we extend our warmest thanks.

Håkan Lundström and Jan-Olof Svantesson
Editors

1
The borderland: singing or speaking or both?

Håkan Lundström and Jan-Olof Svantesson

The aim of this study was to pursue greater knowledge of vocal expressions in the borderland between speech and song through collaboration between researchers with different approaches, with a view to developing an interdisciplinary method for the analysis of such expressions. The research presented here is the outcome of the research project 'In the Borderland between Song and Speech. Vocal Expressions in Oral Cultures' carried out in 2011–14 with support from the Swedish Research Council. The starting point was a conference on endangered languages and musics, *Humanities of the Lesser-Known*, organized in Lund in 2010, which brought together those who came to be the members of the Borderland project.[1]

The material is intercultural and includes a variety of language and music contexts: Kammu (Laos), Akha (Thailand), Seediq (Taiwan), Tanana (Interior Alaska), and Ryukyuan (Okinawa, Japan). A long-term aim has also been to play a part in the revitalization of such oral traditions and to contribute to their sustainability. The languages belong to different language families, Austroasiatic (Kammu), Sino-Tibetan (Akha), Austronesian (Seediq), Athabascan (Tanana), and Japonic (Ryukyuan). They are spoken in different parts of the world, but they also have much in common. Except for Ryukyuan, they lack a written tradition, and most of them are endangered to some degree. Tanana and Ryukyuan have very few speakers, and even Kammu, with at least half a million speakers and Akha with still more, are under constant pressure from the majority languages in their areas. Kammu and Akha are fully fledged tone languages and Tanana and Ryukyuan use lexical tones to some extent.

Our main interest has not been in what is performed – be it 'song', 'recitation', 'prayer', or 'narration' – but in the techniques

---

1 Svantesson, Burenhult, Holmer, Karlsson, and Lundström 2011.

that make improvisation, variation, re-creation, and creation possible in the kind of performances we include in the concept *vocal expression*. Thus, we focus on performance and not on the vocal expressions as artefacts. When we speak of transmission, it is not about the transmission of individual 'poems' or 'songs' but about the intergenerational transmission of the techniques used in order to realize vocal expressions in performance. When we study material from diverse cultures, the goal is not comparison in itself but, rather, understanding the diversity of culturally specific techniques of performance.

Background

The question of how music and language relate to each other, how they are combined or integrated, has been approached from different perspectives which have increased both our knowledge and the number of questions that arise. A recurring subject is the origin of song and speech.[2] Recent theories tend to see a common origin, believing that song and speech have diversified during the evolution of humans as biological and social beings.[3] From another perspective, it has been shown that language and music share the same cognitive resources, and even that the phonology of an individual's native language can influence both musical appreciation and composition.[4] A further approach is the particular study of tone languages and music that involves transcription methods.[5] In this study, we will focus on the language–music relation in sung or recited performances from different, predominantly oral, cultures by combining methodologies from musicology and linguistics.

In everyday situations, the meanings of 'speech' and 'song' are quite commonly agreed upon. However, turning to music traditions in cultural settings where music is mainly orally transmitted, the term 'song' is often problematic. It is, in itself, ethnocentric and may therefore in many ways be misleading. Furthermore, in research about orally transmitted singing the concept of 'song' has been closely associated with the concepts 'original' and 'variant'. These concepts are ideologically burdened, since they imply that it is possible

---

2 See Brabec de Mori 2017: 116–119 for a summary of theories of the origin of song.
3 Brown 2000 and Mithen 2007.
4 Patel 2008.
5 Schellenberg 2017.

The borderland: singing or speaking or both?

to find one original for a number of versions of the same song, which are thus considered as variants of this known or implied original. This approach is relevant in some situations, but there are also contexts where there is no such thing as an 'original'. This has been expressed by Albert Lord in an approach that permits one to understand something as multiform:

> Our real difficulty arises from the fact that, unlike the oral poet, we are not accustomed to thinking in terms of fluidity. We find it difficult to grasp something that is multiform. It seems to us necessary to construct an ideal text or to seek an original. I believe that once we know the facts of oral composition we must cease trying to find an original of any traditional song.[6]

In her discussion about 'oral composition and oral literature', Ruth Finnegan examines Lord's view on oral composition, using examples from oral traditions in the Pacific where she also finds fixity in the pattern composition–rehearsals–performance that involves memorization. This leads her to conclude that there is more than one method of composition in oral contexts.[7]

In the English language, concepts like 'song', 'declamation', 'recitation', 'incantation', and 'chant' are – without being exactly defined – normally used to distinguish different genres of vocal performance. In a similar manner, many cultures use different names for more or less distinctly different forms of expression. In some cases, these different forms are quite clearly defined. In the Kammu language, spoken by an ethnic group in northern Laos, for instance, these terms may be understood as levels of 'speech' or levels of 'song' that represent different positions on a continuum from 'speech' to 'song', in which there is much overlapping in matters like prosody vs. melody, or rhythm vs. rhythmic patterns. What we refer to as the 'borderland between song and speech' is a segment of this continuum.

The term *vocal expression* will be used as a neutral term for expressions that cannot easily be defined as either speech or song.[8] It is a term that is not limited to one culture, but can be used globally. As far as possible, indigenous terms will be used, normally rendered in italics. Sometimes it is necessary to talk about 'song',

---

6 Lord 1960: 100.
7 Finnegan 1988: 86–109.
8 The term was introduced in Lundström 2010: 15.

'recitation', and the like in a very general sense – especially in discussions of, or communication with, related research when referring to the borderland between song and speech or when discussing 'school songs'.

Among ethnic minority groups in South-East Asia, the existence of levels of performance is closely related to the re-creation, extemporization, or improvisation of vocal expressions. This is realized in performance by the combination of traditional sets of words or newly created sentences with pre-existing melodic and poetic templates. This is typical of the *mono-melodic* organization of music culture, in which a limited number of melodic formulae are used for many sets of words.[9] In such cases, the interplay between language and music is crucial.[10] In the special case of tone languages, yet another interplay between language and music occurs, which may take on different forms.[11] Since vocal expressions are closely linked with language, there is a risk that they will disappear as language-knowledge disappears. Most of the languages studied are endangered to some degree, and these musical/poetical traditions are consequently endangered to the same extent as the language they represent.

The borderland between song and speech

Research on the relationship between music and language carried out by musicologists or linguists has a long history. When the ethnomusicologist Steven Feld analysed this field of research in 1974, he found that

> [i]nterest thus far in the language–music relationship occurs at two distinct levels; one being the overlap of musical and linguistic phenomena, the other being the possibilities of applying linguistic models to musical analysis.[12]

In his study of the Kaluli people in Papua New Guinea, Feld worked with a combined ethnomusicological/linguistic approach in order to interpret the social and symbolic levels of Kaluli aesthetics in

---

9 See Lundström 2018: 988–992 for mono-melodic organization and for singing manners among South-East Asian ethnic groups.
10 Lundström 2010: 165.
11 Lundström 2010: 51ff. and Lundström and Svantesson 2008.
12 Feld 1974: 197.

The borderland: singing or speaking or both? 5

which nature metaphors play a central role.[13] In collaboration with Aaron A. Fox a decade later, he recognized four main categories in research on music and language:

1 *Music in language*: the musical dimensions of language (prosody, rhythm, and timing);
2 *Music as language*: application of formal linguistic models to music, creating different 'grammars' of music;
3 *Language about music*: the discourse that surrounds and interacts with musical practice;
4 *Language in music*: different ways in which language and music interact in musical contexts, and especially in song texts.[14]

Our research interest basically falls under the heading 'overlap of musical and linguistic phenomena'. Since we are interested in how language and music interact, though not primarily in 'song texts', our research belongs to the fourth category: *Language in music*. It also relates to the first category: *Music in language*, since we are interested in the musical aspects of prosody, rhythm, phrasing, and lexical tones.

In an article on poetry, Giorgio Banti and Francesco Giannattasio discuss 'Between speaking and singing':

> There are in every culture ways of expression that are ideally intermediate between language and music. They result from different levels of formalization of speech by means of timbric, rhythmic, and/or melodic procedures that heighten and specialize its symbolic effect[.][15]

The vocal expressions they choose in order to exemplify the area between speaking and singing are prayers and magic spells for flat or monotone contour and Maori *haka* for heightened speech, with further examples from children's counting rhymes, funerary lamentations, religious preaching, and political speeches.

In an attempt to organize forms of vocal expression in which music and language overlap, George List placed them in a continuum from 'speech' to 'song' on one axis and from 'monotone' to 'sprechstimme' on the other axis.[16] He used English terms, well aware of the difficulties in translating them to terms in other languages, and

---

13 Feld 1982.
14 Feld and Fox 1994, summarized after Sleeper 2018: 3–6.
15 Banti and Giannattasio 2006: 295.
16 List 1963: 9. This article was preceded by a study of 'Speech melody in song melody in Central Thailand' that also includes a discussion of lexical tones in relation to intonation and melody; List 1961.

his in-between forms include 'recitation', 'intonational recitation', 'chant', and 'intonational chant'.

Anthony Seeger compared several genres of verbal forms of the Amazonian Suyá in a chapter named 'Suyá vocal art: from speech to song'.[17] Under 'textual fixity', he lists the genres on a continuum from 'free text without parallelism' to 'entirely fixed text & parallelism through repetition': everyday speech, plaza speech, myth performance, ceremonial recitative, invocation, and song (*ngére* and *akua*). Seeger summarizes them in a triangular fashion:

> Top corner: *ngére* (song). Priority of melody over text;
> time, text, and melody fixed by non-human source.
> Left bottom corner: *kapérni* (speech). Priority of text over melody;
> text and melody determined by speaker;
> increasing formalization in public performances.
> Right bottom corner: *sarén* (telling) and *sangére* (invocation);
> relative priority of somewhat fixed texts over relatively established melodies.

These are different ways of looking at the overlapping of song and speech, or what we have called the borderland between song and speech, seen as two poles of a continuum with no distinct border between the two phenomena. Consequently, this borderland, in itself, is seen as an area with no distinct borderlines. This is one way to approach the speech/music event as a whole, something that is strongly advocated by Anthony Seeger:

> Far too often music and the other verbal arts are treated in isolation from each other. The separation of the various disciplines that deal with music and speech has had a disastrous effect on the development of our thinking about them [...] Linguists have often ignored the features of oral style that are not grammatical or syntactic; literary scholars have often ignored the linguistic; and ethnomusicologists have spent years analyzing sound structures, but paying insufficient attention to the meaning of the texts. All this has been done in isolation. The failure to recognize the interrelationship of verbal and musical genres and the importance of the ways they are used can result in a dry formalism which reifies the text, performance, or melody and does not [...] account for the richness and use of verbal art forms.

In research on the overlapping of language and music, it is necessary to combine linguistics and (ethno)musicology in order to

---

17 A. Seeger 1987: 25–51. Quotations from pp. 45, 50, and 51.

The borderland: singing or speaking or both?

obtain meaningful results. That this is a growing field of research is evident from the increasing numbers of conferences and workshops that bring researchers together by focusing on this field, as a whole or in certain aspects. Another indication of this is the appearance of special journal issues devoted to this theme.[18]

George List, Steven Feld, and Anthony Seeger developed this area of research as ethnomusicologists, with insights into linguistics and verbal art. But there are also examples of collaboration between ethnomusicologists and linguists. Linda Barwick points to an especially strong tradition of such collaboration in the study of aboriginal music in Australia.[19] In studies of this kind, the expertise of ethnomusicologists and linguists of different specializations is brought together to give a fuller description and analysis of the objects studied. This is rewarding for both sides, partly because there are many interrelations between language and music in vocal expressions where the two overlap and partly because so little is generally known about both the language and the music.

As a result of the developments in combining ethnomusicological and linguistic approaches, new methodologies are being tried out. In a PhD thesis in linguistics titled 'Musicolinguistics: New Methodologies for Integrating Musical and Linguistic Data', Morgan Sleeper uses different technological resources in three case studies in order to integrate the two approaches. These are his starting points:

> Two potential obstacles to combining music and language data in linguistics are (1) a lack of methodological precedents for integrating

---

18 Including the conferences *Humanities of the Lesser-known: New Directions in the Description, Documentation and Typology of Endangered Languages and Music* (Lund, Sweden 2010: see Svantesson, Burenhult, Holmer, Karlsson, and Lundström 2011), *Conference on Diversity and Universals in Language, Culture, and Cognition* (KNAW, Leiden 2013), *The Music of Endangered Languages FEL XIX–NOLA* (New Orleans 2015: see Ostler and Lintinger 2015), *International Council for Traditional Music* (Limerick 2017: see Engelhardt and Amy de la Bretèque 2017) and workshops like *Relationships of Speech Tone and Music* (Vienna 2012: see Schöpf 2014), *Text-setting Constraints in Tone Languages* (Nias, Wassenaar, Netherlands, 2016). Apart from these conference publications, there are special journal issues including *Australian Aboriginal Studies* 2007: 2 (see Marett and Barwick 2007), *Journal of the Phonetic Society of Japan* 22: 3 (see Karlsson, Svantesson, and Lundström 2018).
19 Barwick 2006: 53. See further Marett and Barwick 2001; Barwick, Birch, and Evans 2007; Turpin 2011; Bracknell 2017; and O'Keeffe 2017.

the two, and (2) the belief that musical context does not add to (or change) linguistic analysis. To that end, this dissertation aims to provide the former, and to prove the latter false[.][20]

At Lund University, Sweden, Kristina Lindell (1928–2005), who was a field linguist specializing in the language, narratives, and general culture of the Kammu people in northern Laos, created a research group in the early 1970s. The 'Kammu Language and Folklore' project became a long-lived project under different names.[21] Among the members were the linguist Jan-Olof Svantesson and the ethnomusicologist Håkan Lundström. Together with other researchers, we (Svantesson and Lundström) worked with the same material from different angles, and we collaborated over the documentation of vocal expressions in the material.[22] This background permitted the publication of one person's repertoire of orally transmitted poems used for vocal expressions, with glossing and translations.[23] This person was Kàm Ràw (Damrong Tayanin, 1938–2011), who grew up in a Kammu village and became a key co-worker in the research project. Collaboration with him led to a dissertation in musicology in 1999, with a focus on his technique of re-creating vocal expressions in the mono-melodic tradition of his home area.[24] These results were prerequisites for the 'Borderland' project. There was thus a long tradition of interdisciplinary research in ethnomusicology and linguistics at Lund University, pretty much in line with the general development of the field; and from the time the 'Borderland' project was conceived, around 2009/10, its researchers have played active roles in international developments.

---

20 Sleeper 2018: 1.
21 The research project has been described in Lundström and Svantesson (eds) 2005. The publications include lexicon (Svantesson, Kàm Ràw, Lindell, and Lundström 2014), folk narratives (Lindell, Swahn, and Tayanin 1977, 1980, 1984, 1989, 1995, 1998), grammar (Svantesson 1983, Holmer 2005, Svantesson and Holmer 2014), music (Lundström and Tayanin 1982 and 2006, Lundström 2010), ethnobotany (Engstrand, Widén, M., Widén, B., Kàm Ràw, and Svantesson 2009), mythology, religion, and prosody (Karlsson, House, and Svantesson 2012).
22 See for example Lundström and Svantesson 1996, 2005, 2008.
23 Lundström and Tayanin 2006.
24 Lundström 2010.

The performance template

In our approach, the term *vocal expression* for those expressions in which speech and song overlap serves as a culturally neutral term. It is also chosen as a neutral term in our interdisciplinary research. 'Song', 'recitation', 'narrative', etc. all have a research history and praxis in (ethno)musicology and the various linguistic specializations. Focusing the research on vocal expressions is a way to avoid bias based on existing practices by approaching the object of research as something new that we know very little about.

As regards the composition of oral poetry, Ruth Finnegan discusses 're-creation and re-composition theories' that explain variations in the transmission process.[25] Here we use the term 're-creation' to denote the process of the performance of vocal expressions of material that existed prior to the performance occasion, but which has no normalized 'original version'. In such cases, two or more different versions of the same basic material are thus seen as re-created differently. This kind of process is also described by Francesca Lawson in relation to narrative arts in Tiānjīn, China:

> The prescriptions used by the performers, then, are aural and textual – not notational – and the knowledge of these paradigms is embedded within an oral-aural tradition of apprenticeship [...] Since the aural and textual prescriptive notations are blueprints for countless possible permutations that can be realized in performance, there is no single definitive performance.[26]

Our assumption is that re-creation, in this sense, can be analysed by isolating performance templates. These templates that 'relate to the meter of the text or would directly relate to the text itself' were used by Nigel Fabb in the metrical analysis of poetry.[27] It goes back to the 'delivery instance' of Roman Jakobson concerning vocal renderings of poetry, defined as 'the verse line as it is actually performed'.[28] Here, the concept *performance template* will be widened so as to relate to other aspects of language than metre, and to include music as well.

The performance template is a tool used for analysis of a performer's assumed mental image of a vocal expression, which makes

---

25 Finnegan 1992: 144–145.
26 Lawson 2011: 54.
27 Fabb 1997: 94 exemplifies this by the recitation of Japanese *haiku*.
28 Jakobson 1987: 79.

the principles for the interaction of language and music visible. It is applied when re-created vocal expressions are performed and consists of analysis based on the following parameters: *melody, rhythm, form, phrasing, initial/final formulae, word variations* and *lexical tones*.

This kind of analysis has previously been applied to certain vocal expressions in Kammu culture.[29] One objective of the present research project has been to develop and deepen this approach and, in this process, test the extent to which it can be applied to the material. That material includes vocal expressions that lie close to recitation or rhythmicized speech, i.e. in the borderland between speech and song, though some expressions are more 'song-like'. Some parts of the material are based on syllable-counting poetry, whereas some consist partly or totally of vocables. The material includes vocal expressions that easily fit the concept of re-creation and involve much variation, sometimes improvisation, while others are composed beforehand and are supposed to be performed anew in the same way.

The collaboration

The collaboration between the seven members of the research team has been accomplished at three levels: collectively, in smaller constellations depending on specific topics, and individually. The work has been coordinated throughout. In recurrent working meetings, theoretical and methodological perspectives have been discussed and developed and the results jointly examined. Most of the researchers involved in this collaboration live in different cities in Sweden, and one lives in Alaska. Physical meetings have therefore often been combined with the use of Skype. Tuttle had an opportunity to spend an academic year in Lund, which increased the possibilities of continuous meetings and in-depth communication.

It soon became obvious that there are many differences between linguistics and ethnomusicology, and also between different branches of linguistics. Sometimes we use different terms for the same thing. In other cases, the same term means different things. In addition, some terms are so specific to the field of research in question that they are not easily comprehensible in other fields. In some cases,

---

29 Lundström 2010.

The borderland: singing or speaking or both?

we agreed on new terms: vocal expression, vocal genre, melody-centred, tone-centred, etc. Other terms were listed in a glossary explaining how they are used in this book (see Appendix 3). In some cases, it was necessary to adapt terms. For instance, the term 'phrase' has different meanings in musicology and linguistics – sometimes they coincide, but not always. When the meaning is not clear from the context, we use terms such as musical phrase or linguistic phrase. These adaptations were necessary in our communication in order to avoid misunderstandings; or, rather, it was often through misunderstandings that such problems were identified.

Most steps in the progression of the research have made it necessary to proceed from documented performances, which involves much basic work. In most cases, there is little or no previous research that tackles these matters in the performances studied here. Regarding language, most of our material is complex even at the most basic level of transcription and translation. In many cases, the performers themselves were not able to fully explain the meanings of words or expressions. Musically, the performances are often very open regarding form, as words are often added or subtracted by the performer and as melodic movement is also often varied in combination with speech intonation and, in some cases, lexical tones. As a result, many problems at a basic level of analysis had to be solved in order to achieve any results at a systematic or higher level.

One major challenge has been the combination of linguistic and musicological research. In this process, we have experimented with different formats for representation of the audio recordings that were studied. This has been done partly to facilitate communication between the researchers, and partly in order to present the working methods and results to the reader. Consequently, this book contains a great many graphs, tables, and notations. The software and their use are explained in Appendix 1. Transcription – whether musical notation or various kinds of graphs – and analysis usually make it necessary to break down the sounding totality into segments, sometimes very small ones. All the performances are, of course, totalities, with a flow of sounds and a direction, so one consequence of dividing them into segments is that the conclusions in each case relate to the whole performance. A choice of the actual recordings used is also made available to the reader; see p. xii in this volume.

Presentations at conferences and seminars have been of great importance in several ways. They have not only set useful deadlines and created opportunities to provide information about our research activities or findings, and to benefit from networking and feedback. They have also given us reasons to spend time together in various constellations, enabling us to collaborate on specific themes and to develop a stepwise progression of our research.

The layout of the book

The researchers have worked as a team when discussing methods and outcomes, and they have also worked on specific topics in various sub-groups. The layout of this book basically reflects the chronological order in which the research developed, even though, in reality, there has been considerable overlapping between the different branches of the research. Different sections form chapters, with their separate authors. Parts of these chapters have been published as articles or as presentations at conferences, but this is the first time that we are putting them together as a whole. In so doing, we have chosen to list 26 case studies as 'Analysis 1–26' across the chapters of the book. While the chapters reflect the separate sub-areas of our research, the analyses are intended to reflect totality and continuity. Thus, we attempt to present the results reached concerning each sub-area, as well as the overall results that are presented in the concluding discussion.

As mentioned above, a network of scholars at Lund University has been working on a long-term documentation of the Kammu, an Austroasiatic-speaking people in Laos, starting around 1970 with several research projects targeting different aspects of their language and culture. Chapter 2, 'Kammu vocal genres (Laos)', is based on the fact that the material contains a rather large number of vocal genres performed by a single person. This makes it possible to isolate a number of separate performance templates within one cultural context. The Kammu dialect we studied is a tone language with two lexical tones. The material also permits a detailed study of the role of the lexical tones, as well as their realization in the performance of the different vocal genres.

The research on the Native American Athabascan language and the culture of Interior Alaska carried out at the University of Alaska Fairbanks has likewise produced a substantial material over a number of years.[30] There is also a link to Lund University that dates back

---

30 Including language and culture (Kari 1994, Kari and Fall 2003), music (Pearce 1985), and language and music (Tuttle 1998, 2011).

The borderland: singing or speaking or both? 13

to fieldwork carried out in Alaska in the 1960s and 1970s.[31] Since the available Athabascan material covers a time period of approximately half a century, it is to some extent possible to relate orally transmitted vocal expressions in newly collected material to older samples. However, there had been no actual collaborations between musicology and linguistics before the present studies were commenced. Therefore, Chapter 3, 'Athabascan vocal genres in Interior Alaska', also includes a basic description of vocal expressions. An important aspect of this culture is that of *song-making*, either by instant improvisation or by carefully planned composition.

These chapters report extensive research that was carried out in order to use the combined approach of musicology and linguistics as well as the performance template as an analytic tool. The three following chapters are case studies which aim to test the analysis method that utilizes performance templates. Chapter 4, 'Seediq canonic imitation (Taiwan)', focuses on two related, newly recorded performances. The music of the aboriginal groups in Taiwan has been studied by Taiwanese and Japanese researchers. Our own knowledge was in the area of language.[32] It was therefore necessary to develop a musical understanding of the material before searching for performance templates. A special feature of this genre is imitation between performers.

The Akha minority in northern Thailand is geographically rather close to the Kammu in northern Laos, but the two belong to different language families. Chapter 5, 'An Akha shaman performance (Thailand)', is a study of a section of one performance chosen from an extensive documentation of the Akha language. Our competence was mainly in Akha language and texts, while no collaboration between linguistics and music preceded this study.[33] This performance is very long, and some sections from the beginning, middle, and end were chosen for analysis.

Chapter 6, '*Waka* and *ryūka* performances (Japan/Ryukyu)', uses material from a culture that has had a writing system for a very long time, but where there are still contexts in which the vocal performance of poetry is orally transmitted. The main knowledge of the area was in the field of language, and there had been no preceding collaboration between linguistics and musicology.[34] The

---

31 Rooth 1971, Lundström 1980.
32 For example Holmer 1996.
33 For example Hansson 1983, 1991, 1994, 2014, 2017.
34 Nagano-Madsen 1992, 2015, 2016.

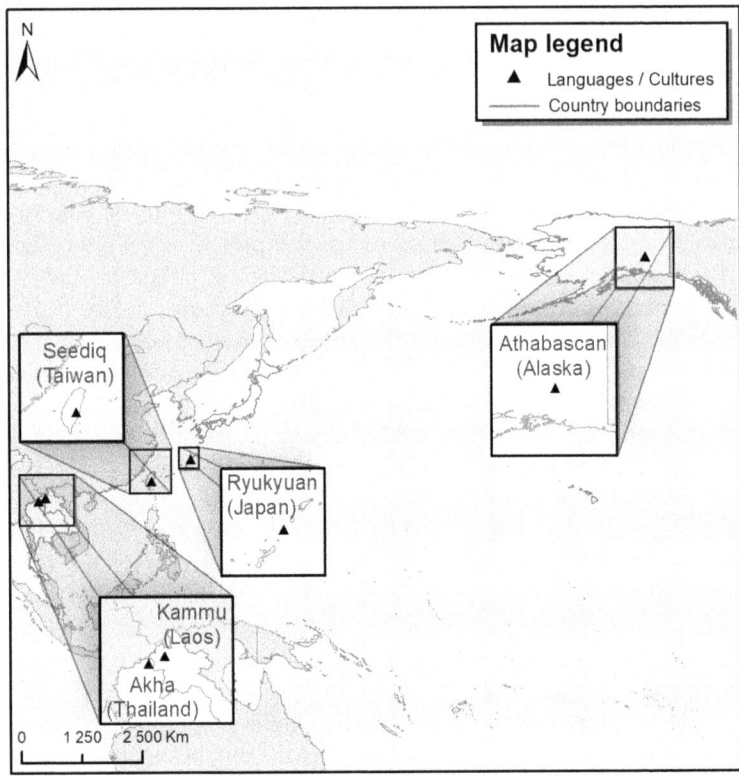

Map 1 The geographical location of the languages and cultures included in the study.

vocal expressions studied are vocal renditions of short poems: *waka* of Japan and *ryūka* of Ryukyu. While the two kinds of performance are very short, with a fixed number of syllables and similar progression of rhythm and pitches, there are differences in their relation to speech intonation.

The source material

The material used is basically of three kinds: field material in individual researchers' collections or in archives; field material gathered in new fieldwork; and material from publications. As regards Kammu traditions there is an extensive material, stemming from the mountain village of Rmcùal in northern Laos, that has been collected and analysed in the long-term project at Lund University.

The borderland: singing or speaking or both? 15

The data contain a considerable amount of narratives and vocal expressions, including information on transmission and also general linguistic and cultural information. Most of this material exists in the form of recordings, in audio media ranging from open-reel tapes and cassette tapes to digital files, and in visual media ranging from drawings, black-and-white photos, colour photos, diapositives, VHS videos, Hi8 and DV to digital videos. During the project period, we have helped to sort out this material for digitization for a database in the 'Rwaai: Digital Multimedia Archive of Austroasiatic Intangible Heritage' project at Lund University, headed by Associate Professor Niclas Burenhult.[35]

Interior Athabascan tales and myths, including vocal expressions, were recorded in Alaska in 1966 and published by Anna Birgitta Rooth. They were analysed in two studies that also described the context of storytelling in Alaska.[36] Descendants of the storytellers are still living there. The source material has been expanded as a result of new information from continuous fieldwork in Interior Alaska carried out by Siri G. Tuttle. Recordings and transcriptions are available at the Alaska Native Language Archive at the University of Alaska, and in publications.[37]

An extensive material of narratives was collected from aboriginal groups in Taiwan in the 1930s by the Japanese scholars Takuji Ogawa and Susuma Asai; it has subsequently appeared in English translation.[38] Recent fieldwork data collected for other purposes include recordings of these and similar narratives from past decades for Seediq, Bunun, and Puyuma. Music of the aboriginal groups has been documented in one study and in recordings. There is a recent study about the present-day musical culture of the Amis minority.[39] New material has been gathered by Arthur Holmer as a result of fieldwork periods, particularly among the Seediq and the Puyuma.

The Akha material basically stems from extensive fieldwork in northern Thailand carried out by Inga-Lill Hansson and commenced

---

35 Internet source: *Rwaai*.
36 Rooth 1971, 1976, 1980. The complete recordings have been digitized with support from the Anér Foundation (Gunvor och Josef Anérs Stiftelse). They are available at the Alaska Native Language Center, Fairbanks, and at Uppsala University Library, Sweden.
37 Pearce 1985, Kari and Fall 2003, Tenenbaum 2006.
38 Baudhuin 1960.
39 Hsu and Cheng 1992, Tan 2012.

in the 1970s. There is an extensive recorded material on partly digitized cassette tapes. All these recordings have been transcribed and translated, and there are also detailed and well-organized field notes. This material is all in Hansson's private archive, which is in the process of being digitized.

For the Ryukyuan study, material in the database 'Okinawa's Old Chant' (Okinawa Cultural Promotion Association) has been used. The information about the Ryukyuan language comes from Yasuko Nagano-Madsen's own fieldwork there, and her subsequent analysis and publications.

In some of the cases, the ethical considerations have been solved naturally by long-term collaboration between researchers and 'informants'. In the case of Kammu, Kàm Ràw (also known by his Thai name, Damrong Tayanin) became a co-worker over more than three decades of collaboration with researchers. The Athabascan elders in Minto, Alaska also took an active part in encouraging the researchers to work with the traditional vocal expressions and spread this knowledge. The work with Akha was conducted in collaboration with knowledgeable individuals over a long time period. Many of these co-workers have passed away, and we feel obliged to continue our commitment to their legacy. Part of the Athabascan materials stem from a currently active *song-maker* and performer, Norman Carlo, who collaborates closely with Tuttle. He has read the text, provided corrections, and approved our description of his work. The work with the Seediq people in Taiwan has taken place in a larger context of preserving and disseminating the Seediq language and culture, with the full support of the speaker community. In the cases where we have used existing recordings, we have, wherever possible, found copyright holders and have their permission to use the material. In the case of the commercial Melodyne software, permission to use the graphs has also been acquired.

The transcriptions

Various methods of transcription of words, pitches, and rhythms have been tested in this study. The choice of method depends on the purpose of the transcription: what it is used for, and what factors are to be communicated. Another factor that influences the choice is how well known the relevant performance is to the researcher(s). In our study, for instance, Western notation was used for the musical transcription of the material in the Athabascan and Seediq sections (Analyses 11–20), basically because we did not know enough about

The borderland: singing or speaking or both? 17

those performance styles to start with. They therefore had to be approached separately as music and as language, with the intention of exploring whether it would be relevant to use the concept of performance templates.

Hence, the use of performance templates as a method leads to different applications depending on the material that is being studied. In some cases, it has been sufficient to transcribe the words and poetic phrases with marks added for lexical tones (Analysis 8). In others, the addition of number notation has been found useful (Analyses 3, 10); see Appendix 2. These forms of transcription have proved practical for the communication of linguistic and musical aspects. We have also experimented with letter notation (see Appendix 1), which may be easier to combine with analysis in the free software Praat and ELAN, as it can fairly easily be written into a tier, like other parameters.

Whatever method is used, each transcription depends on the interpretation made by the transcriber. Musical transcription, whether in musical notation or graphs, tends to approximate pitches musically as fixed tones, i.e. what is interpreted as the main part of a pitch is transcribed, while initial or final movement within a vowel or syllable is normally considered as just that: a sliding motion up to or away from the tone. Thus, a certain pitch is defined as a tone that may be approached or left with downward or upward movements. Changes in pitch during one such tone may be described as embellishments. In sum, the pitch notated is the one that best fits the transcriber's feeling of musical meaning. There is some degree of subjectivity and also ethnocentricity, since the notation system originated in the notation of Western classical music and since the transcriber's cultural musical experience may influence the interpretation. However, the result will be a musically meaningful transcription that communicates the musical sound as experienced by the transcriber and can hence be received by a person with a similar background in musicology.[40] The accuracy increases with the transcriber's knowledge of the music that is being transcribed.

An analysis based on phonetic expertise will approach the sounding material differently, with a stress on exact measurements. In principle, our experience has shown that music transcription adds the important perspective of transcribing motion while being less stringent with

---

40 See further C. Seeger 1964 for an account of a symposium on transcription and analysis organized by the Society for Ethnomusicology and List 1974 for a discussion of different techniques of transcription.

regard to factors that will be more precisely measured in the linguistic analysis. In interdisciplinary work based on musicology and linguistics, these approaches will be combined, and herein lies the strength of our interdisciplinary research. At the same time, this collaboration entails a need to communicate the results of the analyses between researchers of different backgrounds – in this case musicology and linguistics.

In interdisciplinary research involving musicology/ethnomusicology on the one hand and linguistics areas like phonetics or prosody on the other, both these approaches to transcription are necessary for the analysis of the material and for communication between the researchers.[41] As a result, various forms of graphic representations have been found particularly efficient for the analytical aspects, not least because there is software that can produce the underlying graphs. This analysis and the graphs produced are presented in Appendix 1: Software used.

Mechanical transcription has been around for a long time. Around 1900, the kymograph, which had been adapted to linguistic studies and could produce graphs, was used for musical sound as well. Seeger's melograph was an adaptation for the analysis of music. This was paralleled at Uppsala University, Sweden, where a machine for analysing monophonic music was developed in 1964.[42] The output was a paper strip that showed frequency (in Hertz) and amplitude along the horizontal time axis. These graphs could be used for detailed measurements, but it was hardly possible to create notations from them, and while they were useful for measurements, they were too detailed for musical notation. Often the two methods were combined: a slightly simplified graph derived from the mechanical transcription would normally be used, with a parallel transcription in notation.

Since then there have been huge developments with respect to note-editing software, as well as to software that converts digital material like MIDI (Music Instrument Digital Interface) into notation within the tempered tuning system, rhythm notation, and harmony developed in the tradition of Western classical and popular music. When it comes to digital transcription of music belonging to oral traditions, very little has actually happened, and there is still no

---

41 Schellenberg 2017 arrives at a similar conclusion.
42 This device was called Mona. Later, Polly was also developed for polyphonic music, as were additional devices for the specific study of rhythm. Bengtsson, Tove, and Thorsén 1972.

The borderland: singing or speaking or both? 19

software that can do this properly. From the point of view of music transcription, the software used in this study has many advantages and disadvantages in common with the old technology, with the important difference that it is faster and much more flexible when it comes to adjusting the scales of the vertical and horizontal axes. Another major difference is the possibility of watching the analysis in real time.

Some of the programs tested can export graphs, whereas others cannot. In a case of the latter sort, a screen dump must be made. In either case, it has often been necessary to use additional signs to demonstrate certain factors. Though mechanical transcription of sound facilitates the analysis in many ways, it is still time-consuming and involves considerable manual work.

Transcription is also a matter of defining the degree of precision needed for particular ends. In this study, most of the musical transcriptions are more or less rudimentary, and even a rough mechanical transcription would suffice – it could, whenever necessary, be used as a starting point for a more detailed transcription for use in research that would require such accuracy. The Melodyne software captures pitch and movement in a manner that is intuitive for a researcher with a musical approach, but the musical notation generated by the framework does not work for the transcription needed for ethnomusicology analysis. Praat or ELAN adds a great number of factors for detailed analysis of texts, but no musical notation. In the end, then, we had to use different kinds of software and interpolate between them manually.

There is no perfect software for the research method tried out here; but the results could suggest changes or additions to existing software. The development of mechanical transcription that communicates intuitively with researchers in both linguistics and musicology is an important task for the future.[43] It is not so much a question of replacing human transcription with mechanical transcription – this may not even be possible – but more a matter of developing the existing technology as far as possible in a direction that minimizes time-consuming manual work.

---

43 See further Zon 2007.

2
Kammu vocal genres (Laos)

Anastasia Karlsson, Håkan Lundström, and Jan-Olof Svantesson

The Kammu people are one of the ethnic groups in South-East Asia that traditionally live on mountain slopes, where they grow rice and other crops and hunt. They live in northern Laos and adjacent areas in Vietnam, Thailand, and China. The Yùan area, from which most of the material used here stems, is located in the Nalè area in the southern part of the Luang Namtha Province (Map 2). Kàm Ràw (also known as Damrong Tayanin, 1938–2011) was born and grew up in the village of Rmcùal (Figure 1). As a young man, he came to Thailand and eventually to Sweden, where he became a key informant and co-worker in the 'Kammu Language and Folklore' project at Lund University. Most of the vocal expressions studied in this chapter were performed by him, and he also wrote about his life in his home village. Like many other mountain villages, it has been abandoned and the villagers have moved to nearby communities.[1]

> Children didn't sing together with the grown-ups at parties, but in the fields they could do that. At feasts boys at the age of six or seven could sit on their fathers' knees. The elders used to say: 'You will never get good relations with other people if you don't sing. You will stay by yourself. You will never get people for parties and you can not go to another village or play with girls'. So the boys liked to sit on their fathers' knees and to learn. The following morning my father used to ask: 'Did you hear which song we used? Why do you think we used those?' Boys also used to gather by themselves during parties and try to sing like the grown-ups. Women did not join the drinking men but used to sit by themselves. If somebody sings to you then, like a question, you should be able to answer correctly in order not to lose face. At feasting, a singer chooses

---

1 Concerning this development see Évrard 2012.

Kammu vocal genres (Laos)

Figure 1 Kàm Ràw (right) performing a perception test with another Kammu speaker in the village of Thapen, close to Luang Prabang in Laos, 1996.

who should answer by nipping at that person's straw to the wine jar.[2]

In a Kammu village, there should be at least one shaman and one medicine man, since the Kammu people believe in spirits. In my home area, for instance, there were over 20 Kammu villages, but there was only my uncle Sɛ́ɛn who was a shaman in the entire area. Unfortunately he died in 1960. After he had died we had to find a shaman from a distant village when we needed him.

Anyone could become a shaman, depending on who is able to do the work. Both men and women can become shamans. In 1958, my uncle Sɛ́ɛn taught me and one of my cousins, Kàm Mán, how to become a shaman. In fact we knew most of the things already, because we had been together with him for years, but now he gave us extra, intensive training for a few months. To learn how to be a shaman is not easy at all, because one has to learn many different kinds of magic formulas and rites. There are hundreds of different spirits as I said above. There are specific magic formulas to call the various kinds of spirits. The suitable period for learning to be a shaman is when the sesame sets flowers, that is in September and October. This period is the best time for learning the magic formulae. Kammu

---

2 This story is about the vocal expression called *táam* (see Analysis 9). Summarized from Lundström 2010: 36.

Map 2 Map of Laos. The arrow shows the approximate location of the Yùan Kammu area.

people believe that if a person learns the magic formulae during this specific time, the spirits will both respect and fear him or her as a shaman.

When someone catches an illness caused by an evil spirit, that means that a spirit has entered his or her body. A shaman may then chase away the evil spirit from his body. We cannot heal illnesses caused by spirits by giving the patient medicine, the spirits have to be chased away. On the other hand, when someone has caught an ordinary illness or has wounded himself, the medicine man may use plant-medicine to heal the wound or cure the illness.[3]

---

[3] This passage concerns the *krùu* (see Analysis 10). Summarized from Tayanin 1994: 18–20.

Kammu language and vocal expressions

Previous studies of Kammu language and music had made it clear that the analysis of some vocal expressions from the perspective of a performance template is a rewarding pursuit.[4] One main objective at the start of this study was to investigate more vocal expressions in a search for different performance templates, as well as for differences and similarities between them. There was also some prior knowledge about the interplay of melody and lexical tones.[5] Another objective was to investigate how this interplay was practised in the various performance templates. Other factors, such as thematics in narratives, intonation, and reduplication of syllables, had not been studied before. Different methods of description or transcription of performances have been employed in this study, depending on the aims of the analysis in question, but also in order to communicate detailed information in a way that would be easily understandable for both linguists and musicologists.

The Kammu (Kmhmu', Khmuʔ, etc.) language belongs to the Mon–Khmer branch of the Austroasiatic language family and is spoken by some 600,000 people in northern Laos and adjacent areas of Vietnam, Thailand, and China.[6] There are three major dialects: Northern, Western, and Eastern Kammu. The Yùan variety of Kammu treated here is a sub-dialect of Northern Kammu, spoken in the Nalè area in the southern part of the Luang Namtha Province. Northern and Western Kammu have developed a system of two lexical tones, High and Low (denoted ´ and `, respectively), while Eastern Kammu, spoken further to the east and south in Laos, and also in Vietnam, retains the original state without distinctive lexical tones. These tones have developed from voiceless and voiced initial consonants, which gave rise to High and Low tone, respectively. For example, the Eastern Kammu minimal pair *klaaŋ* 'eagle' ~ *glaaŋ* 'stone' with a voiceless vs. voiced initial consonant corresponds to Northern Kammu *kláaŋ* ~ *klàaŋ* and Western Kammu *kláaŋ* ~ *kʰlàaŋ* with High vs. Low tone. Similarly, the Eastern Kammu pair *hraaŋ* 'tooth' ~ *raaŋ* 'flower', with a voiceless vs. voiced initial sonorant,

---

4 Lundström 2010.
5 Lundström and Svantesson 2008.
6 For information about Kammu culture, see Svantesson, Kàm Ràw, Lindell, and Lundström 2014 and references given there.

corresponds to Northern and Western Kammu *ráaŋ* ~ *ràaŋ*.[7] Our analysis here concerns the tonal Northern Kammu dialect; material from other dialects is shown only for comparison, in certain cases.

Northern Kammu words are written in the practical orthography used in other publications from the Kammu project at Lund University. In this orthography, *ñ* and *y* are written for IPA [ɲ] and [j]. Aspirated stops are written *kh* [kʰ], etc. Words with an initial vowel have a glottal stop as onset (e.g. *àn* [ʔàn]), and words ending in a short vowel have a glottal stop coda (*pə̀* [pə̀ʔ]).

Syllables and tones in Kammu

Like many other Mon-Khmer languages, Kammu has two kinds of syllables, usually called major and minor syllables. Minor syllables are unstressed pre-syllables with no phonemic vowel. Most words are either monosyllabic, consisting of one major syllable (e.g. *tís* 'mushroom'), or sesquisyllabic, consisting of one minor and one major syllable, e.g. *km̀mú* [kə̀m.múʔ] 'human being, Kammu' and *kmúul* [kə̀.múul] 'silver'. In careful pronunciation, minor syllables are often pronounced with a schwa vowel [ə], not indicated in the phonemic transcription.

Like major syllables, minor syllables also carry a tone in the northern tonal dialect. In most cases, the minor syllable tone can be predicted from the segmental composition of the word. There is a potential minor syllable tone contrast only when the minor syllable consists of two consonants and has an unaspirated stop as onset. Examples of minimal pairs are *pŋ́kà* 'to wear by the ear' vs. *pŋ̀kà* 'shy' and *pŕnɔ̀* 'broom' vs. *pr̀nɔ̀* 'carrying-sling'. Only about 30 minimal pairs have been found, whereas there are more than 900 minimal pairs (such as *ráaŋ* 'tooth' vs. *ràaŋ* 'flower') for the major syllable tone. In the transcription used here, the minor syllable tone is usually not indicated.[8]

---

7 See further Svantesson and Holmer 2014, and for more information on Kammu lexical tones and tonogenesis Svantesson 1983 and Svantesson and House 2006.

8 See further Svantesson 1983 and Svantesson and Karlsson 2004 for minor syllables and tones.

Intonation

The main function of intonation in Kammu is to signal prosodic phrasing.[9] The words in an utterance are grouped into phrases, and the end of each phrase is marked by a high (rising–falling) boundary tone. Here, 'phrase' is defined in prosodic terms, not to be confused with musical phrase. New information is placed utterance-finally, coinciding with the place of the boundary tone. This intonation pattern is found in both the tonal and the non-tonal dialects.

The lexical tones in the tonal dialects may interfere with the realization of the intonation pattern, but they do so only when the identity of a lexical tone is jeopardized. Example 1 is a schematized illustration of the intonation pattern (smooth curve) common to all Kammu dialects. Short horizontal bars show how the utterance intonation adapts to lexical tones. The high (rising–falling) phrase-final boundary tone is changed to low only when the combination of lexical tones in the final words is High–Low, since the identity of the Low lexical tone would be blurred by a high boundary tone.

Example 1 Stylized intonation pattern in Kammu. The curved lines show the dominating intonation pattern in both dialects. The shorter horizontal lines show how this pattern may be perturbed owing to the influence of the lexical tones (marked as H(igh) and L(ow)); in particular, a phrase-final High–Low lexical tone pattern (as in the final phrase) may eliminate the final rise.

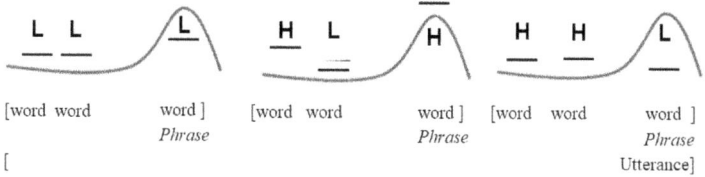

L L	L	H L	H	H H	L
[word word	word]	[word word	word]	[word word	word]
	Phrase		*Phrase*		*Phrase*
[					Utterance]

---

9 The way in which the intonation systems differ in non-tonal and tonal Kammu dialects was investigated in the 'Separating Intonation from Tone' project, supported by the Swedish Research Council, based on data collected in northern Laos in November 2007 and in northern Thailand in March 2008. A total of 24 speakers ranging in age from 14 to 72 were recorded. It was found that the main function of intonation in Kammu is to signal prosodic phrasing.

The realization of lexical tones is relational (linear): a High tone is higher than a preceding Low tone, and a Low tone is lower than a preceding High tone. Low and High tones tend to be realized in different pitch regions.[10] Henceforth, the terms low and high pitch region denote the different frequency areas used for Low and High tones in speech. A third, neutral pitch region is recognized in singing.

In addition to differences in F0,[11] timing of tones expressed as synchronization of the F0 peak in the syllable is relevant for describing lexical tones in Kammu. The tone is usually regarded as being realized in the entire rhyme (vowel + coda), at least in 'typical' Asian tone languages, such as Chinese or Thai. In Kammu, with no contour tones, the vowel kernel is a sufficient domain for realizing the tones, and tone is synchronized near the vowel onset, probably reflecting the involvement of syllable-initial consonants in tonogenesis.

Syllable reduplication and prolongation

A special kind of syllable reduplication, where the vowel of the base syllable is repeated, often occurs in recitation and song but not normally in speech. The reduplicated vowel may be short or long, sometimes longer than the vowel of the base syllable. Prolongation of the vowel or of a final sonorant is also common. Occurrences of reduplication and prolongation are genre-dependent.

Syllable reduplication is illustrated in Example 2, where vowel length is not indicated in the reduplicated form, as the duration may vary with the vocal genre. A dot (.) represents the syllable boundary. The coda of the base syllable often becomes the onset of the reduplicant (a). The reduplicant can also acquire the onset *h* or *ʔ*, especially when the base syllable is open, lacking a coda (b), but in other cases as well (c). Prolongation of syllables takes two different forms, either as a lengthening of the vowel or as a lengthening of a final sonorant: *nàaŋ* >*nàa.ŋŋ*. In very few cases, a sonorant onset is prolonged. The patterns of reduplication and lengthening differ between the different vocal genres.

---

10 For more details on pitch regions, see Karlsson, Lundström, and Svantesson 2018.
11 F0 = fundamental frequency (first harmonic) of, e.g., the sound of a voice.

Example 2 Syllable reduplication in Kammu.

(a) nàaŋ   >nà.ŋa   'dear'
    pɔ́ɔ́c   >pɔ́.cɔ   'bamboo'
    lès   >lè.se   'close'

(b) tàa   >tà.ha   'at'
    yʌ̀ʌ   >yʌ̀.ʔʌ   'with'

(c) àn   >àn.ha   'let'
    yèt   >yèt.he   'stay'

Phonetic measurements

The main principle in analysing vocal expressions in Kammu was to regard the tonal phrasing pattern in speech (Example 1) as the underlying melodic default pattern for both tonal and non-tonal dialects.[12] The description concentrates on the extent to which the vocal genres retain the intonation of ordinary speech, and also on how they differ from speech in the treatment of lexical tones. In this way we can identify more or less speech-like vocal expressions. Pitch was measured in Praat, noting the measurements in Microsoft Excel and constructing graphs in Microsoft PowerPoint. For each syllable, F0 was measured at the vowel onset and at the next two turning points of the pitch movement within the rhyme. These F0 values were measured both in the original syllable and in the reduplicant (the reduplicated syllable). In some genres, syllables can have more than three turning points of pitch, especially in prolonged and reduplicated syllables resulting from the singer's vibrato that belongs to the musical performance. Three turning points were measured, irrespective of the number of turning points within the syllable. In cases with less than three turning points, two points were taken. All measurements were performed manually. Furthermore, to compare genres the following parameters were taken into account:

- the amount of reduplication;
- the syllabic location of prolongations (onset, nucleus, or coda);
- tonal movements and their syllabic location (in original syllables or reduplicants) and their alignment (early/late within the syllable);

---

12 Based on Karlsson, House, and Svantesson 2012.

- the realization of lexical tones: by using separate pitch regions or by local pitch changes (relational realization).

The melodic transcription for each genre was checked for its relation to lexical tones. Melodies were analysed as underlying patterns of performance templates, similar to intonation in speech, and lexical tones as a separate level. This approach was used in order to establish whether melody only consists of lexical tones; whether there is a melodic pattern, separate from lexical tones, to which lexical tones are modulated; or whether the melodic pattern itself is modulated when conflicting with tones, as was seen to happen with speech.

An example of vibrato and measurement points is given in Example 3. The word is *síi-pàay* 'bean'. The first syllable *síi* has High tone, the second syllable has Low tone, and both syllables are reduplicated: *síi-ʔi-pàa-yaa*. Vibrato occurs in the reduplicant *yaa*. $f0_1$, $f0_2$ and $f0_3$ indicate the points of measurement in each syllable: $f0_1$ is measured at the vowel onset, and $f0_2$ (and $f0_3$) are measured at the next F0 turning points.

Example 3 Illustration of vibrato and measurement points of F0. The word is *síi-pàay* 'bean' with reduplicated syllables: *síi-ʔi-pàa-yaa*. Female singer. Genre: *tə̀əm*.

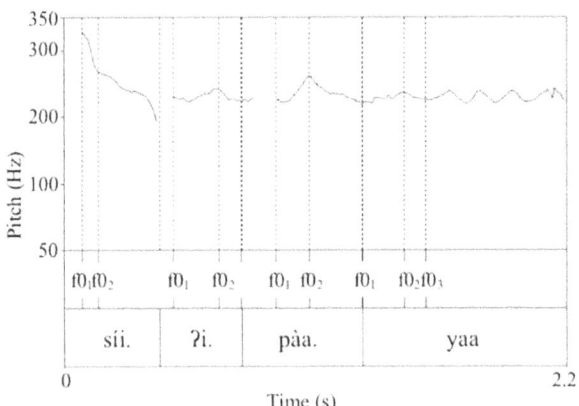

The vocal genres

The borderland between song and speech that is the focus of our research can be described as a section of a continuum of vocal expressions spanning from speech to 'song'. When the Kammu vocal expressions are ordered on such a continuum, the poetic and musical complexity appears to increase the closer we get to 'song'. Naturally, there will be some overlapping and other inconsistencies; but the image provides a useful overview. In this chain, each poetic technique may be seen as a special and more complex case of the preceding one: *Reduplication* → *Lexical parallelism* → *Pivot-rhyme* → *Chain-rhyme* → *Cross-rhyme*. Musically, the metrical and rhythmic organization becomes more fixed the closer we come to 'song', and this is paralleled by increased range and an increase in stable pitches (Table 1).[13]

The Kammu source material

Except where otherwise noted, the material referred to in this study stems from the Kammu research project at Lund University, which dates back to 1972 and lives on in the form of individual research and various short-term projects.[14] The vocal expressions discussed here are unique in the sense that they all come from one performer, Kàm Ràw, born in the village Rmcùal in northern Laos, and were recorded over a long period of time. This repertoire has been chosen because many genres are represented and because it permits study of variations within the repertoire without the uncertainty that may be caused by individual variations. However, this does not mean that the research has been limited to this repertoire. On the contrary, many performances by representatives of the same dialect area, and other areas as well, have been analysed in order to verify the reasonableness of our results.

---

13 This continuum was discussed in Lundström 2014.
14 See further Lundström and Svantesson (eds) 2005.

Table 1 Vocal genres in the speech–song continuum with regard to the poetic techniques used in this study

← SPEECH								SONG →
Lòɔŋ (narratives)	*Kàm à-thí-tháan* (prayers)	Ceremonial expressions (*Ɔɔc*, etc.)	*Krùu* (spells)	*Hrlii*	*Hruvà, Húuwà*	*Yàam*	*Yùun túŋ*	*Tàəm*
Analysis 1	Analysis 2	Analyses 3, 8a	Analysis 10	Analysis 4	Analyses 5–6	Analysis 7	Analysis 8b	Analysis 9

Anaphora
Parallelism
Vowel or consonant rhymes

Pivot rhymes

Chain-rhymes

Cross-rhymes (*trnàəm*)

Rhymed words of address

Analysis 1 Lɔ́ɔŋ, narrative style

Meaning approximately 'chanting', lɔ́ɔŋ is, in a general sense, used for various vocal genres. Here it will be exemplified by a specific style of vocal expression that occurs in narratives about daily activities, and in one prayer with the aim of showing the soul of a deceased person the way to the village of the dead.

By analysing syntactic and tonal properties of everyday speech, some types of narratives were found to have similar information and prosodic structure not found in other genres, for instance folktales. These narratives typically list certain types of activities. Most of the recordings are spontaneous accounts of rice-growing, from which it was possible to establish features typical for this genre. Compared to other speech genres, a high degree of rhythmization is found in the narrative accounts. Rhythmization is attained by tonal, segmental, and syntactic means. The same features were found in Lɔ́ɔŋ ŋɔ́ɔr, a prayer to guide the soul of a deceased person to the spirit village of his/her ancestors. Though 'rice narratives' belong to everyday speech and Lɔ́ɔŋ ŋɔ́ɔr has a ceremonial context, both are lists of activities and share similar syntactic and tonal patterns. This leads to systematic long-term mutual relations of boundary tones marking information units and thematic shifts. Structural means of signalling information structure are uniform through this kind of narrative. In this case, we may speak about a fixed performance template used in narrative accounts.

Informational structuring of rice narratives

The speech material analysed here consists of 'rice narratives', spontaneous accounts of rice-growing, from the first period of work in the field until the rice is steamed and eaten. Rice narratives related by 14 tonal and 10 non-tonal speakers were recorded in Laos in 2007 and in Thailand in 2008.[15]

Very few disfluencies (interruptions, hesitations, etc.) are found, as speakers are describing the growing of rice, an everyday activity well known to most of them. Although spontaneous, this material is structured in the same way by all speakers: new information is

---

15 See further Karlsson, Svantesson, and House 2013.

given at the end of an utterance (underlined in Example 4) and is then repeated as old information in the immediately following utterance. Using square brackets to mark prosodic phrases, the informational structuring is: [anchor + new$_1$] [old new$_1$ + new$_2$] [old new$_2$ + new$_3$] ... The new information becomes an anchor point (old information) in the next utterance. There are thus a considerable number of repeated words in the speakers' monologues, while anaphoric reference is not used as in this example: *Before there is rice we have to clear the field* [...] *After clearing the field we burn the field* [...] *After burning we sow*. The verbal contents can thus be seen as a list of successive events. Some speakers use only one utterance per event, while some include much additional information.

Example 4 Segments of a rice narrative. Each line marks [given + new] units. There are three such units in this case. New information at the end of each unit is underlined. Prosodic phrases are marked by brackets. Female speaker, Nang An from the Namyɔɔn Meey village, tonal dialect.

[hóoc	nì	yɔ̀h	kíaw]		
[finish	then	go	harvest]		
[kíaw	ŋɔ́]	[kíaw	hóoc	yɔ̀h	tíi]
[harvest	rice]	[harvest	finish	go	beat]
[tíi	ɔ̀ɔr	wèc]	[tàa	yùuŋ]	
[beat	bring	return]	[to	barn]	

Structuring of the informational flow into [given + new] units is systematically cued by prosodic means. Thus, the tonal prosodic phrase boundaries in the [given + new] units are upstepped in relation to one another: each succeeding boundary is phonetically realized with a higher F0 value.[16] The final word of the last prosodic phrase gets the highest F0 value, coinciding with the [new]. This is fully realized when no conflict with lexical tones occurs. The high boundary tones are on the right edge of prosodic phrases in Kammu, as illustrated in Example 1. This is also the case for rice narratives, as shown in Example 5 by the tonal course of the utterance in Example 4 spoken by a female tonal speaker.

---

16 Prosodic phrasing by phrase-final boundary tones occurs in many languages. Kammu, though, is characterized by only one tonal type of boundary tone and thus by a rather fixed phrase tune.

Kammu vocal genres (Laos)

Example 5 Tonal course of the utterance in Example 4. The division into three [given + new] units is shown by vertical lines. The high boundary tones of focused phrases, occurring on the underlined words in Example 4, are shown with arrows. Note that the final syllable starts rising, as expected for a boundary syllable. A Low lexical tone may suppress the rising movement. • **01 Rice narrative**

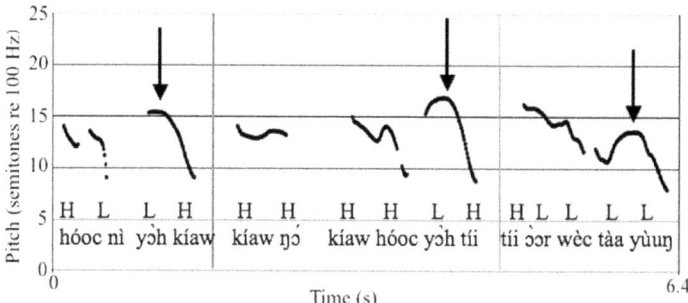

The following part of a rice narrative stems from a male speaker of a non-tonal Kammu dialect. The basic structure is the same as in Example 4. Activities mentioned at the end of one phrase are immediately repeated at the beginning of the next phrase (Example 6).

Example 6 A section of a rice narrative related by a non-tonal male speaker, Siang Khamma from the Yang Tuey village, Muang Kwaa, Phongsaly Province, who lists: field-house, burn, sow and weed. Each [given + new] unit is shown by a new line.

waay	ni	ləə	əh	cʔo		
After	that	then	make	field-house		

əh	cʔo	lɛɛw	gɔɔ	puur		
make	field-house	ready	then	burn		

puur	hooc	lɛɛw	gɔɔ	cmɔɔl		
burn	finish	ready	then	sow		

cmɔɔl	hŋɔ	rəh	lɛɛw	gɔɔ	ɨ	hɛɛl
sow	rice	grow up	ready	then	oh	weed

In this case, too, the tonal course of the utterance shows the same characteristics with high boundary tones at the end of prosodic phrases (Example 7).

Example 7 Tonal course of the utterance in Example 6. The end of each [given + new] unit is indicated by an arrow.

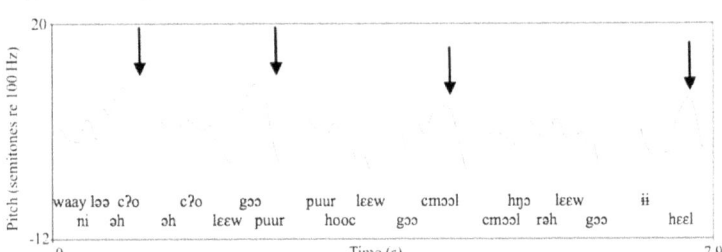

In Melodyne a thin curve shows the detailed movement, and pitches are approximated as straight lines of varying width, so-called 'blobs', which serve as a base for the automatic notation. This process is similar to what happens in the manual transcription of music. When applied to rice narratives, the tonal course is clearly visible and the musical notation is fairly accurate. The automatic score notation gives a reasonable description of the melodic and rhythmic movement, though one should be aware that bars and barlines are not optimal (Example 8).[17] The pitches are relatively fixed but not organized in a tonal system. The rhythmic pattern is notably regular, without having a regular beat. In these respects lɔ̀ɔŋ differs from ordinary daily language and also from vocal music.[18]

In the illustration of the non-tonal speaker in Example 9 the same characteristics are obvious, but there is a definite difference between the two performances in tonal range: 8 semitones in Example 8, compared to 13 in Example 9. There are no cases of syllable reduplication, but the number of syllables in the phrases differs. The corresponding numbers of syllables are 4–6–5 in three phrases and 6–6–6–8 in four. The manner of performance thus permits varying phrase lengths, which produces some rhythmic irregularities.

---

17 There are ways, however, in Melodyne to change the bars at will.
18 This is supported by Karlsson, House, and Svantesson 2015, who found that, apart from differences from ordinary speech, there were also differences between the narrative accounts lɔ̀ɔŋ and folk narratives.

Kammu vocal genres (Laos)

Example 8 The segment from the rice narrative in Examples 4–5 in a Melodyne graph. Arrows show boundary tones of focused phrases. The words and the lines in the notation that show downwards sliding motion have been added manually. • **01 Rice narrative**

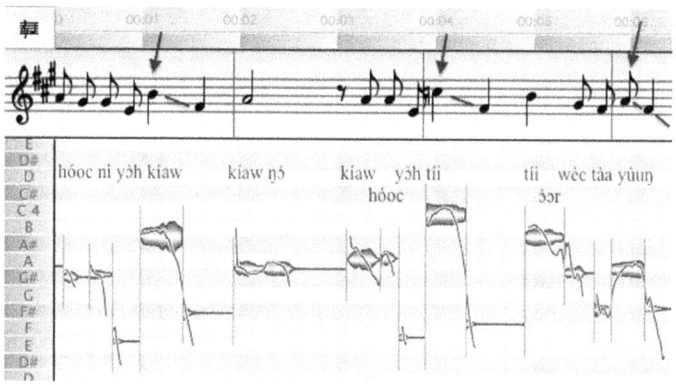

Example 9 The segment from a rice narrative in Examples 6–7 in a Melodyne graph. Arrows show boundary tones of focused phrases.

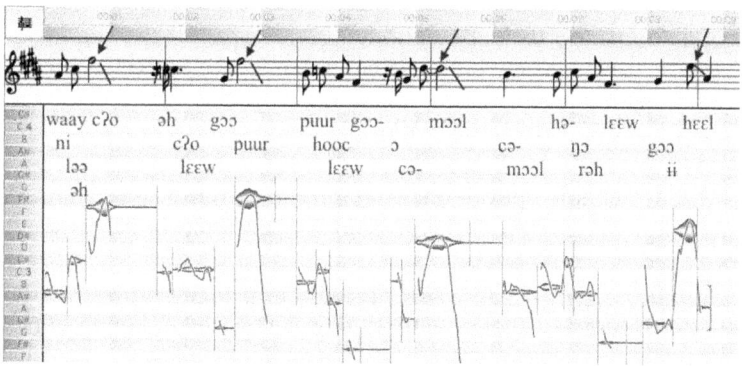

Division of narratives into topics

A *thematic episode* is seen as an informatively coherent part of discourse, with a clear beginning and end.[19] Each episode has one central topic. As we are dealing with narratives about a traditional activity, the Kammu agricultural calendar as described by Kàm

---

19 See e.g. Chafe 2001.

Table 2 Rice-narrative topics (left) compared to the main agricultural seasons of the Kammu farming year (right)

Rice narrative topics	Agricultural periods
1) Clearing	1) Clearing
2) First and second burning	2) First burning
	3) Second burning
3) Sowing	4) Sowing
4) Weeding	5) First weeding
	6) Second weeding
	7) Third weeding
5) Ripe rice	
6) Harvesting	8) Harvesting
7) Putting in barns	
8) Pounding rice	9) Finishing off the year
9) Soaking rice	10) Starting to eat the new rice
10) Steaming rice	
11) Eating rice	

Ràw (Table 2, right column)[20] was used as a reference framework for division into thematic episodes. Most speakers use the topics listed in Table 2, left column. Some speakers have additional topics, such as making field-houses, protecting crops from animals, or different ways of cooking rice. All topics in the left column except (5) and (7) occur with all speakers.

Each thematic episode includes several [given + new] units. A schematic illustration of the prosodic organization of narratives is provided in Example 10.

Speakers structure thematic episodes in their narrative account as [description + name of activity that is described]. For example: *We go to seek a field, seek in the forest, after finding the field we clear*, the part before *clear* being the description. *Clear* is the name of the activity and coincides with the end of the thematic episode. *Clear* is thus the topic of the thematic episode, and all the previous descriptions (*seek a field, seek in the forest*) are about what is included in *clearing*. However, in some cases there is another type of structuring of topics, where the topic is introduced at the beginning and then described; here is an example: *We seek a place we will*

---

20 For calendar and farming year, see Lindell, Lundström, Svantesson, and Tayanin 1982.

Kammu vocal genres (Laos)

Example 10 A schematic illustration of the performance of /hɔɔŋ/. Right-edged boundary tones of prosodic phrases (p-phrase) are organized in a template that marks the informational structure of the narrative. Smooth lines illustrate the approximate tonal contour. The template is similar for tonal and non-tonal dialects, but is perturbed by lexical tones in the tonal dialect.

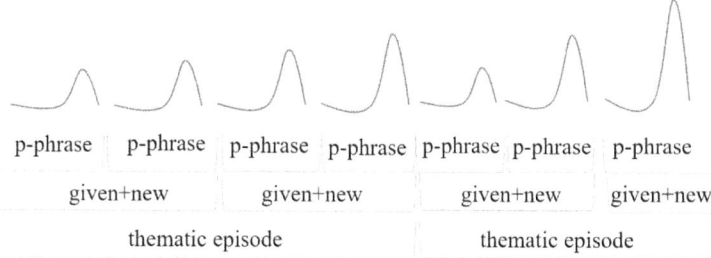

clear, yes, search the forest, look for a place that will be good for the rice and we clear. In this case, *clear* is introduced in the beginning as a new topic, and its development comes afterwards. This kind of topic gets the highest F0 at the beginning of the topic instead of at the end. It should be observed that *clear* is repeated at the end, obviously indicating that the episode about clearing is finished here.

Tonal structuring of rice narratives by boundary tones is exemplified in Examples 11 and 12. As the narratives are long, only the last words in [given + new] units are included. A non-tonal speaker (Example 11) has 10 episodes in his narrative. He was living in a village in Laos and is familiar with work in the field.

Example 11 Rice narrative related by a non-tonal male speaker, Phet Smai from the Konkeo village, Vientiane Province. *Top:* Phrase final words coincide with new information. Square brackets show the division into thematic episodes. *Bottom:* Tonal movement with tonal boundaries marking ends of thematic episodes, indicated by arrows.

[psɨm]   [cmɔɔl, hreʔ]   [hɛɛl]   [ple, hɔɔt]   [kiaw, cʔoʔ]   [hntaar, hic]
[plant] [sow, field]   [weed]   [fruit, harvest] [cut, barn] [dry, pound]

[gual, tiʔ, guum]   [ɟam, ruŋ]   [hmpial, muut]   [ʔɛɛp niʔ]
[rice-mortar, hand, winnow]   [soak, steam]   [turn, knead]   [rice-basket thatᵃ].

Note: ᵃSteamed rice is placed in rice baskets to be eaten.

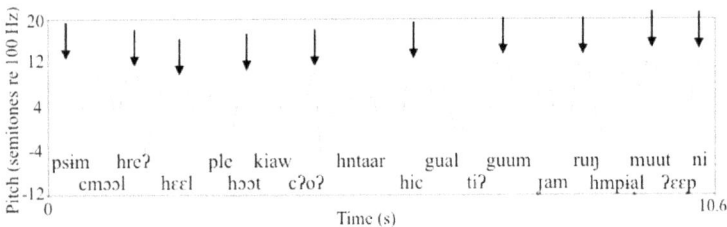

One tonal speaker had moved to a town in Thailand and only knew about rice-growing from his parents. His narrative is shorter with fewer details, consisting of 5 episodes (Example 12). Nonetheless, the melodic movement is similar to that of the non-tonal speaker in Example 11. The highest boundary tones (shown by arrows) mark the end of thematic episodes.

Example 12 Rice narrative related by a tonal male speaker, Somswàt Búnkə̀ət from the Òm Kɔ́ɔ village, Bo Keo province, Kwɛ̀ɛn dialect. Tonal boundaries marking ends of thematic episodes are indicated by arrows.

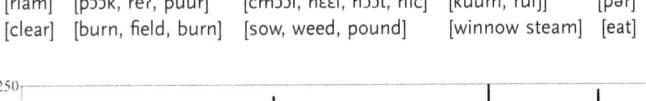

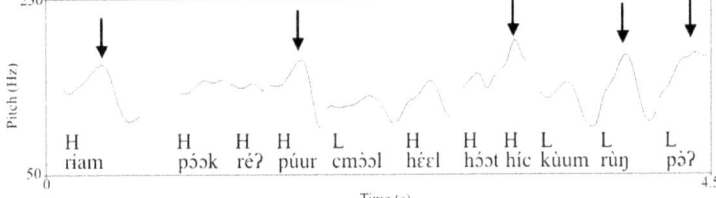

Lɔ̀ɔŋ ŋɔ̀ɔr, 'Showing the way'

A syntactic structure similar to that of rice narratives is found in the Kammu *Lɔ̀ɔŋ ŋɔ̀ɔr*, literally, 'chanting the way', which belongs to the funeral wakes where it was performed in order to guide the soul of the deceased to the spirit village where he/she would then live as an ancestral spirit. The extract in Example 13 consists of three lines from a performance of a total of 86 lines.[21]

Example 13 A section of *Lɔ̀ɔŋ ŋɔ̀ɔr* performed by Sét Mán, Yùan area, ca. 1980, in the presence of other mourners. Sét Mán is a nephew of Kàm Ràw who performed many of the vocal expressions in this chapter.

Còh   Klàaŋ   Ktéey   cùur   ənsú   rɔ̀ɔt   Òm   Críil.
from   stone   *Kteey* go down down   arrive   water golden
Go down from the Ktéey cliff to the Golden Brook

Còh   Òm   Críil   lɔ̀ɔŋ   ənsú,   rɔ̀ɔt   Wàk   Kntɔ̀.
from   water   golden   follow down,   arrive   waterfall rainshield.
Go along the Golden Brook down to the Rainshield Waterfall

Kháam   Wàk   Kntɔ̀   ənsú   rɔ̀ɔt   Òm   Cùk.
pass   waterfall rain shield down   arrive   water fishtail palm.
Go past the Rainshield Waterfall down to the Fishtail Palm Brook

The initial part is structurally similar to the rice narratives: new information is given at the end of prosodic phrases and repeated in the beginning of the following phrase. The phrases achieve a high tonal boundary (Example 14, bottom panel).

A similar pattern is found in a performance of *Lɔ̀ɔŋ ŋɔ̀ɔr* in the Rɔ̀ɔk dialect area, south of Yùan. This performance is realized as a call-and-response pattern, where the lead performer's lines are immediately repeated by those present. As illustrated in the top panel of Example 14, the right phrase boundary is marked by a high boundary tone (suppressed by a Low lexical tone in the second phrase), and phrases comprising new information (the second and the last one) are realized in a lower pitch area. This is also the case in the Yùan-area example at the bottom panel of Example 14; in addition, it is clearly shown by the graph in Example 15. As was

---

21 See Tayanin 2006: 78–88 or Svantesson, Kàm Ràw, Lindell, and Lundström 2014: 181–182. In several previous publications, this has been referred to as 'the guiding song'.

Example 14 Tonal course of two *Lɔ̀ɔŋ ŋɔ̀ɔr* performances showing alternating high and low pitch areas related to a call-and-response performance manner. The horizontal line indicates an approximate division into high and low pitch levels and arrows show ends of phrases. The performers are Tá Khám, Lwà village, Rɔ̀ɔk dialect area, ca. 1980 (top) and Sét Mán, Yùan area, ca. 1980 (bottom). Both are male tonal speakers. • **02 Lɔ̀ɔŋ ŋɔ̀ɔr**

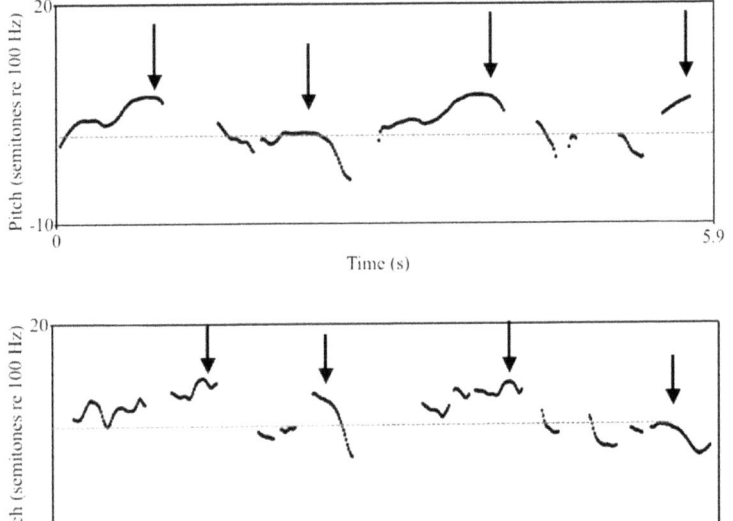

the case with the rice narratives, pitches appear to be quite stable, and the performance is rather rhythmic.

As mentioned above, everyday spoken narratives (rice monologues) are highly rhythmic, and their prosodic and syntactic features are very similar to those of *Lɔ̀ɔŋ ŋɔ̀ɔr*. Tonal phrasing and the use of lengthening are similar in the two genres. The main difference is the use of pitch levels. In *Lɔ̀ɔŋ ŋɔ̀ɔr*, the speaker shifts between higher and lower pitch levels (registers) by performing every second phrase at a lower level. This comes out quite naturally in the call-and-response pattern of the Rɔ̀ɔk-area performance (Example 14 top), where those present repeat each new sentence in unison at a lower pitch. Kàm Ràw would never perform *Lɔ̀ɔŋ ŋɔ̀ɔr* outside its actual function at a funeral, but he said that this alternation was the normal way of performing it in the Yùan area. This might explain why the Yùan-area performance (Examples 14 bottom and 15) also

Kammu vocal genres (Laos)

Example 15 The melodic movement of the excerpt of Lɔ̀ɔŋ ŋɔ̀ɔr from the Yùan area in Example 13 showing alternation in pitch register where prosodic phrases in a high register (boxes with solid lines) are followed by phrases in a lower register (boxes with dashed lines). Notes within brackets are sobs or spoken words. • 02 *Lɔ̀ɔŋ ŋɔ̀ɔr*

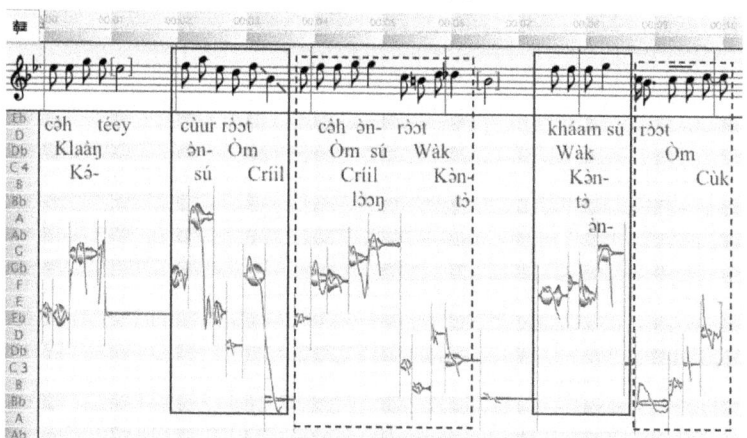

has lines alternately in a higher and lower pitch area, even though there is only one person who performs it. Both the narrative accounts and Lɔ̀ɔŋ ŋɔ̀ɔr may be rather long. Perhaps the alternation of phrases in a high and a low pitch area in Lɔ̀ɔŋ ŋɔ̀ɔr may be seen as an organizing principle.

The lɔ̀ɔŋ performance template

The difference between language and music – or spoken language and vocal music – is often expressed by the pulsating-rhythm and tonically ordered pitch parameters. While these are generally lacking in spoken language, they are present in vocal music. In these respects, lɔ̀ɔŋ is closer to spoken language than to vocal music; but it has a tendency towards repeated rhythm and pitch patterns, which are comparatively stable. Lɔ̀ɔŋ differs both from spoken language and from vocal music and fits into the borderland under study here.

Melody
- Melodic movement with relatively fixed pitches without a tonal centre (see Examples 8–9, 15).
- Range: 8–13 semitones.

Rhythm
- Rhythmic movement in rather uniform repeated patterns without a regular beat.

Form
- Litany: succession of prosodic phrase-pairs connected by repeated word(s).
- Call (higher pitch level) and response (lower pitch level) pattern occurs (Lòɔŋ ŋɔ̀ɔr).

Phrasing
- Successive right-edged phrase boundary tones, with the highest phrase boundary tone coinciding with the end of each episode.
- New information is given at the end of an utterance and is then repeated in the immediately following utterance: [anchor + new$_1$] [old new$_1$ + new$_2$] [old new$_2$ + new$_3$] …

Word variations
- Schwa vowels (ə) are usually not audible.

Lexical tones
- Low lexical tone may make the boundary tone at the end of an episode low.

Analysis 2 *Kàm à-thí-tháan*, prayer

Prayers directed at a large number of spirits, *róoy*, accompany many activities in Kammu life.[22] Numerous Kammu prayers have been published, but there are fewer recordings. Two prayers used in shaman ceremonies are discussed in this analysis.[23]

Ì càk cə̀ən, 'We called you'

These words may also be referred to as *Krùu kʔə́əy mà krùu*, 'Spell for apologizing to the magic power'. They belong to the part of a shaman ceremony when the shaman spirits have arrived and sing through the shaman as a medium asking why the people called the spirits: *Mɔ́ɔ rɔ̀ɔt màañ*, 'The shaman arrives and asks'. The people may reply with these words:

Example 16 Words and translation of *Ì càk cə̀ən*.

əə cép bɔ́ɔ kháat, pyàat bɔ́ɔ thɔ́ɔy
əə, ì càk cə̀ən, ə̀ən màa
rɔ̀ɔt pía rɔ̀ɔt pát, pát pía tlhát, pát àn kséh
pía ùun tlhát, pát ùun k'rúk

yes, pain does not end, illness does not vanish
yes, we called you, we asked you to come
come to cure, come to heal, heal and let disappear
cure and let it bounce away, heal and let it fall

Prosodically *Ì càk cə̀ən* resembles ordinary speech, and prosodic phrasing is built on syntactic groups (Example 17). The syntactic groups consist of two parts linked by pivot rhymes (*kháat/pyàat, cə̀ən/ə̀ən, pát/pát, tə̀lhát/pát*).[24] Schwa or epenthetic vowels are pronounced ə (*tə̀lhát* and *kə̣séh*).

---

22 For words of prayers see, for example, Lundström and Tayanin 1982: 138–152 concerning the farming year, Tayanin 2006: 123–162 concerning funerals and Tayanin and Lindell 2012: 167–174 concerning hunting. Svantesson, Kàm Ràw, Lindell, and Lundström 2014: 439 has an index of prayers contained in the dictionary.
23 See further *Krùu* in Analysis 10.
24 The term pivot rhyme goes back to Lindell 1988, which deals with Kammu sayings and proverbs.

Example 17 Smaller syntactic groups [ ] and larger prosodic phrases ( ) in *ì càk càən*.

([əə cép bɔ́ɔ kháat] [pə̀yàat bɔ́ɔ thɔ́ɔy])
([ə̀ə] [ì càk càən] [ə̀ən màa])
([rɔ̀ɔt pía] [rɔ̀ɔt pát] [pát tə̀lhát, pát àn kə́séh])
([pía ùun tə̀lhát] [pát ùun kə́rúk])

([yes, pain does not end] [illness does not vanish])
([yes] [we called you] [we asked you to come])
([come to cure] [come to heal] [heal and let disappear])
([cure and let it bounce away] [heal and let it fall])

The performance starts high, and the first line falls (Example 18). The remainder is within the rather narrow range of approximately 6 semitones, and the intervals between syllables are small. The smaller prosodic groups are cued by a high boundary tone at their right edge. Lines 3 and 4 end on high boundary tones, The last of them is the highest, which is the normal way of marking the end of a continuous narration in Kammu. It should be noted, however, that line 2 ends on a Low lexical tone while the other lines end on a High. The small prosodic phrases are grouped into larger prosodic phrases[25] which, in addition to the final high boundary tone, are also marked by lengthening the final syllable. After the opening phrase, there is a fairly regular rhythm. The tempo is fast, with 33 syllables in 9 seconds – an average of nearly 4 per second, compared to an average of 2.3 in the *Lɔ̀ɔŋ ŋɔ̀ɔr* in Example 15. In lines 2–4, the average is 5 per second.

The overall shape of this vocal expression is that of a high and falling start, beginning with a possibly vocative *əə*. Then follows a swift, gradually rising delivery of words at fairly narrow intervals, where phrasing is marked by starting each prosodic phrase on a slightly higher F0 than the last word of the preceding phrase (Example 18). The prayer then ends with an upward motion. It may be noted, however, that there are several examples of movement contrary to lexical tones and that the tones and pitches tend to coincide on the final syllable of a syntactic group. For the most part, the tonal movements within syllables are flat or falling.

---

25 This is in accordance with accounts of prosody as a hierarchical structure, which is not discussed here. For references, see e.g. Gussenhoven 2004.

Kammu vocal genres (Laos)

Example 18 Melodic movement of the prayer *ì càk càan*, 'We called you'. The arrow indicates gradually rising phrases. Performed by Kàm Ràw, ca. 1983/84.

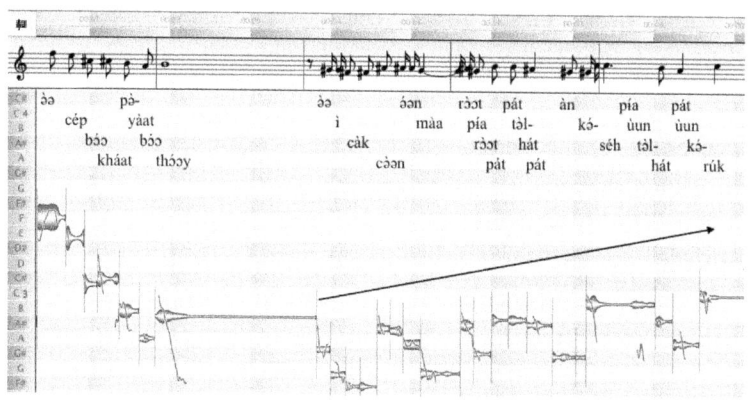

Wéey mὲɛ krùu, 'Worship one's power'

The shaman speaks these words, also referred to as *Krùu kʔɔ́ay mà krùu* 'Spell for apologizing to the magic power', in the form of a prayer after having made a mistake in a spell, or before starting in order to prevent punishment if a mistake should occur:

Example 19 *Wéey mὲɛ krùu*, 'Worship one's power'. Kammu words and translation.

 sáa-thú, khúu báa, àay-cáan
 Àay Púun hə́ə súu krùu
  kúu déey krùu, déey mòn pɔ̀ɔ cáw, mὲɛ cáw
  kúu déey hám, déey hían pɔ̀ɔ krùu, mὲɛ krùu
  [pɔ̀ɔ...] lòŋ sɔ́ɔŋ tìa héey háa kúu
  lòŋ sáam tìa... héey háa kúu
 súu-màa, sáa-thú, khúu báa, àay-cáan

 forgive me, sādhu, teacher, scholar
 Master Lime has taught me the spells
  I received the spells, received the mantras of your father, of your mother
  I received the teaching, the lessons of the father of spells, of the mother of spells
   when you come down for the second time, [come to me]
   when you come down for the third time, [come to me]
 forgive me, sādhu, teacher, scholar

The first and last lines are addressed to the shaman spirits. The underlined final word of the second line (*krùu*), rhymes with the first word of the third line (*kúu*). Lines 3 and 4 are linked by parallelism, as are lines 5 and 6. The introductory word *sáa-thú* is performed rather slowly as an opening, and with a falling interval. The speed is high, similar to the previous prayer.

Example 20 Prosodic phrases in *Wéey mɛ̀ɛ krùu*, 'Worship one's power'.

[sáa-thú, khúu báa, àay-cáan]
[Àay Púun hə́ə súu krùu]
[kúu déey krùu, déey mòn
  pɔ̀ɔ cáw, mɛ̀ɛ cáw]
[kúu déey hám, déey hían
  pɔ̀ɔ krùu, mɛ̀ɛ krùu]
[... lòŋ sɔ́ɔŋ tìa héey háa kúu
lòŋ sáam tìa... héey háa kúu
súu-màa, sáa-thú,
  khúu báa, àay-cáan]

As regards phrasing (Example 20), there is no resemblance to daily speech or rice narratives, so the ending of prosodic phrases have no high boundary tones. Syllable lengths within phrases are short or long, and the final syllable of a phrase is lengthened, marking the end of a phrase. In addition, the initial syllables consisting of the vocative *sáa-thú* are lengthened. Compared to other genres that are delivered at a slower tempo, as for instance in *tə́əm* (Analysis 9), the fast tempo does not allow room for syllable reduplication. Though lexical tones are sometimes realized, every syllable is performed with a falling pitch, which is unusual in Kammu genres (Example 21).

Example 21 *Wéey mɛ̀ɛ krùu*, 'Worship one's power'. Because of a high tempo, many words are performed in very short time spaces. Therefore, some parts of the transcription have been omitted. Performed by Kàm Ràw, ca. 1983/84.

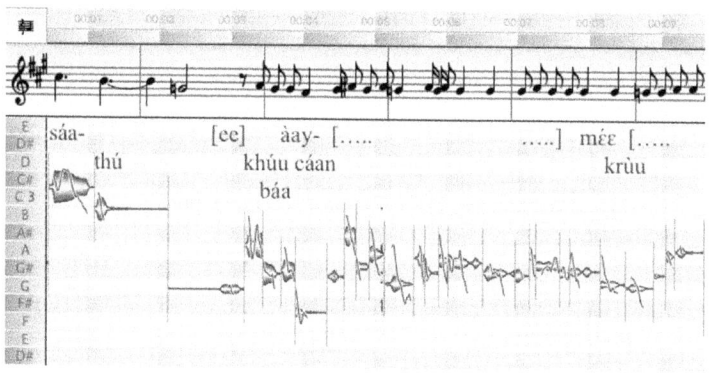

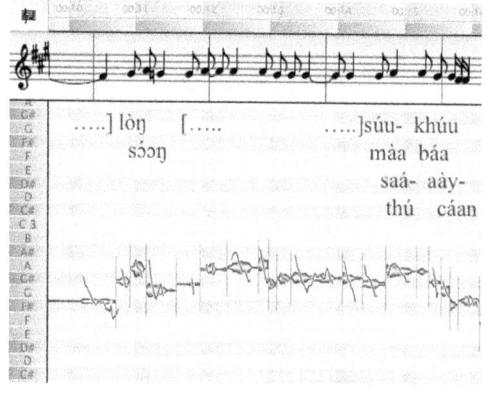

If the introductory word is disregarded, the melody has less movement than the prayer *Ì càk cə̀ən*, 'We called you' (Example 18); and although the prosodic phrases produce a certain regularity, it is not as clearly organized into distinct rhythmic units as the genre *lɔ̀ɔŋ* (Analysis 1). Most of the time, it moves in the narrow space of approximately 4 semitones, and boundary tones are not particularly marked. Especially the end of the melody is falling, independently of the lexical tones. The feeling is that of a rather flat melody with very little room for intonation.

The *kàm à-thí-tháan* performance template

Melody
- Melodic movement is rather level but slightly rising (disregarding initial formula), with no tonal centre (see Examples 18, 21).
- A narrow range of 4–6 semitones (disregarding initial formula).

Rhythm
- Fast tempo.
- Rhythmic movement is basically created by the lengthening of final syllables in prosodic phrases.
- Rhythmic movement in rather uniform repeated patterns, with no regular beat.

Form
- Litany: consecutive prosodic phrasing built on syntactic groups with pivot rhymes.

Phrasing
- Smaller syntactic groups end on a high boundary tone, each slightly higher than the preceding group, with a lengthening of the final syllable.
- Larger prosodic phrases are marked by the lengthening of the final syllable.

Initial/final formulae
- The initial phrase is vocative, starting at a high pitch and falling with lengthened syllables.

Word variations
- Schwa vowels (ə) are very short and hardly audible.

Lexical tones
- Lexical tones are not very pronounced.
- Movement contrary to lexical tones is common.
- The melodic movement within syllables is flat or falling.

Analysis 3 Ɔɔc, 'Begging', at New Year

In late autumn, when the rice had been harvested and the master of the house had sacrificed taro, sweet potato, and elephant grass to the ancestor spirits in order to inform them that the old year was ended, young people used to gather in small groups and wander all over the village to collect gifts. This wassail went on for three consecutive evenings, and each household would have several visits.

The youths sang outside the houses of the village, expecting gifts consisting of taro, sweet potato, and peanuts which the house owner would first hold over the stove and over the table while praying to the spirits of waste to leave those places and to leave his house. The wassail was thus intended to drive out the spirits of waste, i.e. *róoy yáap* and *róoy hʔéep*, which are the spirits of stillborn babies and of those who died in accidents. It was believed that these spirits could not find repose in the village of the dead, but were doomed to roam around alone. Unlike other spirits, the spirits of waste did not receive blood sacrifices. Therefore, people believed that these spirits were constantly hungry, that they would be attracted to the fields by the growing rice and that they might follow the harvested rice into the village, houses, and barns. In such a case the crop would not last long, or it would rot.

On the evening of the third wassail day, the youths would gather in one of the common-houses of the village to have a feast on the food they had collected. A little of each offering was saved, however, and carried to the village boundary, where it was thrown away towards the west – that is, where the sun sets. This was how they disposed of the waste spirits.

This wassail was called *Ɔɔc*, 'Begging'. The words are organized into units, within which one of the final words of a line rhymes with one of the first in the following line. Each line consists of 5 syllables followed by the non-lexical word *ís*, which makes 6 syllables. The only exception is the first line (A in Example 22), which consists of 3 + 1 syllables. The non-lexical word *ís* that occurs at the end of each line should probably be seen as a 'song-word'. Since this is the only known occurrence of the syllable *ís*, it has been assigned a High lexical tone based on the way it is performed in *Ɔɔc*.

The melody used in the village of Rmcùal consists of a short motif that is repeated over and over with minor variations. The range is a sixth (9 semitones), and the rhythm is even and suitable for walking. The syllables 2, 4, 5, and 6 have fixed pitches throughout the performance. Since each of these (except syllable 6) is combined with High or Low lexical tones, agreement between pitch and lexical tone is accidental. Syllables 1 and 3 have two possible pitches, which permits adaptation to High or Low lexical tone as shown by the arrows in Example 22. Lexical tones are thus only partly realized in the performance.

Example 22 The three variants of the ɔ̀ɔc melodic motif. A is the initial formula; B and C are repeated throughout. Arrows mark the only pitches that vary and can be adapted to High or Low lexical tone. • **03 ɔ̀ɔc**

As can be seen from the translation (Example 23), the verbal content of the song is an enumeration of details that explain why the singers are visiting a household. Except for the initial formula built on words without lexical meaning, the prosodic phrases are organized in pairs. These phrase-pairs are held together by parallelism and rhymes arranged so that one of the last syllables of a line rhymes with one of the first in the following line: for instance lines 6/7: *tə̀-làa / pə̀-yàa* or 10/11: *lə̀m-táas / kráas*. The vowel *ə* is a schwa vowel that is more or less inaudible in ordinary speech. The word *tə̀-làa* is normally written *ìlàa*, but since the schwa vowel is given the same length as any other vowel in the performance, it is written out in this transcription.

In Kammu practice, most melodic phrases end on a low pitch. The rising pitch at the end of the ɔ̀ɔc melodic motif is hence unusual. The enumeration in the verbal contents and the paired phrases probably reflect the same prosodic practice as the *lɔ̀ɔŋ* narrative style (Analysis 1), but are here combined with a melodic motif with a regular rhythm and a tonal centre.

Number notation is used for the transcriptions, since it provides a description of melodic and rhythmic features that is sufficiently

Kammu vocal genres (Laos)

Table 3 Number notation limited to the signs used in the following examples*

Half note (minim):	♩	1 –
Quarter note (crotchet):	♩	1
Dotted quarter:	♩.	1·
Eighth note (quaver):	♪	<u>1</u>
1 = tonic.		
If 1 = c then 1–2–3–4–5–6–7 corresponds to c–d–e–f–g–a–b		
Pause:		0
Lowered (by a semitone):		♭1, ♭2 etc.
Glissando (sliding between tones):		⇒

Note: *For a complete description, see Internet reference: Numbered musical notation in the References.

Example 23 ɔ̀ɔc, village Rmcùal version in number notation. The lexical tone of the syllable *heel* in line 4 is uncertain. Performed by Kàm Ràw, ca. 1977. Original pitch: 4 ≈ 135 Hz. • **03 ɔ̀ɔc**

Bold italics indicate realized lexical tone.
For number notation signs, see Appendix 2.

Line No.

(1)	*4* crlíŋ 0		*1* cràaŋ 0		4· <u>5</u> crɔ̀ɔc 0	<u>6</u> ís oh

(2)	*1* ɔ̀ɔc beg	4 sɔ́ɔŋ two	*1* kràm time	1 sáam three	4· <u>5</u> kràm time,	<u>6</u> ís oh

(3)	4 kràm time	4 pían get	*4* ŋɔ́ rice	1 pían get	4· <u>5</u> màh cooked rice,	<u>6</u> ís oh

(4)	*1* kə̀n - slap	4 táh	2 plù thigh	[1] heel - 0	4· 5 wèel	<u>6</u> ís oh

(5)	4 wèel 0	4 thán big as	4 plù thigh	1 thán big as	***4· 5*** plɔ́ɔŋ calf of leg,	<u>6</u> ís oh

(6)	4 cáak tear	4 cáak tear	4 lá leaf	1 tə̀ - bamboo,	4· <u>5</u> làa	<u>6</u> ís oh

	4	4	4	1	4. 5	6		
(7)	pə̀ - *title*	yàa	ùun let	ì us	yɔ̀h* go,	ís oh	*alt:	cáa tell
	4	4	4	1	4. 5	6		
(8)	cáak tear	cáak tear	lá leaf	kə̀l - plant,	púun	ís oh		
	4	4	4	1	4. 5	6		
(9)	lə̀ - *title*	kùun	ùun let	ì us	yɔ̀h go,	ís oh		
	1	4	2	1	4. 5	6		
(10)	lìan come	crɔ́ŋ give	tàa at	làm - balcony,	táas	ís oh		
	1	4	2	1	4. 5	6		
(11)	lìan come	kráas smile	tàa at	pə́r - door,	lòŋ	ís oh		
	1	4	2	1	4. 5	6		
(12)	píñ shoot	kró bulbul	tə́r - double	tɔ̀	kám arrow,	ís oh		
	1	4	2	1	4. 5	6		
(13)	phɔ́ɔŋ repay	ràm debt	yʌʌ with	rə̀ŋ - rice-grain,	kó	ís oh		
	1	4	2	1	4. 5	6		
(14)	ùun give	cró taro	ì we	pə́ - return,	káay	ís oh		
	1	4	2	1	4. 5	6		
(15)	ùun give	kwáay batata	ì we	cə̀ə will	ràp keep,	ís oh		

Interpretation:

Críiŋ, cràaŋ, crɔ̀ɔc, oh
Begging twice and thrice, oh
   For seeds and cooked rice, oh
Bigger than your thigh, oh
   Bigger than the calf of your leg, oh
Tear, tear bamboo leaves, oh
   The *Pyàa* sent us out, oh
Tear, tear *klpúun* leaves, oh
   The *Lkùun* sent us out, oh
Come give it from your porch, oh
   Come smile by your door, oh

> Shoot two birds with one arrow, oh
> > Pay your debts with pounded rice, oh
> Taro we will return, oh
> > Batatas we will keep, oh

detailed for our purpose, which in this case is to determine whether lexical tones are realized in the performance or not (Table 3; for more details see Appendix 2). The aim has been to try out a simple transcription that is easily communicated and yields a clear picture of musical pitch vs. lexical tone, and also of metre and poetic form. The transcriptions are therefore also arranged so that parts that can be interpreted as initial and final formulae of a line are directly aligned below each other and can easily be compared.

The Ɔɔc performance template

In our material, this melodic formula is only used with the words of the Ɔɔc wassail festivities. The short melodic formula is repeated for each line of the words which, in principle, are organized as phrase-pairs connected through rhymes. It might be discussed whether the concept 'performance template' is relevant for this melodic formula. On the other hand, it cannot be ruled out that this melodic formula could function as such, for it has some characteristics that generally occur in Kammu performance templates.

Melody
- A short melodic formula with a tonal centre (see Example 22).
- Melodic range: 9 semitones.

Rhythm
- Regular pulse.
- Syllabic.

Form
- Litany: prosodic phrase-pairs generally connected through rhymes.

Phrasing
- A high boundary tone coincides with the end of a phrase.
- Prosodic and musical phrases are aligned.

Initial/final formulae
- An initial formula at the very beginning
- A final song-word in each phrase (*ís*).
- The penultimate syllable of a line is lengthened.

Word variations
- A song-word without lexical meaning at the end of each line: *ís*, which is always performed high.
- The initial formula consists of song-words.
- Same duration for long and short vowel, minor and major syllable.
- Schwa vowels (normally ə) have the same duration as all other vowels that are performed as short.

Lexical tones
- Melody-centred.
- Lexical tones only partly realized.

Analysis 4 The vocal genre *hrlɨɨ*

In the Kammu village of Rmcùal in northern Laos, the predominant vocal expression in feasting situations was *tɔ́ɔm*, which could be used only in such situations. If the same kind of orally transmitted poems – called *trnɔ̀ɔm* – were to be performed at other times, the vocal genre *hrlɨɨ* would be used instead. *Hrlɨɨ* could also be used outside the village, not least in the fields where many young people spent much time watching over the growing rice. It also functioned as a mnemonic tool for learning and remembering the *trnɔ̀ɔm* poems. Generally speaking, *hrlɨɨ* is a rhythmicized way of performing a *trnɔ̀ɔm* freed from speech intonation, but with the lexical tones realized.

Example 24 shows the words of a typical *trnɔ̀ɔm*, which is the kind of orally transmitted poem used for *hrlɨɨ* and some other vocal genres. It is organized into two stanzas. Generally, the second stanza contains a more or less concrete message, whereas the first stanza is more metaphoric and serves as a 'poetic parallel' to the second. A high degree of parallelism is evident from the repetition of phrases in which only a few words are exchanged in the repetitions. The words that are exchanged are most often rhyme words, and the rhyme pattern stretches over both stanzas. This particular *trnɔ̀ɔm* is of the kind that would be used when visiting somebody in another village more or less uninvited.[26]

The symbols after each line are used to identify lines of stanzas. The numerals stand for stanzas (1, 2, and so on), the letters for lines within stanzas (a, b, and so on), and the index for variations of lines ('). In the 'basic' form of the *trnɔ̀ɔm* in Example 24, the order of lines is: 1a–1b–1a–1b', 2a–2b–2a–2b'. In Example 25, the same *trnɔ̀ɔm* has been reorganized and the lines of the poem have been regrouped into 1a–1a–2a–2a, 1b–1b'–2b–2b'. This happens in performance, but here it serves to show consistencies in the intonation of lexical tones and to bring out the pattern of parallelism and rhymes.

Hrlɨɨ is strictly syllabic, i.e. each tone corresponds to one syllable. For the most part, it employs one tone duration only and has a regular pulse – the exceptions are the penultimate syllable of a line,

---

[26] For the use and meaning of this *trnɔ̀ɔm*, see further Lundström and Tayanin 2006: 52.

Example 24 A *trnə̀əm* in Kammu and English translation. The rhyme words (end rhyme) are ɔ̀ɔn/kɔ́ɔn, pùun-pùun/k̄-núun, kì-tàak/hń-tàak, tr̩̀-kíl/rr̩̀-kíl.

Àay mə̀h krὲ nɔ́ɔŋ ɔ̀ɔn	I am still weak like a plaited table	1a
Krὲ nɔ́ɔŋ ɔ̀ɔn pùun-pùun kì-tàak	Like a plaited table, like a stepped-on tree-trunk	1b
Àay mə̀h krὲ nɔ́ɔŋ ɔ̀ɔn	I am still weak like a plaited table	1a
Krὲ nɔ́ɔŋ ɔ̀ɔn pùun-pùun tr̩̀-kíl	Like a plaited table, like a stepped-on tree-stump	1b´
Àay mə̀h kɔ́ɔn nɔ́ɔŋ nὲ	I am still small like a little child	2a
Kɔ́ɔn nɔ́ɔŋ nὲ hń-tàak k̄-núun	Like a little child, less than knee-high	2b
Àay mə̀h kɔ́ɔn nɔ́ɔŋ nὲ	I am still small like a little child	2a
Kɔ́ɔn nɔ́ɔŋ nὲ rr̩̀-kíl k̄-núun	like a little child, just about knee-high	2b´

which is longer, and occasionally also the very last syllable of a stanza. With these exceptions, each syllable is given the same duration, regardless of vowel length. A minor syllable is, without exception, treated in the same way as a major syllable and is thus given a much longer relative duration than in speech.[27]

Prolongation takes place in syllable-final sonorants (*nɔ́ɔŋ* 'still' > *nɔɔŋŋ*) and by inserting epenthetic vowels into minor syllables and prolonging them (*rŋ.kìl* 'no more than' > *rəŋŋ.kìl*). Thus, prolongation is achieved using positions in which the length contrast does not occur. This differs from the situation in normal speech, where minor syllables are unstressed and have a very short epenthetic vowel that often disappears completely.

A *hrlìi* performance has three pitch levels: high, low, and neutral, and a tonal centre. The main part of the performance is limited to two pitch levels, high and low – the only exception being a few syllables at the beginning of a poetic line after a pause, which are performed as neutral tones at lower pitch and may be considered as an initial formula. The size of the interval between the two dominating pitches varies from a second to a minor third (2–3 semitones), which means that the pitches can be easily recognized by ear. The high and low pitches are almost invariably used for High and Low lexical tone respectively. In Example 25, the repetitions of words in this performance are grouped in boxes to demonstrate

---

27 See further Lundström and Svantesson 2008.

Kammu vocal genres (Laos)

Example 25 An approximate transcription of a *hrlɨ̌* performance of the *trnə̀əm* in Example 24, in which the lines have been reorganized so that the consistent realization of L = Low and H = High lexical tones can be readily seen. After a performance by Kàm Ràw.

that the same lexical tones are performed in the same way each time they occur.

In the investigation, we used a material consisting of performances by one Kammu speaker, Kàm Ràw (Damrong Tayanin), speaking the Yùan sub-dialect of the Northern dialect.[28] A 'studio sample', which was performed at the informant's own initiative, consisted of 12 performances and 909 syllables in total. A 'laboratory sample',

---

28 Reported in Lundström and Svantesson 2008.

which was performed at the request of the researcher (HL), consisted of 24 performances and 1,393 syllables. Finally, there was an 'experiment sample' consisting of another 12 performances that the informant had not performed in this style before. This was made in order to test predictions about rhythm and pitch relative to lexical tones. A fourth sample consisted of 2 performances by other Yùan informants, bringing the total up to 50 performances.

The results showed that the *hrlìi* material followed the linguistic analysis of syllabification and of the individual tones, both on major and minor syllables. There were no mismatches at all in syllabification and the tonal mismatches were extremely few, less than 0.5%.

The *trnə̀əm* presented in Example 26 praises a woman's beauty. This is made clear in the second stanza. The poetic form is similar to that of Example 24. This *trnə̀əm* will be used as an example of several vocal genres starting with *hrlìi* in Example 27, since, by using lines from the same *trnə̀əm*, the differences between vocal genres will become clearer.

Example 26 A *trnə̀əm* in Kammu and English translation. Rhyme words (end-rhyme) are mɔ̀ɔn/kɔ́ɔn, ɔ̀ɔn-crɔ̀ɔn/rɔ̀ɔn, cùut/sî̓yúut.

• 04 *Nàaŋ mɛ̀ɛn, hrlìi*

Nàaŋ mɛ̀ɛn trə́ mà mɔ̀ɔn	What silkworm's fruit are you, dear,	1a
Ɔ̀ɔn-crɔ̀ɔn nàaŋ kɔ́ɔn mían ɔ̀ɔn cùut	Beautiful and tall like a *cùut* plant?	1b
Nàaŋ mɛ̀ɛn trə́ mà mɔ̀ɔn	What silkworm's fruit are you, dear,	1a
Ɔ̀ɔn-crɔ̀ɔn nàaŋ kɔ́ɔn mían ɔ̀ɔn yòl	Beautiful and tall like a banana flower?	1b′
Nàaŋ mɛ̀ɛn kɔ́ɔn mà mə̀ Sî̓yúut nàaŋ kɔ́ɔn mían ràaŋ rɔ̀ɔn	What mother's child are you, dear, Rosy and sweet like a cockscomb flower?	2a 2b
Nàaŋ mɛ̀ɛn kɔ́ɔn mà mə̀ Sñ́tùuñ nàaŋ kɔ́ɔn mían ràaŋ rɔ̀ɔn	What mother's child are you, dear, Rosy and fair like a cockscomb flower?	2a 2b′

In Example 27, musical notation has been used for the transcription in order to indicate the sound of a *hrlìi* performance. No bar-lines have been used as the musical phrases evidently depend on the poetic lines, in this case combinations of 5 and 7 syllables. For the same reasons, the staffs are aligned after the phrase-endings. When lexical tone and musical pitch coincide, this is indicated by capital letters, L and H, respectively. In this performance, they always coincide; but there are examples where High lexical tones are performed to the lowest, 'neutral', pitch which functions as an initial formula – in this case, the first notes of lines 1, 3, 5, and 8. Lines 3, 5, and 8 start with the short added word *sáh*, 'I say', at the lowest, 'neutral', pitch level. This is a common auxiliary word in *hrlïï* and some other vocal genres. It has not been transcribed in the example. The last two tones of a line are performed in the same way, regardless of lexical tone, and hence function as a final formula.[29]

Example 27 *Hrlïï* performance in notation. The word *sáh*, approximately 'I say', is an extra word often used at the beginning of lines. It is very short and does not affect the rhythm. Performed by Kàm Ràw, ca. 1979/80. Original pitch: c ≈ 130 Hz. • **04 Nàaŋ mὲɛn, hrlïï**

H: High lexical tone and high pitch level coincide.
L: Low lexical tone and low pitch level coincide.
l, h: Lowest pitch level used in initial formula regardless of lexical tone (parentheses show the initial formulae).

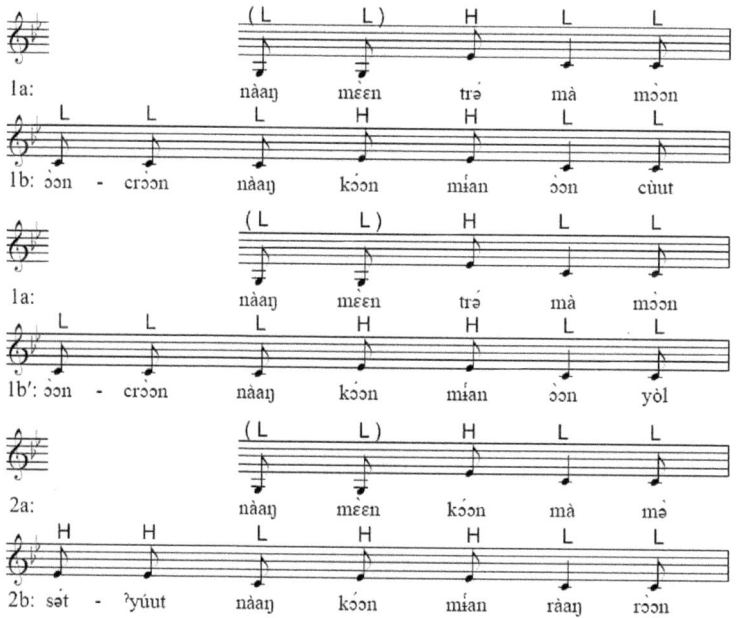

---

[29] For more details, see Lundström and Svantesson 2008 and Lundström 2010: 62–63.

In the borderland between song and speech

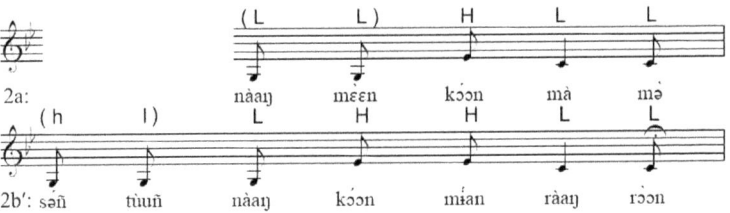

This particular *trnə̀əm* will be often referred to in the following, as it will be used for analysing several Kammu genres. In Example 28, the first stanza is employed in order to demonstrate some basic characteristics of *hrlìi* performance. It demonstrates that the majority of the words are performed at two pitches (around C3 and D3, respectively). The former are all syllables with Low lexical tone and the latter with High. It may also be noted that the initial 2–3 syllables of lines 1 and 3 are much lower – these sections serve as initial formulae at the beginning of lines, usually after a breathing pause.

Example 28 A Melodyne graph of the first four lines (= first stanza) of the performance in Example 27. High lexical tone is realized at a rather fixed high pitch relative to the Low. [ ] = the extra word *sáh* with High tone is normally performed low in the initial formulae. Vertical: pitches, horizontal: time (one column = 1 second).

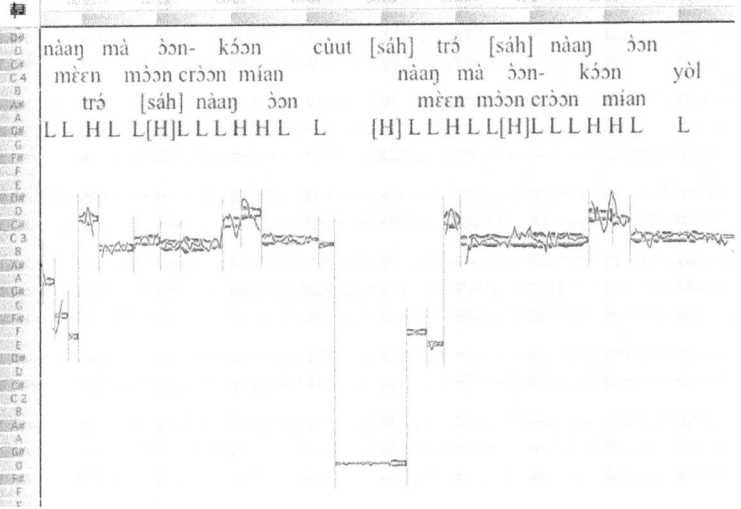

Kammu vocal genres (Laos)

The performer realizes High tones in the region above approximately 130 Hz, while Low tones are between 100 and 130 Hz. Lines start below 100 Hz and the separation between the tones is rather limited in this region. Examples 29–31 show the details of the lexical tone as well as the movement within them. It may be noted that there is very little movement in those words with Low lexical tones that are realized as low, while there is movement in words with High tone.

Example 29 Pitch measurements of lexical tones and movements within syllables in phrases 1–4 of the performance in Example 27. In this graph, tone length is disregarded. Vertical: Hz, horizontal: time.

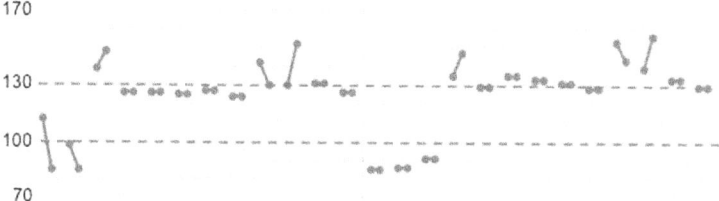

L L H L L L LL H H L L H L L H L L L L L H H L L
nàaŋ trɔ́ mɔ̀ɔn crɔ̀ɔn kɔ́ɔn ɔ̀ɔn   sáh mèɛn mà   ɔ̀ɔn- nàaŋ mían yòl
mèɛn mà ɔ̀ɔn- nàaŋ mían cùut nàaŋ trɔ́   mɔ̀ɔn crɔ̀ɔn kɔ́ɔn ɔ̀ɔn

In Examples 30 and 31, phrases 5–6 and 7–8, respectively, are illustrated in the same manner. Two measurement points per base syllable are shown: the initial F0 and the first subsequent F0 maximum within the same syllable. Dashed lines show approximate pitch registers for low and neutral (below 100 Hz) lexical tones. It can be noted that High lexical tones are performed with a sliding upward motion when approached from the lowest 'neutral' pitch register (Example 30: the fourth syllable kɔ́ɔn and Example 31: the tenth syllable kɔ́ɔn). Similarly, a High lexical tone followed by a Low can be performed with a sliding downward movement (Example 30, the eighth syllable ʔyúut).

Example 30 Pitch measurements of phrases 5–6 of the performance in Example 27.

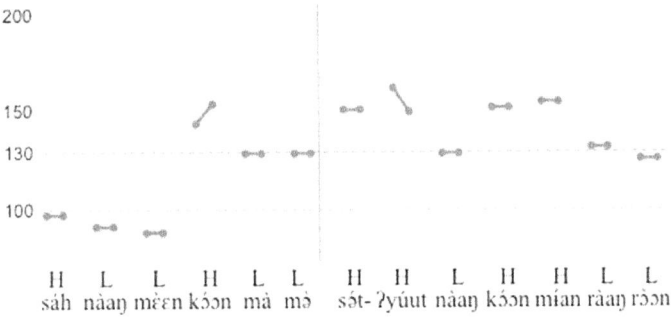

Example 31 Pitch measurements of phrases 7–8 of the performance in Example 27. The auxiliary word *sáh* (syllable 6) with High lexical tone is performed in the higher area of the lowest pitch and glides downwards.

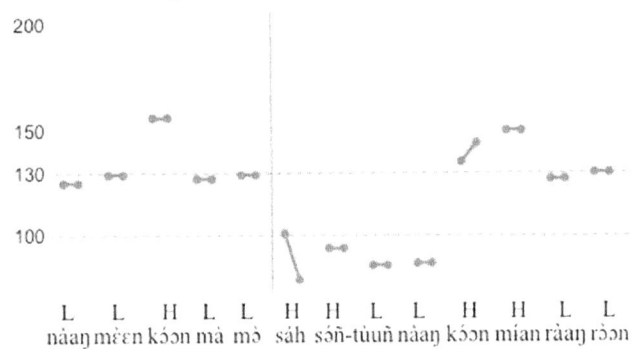

The *hrlíi* performance template

Melody
- Level melody without speech intonation with a tonal centre (see Example 27).
- Two pitch levels for the main part of the performance (high and low) with an interval of about 2–3 semitones.
- Melodic range: 9 semitones.

Rhythm
- Strictly syllabic, with a regular pulse.
- One tone duration dominates.

Form
- Strophic (*trnàəm* poem).

Phrasing
- Prosodic and musical phrases are aligned.
- Verbal phrasing dominates (a 7-syllable line is two tone durations longer than a 5-syllable line, etc.).

Initial/final formulae
- In an initial formula, syllables at the beginning of a poetic line are performed at an extra-low tone. Occurs at the very beginning and when a line starts after a pause.
- The penultimate syllable of a phrase and the very last syllable of a stanza are longer.

Word variations
- Same duration for long and short vowel, minor and major syllable.
- An auxiliary word *sáh*, 'I say', often occurs at the start of phrases, performed very short and at an extra-low level.
- Schwa vowels (normally ə) have the same duration as all other vowels that are performed as short.

Lexical tones
- Lexical tones are realized, except in the initial formula.
- High and low pitch levels correspond to lexical tones.
- Tones are realized within separate pitch regions (Low tones in the 100–130 Hz region, and High tones above 130 Hz).
- High lexical tones are performed with a sliding upward motion when approached from a lower pitch. A High lexical tone followed by a Low is performed with a sliding downward movement.
- There is very little movement in words with Low lexical tones that are realized as low, while there is movement in words with High tone.

Analysis 5 The vocal genre *hrwə̀*

Hrwə̀ is used particularly by young people, especially when away from the village, out in the fields, or in the forest. It was used for *trnə̀əm* with contents that fitted these contexts. The performance is built on a short melodic motif that is repeated with small variations (Example 32). It makes use of three basic pitch levels. In details, there is much variation in the execution of pitches and in the rhythmic delivery. The highest and the lowest pitch levels are approximately a fourth (5 semitones) apart. The middle pitch is normally a minor third (3 semitones) above the lowest. The last note has a downward slur with an indefinite final pitch approximately a fourth below.

Example 32 *Hrwə̀* musical phrases of a 5- and a 7-syllable line (for comparative reasons the syllables are numbered backwards). 'V' refers to vowel reduplication and 'v' to prolongation (with glissando).
• 05 *Nàaŋ mɛ̀ɛn, hrwə̀*

Using two lines from the *trnə̀əm* in Example 26, a Melodyne graph is shown in Example 33. The melodic shape is clear and the graph also demonstrates the difference between 5- and 7-syllable lines: the 5-syllable line is prolonged by adding two more syllables. When a line is prolonged by added syllables, they are added in the middle of the line without affecting the initial or final formulae. On the other hand, the long final tone is shortened so that the length of each phrase is approximately 7 seconds. In that way the musical metre is preserved.

Kammu vocal genres (Laos)

Example 33 *Hrwə̀* performance of the *trnə̀əm* Example 26. Phrase 3: *Nàaŋ mɛ̀ɛn trɔ́ mà mɔ̀ɔn* (5 syllables not counting reduplicants) and phrase 4: *Ɔ̀ɔn-crɔ̀ɔn nàaŋ kɔ́ɔn mían ɔ̀ɔn yòl* (7 syllables). Performed by Kàm Ràw, ca. 1979/80. Original pitch: final tone ≈ 130 Hz.

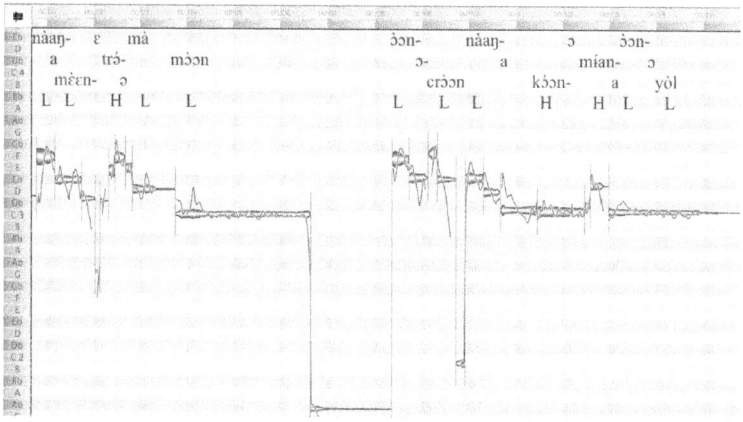

In some genres of vocal expressions in Kammu culture, there is vowel reduplication. This means that the vowel of a syllable is repeated, and the reduplicant is often much longer than the original vowel. In this particular case reduplication takes the following form (the reduplicant is underlined). For full text and translation, see Example 26:

Nàaŋ mɛ̀ɛn trɔ́ mà mɔ̀ɔn	*can become:*	Nàaŋ-<u>a</u> mɛ̀ɛn-<u>ɛ</u> trɔ́-<u>ɔ</u> mà-<u>a</u> mɔ̀ɔn
What silkworm's fruit are you, dear,		
Ɔ̀ɔn-crɔ̀ɔn nàaŋ kɔ́ɔn mían ɔ̀ɔn cùut	*can become:*	Ɔ̀ɔn-<u>ɔ</u>-crɔ̀ɔn-<u>ɔ</u> nàaŋ-<u>a</u> kɔ́ɔn-<u>ɔ</u> mían-<u>a</u> ɔ̀ɔn-<u>ɔ</u> cùut
Beautiful and tall like a *cùut* plant?		

In *hrwə̀*, every line is divided into two or three prosodic groups marked by a higher first lexical tone irrespective of L or H and by successive lowering (declination) of pitches within each prosodic group (Example 34). Lines visualize pitch declination. Each new prosodic group starts with a high pitch which is usually lower than in the previous group. Within a declining group, High tones are usually performed lower than preceding Low tones. If the first lexical tone in a phrase is High, it is boosted, as in the case of the word *kɔ́ɔn* in Example 34.

Example 34 *Hrwə̀*. First phrase of the *trnə̀əm* Example 26 showing melodic descent and a case where a high lexical tone (*kɔ́ɔn*) is boosted so that the second phrase starts higher than the preceding one.

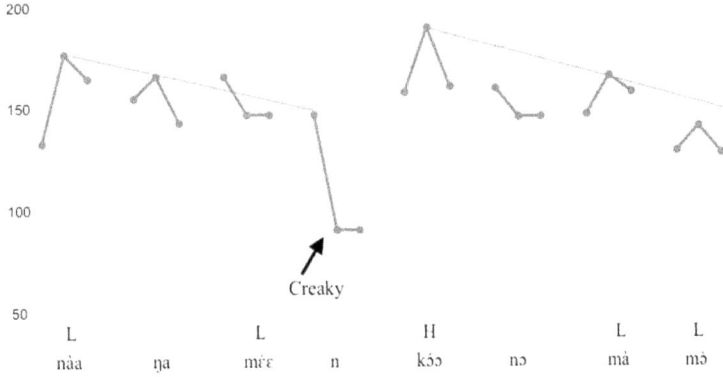

Example 35 displays F0 measurement points for each syllable, including reduplicants, and also in sonorant codas (when prolonged). For example, in *nàaŋ*, six points were measured: start, middle, and last, both in the original syllable *nàa* and in the reduplicant *-ha*. Frequencies (in Hz) are shown on the vertical axis. Lines visualize pitch declination through each of the three prosodic groups. Creakiness often occurs at the end of a prosodic group and might signal a phrase boundary, as happens with regard to speech in several languages.

Example 35 *Hrwə̀*. First phrase of the *trnə̀əm* Example 26.
• 05 *Nàaŋ mɛ̀ɛn, hrwə̀*

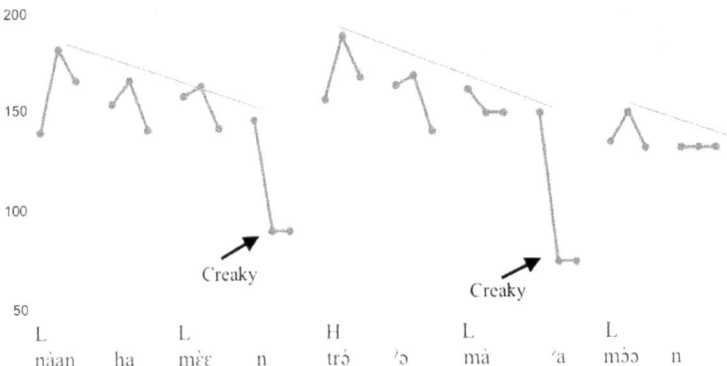

The *hrwə̀* performance template

Melody
- Formulaic descending melody with a tonal centre (see Example 32).
- There is successive lowering or declination of pitches within each prosodic group.
- Syllables have a rising-falling pattern.
- Melodic range: 5 semitones.

Rhythm
- Regular pulse.
- One tone duration except at phrase endings.

Form
- Strophic (*trnə̀əm* poem).

Phrasing
- Prosodic and musical phrases are aligned.
- Verbal phrasing dominates (a 7-syllable line is proportionally longer than a 5-syllable line, etc.).
- Lines are divided into prosodic groups marked by a higher first lexical tone.
- The last word of a phrase is prolonged and lower, regardless of tone.
- Creakiness occurs at the end of a prosodic group and might signal a phrase boundary.

Word variations
- Same tone duration for long and short vowels, minor and major syllables.
- Coda prolongation is frequent.
- Syllabic reduplication is frequent. Reduplicants are generally lower than the original vowel.
- Schwa vowels (normally ə) have the same duration as all other vowels that are performed as short.

Lexical tones
- Lexical tones are often ignored. When realized, lexical tones are relative.
- Because of declination, a High tone can start lower than a preceding Low tone in the same prosodic group.

Analysis 6 The vocal genre *húuwə̀*

Húuwə̀ also belongs to the young people – especially young girls – and is used in the fields or the forest. It was used for *trnə̀əm* with contents that fitted these contexts. The melodic formula is similar to that of *hrwə̀*, but the phrases start low and have a recurring refrain (Example 36, for full text and translation see Example 26).

Example 36 *Húuwə̀* performance of the *trnə̀əm* Example 26. Phrase 3: *Nàaŋ mɛ̀ɛn trə̀ mà mɔ̀ɔn* (5 syllables not counting reduplicated vowels) and phrase 4: *ɔ̀ɔn-crɔ̀ɔn khɔ́ɔŋ kɔ́ɔn mían ɔ̀ɔn yòl* (7 syllables), thus demonstrating the difference between lines with 5 and 7 syllables. In contrast to *hrwə̀* (Example 33) the first syllable(s) of a line is/are always performed low. Performed by Kàm Ràw, 1978. • **06 Nàaŋ mɛ̀ɛn, húuwə̀**

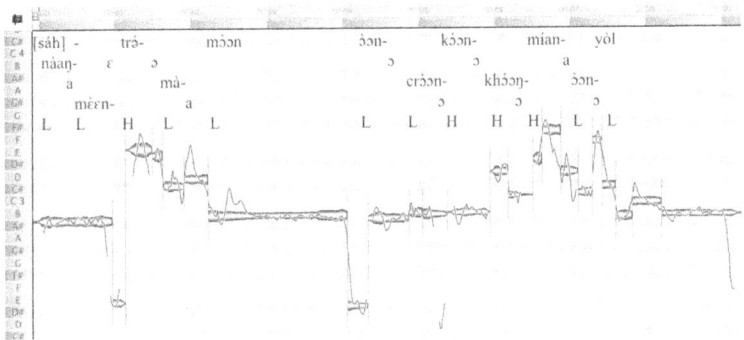

The refrain is performed to the syllables *húu wə̀* in the beginning and after each stanza (Examples 37–38). In the neighbouring Kwɛ̀ɛn area, the corresponding genre was called *əə ləə* after its refrain in that area.

The refrain is very similar to the refrain of a lullaby, the words *tuul luul* being used for lulling a child.

Example 37 *Húuwə̀* refrain. Performed by Kàm Ràw, 1978. Original pitch: c ≈ 145 Hz.

Kammu vocal genres (Laos)

Example 38 *Húuwə̀* refrain.

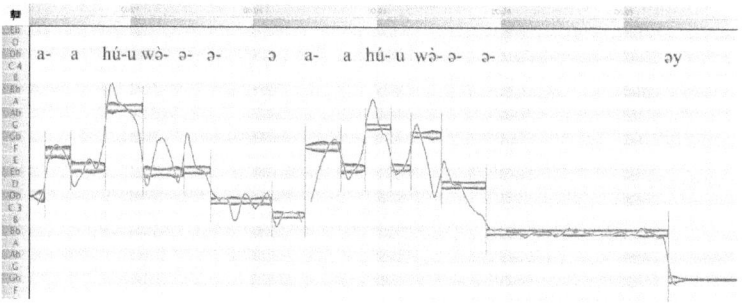

Húuwə̀ involves many reduplications and tonal movements in all syllables, both main and reduplicants. There is no use of separate pitch regions to realize tones. Instead, the tonal movement is rising-falling in base syllables, where the highest F0 point in High tone syllables is higher (starting from 200 Hz for our performer) than for words with Low tone. Reduplicants ignore lexical tones. The tonal contour is declining, building on the lowering of succeeding Low tones with High tones performed higher than this 'melodic' base line. The first High tone that occurs tends to be the highest within each line. These characteristics are easily observed in the graphs based on measuring height in the mid-point of the syllable (Example 39).

Example 39 *Húuwə̀*: the first two lines of the *trnə̀əm* Example 26, showing declining movement and realization of lexical tones.

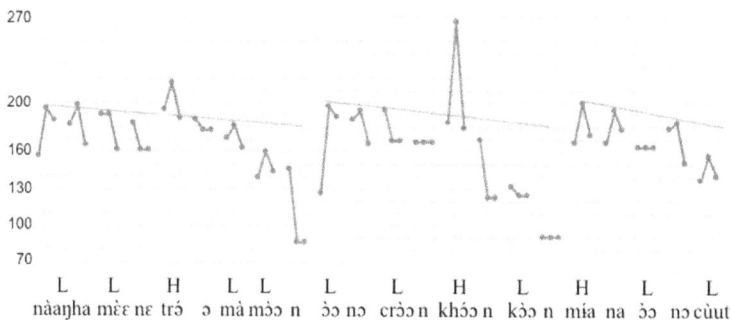

Example 39 displays F0 measurement points for each syllable, both base and reduplicant, or within a sonorant coda when prolonged. For example, six points were measured in *nàaŋ*: start, middle, and last, both in the base syllable *nàaŋ* and in the reduplicant *-ha*. Frequencies (in Hz) are shown on the vertical axis. This performer realizes High tones from or above 200 Hz. Example 40 displays measurements of the maximum pitch for each base syllable.

Example 40 *Húuwà:* the sixth line of the *trnàəm* Example 26, showing realization in base syllables of 5 consecutive High lexical tones: *Sɨ́ʾyúut khɔ́ɔŋ kɔ́ɔn mían* performed: *Sà-tə ʾyúu-tu khɔ́ɔŋ kɔ́ɔn mía-na ràa-ŋa rɔ̀ɔn* (in this line the word *khɔ́ɔŋ* has replaced the synonymous word *nàaŋ*).

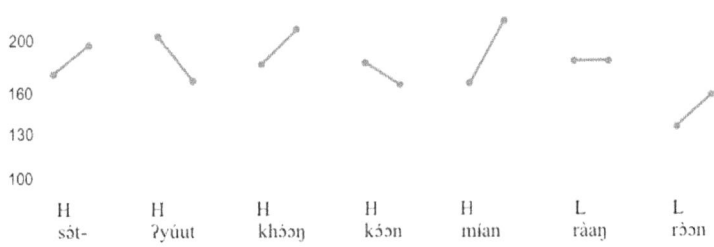

There are many reduplications and syllable prolongations; for example, the first phrase *nàaŋ mɛ̀ɛn trɔ́ mà mɔ̀ɔn* is realized as *nàa-ŋa mɛ̀ɛ-nɛ trɔ́-ʔə màaa mɔ̀ɔnnn*. Tonal movements occur in every syllable, both base and reduplicant. The tonal properties of base syllables are illustrated in Example 41.

Example 41 Illustration of tonal properties within each syllable of the two first phrases in a *húuwà* performance of the *trnàəm* Example 26. Three F0 points in every base syllable are shown. Reduplicants are not shown.

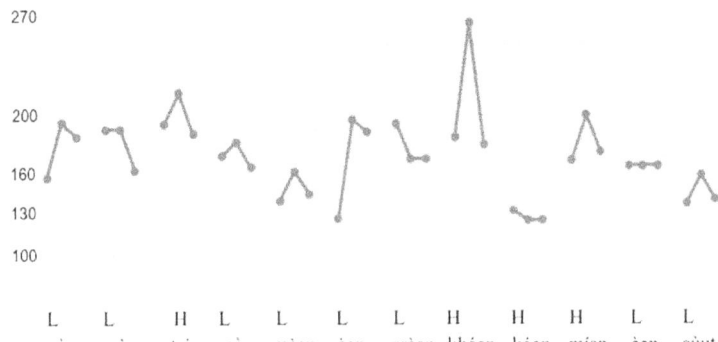

The lexical tones are realized, but by a different technique from the one in *hrlɨɨ*. In *hrlɨɨ* tones are realized within separate pitch regions (Low tones in the 100–130 Hz region, and High tones above 130 Hz); but the realization of tones in *húuwɔ̀* is relative: a High tone is higher than a preceding Low tone, and a Low tone is, with few exceptions, lower than a preceding High tone.

The *húuwɔ̀* performance template

Melody
- Formulaic descending melody moving with a tonal centre.
- Successive lowering or declination of pitches within each prosodic group.
- The tonal movement in base syllables is rising-falling.
- Melodic range: 5 semitones.

Rhythm
- One tone duration, except at phrase endings.
- Regular pulse.

Form
- Strophic (*trnɔ̀ɔm* poem) with refrain (see Example 37).

Phrasing
- Prosodic and musical phrases are aligned.
- Verbal phrasing dominates (a 7-syllable line is two tone durations longer than a 5-syllable line, etc.).
- The last word in a phrase is prolonged and lower, regardless of lexical tone.
- Creakiness occurs at the end of a prosodic group and might signal a phrase boundary.

Initial/final formulae
- The first syllable(s) of a line is/are performed low.

Word variations
- Same tone duration for long and short vowels, minor and major syllable.
- Coda prolongation is frequent.
- Syllabic reduplication is frequent.
- Schwa vowels (normally ə) have the same duration as all other vowels that are performed as short.

Lexical tones
- Mainly tone-centred.
- The realization of tones is relative: a High tone is higher than a preceding Low tone, and a Low tone is, with few exceptions, lower than a preceding High tone.
- Reduplicants ignore lexical tones.

Analysis 7 The vocal genre yàam

Yàam, 'weeping', is used particularly by women: in the village it was used for soothing babies and called Táa yàam, 'Don't weep'; for dirges belonging to funeral wakes (Yàam róoy); and for guiding the soul of the deceased to the land of the dead (Lɔ̀ɔŋ ŋɔ̀ɔr) (Analysis 1). If somebody had died in a rice field, the clothes of the deceased would be laid in that place, and women would regularly go to yàam there. After the harvesting, a ceremony would be held in the field, and the women would perform dirges.

Even though yàam is particularly connected with female activities and funeral practices, this was not exclusively so, as is demonstrated by the existence of a Tɔ́əm yàam, 'Weeping tɔ́əm'. Kàm Ràw performs this in the yàam vocal genre. In this case, the words are not arranged in stanzas, as is the case with trnɔ̀əm, but constitute about 20 lines which are tied together by chain-rhymes. It is more similar to certain ceremonial vocal expressions. Actually, the latter half is identical to the 'Tiger dance' (Yùun rwàay) that is associated with a ceremony for driving out the 'Tiger spirit' (róoy rwàay), a kind of vampire spirit. The Tɔ́əm yàam was performed with an unfaithful lover in mind. According to Kàm Ràw, it is very serious and was actually used with the intention of sending away the soul of the person in question to the land of the dead.

Outside the village yàam was also used for trnɔ̀əm, for instance when women were by themselves while washing in a river, fishing, or catching frogs. Young girls and boys would use it occasionally. In these cases, yàam was not used for praise or deprecation but rather for joking or for youth trnɔ̀əm. Boys and girls could also use yàam for a different kind of rhyme that might often be spoken.

Yàam is based on a short musical motif that may be prolonged by adding new word-pairs and repeating the penultimate 'bar' (Examples 42 and 43). The melody is arch-shaped: it starts low, rises and falls again. It ends a second (2 semitones) below (B♭) at what might be perceived as the tonic (C), and feels like a 'blue ending'.

Example 42 *Yàam* melodic formula for a line of 5 syllables. 'V' stands for a reduplicated vowel, 'v' for a less frequently reduplicated vowel.
• **07 Nàaŋ mɛ̀ɛn, yàam**

Example 43 *Yàam*. First phrase of the *trnə̀əm* Example 26. Performed by Kàm Ràw, 1978. • **07 Nàaŋ mɛ̀ɛn, yàam**

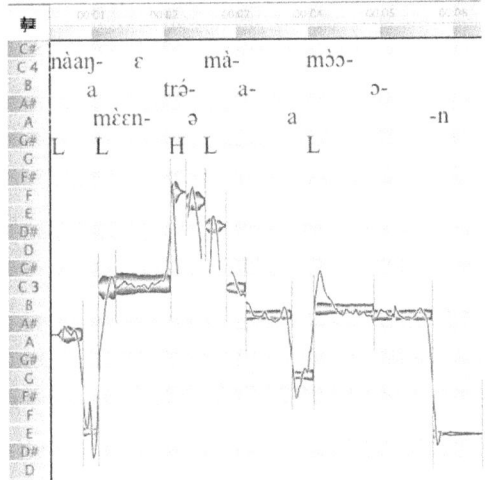

Lexical tones are realized at the vowel onset of the base syllables (Example 44). Tonal movement occurs in almost every base syllable, and this involves pitch going up or down, or up–down, down–up. High lexical tones start at a high pitch level or occasionally at a medium pitch level, in which case the high pitch occurs within the vowel. In initial formulae, all words are performed at low pitch level, regardless of lexical tone.

Kammu vocal genres (Laos)

Example 44 *Yàam*. The second phrase of the *trnə̀əm* in Example 26, demonstrating tonal movement in base syllables. The tonal movement in some prolonged codas (ŋ, n) is shown separately.

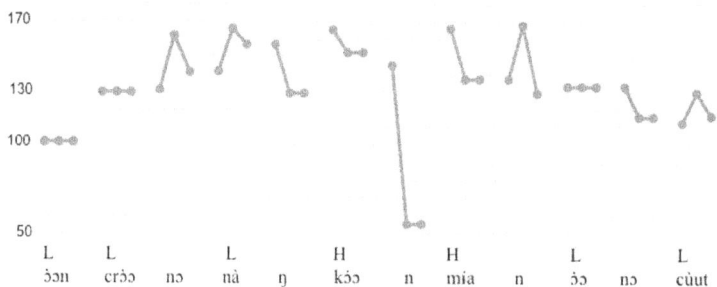

The *yàam* performance template

Melody
- Formulaic arch-shaped melody with a tonal centre ending 2 semitones below the tonic (see Example 42).
- Melodic range: 9 semitones.

Rhythm
- Regular pulse.
- Iambic movement dominates.

Form
- Strophic (*trnə̀əm* poem) [litany also occurs].

Phrasing
- Prosodic and musical phrases are aligned.
- Verbal phrasing dominates (a 7-syllable line is two tone durations longer than a 5-syllable line, etc.).
- The last word in a phrase is prolonged and lower, regardless of lexical tone.

Word variations
- Same tone duration for long and short vowels, minor and major syllable.
- Coda prolongation is frequent.
- Syllabic reduplication is frequent.
- Schwa vowels (normally ə) have the same duration as all other vowels that are performed as short.

Lexical tones
- Mainly tone-centred.
- Low lexical tones start at a low or medium pitch level and continue to high.
- High lexical tones start at a high pitch level, or occasionally at a medium pitch level, in which case the high pitch occurs within the vowel.
- Lexical tones are realized at the onset of base syllables.
- Tonal movement in almost every base syllable (pitch goes up or down, or up–down, down–up).
- Reduplicants ignore lexical tones.

Analysis 8 The vocal genre *yùun tìiŋ*

8a: *Yùun tìiŋ*, 'Water-tube dance'

In a Kammu village, the period that preceded the sowing season was the most common season for repairing houses and building new ones. When people worked on the houses, many water-containers, called *tìiŋ*, were constructed. Made from bamboo, they were about one or one and a half metres long. At feasts during the house-building, young boys and girls used to perform the words and movements of *Yùun tìiŋ* (*yùun* means 'dance'), so it can be translated 'Water-tube dance'. It was accompanied by the water-containers, which served as stamping tubes when struck against the ground. The dancers stood behind one another in a circle, each person holding a water-tube; and they walked around striking the tubes, making a curtsy rhythmically. The version in Example 45 stems from the Rmcùal village, but there are also a few recordings from neighbouring villages with variants of the words and melody.

Lexical tones might be expected not to be systematically performed in this melody type. Therefore, an approximate method of representation has been chosen that would make it easy to spot the relationship between lexical tones and pitches. This involves transcription – including reduplication of syllables – and parallel translation of the words. Initial and final formulae with regard to which it may be expected that lexical tones are not always reflected in performance are marked. The length of tones is not shown in the transcription but may be understood from Example 46. Pitches are given in the high (H), low (L), and neutral (N) categories. Neutral is in this case located between the high and the low pitches. A higher octave is marked with a + sign. When High and Low lexical tones coincide with high and low pitch, respectively, they are indicated in bold italics: *H, L*.

Even though many lexical tones coincide with musical pitch, one may interpret such occasions in the initial and final formulae as accidental. For the remaining portion of the lines, there are as many cases when they do not coincide. Often a High or Low slides to the neutral pitch. One may conclude that this melody has a more fixed melodic and rhythmic structure and is less flexible where the realization of lexical tones is concerned.

The schwa (ə) is short but clearly audible. Like all vowels, it can be reduplicated and performed to the long second tone of an iambic unit. Two examples of this occur in the first line of Example 45 (reduplicated schwa underlined; other vowels that fall on the long tone are also doubled): *Kə̀n-əə-tíik-ii tìiŋ-hee rə̀-əə-háaŋ-aa* [...]

Example 45 *Yùun tìiŋ*, Water-tube dance, with realization of lexical tones. Performed by Kàm Ràw, ca. 1977. • **08 Yùun tìiŋ**

H = high pitch.
N = neutral pitch.
L = low pitch.
L+, H+ = low, high in a higher pitch level (initial formula).
N–L = gliding from N to L.
L–N = gliding from L to N, etc.
H = High lexical tone performed high.
L = Low lexical tone performed low.

Initial formula

[L+	H+	L+–N]	N	L	N	H–N		[N–L–N	H–N]
kə̀n-ə-ə strike down	tíik-i tube	tìiŋ-he-e	r̀-ə- bamboo	háaŋ-a	tə́ən-ə- bounce	trə́-ə		tə́ən-ə- bounce	trə́-
[L+	H+	L+–N]	N	N–L	L–N	*H*		[L–N	H–N]
kə̀n-ə- strike	tíik-i down	tìiŋ-hə-ə tube	rə-ə- tree	yə̀-ə	hm̀-m- rebound	píal-i		hm̀-m- rebound	píal-i
[L+	H+	L+–N]	*L*	N	H–N	*L*	N	[*L*–N	H–N]
yùun-u, dance,	tìiŋ-i, tube,	yùun-hu-u dance	tìiŋ-i tube	pə́ə not	yùun-u dance	tìiŋ-i tube	tə́-ə broken	tìiŋ-i tube	tə́-ə broken
[L+	H+	L+–N]	*L*	N	H–N	*L*	N	[N–H	H–N]
yùun-u, dance,	tìiŋ-i, tube,	yùun-hu-u dance	tìiŋ-i tube	pə́-ə not	yùun-u dance	tìiŋ-i tube	páak-a split	tìiŋ-i tube	páak-a split
[L+	H+	L+–N]	N–H	*H*–N	N–L	N		[N–L–N	H–N]
kə̀n-ə- strike	tíik-i down	tìiŋ-he-e	r̀-ə- tube	háaŋ-a bamboo	tə́ən-ə-	trə́-ə bounce		mm	nàaŋ dear
[*L*	H–N	H–L]	N–L	*L*	N	H–N		[N–L–N	H–N]
kə̀n-ə- strike	tíik-i down	tìiŋ-hə-ə tube	(t)ə-ə-ə tree	yə̀-ə	hm̀-ə- rebound	píal-i		hm̀-m- rebound	píal-i
[L+	H+	L+–N]	*L*	N	H–N	*L*	L	[N–H	N]
yùun-u, dance,	tìiŋ-i, tube,	yùun-hu-u dance	tìiŋ-i tube	pə́ə not	yùun-u dance	tìiŋ-i tube	tə́-ə broken	tìiŋ-i tube	tə́-ə broken

Final formula

[L+	H+	L+–N]	L	N	H–N	L	N	[N–H	H–N]
yùun-u,	tliŋ-i,	yùun-hu-u	tliŋ-i	pá-ə	yùun-u	tliŋ	páak-a	tliŋ-i	páak-a
dance	tube	dance	tube	not	dance	tube	split	tube	split

Interpretation:

> Strike down bamboo tubes, bounce
> Strike down wooden tubes, rebound
> The one that doesn't dance is broken, is broken
> The one that doesn't dance is split, is split [etc.]

8b: The vocal genre *yùun tlìŋ*

The melody used for *yùun tlìŋ* also commonly served as a basic melody for a style of performing non-ritual *trnə̀əm* (Example 46). This particular performance style differs from the majority of basic melodies used for *trnə̀əm* in most Kammu dialect areas in northern Laos. According to Kàm Ràw, it was originally used in the so-called Cwàa area to the north-east of the Yùan area on the east side of the Nam Tha river and then spread into the Yùan area, probably in the 1960s. The melody may be historically related to the *cèem ə̀əy* style, commonly used among the Kammu who live around Luang Prabang.[30]

Example 46 The basic melody of the vocal genre *yùun tlìŋ*. The example shows two kinds of musical phrases: a and b, and three phrase lengths: 11 (or 10), 9, and 7 syllables, respectively, numbered backwards in order to show how syllables are added in the middle of lines while the beginning and ending are unaffected.

---

30 See further Proschan 1989: 239–240. For a musical transcription of a *cèem ə̀əy* performance, see Lundström 2010: 218.

The longer the phrase to be performed, the more tones are put into the middle of the template, while its beginning and end function as formulae and are stable in either of two variants (a and b in Example 46). In the vast majority of cases, High lexical tones are not realized by higher pitch (Example 47). Schwa vowels (ə) are clearly audible and normally short, but they are long when they fall on the second syllable of an iambic unit (underlined). This is the case in the first line of Example 47: *pà kə́ə-tóŋ-hoo* […]

Example 47 *Yùun tìiŋ* genre with lexical tones. A suite of three *trnə̀əm*: *Yèm àay yèt tàa lès pŋkà* (When close to you I'm shy) > *Mà àay àn àay tèn wáay wèc* (Mother asked me to go and to hurry home) > *Prɔ́ àay yèt rùam kúŋ* (I wish we could live together in the village). Performed by Kàm Ràw, ca. 1977.

H = high pitch level.
h = medium high pitch level.
l = medium low pitch level.
L = low pitch level
L+, H+ = low, high in the higher octave (initial formula).
H–L etc. = gliding from H to L, etc.
H, L, h, l = lexical tone and tone-level coincide.

Initial formula

[l+	h+	l+–l]	l	L	L–l	h–L
pà	ká-	tóŋ-ho	llit-e	théeŋ-e	làm-a	ŋà
eat	egg		beetle		tasty	itching

[l+	h+	l+–l]	l	L	L	l
pà	ká-	tóŋ-ho	sén-	wà	làm-a	tées-e
eat	egg		beetle		tasty	itching

[l+	h+	l+–l]	L	L	L–L–l	l
yèm-e	àay-a	yèt-e	tàa	lès-e	kàay-a-a	sáh
when	I	stay	at	close	then	say

[l+	h+	l+–l]	l	L	L	l
yèm-e	àay-a	yèt-e	tàa	cà-a	kàay-a	sáh
when	I	stay	at	far	then	say

[l+	h+	l+–l]	l	h–L		
mà	àay-e	àn-ha	àay-a	téc-e		
mother	my	let	me	sell		

[L	h	H–h]	h–l	l–h		
mà	àay-e	àn-a	àay-a	téc-e		
mother	my	let	me	sell		

Final formula

L–L–l	h
làm-a	ŋà
tasty	itching

L–L–l	h
làm-a	èes
tasty	itching

h-L	L-h	H-L	h–l
pǹ-ə-	kà	pǹ-ə-	kà
embarrassed		embarrassed	

H–l	h–L	L–L–l	h–l
sí-e	èeŋ-e-	sí-	èeŋ-e
yearn		yearn	

L–L–l	h–l
pháay-a	lɔɔ
cotton	bobbin

H–l	h–l
pháay-a	làn
cotton	reel

Kammu vocal genres (Laos)

[l+	h+	l+–]	l	L			l–h	H–l
mà	àay-e	àn-ha	àay-a	tèn-e			wáay-a	wèc-e
mother	my	let	me	stay			hurry	return

[L	h	H–h]	h–l	L			h	L
mà	àay-e	àn-a	àay-a	tèn-e			wáay-a	kàay-a
mother	my	let	me	stay			hurry	return

[l+	h+	l+–l]	l	L	l–h	H–l	L–L–l	h–l
ò	lə̀ə	pàt-ha	pɔ̀ɔc-ɔ	tàa	sń-ə-	trùh-u	lɔ̀ɔc-ɔ	kɔ́ɔŋ-ɔ
I	then	cut	*bamboo*	at		downstream	forget	cook

[L	h	H–h]	h–L	L	l–h	H–l	h–L–l	h–l
ò	lə̀ə	pàt-ha	pɔ̀ɔc-ɔ	tàa	sń-ə-	trùh-u	lɔ̀ɔc-ɔ	cáa
I	then	cut	*bamboo*	at		downstream	forget	all

[l+	h+	l+–l]	l	L	h	H–l	l–L–l	h–l
àay	lə̀ə	tḿ-hə-	pùh-u	kɔ́ɔn-ɔ	pŕ-ə-	yɔ́ɔŋ-ɔ	lɔ̀ɔc-e-e	wèc
I	then	run	across	child		dragon	forget	return

[L	h	l+	h+	l+–l]	l	h–l	L–l	h
àay-a	lə̀ə	tḿ-hə-	pùh-u	kɔ́ɔn-ɔ	pə̀-	yàa	lɔ̀ɔc-e	kàay-a
I	then	run	across	child	*title*		forget	return

[l+	h+	l+–l]	l	h–L	L–l	h–L	L–l	h
prɔ́	àay-a	plúŋ-hu	rùam-m	cét-e	dèɛ	nàaŋ-a	dèɛ	nàaŋ
wish	we	sprout	together	sour	oh	dear	oh	dear

[l+	h+	l+–l]	l	L	L–l	h–L	L–l	h
prɔ́	àay-a	plúŋ-hu	rùam-m	èn-e	dèɛ	khɔ́ɔŋ-ɔ	dèɛ	khɔ́ɔŋ
wish	we	sprout	together	0	oh	dear	oh	dear

[l+	h+	l+–l]	l	h–L			L–l	h–L
prɔ́	àay-a	yèt-he	rùam	kùŋ-u			dèɛ	nàaŋ
wish	we	stay	together	village			oh	dear

[L	h	H–l]	h–L	L			L–l	h–L
prɔ́	àay-a	yèt-he	rùam	kàaŋ-a			dèɛ	cùu
wish	we	sit	together	house			oh	dear

Interpretation:

Beetle eggs taste sour, sour, oh, dear
Spider eggs taste bitter, bitter
When close to you I'm shy, I'm shy
When far from you I yearn, I yearn

Mother asked me to go and sell bobbins
Mother asked me to go and sell reels
Mother asked me to go and hurry back
Mother asked me to go and hurry home

I cut bamboo downstream and forgot to cook it
I cut bamboo downstream and forgot everything
I met a mighty Dragon and forgot to go back
I met a wealthy Lord and forgot to go home

I wish we could sprout together bitterly, oh dear, oh dear
I wish we could sprout together happily, oh dear, oh dear
I wish we could live together in the village, oh dear, oh dear
I wish we could sit together in the house, oh dear, oh dear

The *yùun tîiŋ* performance template

Melody
- A fairly long melody with a descending contour, tonal centre, and triadic melodic movement (see Example 46).
- Melodic range: 15 semitones.

Rhythm
- Regular pulse.
- Iambic delivery of the words.

Form
- Strophic (*trnɔ̀ɔm* poem) [litany also occurs].

Phrasing
- Prosodic and musical phrases are aligned.
- Verbal phrasing dominates (a 7-syllable line is two tone durations longer than a 5-syllable line, etc.).
- The poetry may be varied by the addition of polite words or phrases.

Initial/final formulae
- Initial and final formulae.

Word variations
- Same tone duration for long and short vowel, minor and major syllable.
- Song-words with lexical meaning: *dɛ̀ɛ nàaŋ, dɛ̀ɛ khɔ́ɔŋ* (approximately 'oh, dear'), each pair of words corresponding to an iambic unit.
- Reduplication is frequent: in principle one word with a long vowel or with reduplication per iambic unit.
- All vowels, including schwa (ə), have approximately the same duration. In addition, schwa vowels are long when falling on the second long tone of an iambic unit.

Lexical tones
- Predominantly melody-centred.

- Most of the phrases circle around high, 'neutral', and low pitch levels. Lexical tones are often realized in these phrases, but contrary motion occurs.
- A 'neutral' pitch (n) is often used both for High and Low lexical tones, but Low, and more often High, lexical tones can be realized by sliding from the initial pitch: Low may be performed l–n or n–h, High may be performed h–n.
- A lexical tone is often realized at the beginning of a syllable.
- Lexical tones are not realized in initial formulae that usually comprise the first three words of a line.

Analysis 9 The vocal genre *tə́əm*

Tə́əm is an elaborate form of performing the orally transmitted *trnə̀əm* poems. The performer may also elaborate the words by prolonging or contracting them, or by adding sets of words that may be traditional or made up on the spot. A *tə́əm* melody basically consists of a melodic formula that varies between the Kammu dialect areas, but it also varies in details between villages and even between individuals. There are usually rather distinct initial and final formulae, performed for various words that may be translated 'hey' or 'oh'. A common final formula in the Yùan area is *kàay sáh*, 'this I say', and the word *sáh*, 'I say', which is often squeezed in at the start of lines within the *trnə̀əm*. Apart from these portions, the melody moves forward in rather narrow intervals that are more or less compulsively determined by the lexical tones.

In the research on related vocal expressions in South-East Asia, words or syllables that seem to be added in performance are normally treated as 'fillers' with the function of making the words of a poem fit a melody. Without denying the fact that fillers do exist, this view is based on an assumption that an existing poem with a stable form is fitted to a stable melody when performed. The process of performance is, however, a more complex creative activity which involves linguistic, poetical, and musical aspects that do not have stable forms, but are fluid. When looking at the graph in Example 48 as a formula used for a performance template, it is clear that some such words may actually be integrated and even necessary parts of the performance template, with the function of making people recognize that the performance is special for a particular area, village, or individual. The words *hə̀əy*, *eee* and *kàay sáh* thus define *tə́əm* Yùan. Other tonal dialects in the area, like Kwɛ̀ɛn, have similar patterns using their specific words.[31] The primary conclusion is that these are not random words put in to fill blank spaces in the melody, but necessary constituents for performance.

In major aspects of the performances, the words are grouped two by two and performed in an iambic pattern (short + long). In the case of parts where lexical tones and musical pitch coincide, we use the term *tone-centred*, whereas the other parts are referred to

---

31 See further Lundström 2010: 85ff.

as *melody-centred*.[32] After subtracting initial and final formulae (i.e. the parts where melody centration dominates), the remainder of the performance is more dominated by lexical tone centration.

Example 48 shows the main outline of a performance with the initial and final formulae. In its basic form, a *trnə̀əm* consists of two stanzas, the first one starting with a high-pitched *Həəy* and the second with *Eee* in the lower region. Each stanza normally consists of four musical phrases marked α, β, γ, δ. The α and δ musical phrases are initial formulae and the γ-phrase includes final formulae. These sections are mainly melody-centred. The tone-centred β-phrases are the major part of the performance. In reality there will be much variation that includes the length and order of the musical phrases.

Example 48 An outline of *Yùan tə̀əm* musical phrases in a performance of two stanzas based on the poetic lines 1a, 1b, 2a and 2b (cf. Examples 24 and 26). Arrows indicate response by listeners.

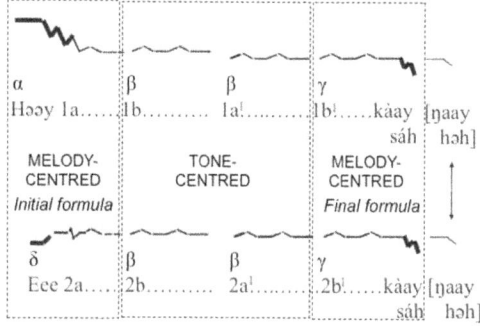

Example 49 is an approximate graph of one stanza of a *tə̀əm Yùan* performance (for full text and translation, see Example 26). The shaded parts show the areas in which words can be predicted to be performed if the lexical tones were different from this particular performance. This type of graphic representation was used in the initial phase of our research. It was devised in order to communicate musical characteristics in a manner that did not presume knowledge of musical notation and therefore served as a good starting point for discussions, while being easy to carry out with the use of an ordinary computer, basically using Microsoft Word for tables.

It should be noted that the first and third lines of the *trnə̀əm* are 5-syllable lines that are made into 7-syllable lines through

---

32 These terms were introduced in Lundström 2010: 48.

prolongation: the added 'padding words' *dὲɛ nàaŋ* (dashed underlining), meaning approximately 'oh dear'. Conversely, the last 9-syllable line, with the added 'song-words' *kàay sáh*, is turned into a 7-syllable line by means of contraction: four syllables are squeezed into a 2-syllable iambic unit (*mían ɔ̀ɔn yòl kàay*). These are common devices in *tə́əm* performance.

Example 49 One stanza of a *tə̀əm Yùan* performance of the *trnə̀əm* Example 26 in a simplified graphic transcription. H = high lexical tone, L = low. Vertical: pitch, horizontal: beats (1 square ≈ 1 eighth note). Performed by Kàm Ràw, ca. 1979/80. Original pitch: c ≈ 130 Hz.
• **09 *Nàaŋ mὲɛn, tə́əm***

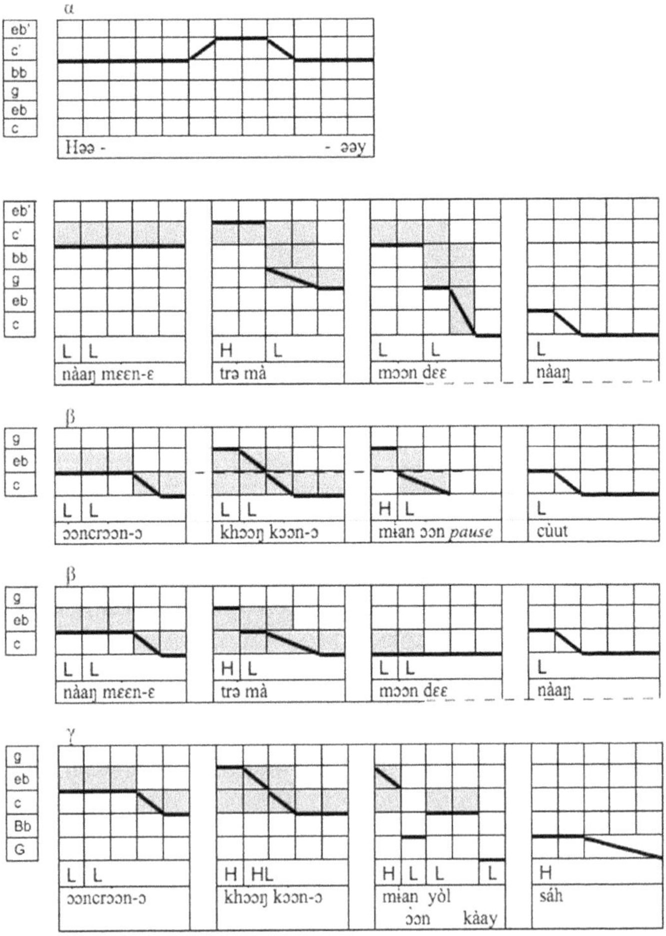

Kammu vocal genres (Laos)

When performed in the vocal *tɔ́ǝm* genre, the words are fitted into the model in Example 48. Reduplication of vowels and coda prolongation are frequent. The musical transcription in Example 50 is based on the same performance as Example 49, but it also includes the second stanza. The order of the musical phrases follows the basic pattern: α–β–β–γ for the first stanza and δ–β–γ for the second. The initial long-drawn-out *hǝǝǝy* and the final *kàay sáh* are also in agreement with the model in Example 48. Most lines are preceded by the word *sáh*, but it serves as a very short upbeat to the next syllable and steals time from the preceding syllable. There are breathing pauses in two of the β-phrases, and the first three 5-syllable lines are made into 7-syllable ones by the addition of 2 syllables (underlined). It should be observed that the two final lines of 5 and 7 syllables plus the 2-syllable *kàay sáh*, 14 syllables altogether, are compressed into a δ-phrase of 6 iambic units, which would otherwise contain 7 syllables or less. It is a common stylistic device to shorten the stanzas in this manner, particularly the final stanza of a performance.

Example 50 *Tɔ̀ǝm Yùan* performance of the *trnɔ̀ǝm* Example 26. Dotted barlines mark divisions betweeen iambic units. Musical phrases are marked α, β, γ, δ (cf. Example 48). Added words are underlined. The word *sáh* is notated with an 'x'. Performed by Kàm Ràw, ca. 1979/80. Original pitch: c ≈ 130 Hz. • **09 Nàaŋ mὲɛn, tɔ́ǝm**

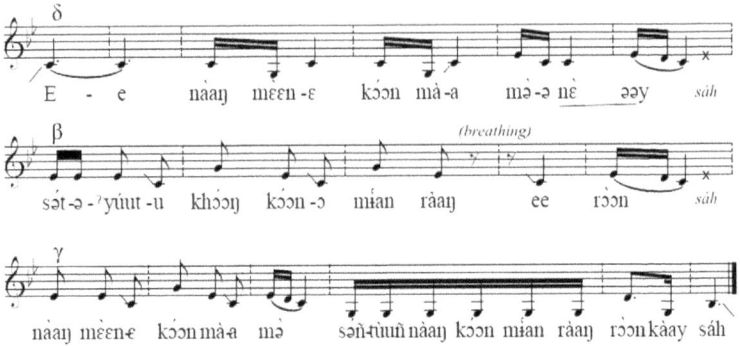

1 Pàh mòŋ cŋkwá ŋɔ̀ɔr, 'Bright moon, widen my path'

A *trnə̀əm* is an orally transmitted poem that may be performed as *tə́əm* or in many other genres. It can often easily be divided into two stanzas, the first usually being an associative parallel to the second one. This means that the meaning can be expected to be clearer in the second stanza. In Example 51, it is a person walking on a forest path in the dark, wishing for the moonlight to light it up. But a *trnə̀əm* like this one can be performed on other occasions as well.

Within each stanza, there is much repetition or parallelism, which leads to considerable play on consonants and vowels (Example 51). In this case, the first stanza is dominated by *c* and *a* ~ *ɔ* and the second stanza by *p* and *o* ~ *ɔɔ*. There are also end rhymes that tie the two stanzas together, since the first word of a rhyme-pair comes in the first and the second rhyme-word in the second stanza (the syllables *kɔ̀ɔr/ŋɔ̀ɔr*, *kɔ̀/kwá* and *kèer/kléɛr*).[33]

Example 51 The *trnə̀əm Pàh mòŋ cŋkwá ŋɔ̀ɔr*, 'Bright moon, widen my path'. End-rhymes are *cŋkɔ̀ɔr/ŋɔ̀ɔr, kɔ̀/cŋkwá, kèer/cŋkléɛr*. In the actual performance quoted in Examples 51–55, minor variations occur concerning specific words.

Còŋ pə̀ cráh còŋ pə̀	High pale, oh, high pale
Còŋ cráh cỳkɔ̀ɔr kɔ̀	High pale, sister-in-law got heartburn
Còŋ pə̀ cráh còŋ pə̀	High pale, oh, high pale
Còŋ cráh cỳkɔ̀ɔr kèer	High pale, star fruit gives you heartburn.

---

33 For more information on the poetics of *trnə̀əm*, see Lundström and Tayanin 2006 and Lundström 2010.

Pàh pə̀, mòŋ, pàh pə̀ — Bright moon, oh, bright moon
Pàh mòŋ cŋ̀kwá ŋɔ̀ɔr — Bright moon, widen my path
Pàh pə̀, mòŋ, pàh pə̀ — Bright moon, oh, bright moon
Pàh mòŋ cŋ̀klɛ́ɛr ŋɔ̀ɔr — Bright moon, peep down on my path

The following examples illustrate the realization of the lexical tones in certain melodic positions. Example 52 demonstrates that High lexical tones are realized higher than Low lexical tones, with only one exception: the fourth syllable in line δ, which is the first line after a breathing pause, usually the third line of a stanza (see Example 48), which is always performed low even if the lexical tone is High.[34] This is a case of exceptional melodic dominance that sometimes occurs close to a phrase ending. Note that the graph (Example 52) has four high pitches: H, H2, H3, and H4 and three low pitches: L, L1, and L2. This is designed to cover the melodic contour which descends more than one octave.

Example 52 Four lines from the first *tə̀əm* stanza of *Pàh mòŋ cŋkwá ŋɔ̀ɔr* in Example 51, schematically showing how lexical tones are realized (the lines in this performance are line 1 of stanza 1, line 1 of stanza 2, line 4 of stanza 1, and line 4 of stanza 2, with variations). H = high lexical tone, L = low. Performed by Kàm Ràw, 1981. Vertical: pitch levels, horizontal: beats (1 square ≈ 1 eighth note). Original pitch: L ≈ 110 Hz.
• 10 *Pàh mòŋ*, B1a

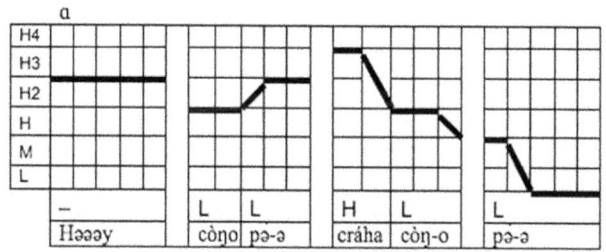

---

34 For words and translation of this *trnə̀əm*, see Lundström and Tayanin 2006: 163.

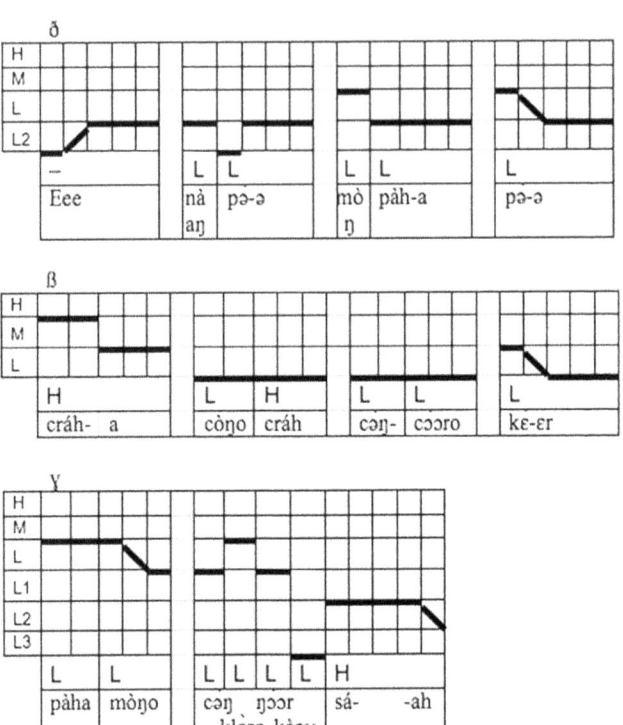

This particular *trnɔ́ɔm* was chosen as it has very few words with High lexical tones, so it is fairly easy to spot how they are realized. There is actually one line that consists only of words with Low lexical tone. In a β-phrase, these are evidently performed either at low or medium pitch (Example 53). The β-phrases are tone-centred parts of the performance and therefore dominated by the lexical tones, while the melody plays a smaller role.

Kammu vocal genres (Laos)

Example 53 The realization of a β-phrase of *Pàh mòŋ cŋkwá ŋɔ̀ɔr*, Example 51, made up of words of only Low lexical tones. For the β-phrase, see Example 48. Vertical: pitch levels, horizontal: beats (1 square ≈ 1 eighth note).

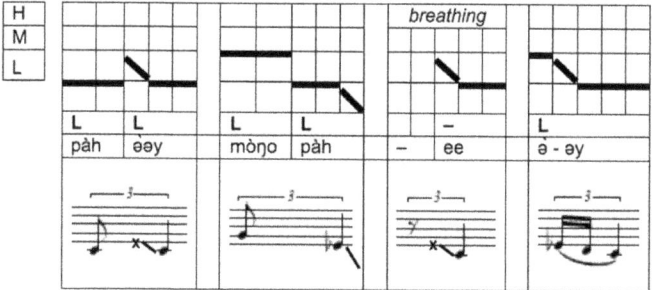

The different iambic units that occur in β-phrases in the same *trnə̀əm* are listed in Example 54. It shows that High lexical tone can be performed high, or high sliding to low. In certain positions both High and Low can be realized at medium pitch.

Example 54 The different iambic units that occur in β-phrases in the same *trnə̀əm* as the previous examples: *Pàh mòŋ cŋkwá ŋɔ̀ɔr*, Example 51. H = High lexical tone, L = Low. Vertical: pitch levels, horizontal: beats (1 square ≈ 1 eighth note).

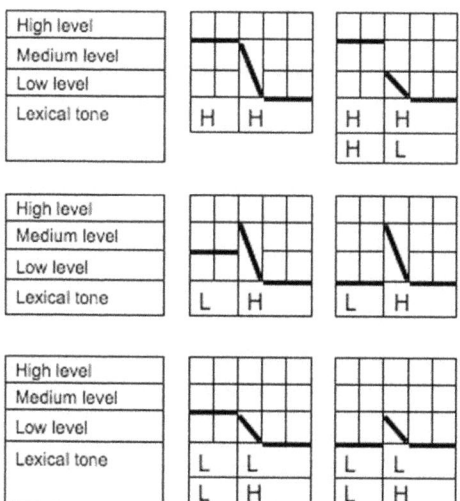

Musical transcription – whether in musical notation or graphs – tends to approximate pitches musically, i.e. the main part of a pitch that corresponds to a linguistic unit is transcribed. Initial or final movement within a sound is normally considered to be just that: a tone is reached or left by a sliding motion. The result will be a musically relevant transcription that communicates the musical sound as experienced by the person who is transcribing. An analysis based on phonetic expertise will approach this differently, and this is one of the advantages of cross-disciplinary work.

In Example 55, a section of the α-phrase in Example 52 has been measured with regard to the realization of lexical tones. This measurement adds the information that, in tɔ́əm, the lexical tones are realized at the vowel onset, while all other pitch movements are in the coda or in added syllables.

Example 55 An α-phrase of *Pàh mòŋ cŋkwá ŋɔ̀ɔr*, Example 51. Arrows demonstrate lexical tones that are realized at the vowel onset in *tɔ̀əm*.

High level					↓					
Medium level		↓						↓		
Low level	↓									
Lexical tone	L		L		H		L			
Realization	còŋ-	ə	pɔ̀-	ə	crá-	ha	còŋ-	ə		
Words	còŋ		pɔ̀		cráh		còŋ			
Translation	high		oh		pale		high			

2 *Táa píc àay yʌ̀ʌ prìaŋ*, 'Don't abandon me to stay with others'

This is a widely spread *trnɔ̀əm* that belongs to the social situation when the performer asks people to let him/her be included, or stay included, in their friendship group (Example 56). It basically says: don't force me to stay among strangers. It shares the general poetic characteristics of *trnɔ̀əm*.

Example 56 The *trnɔ̀əm Táa píc àay yʌ̀ʌ prìaŋ*, 'Don't abandon me to stay with strangers'. End-rhymes are in italics or underlined.

Táa *thíaŋ* àay yʌ̀ʌ r̲ì̲c̲	Don't discard me to stay with the munia-birds
Thíaŋ yʌ̀ʌ rìc tə̀ŋ mə̀h nə̀ŋ rìc	If you do, I will surely be but a munia-bird

Kammu vocal genres (Laos)

Táa thíaŋ àay yʌ̀ʌ kɔ̀ɔy	Don't discard me to stay with the tree shrews
Thíaŋ yʌ̀ʌ kɔ̀ɔy tə̀ŋ mə̀h nə̀ŋ kɔ̀ɔy	If you do, I will surely be but a tree shrew
Táa píc àay yʌ̀ʌ prìaŋ	Don't abandon me to stay with strangers
Píc yʌ̀ʌ prìaŋ tə̀ŋ mə̀h nə̀ŋ prìaŋ	If you do, I will surely be but a stranger
Táa plɔ́ɔy àay yʌ̀ʌ plɔ́ɔy	Don't desert me to stay with strangers
Píc yʌ̀ʌ prìaŋ tə̀ŋ mə̀h nə̀ŋ prìaŋ	If you do, I will surely be but a stranger

The performance includes frequent reduplications and coda prolongations. The lexical tones are often realized, and it is possible to distinguish three pitch areas: ≤130 Hz, 130–180 Hz and ≥180 Hz. High lexical tones lie in the highest pitch area and Low tones in the middle pitch area. Then there are portions with even lower pitch. The initial formula that starts at a high pitch covers the first 3–4 words (Examples 57–58). In this case, all the words have High lexical tone; but in the case of Low lexical tones, or a mixture, the pitch will also zigzag down to the low pitch area, and the realization of the lexical tones will be relational. It then stabilizes in the middle area where the Low lexical tones are realized.

Example 57 Realization of lexical tones in the first phrase, the α-phrase, of *Táa píc àay yʌ̀ʌ prìaŋ*, Example 56.

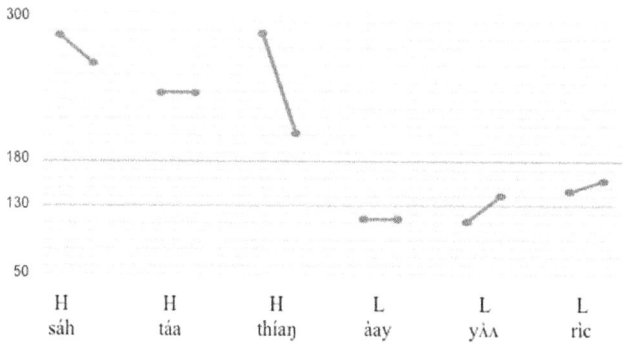

Example 58 Realization of lexical tones in the same first phrase, the α-phrase, of *Táa píc àay yìʌ prìaŋ* as in Example 57. The tonal movement within each word is shown. Vertical lines show word boundaries. The initial *həəəy* (not shown in Example 57), with a short *sáh* squeezed in before the first word of the *trnə̀əm (táa)*.

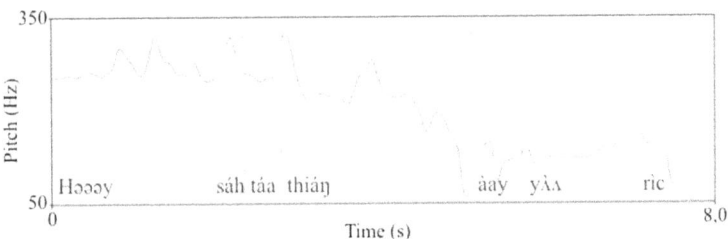

Examples 57–58 show the realization of lexical tones in the first phrase of a Yùan *tə́əm* performance. This is a melody-centred section, but lexical tones can still be seen to be realized in the performance. In this case, High lexical tones are performed higher than 180 Hz and Low tones mainly in the middle area. As shown in Example 59 this is even more evident in the second phrase, which is a tone-centred section. As these examples show, High syllables have falling tone, whereas Low syllables have rising tone in most cases.[35]

Example 59 Realization of lexical tones in the second phrase, β-phrase, of *Táa píc àay yìʌ prìaŋ*, Example 56.

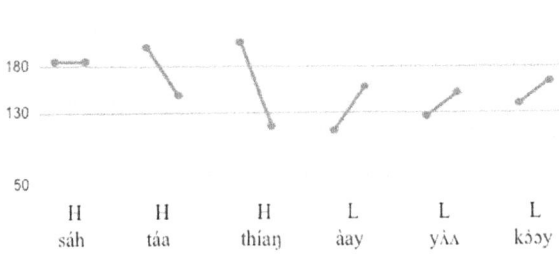

Example 60 shows the final phrase. Like all *tə́əm* performances of the Yùan style, it finishes with a falling movement in the lowest

---

35 This was shown to be statistically significant in Karlsson, House, and Svantesson 2015.

pitch area with the words *kàay sáh*, meaning 'this I say'. The whole phrase is performed low. Even the initial *plɔ́ɔy* with a High lexical tone is performed in the middle pitch area but still high, relatively speaking. Here the performance moves downwards, and 5 (or 6) syllables are performed in the lowest pitch area. They all happen to have Low lexical tones, but it can also be seen that there is no movement within the tones. This technique of flattening out the melody – and the tones – appears particularly when the tempo increases and the performer is exhausting the last remaining air in his lungs.

Example 60 Realization of lexical tones in the final phrase, y-phrase, of *Táa píc àay yʌ̀ʌ priaŋ*, Example 56. • **11 *Táa píc*, Last phrase**

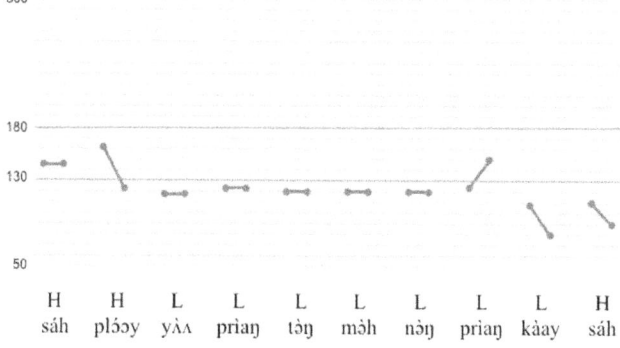

The *tə́əm* performance template

Melody
- A fairly long descending melody with a tonal centre (see Example 48).
- Melodic range: 16 semitones.

Rhythm
- Regular pulse.
- An iambic pattern dominates: normally one word-pair or one word with reduplicant per iambic unit.

Form
- Strophic (*trnə̀əm* poem).

Phrasing
- Prosodic and musical phrases are aligned.
- Verbal phrasing (syllables added through prolongation or contraction) and musical phrasing of approximately equal weight.
- The poetry can be varied by the addition of lines or stanzas.

Initial/final formulae
- An initial formula consists of an initial, long high-pitched tone (*Hǝǝǝy*) and falls with the very first syllables.
- An initial formula of phrases inside a stanza (generally the third line) consists of an initial, long low-pitched tone (*Eee*) and rises with the very first syllables.
- There is a final formula with the words *kàay sáh* (approximately 'this I say'), ending approximately 2 semitones below the tonic.

Word variations
- Song-words with or without lexical meaning.
- An auxiliary word *sáh* ('I say') often occurs at the start of initial phrases, performed at approximately the same pitch as the first syllable of the phrase.
- Same tone duration for long and short vowels, minor and major syllables.
- Coda prolongation is frequent.
- Syllabic reduplication dominates.
- All vowels, including schwa (ǝ), are of approximately the same duration. In addition, schwa vowels are long when falling on the second long tone of an iambic unit.

Lexical tones
- Contains both melody-centred and tone-centred features.
- Lexical tones are realized at three pitch levels.
- A medium pitch (M) is often used both for High and Low lexical tones.
- A lexical tone is often realized at the beginning of a syllable.
- Low and more often High lexical tones can be realized so that they slide from the initial pitch: Low may be realized as L–M or M–H, High may be realized as H–M.
- Lexical tones are sometimes ignored in the middle of the second part of a stanza when all syllables are performed L. There is no contrary movement in these passages.

Analysis 10 Krùu, 'spells'

The Kammu shaman is called *mɔ́ɔ*. This term can also be used for a physician. More specifically, the Kammu shaman is called *mɔ́ɔ rɔ́oy*, 'spirit doctor'. The shaman is a specialist in communicating with the spirit world. At the beginning of a seance, he/she calls for the assistance of the shaman spirits or *kɔ́ɔn rɔ́oy*, 'spirit children', the spirits of previous shamans. Apart from the sick person, a traditional shaman ceremony included the shaman, one or more helpers, and an 'audience'. The aim of the seance was for the shaman to diagnose and cure illness by functioning as a medium for certain spirits, by visiting the land of the dead and/or driving out bad spirits.

The contextual information has been obtained from interviews with Kàm Ràw, and the *krùu* were not recorded in an actual seance. He had substantial knowledge of Kammu shamanistic rituals, knowledge that appears to be rapidly disappearing among the Kammu people in his home area. In northern Kammu tradition, the musical instruments used were the knobbed gong, *mòoŋ*, in combination with the cymbals, *créeŋ*. Apart from these instruments the shaman, and others present at a seance, perform various vocal expressions. The shaman may also whistle, either in communication with certain spirits or when certain spirits are considered to have entered his body and are talking through him. In Kammu tradition, the *rɔ́oy hʔéep* (i.e. the spirits of those who died in accidents) are particularly believed to whistle in a special manner.

The *krùu* are known only to those who (like Kàm Ràw) were taught to be shamans. Almost all words in the *krùu* are loans from Old Lao or Proto-Southwestern Tai, the ancestor language of modern Lao, Thai, and Lü.[36] Although some of these words occur in ordinary Kammu, most of them cannot be understood by ordinary Kammu speakers. Some of the words are ultimately of Indic origin, including the word *krùu* itself, which is etymologically related to Sanskrit *guru*, 'teacher'.

One focus in this section is on the relationship between prosodic and musical phrasing in the performances. For this reason, rather long performances need to be examined. In order to facilitate this, number notation has been used for the transcriptions (see Appendix 2).

---

36 Svantesson 2011.

This is also useful for the other focus, which is on the realization of lexical tones in this genre.

Vocal expressions in a Kammu shaman seance

There are different forms of vocal expressions during a shaman seance.

Calling shaman spirits

- *Kʔə́əy kɔ́ɔn mɔ́ɔ* 'Call the shaman spirit(s)'. The shaman calls the spirits of dead shamans through these vocal expressions that start in a somewhat similar manner to the vocal genre *tə́əm* (used in social situations), but continue more like a polite *krùu* (see below). (Figure 2)
- *Tə́əm*. Those present may perform ordinary *trnə̀əm* of the type used at parties in order to encourage the shaman spirits to come (Analysis 9).
- *Mɔ́ɔ rɔ̀ɔt màañ* 'Shaman arrives and asks'. When the shaman spirits have arrived, i.e. entered the body of the living shaman, they ask why people called using the same vocal genre as *Kʔə́əy kɔ́ɔn mɔ́ɔ*.
- *Kʔə́əy hrmàal* 'Calling a soul'. The shaman may call a sick person's lost or wandering souls back. The same vocal genre as *Mɔ́ɔ rɔ̀ɔt màañ*.
- *Mɔ́ɔ krɔ́ɔ ùun róoy cɔ̀ɔy tèe* 'Shaman asks spirits for help'. A shaman may address the shaman spirit(s) for support. The same vocal genre as *Mɔ́ɔ rɔ̀ɔt màañ*.

Kàm à-thí-tháan, *prayers*

- *Ì càk cə̀ən* 'We called you'. The people may reply *Mɔ́ɔ rɔ̀ɔt màañ* 'Shaman arrives and asks'. These words are spoken quickly, like a prayer, without much intonation or marked pronunciation of lexical tones (Analysis 2).
- *Krùu kʔə́əy mà krùu* 'Spell for apologizing to the magic power' or *Wéey mɛ̀ɛ krùu* 'Worship one's power'. The shaman speaks these words in the form of a prayer after having made a mistake in a spell, or before starting in order to avoid punishment, should a mistake occur (Analysis 2).
- *Mìa tàaŋ ròoŋ cét khát mìŋ nə́ə* 'Go back to your seven-roof building'. These are words for seeing the shaman spirit(s) off. It is not among the recordings. This may indicate that it would be spoken as a prayer.

Krùu, spells

There are a great number of *krùu*, 'spells', for certain situations. They are mainly performed in a rhythmic manner, with a degree of melodic movement generally relating to the lexical tones. There are two major types of *krùu*:

1. *Polite krùu* are performed rather slowly in order to ɔ̀ɔy, 'lure out' or 'call out', a spirit that the shaman thinks is the reason for a problem without angering it. They include:
   - *Krùu ɔ̀ɔy róoy*, Calling out spirits
   - *Krùu ɔ̀ɔy róoy phíi pàa*, Calling out the sky spirit
   - *Krùu plɔ́ɔŋ rúu*, Opening your mind [= remember]
   - *Krùu ràaŋ húum*, Making someone appreciate a person.
2. *Impolite krùu* are performed in a very rapid manner in order to *ptú*, 'drive out', a dangerous spirit by scaring it. These include:
   - *Krùu ptú róoy*, Driving out a spirit
   - *Krùu ptú róoy rwàay ɔ̀ɔk*, Driving out the tiger spirit
   - *Krùu ptú róoy cntràas*, Driving out the lightning spirit

Figure 2 Kàm Ràw demonstrating the simultaneous playing of gong and cymb, *créɛŋ*, when singing the song *Kʔɔ́əy kɔ́ɔn mɔ́ɔ*, 'Calling the shaman spirits', of the shaman seance. The gong is hung on the right arm and struck with a drumstick in the right hand, while one cymbal is held between the big toe and the next toe of the left foot and struck with the other cymbal held in the left hand. The photograph was taken in Lund, Sweden, in 1999.

Krùu performances

The performer, Kàm Ràw, said that *krùu* relates to *à-thí-tháan* ('pray') as *tɔ́ɔm* (Analysis 9) relates to *hrlìi* (Analysis 4), which means that they are two ways of addressing an entity: *krùu* and *à-thí-tháan* address spirits, whereas *tɔ́ɔm* and *hrlìi* address people. It also means that *à-thí-tháan* and *hrlìi* are close to speech, while *krùu* and *tɔ́ɔm* are musically – and poetically – more complex. The relationship between lexical tones and musical pitch in *krùu* is rather complex, and closely related to the poetical form and poetical variation. The realization of the lexical tones in *krùu* is relative rather than expressed by exact pitch. In this respect, *krùu* has parallels with performances in the *tɔ́ɔm* genre, but also with *hrlìi*. The performer, Kàm Ràw, uses the same frequency area (F0) that he uses in speech, which differs from those he uses in performing *tɔ́ɔm* (Analysis 9), for example.

Many *krùu* start and end with a vocative phrase. Apart from this, prosodic phrases are often paired in a manner similar to the *lɔ̀ɔŋ* narratives (Analysis 1). The second phrase of a pair partly parallels the first phrase, either antithetically, as question and response, or by repetition, with one or two words exchanged. These pairs are indicated in the translations in Examples 62 and 63, in which the second phrase of a pair is indented. Longer *krùu* have two or more sections (A, B, C, etc.). These sections function as *thematic episodes*, which means that several prosodic phrases are tied together into one thematic episode, closer to speech.

- Some *krùu* are very short. Most are long, however, and the long *krùu* are divided into more than one section.
- The end of a section is usually marked by breathing and by the performer clearing his throat (transcribed 'hrm'). This is called *km̀rèh* and is intended to scare spirits away.
- Each section is performed in one breath.
- The tempo usually increases with each section.
- Some *krùu* start with lines of 3 syllables that are performed with long note values, i.e. more slowly than the rest.
- Basically, the *krùu* consists of lines of 5, 7, or 9 syllables, musically marked by a long final tone.
- Musical phrases generally end with ♭3⇒1 or with 1, which often, but not always, reflect lexical tone.
- The first two lines of a section are often tied together: For instance two lines of 5 syllables may be performed as 10 syllables, before finishing with a long final tone.

Kammu vocal genres (Laos)

- In long *krùu*, it is becoming more common for lines to be tied together, in some cases into very long units.

Krùu ɔ̀ɔy róoy (Examples 61–62) is a polite type of *krùu*, which is used when the shaman is asking a spirit to leave a person's body or when something is gently requested. This type is more melodious, long-drawn-out and slower compared to the *krùu* for driving a spirit out by scaring it. It has four sections of increasing speed. Section A is the most melodious one and has a tempo of 75 beats per minute, only slightly faster than a resting heartbeat. In comparison, the tempo of 'standard' *krùu* is 150–190, more than twice as fast. The tempo increases in the later sections: B has 96, C 115, and D 164. Musical phrases centre on the tonic (1 in number notation).

Example 61 The 2nd and 3rd prosodic phrases of *Krùu ɔ̀ɔy róoy*, Spell for calling out spirits (cf. Example 62). A vertical line indicates the break between the prosodic phrases. High and Low lexical tones are indicated below the words. Arrows show the realization of Low and High lexical tone at the phrase endings. The corresponding number notation is given at the bottom of the graph. Performed by Kàm Ràw, ca. 1983/84. Original pitch: 1 ≈ 139 Hz. • **12** *Krùu ɔ̀ɔy róoy*

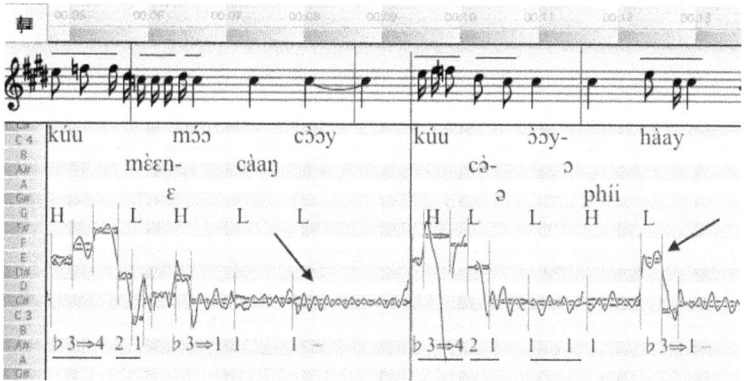

As illustrated in Example 61, High lexical tones are normally performed at a higher pitch (approximately ♭3 or 4). A musical phrase generally ends on the tonic, which is indicated by arrows. If the last syllable is Low the musical phrase will end on a low pitch (1), and if the last syllable is High it will usually end high and falling (♭3⇒1). In the graph, a vertical line shows the division between the two prosodic phrases. In this case the prosodic and musical phrases coincide. Each phrase consists of 5 syllables (6 or 7 syllables if reduplicants are counted). In performances, there may be a lower or a higher number of syllables in a phrase.

Example 62 *Krùu ɔ̀ɔy róoy*, Spell for calling out spirits, Number notation. Performed by Kàm Ràw, ca. 1983/84. Original pitch: 1 ≈ 139 Hz.

See Appendix 2 for number notation signs.
    Coincidence of lexical tone and musical pitch is marked in **bold italics**.
    Glissando is marked with ⇒. For example: *b3*⇒1 denotes glissando from a pitch where tone and musical pitch coincide (*b3*) to a pitch where they do not coincide (1).
[ ] = uncertain word or lexical tone.
( ) = uncertain pitch.

A Tempo: 1 ≈ 75/minute
Prosodic
phrase
No:

1	*1* àk-	*1* àk-			*b3*⇒ *1* — ʌ́ʌy	
2	*b3*⇒*4* kúu	*2 1* mɛ̀ɛn-ɛ	*b3*⇒1 cɔ́m	*1* càaŋ	*1* cɔ̀ɔy	
3	*b3*⇒*4* kúu	*2 1* cə̀ə	*1 1* ɔ̀ɔy-	1 ɔ	*b3*⇒*1* phíi	*b3* — hàay
4	1 kúu	*1* cə̀ə	*1 1* pàay-a	*b3*⇒1 phíi	(*b3*)⇒1 sía	Hrm

B Tempo: 1 ≈ 95/minute

5	4 mía	4 yə̀ə,	*5*⇒*4* phíi	*b3*⇒*1* mía	*1* — yə̀ə	
6	*1* mía	*1* yàam	*b3*⇒1 kúu	*1* wàa	*b3*⇒1 — dáay	
7	*1* pàay	*1* yə̀ə,	*b3*⇒1 phíi	(*b3*)⇒*1* pàay	*1* — yə̀ə,	
8	4 pàay	*1* yàam	*b3*⇒1 kúu	1 wàa	*3*⇒1 díi	Hrm

Kammu vocal genres (Laos)

C Tempo: 1 ≈ 115/minute

1	1	*1*	♭*3*⇒*1*	♭3⇒*1*	–	
9 kríaŋ		díi,	pə̀ən	péɛŋ	lɛ̀ɛw	

1	♭*3*	♭*3*⇒*1*	*1*	♭*3*⇒1	–	
10 Nàaŋ	Kɛ́ɛw	ɔ̀ɔk-ɔ	màa	kín		

1	*1*	*1*	♭*3*⇒*1*	♭*3*⇒1	1	
11 níi	yə̀ə,	Àay	Khóŋ	Khóot-	ɔ	

1	*1*	*1*	♭*3*		*1*	
12 níi	yə̀ə,	Àay	Khóot [Khóŋ?]		Míaŋ	Hrm

D Tempo: 1 ≈ 165/minute

4	**5⇒4**	**5⇒4**	♭*3*⇒1		*1*	–
13 míŋ	bɔ́ɔ	ʼyáan	kúu		rɨ́	

4	***4***	***4***	♭*3*⇒1		1	–
14 tíin	kúu	tém	cə̀-		khép	

1	*1*	1	♭*3*	***4***	♭*3*⇒*1*	♭*3*⇒1	1
15 lèp	mɨ́	kúu	lə̀ə	tém	mɛ̀ɛŋ	pɔ́ɔŋ-	ɔ

1	1	♭*3*	1		♭*3*⇒1	–
16 tíin	kúu	tém	cə̀-		khép,	

1	*1*	1	*1*	♭*3*	*1*	*1* –
17 lèp	mɨ́	kúu	lə̀ə	tém[kúu?]	ŋùu	líam

1	*1*	♭*3*	1	♭*3*⇒1	1	1	–
18 ɔ̀om	rə̀-	sáp,	Prà	báŋ	khán	kúu	Hrm

Interpretation:

[A]   Àk-àk-ʎʎy,
      I am a shaman who can help
      I shall call out the evil spirits
      I shall drive away the tiger spirit
      Hrm

[B]   Go back, spirits, go back
         Leave while I speak politely
      Go back, spirits, go back
         Go back while I speak nicely
      Hrm

[C] People have made good food for you
　　 Miss Kɛ́ɛw come out and eat
　　 Go away Master Khóng Khóot
　　 　Go away Master Khóot Míaŋ
　　 Hrm

[D] Do you not fear me?
　　 My feet are full of centipedes
　　 　My nails are full of scorpions
　　 My feet are full of centipedes
　　 　My nails are full of pythons
　　 [Go away while I speak politely
　　 　Go away while I speak nicely]
　　 om close, Buddha protect my tray

Characteristics of *Krùu ɔ̀ɔy róoy*

- The dominating pitch is 1. Range: 7 semitones.
- Syllabic and the last syllable of a line is long and generally glides upwards or downwards.
- Most lines start at a low pitch 1, independent of lexical tone. There may be 2–4 consecutive syllables like this. This is interpreted as an initial formula similar to the practice in *hrlii* (Analysis 4).
- Final syllables are performed 3⇒1 or 1 regardless of lexical tone. This can be considered a final formula in which lexical tone does not matter, similar to *tɔ́əm* (Analysis 9) and several other genres.
- High lexical tones are realized as ♭3, 4 or 5, often gliding to or from these pitches upwards: ♭3⇒4, 5⇒4, or downwards: ♭3⇒1.
- Low lexical tones are generally 1, but may be higher.
- The first lines of sections B, C, and D begin without an initial formula, so that the lexical tones are realized in musical pitches from the very start. The pitches are higher here. The patterns are 4-5-4-3-1, 4-4-5-3-1, 4-4-4-3-1. The range is one factor that gives *Krùu ɔ̀ɔy róoy* a more melodic touch, in combination with a rather low speed. These may be the features that make it 'polite'. In these passages, words with Low lexical tone may be realized as high as 4. The principle seems to be that it is not higher than the adjacent High lexical tone.

Krùu ptú róoy rwàay ɔ̀ɔk (Example 63) is intended to drive out the tiger spirit, *róoy rwàay*, which is a vampire spirit considered to be very evil and dangerous. In contrast to the previous *krùu*, which talks fairly pleasantly to a spirit, this *krùu* is not at all polite but very direct or even rude, using strong words to scare out the spirit. It is longer and consists of 8 sections (6 of which were transcribed) and about 70 lines, compared to less than 20 for the previous one. The tempo is faster, equalling approximately 232 beats per second from the start. Section B has 257, compared with an average of 95 for the polite *krùu* (Example 62). The remainder averages around 260, which means that the tempo does not increase much but is rather fast from the start. The tonal range is smaller, encompassing 3 semitones (pitches 1–3), whereas the polite style has 7 semitones (1–5). This means that the High lexical tones, though clearly audible, are not very salient. The intervals between the pitches also tend to be narrower. Reduplication of vowels occurs only in the very first line. The musical phrases are constructed as in the previous *krùu* and as described in Example 61. One exception is that the final phrase of a section generally ends with an upward sliding motion (1⇒♭3 or 2⇒♭3).

In Example 63, vertical lines are added in the margins. A line in the left margin marks a prosodic phrase-pair. A line in the right margin marks a musical phrase that is prolonged to encompass two or more prosodic phrases. For practical reasons, solid and dashed lines are alternated. In this way, it is possible to obtain an overview of how prosodic and melodic phrases are combined.

The first 8 prosodic phrases coincide with the musical phrases in the same manner as in Example 62. The prosodic phrase No. 9, however, ends on a High syllable (ʔγóoη) that is performed low (1), while the musical phrase ends in No. 10, the last syllable of which is High and performed high–low (♭3⇒1). This results in one melodic phrase being prolonged to encompass two prosodic phrases (9–10). There are several cases of a musical phrase being prolonged to encompass 2–5 prosodic phrases. In prolonged musical phrases, long sequences of syllables will often be performed low (pitch 1), regardless of lexical tone. This practice can partly be explained by the fact that each section (A, B, C, etc.) is performed in one breath. When a section gets 'wordier', more words need to be squeezed in, since the performer needs to save the air in his lungs, and prosodic phrases are then tied together into prolonged musical phrases.

There is only one case where a prolonged musical phrase corresponds exactly to one prosodic phrase-pair (39–40), but there are more cases when a prolonged musical phrase includes a prosodic phrase-pair (16–17, 18–19, 30–31, 35–36). It may be concluded that prosodic and musical phrases often coincide; but when the tempo is fast and the number of words in a section increases, musical phrasing tends to dominate.

This *krùu* shares many of the characteristics of the former one (Example 62), but some differences may be noted:

- Range: 3 semitones.
- In most cases the final syllable of a section is performed with an upward glissando: 1⇒3 or 2⇒3.
- High lexical tones are realized at 3 or 2.
- Several sections start without an initial formula (sections B, D, E, H).
- In several cases whole lines are performed at one pitch (1) regardless of lexical tones, particularly in the latter part of sections.
- In several cases three lines are grouped together so that lines 2 and 3 begin without an initial formula.

Example 63 *Krùu ptú róoy rwàay ɔ̀ɔk*, Spell for driving out the tiger spirit. Number notation. Performed by Kàm Ràw, ca. 1983/84. Original pitch: 1 ≈ 139 Hz.

For number notation signs, see Appendix 2.
Vertical line left margin = prosodic phrase pairs.
Vertical line right margin = musical phrase longer than a prosodic phrase.
Coincidence of lexical tone and musical pitch is marked in **bold italics**.
Glissando is marked with ⇒. For example: *b*3⇒1 denotes glissando from a pitch where tone and musical pitch coincide (*b*3) to a pitch where they do not coincide (1).

A Tempo: 1 ≈ 232/minute

	1–	1	1	*b*3	2	*1*	1	*b*3⇒1 –	
1	òom	cúk-	u	cík-	i,	Prà	cá-	kháan	

	*b*3	1	*1*	1				*b*3⇒1 –	
2	sáaŋ	wáan,	Prà	cá-				khóo	

	*b*3	*b*3	1	1				*b*3⇒1 –	
3	phák	khóo-	mòo	àa-				cáan	

	1	*1*	1	1	1	*1*	2⇒*b*3 –	
4	wáan	àn-	nì	pén	wáan	àa-	sáŋ	Hrm

B Tempo: 1 ≈ 257/minute

	*b*3	2	1	1	1	*1*	*1*	*1*	*b*3⇒*1* –
5	wáan	àn-	nì	pén	wáan	lì-	lì	lì-	lì

	*b*3	*b*3	2	2			2⇒1 –	
6	híin	khóp-	khép	khɔ́ɔ-			khɛ́ɛ,	

Kammu vocal genres (Laos)

	1	1	1	1			b3⇒1 –	
7	nàm	cók-	cék	cɔ́ɔ-			céɛ	

	b3	2	1	1			b3⇒1 –	
8	kúu	cə̀ə	sá	phíi			pɔ́ɔp	

	1	1	1	1			1 –	
9	phíi	pɔ́ɔp	màa	ʔyóoŋ-			ʔyóoŋ	

	1	1	b3	2			b3⇒1 –	
10	kúu	cə̀ə	sá	phíi			phóoŋ	

	b3	2	1	1			1 –	
11	phíi	phóoŋ	màa	ʔyáay-			ʔyáay	

	1	1	1	1			2⇒b3 –	
12	kúu	cə̀ə	sá	phíi			[pháay|haay]	Hrm

C Tempo: 1 ≈ 240/minute • **13** *Krùu ptú róoy rwàay ɔ̀ɔk*, **C–D**

	1	1	1	1			1 –	
13	phíi	pháay*	màa	ʔyá-			ʔyá	[* haay?]

	1	1	b3	b3			b3⇒1 –
14	kúu	cə̀ə	sá	phíi			ká

	b3	2	1	1			1 –
15	phíi	ká	màa	ʔyɨ́a?-			ʔyɨ́a?

	1	1	b3	b3	2⇒1	1	1 –
16	phíi	lə̀ə	kép	sḿ-	pɔ́ɔy	tàaŋ	dèey

	1	1	1	1	2	1	1 –
17	phíi	lə̀ə	kép	sḿ-	pɔ́ɔy	tàaŋ	kók

	1	1	1	1	1	1	1⇒b3 –
18	kìi	lə̀ə	yòk	sḿ-	pɔ́ɔy	tàaŋ	dèey

	b3	2	1	2	1	1	b3⇒1 –
19	phíi	lə̀ə	yòk	sḿ-	pɔ́ɔy	tàaŋ	háak

	b3	2	b3	1			1 –
20	máak	màn	tók	tàaŋ			dèey

	1	1	1	1	1	1	1⇒b3 –
21	máak	màn	tók	sáam	sú	sáam	sáay

	b3	b3	b3	2			1 –
22	Mɨ̀ɨn	kɔ́ɔn	kép	bɔ́ɔ			dèey

	b3	b3	b3	2			1 –
23	Séɛn	kɔ́ɔn	kép	bɔ́ɔ			dèey

	1	1	1	1			1⇒b3 –	
24	Kúu	kép,	kúu	yàŋ			dèey	Hrm

In the borderland between song and speech

D Tempo: 1 ≈ 282/minute • **13 Krùu ptú róoy rwàay ɔ̀ɔk, C–D**

	♭**3**	**2**	**1**	1				♭**3** –		
25	Phíi	làə	wàa	p-				sáŋ		

	♭**3**	**2**	**1**	1				♭**3**⇒1 –		
26	phíi	làə	wàa	sḿ-				pɔ́ɔy,		

	1	1	**1** –	**1**	♭**3**			♭**3**⇒1 –		
27	kúu	[bɔ́ɔ]	wàa	lɛ̀	sḿ-			pɔ́ɔy		

	1	**1**	**1**	1				♭**3** –		
28	kúu	càə	wàa	sóm-				pá		

	2	**2**	♭**3**	**2**	1	1	1	1 –		
29	kúu	càə	sá	nàm	tóo-	róo	tée-	rée		

	♭**3**	**2**	♭**3**	**2**	**3**	**1**		1 –		
30	phíi	pɔ́ɔp	ʔyúu	nèey	púum	kɔ̀ɔ		lèey		

	1	1	1	**1**	⇒♭**3**	**1**		⇒♭**3** –		
31	phíi	pɔ́ɔp	ʔyúu	nèey	séey	kɔ̀ɔ		ɔ̀ɔk	Hrm	

E Tempo: 1 ≈ 260/minute

	♭**3**⇒ –	[**2**⇒] –	**2**⇒1 –							
32	Kín	kɛ́ɛŋ	khéɛ							

	♭**3**	**1**	**1**	1	♭**3**⇒1 –			♭**3**⇒1 –		
33	Kúu	càə	[tɔ̀ɔ]*	táa	phíi			[pɔ́ɔp|bɔɔt?]	[* tɔm?]	

	1	**1**	**1** –							
34	Méey	wàn	ñɔ̀ɔt							

	1	**1**	**1**	1	1⇒**2** –			[**2**⇒♭**3**] –		
35	Kúu	càə	tɔ̀ɔt	táa	[phíi|hɨ̈]			paaŋ		

	♭**3**	♭**3**	[1	1]	**1** –	[1]	**1**	**2**⇒♭**3** –		
36	phíi	pɔ́ɔp	sá-	wáay	lɔ̀ɔŋ,	laaŋ	kɔ̀ɔ	hán		

	♭**3**	**2**	1	1	♭**3**	**1**		**2**⇒1 –		
37	Phíi	táa	dám	táa	khám	màa		khɨ̈n		

	[1	1]	**1** –	[♭3]	**1**			**1** –		
38	Ra	raam	ràay,	seey	yàam			ràay	Hrm	

H Tempo: 1 ≈ 260/minute

	♭**3**	♭**3**	♭**3**	**2**	**1**	**1**		♭**3**⇒1 –	
39	sɔ́ɔŋ	wák	hɛ́ɛ	kúu	mìi	mɛ̀ɛŋ		pɔ́ɔŋ	

	♭**3**	♭**3**	**2**	1	**1**	1		♭**3**⇒1 –	
40	sɔ́ɔŋ	tɔ̀ɔŋ	tɔ́ɔm	kúu	mìi	khwán		pháa	

Kammu vocal genres (Laos)

	1	*1*	1	[1]	1	*[1]*	[1⇒2] –
41	pàən	lǐi-	sáa	kə́-	tháa	[mòn]	[dǐi]

	♭3	*2*					*1* –
42	kúu	tə̀ŋ					mǐaŋ

	♭3	*2*	1	*[1]*	*1*	1	*1* –
43	phǐi	táa	líaŋ,	tə̀-	nə̀ŋ	khǐi-	mìn

	1	1	1	*1*			1⇒♭3 –
44	sá	phǐi	nǐi	tə̀ŋ			khám

	1	*1*					♭3⇒1 –
45	cám	nɔ̀ɔk					pháa

	1	[1]	*1*	*1*	*1*	1	1⇒♭3 –	
46	òom	[rə̀-	tàa	Prà	mòn]	khàn	kúu	Hrm

Interpretation:

[A]   Buddha, ckháan pepper
Arrange medicine, Buddha ckhóo
Herb teacher
This medicinal plant, what medicinal plant is it? Hrm

[B]   This medicinal plant is a real, real medicinal plant
Khóp-khép khɔ́ɔ-khɛ́ɛ stone
Cók-cék cɔ́ɔ-cɛ́ɛ water
I shall drive away the tiger spirit
    The tiger spirit returns again and again
I shall drive away the spirits of waste
    The spirits of waste return again and again
I shall drive away the miscarriage spirit. Hrm

[C]   The miscarriage spirit returns again and again
I shall drive away the tiger spirit
    The tiger spirit returns again and again
Where do the spirits collect holy fruits?
    The spirits collect holy fruits at the tree trunk
Where do the spirits collect holy fruits?
    I shall collect holy fruits at the root
Where do the betel nuts fall?
    The betel nuts fall everywhere
Ten thousand people cannot pick them up
    A hundred thousand people cannot pick them up
Only I can pick them up. Hrm

[D] Some call it holy fruits,
         Some call it holy water
     I do not call it holy water
         I shall call it sóm-pá
     I shall pour out the tóo-róo tée-rée water
     The tiger spirit in the stomach will be driven out
         The tiger spirit in the guts will come out. Hrm

[E] Eating khɛ́ɛ soup
     I will hit the tiger spirit's eye
         A wicker twined around the tree's top
     I will hit the tiger spirit's eye blind
         I indeed see the tiger spirit deep down in the stomach
     The black spirit eyes, the golden spirit eyes are coming up
     This is a hard time starting for the spirit. Hrm

[H] There are scorpions on my casting-net hook
         There are heavenly souls on my tɔ̀ɔŋ tɔ́ɔm hook
     All around the country my magic is praised
     Yellow-eyed spirit,
     Shaman's helper khíi-mìn
     Drive out the spirit so that it runs all night
     Goes behind the sky
     Òom rtàa, Buddha mantra, protect my tray

The lexical tones in *krùu*

Measurements were made and represented in graphs in order to see how the linguistic phrases occur in this *krùu* and how the lexical tones are handled. The number notation above the text is transcribed after what can be heard musically, that is the tonal 'centre' or 'musical approximation' of a performed tone, while the exact measuring focuses on the maximum points. These two do not always coincide. In many *krùu*, the separate sections are marked by a higher and louder ending, much like the rice narratives. In these cases, the melodic contour is hence dominated by the intonation at the endings.

In the following graphic representations of phrases from *Krùu mòn òm smpɔ́ɔy*, Spell for making holy water (Example 64), the maximum pitch of each syllable is shown. The prosodic phrases are grouped in phrase-pairs and the axis on which two phrases are mirrored, the mirror break, is marked with a vertical line. Example 64A shows the first two lines that constitute one thematic episode mirrored in meaning, as the vertical line shows. In this case, the thematic

Kammu vocal genres (Laos)

episode coincides with a musical phrase. The main melodic outline is often mirrored, too: the first part goes from high to low and the second part from low to high.

Example 64B shows a different melodic contour. The first part goes from low to high and the second part from high to low. In this part of the performance, the tempo has increased and the performer has started to combine more than two prosodic phrases into one musical phrase. The first part in this figure is actually the final part of a single musical phrase (ending high), and the second part is the beginning of the next musical phrase (starting high and ending low). It can also be noted that in the first part all syllables except the last one are performed low, regardless of tone. This occurs in *krùu* – as in *tɔ́ɔm* – in final musical phrases when the performer is running out of breath. This is also obvious in the final phrase of the performance, shown in Example 64C.

Example 64 Prosodic phrase pairs and musical phrases from *Krùu mòn òm smpɔ́ɔy*, Spell for making holy water. Performed by Kàm Ràw, ca. 1983/84. Original pitch: 1 ≈ 140 Hz.

Graphs: Vertical: Hz, horizontal: time (unspecified). The mirror break is marked by a vertical line.

Number notation: For number notation signs see Appendix 2.

A Speed: 1 ≈ 192/minute

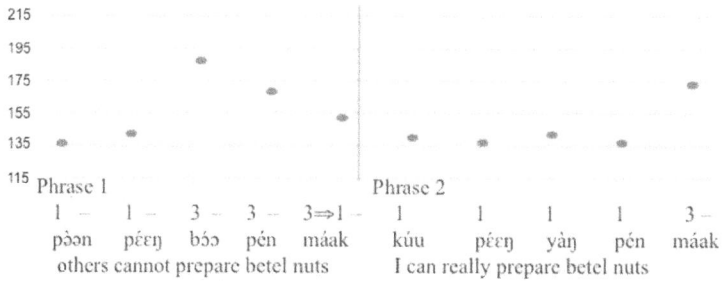

B Speed: 1 ≈ 228/minute

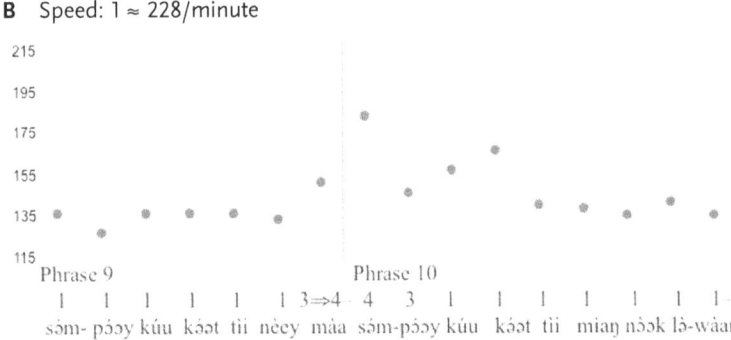

C Speed: 1 ≈ 240/minute

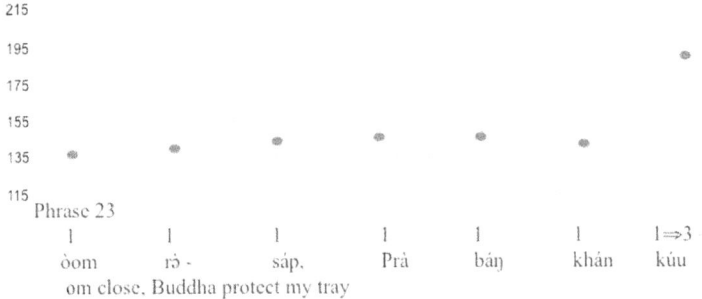

This genre is melody-centred, and lexical tones accommodate to the rising or falling general tonal contour. The situation is similar to that of speech, with a fixed melodic formula and lexical tones accommodating to it. The main difference is that tonal identities are neutralized in *krùu* by levelling the transitions between tones when in direct conflict with the melody. The realization of the lexical tones in *krùu* is thus relative, rather than an exact pitch. Using our approach with a performance template in which melodic movement and tones can be studied as two separate phonetic levels, differences in the realization of lexical tones can be accounted for systematically.

Kammu vocal genres (Laos)

Example 65 Illustration of two phrases without conflicts between lexical tones or between lexical tones and melody. The melodic outline is indicated by a line. Arrows point to transitions discussed in the running text. Only the F0 values at the beginning of the vowels in each syllable are shown, as this is the point at which the identity of lexical tones is phonetically anchored.

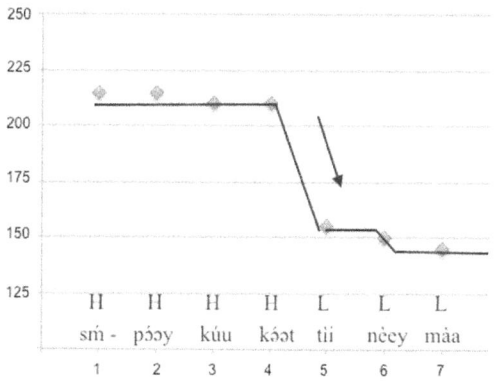

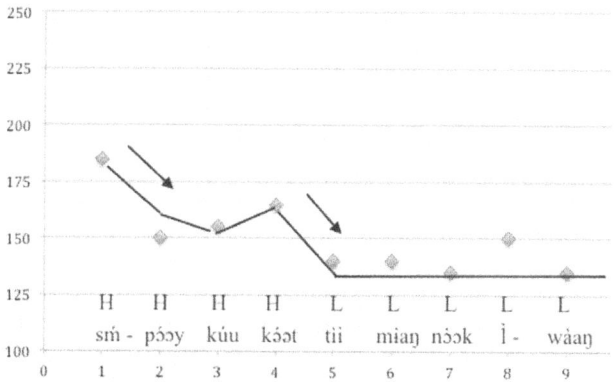

In Example 65, two phrases without conflicts between tones or between tones and melody are illustrated. The melody falls towards the end. Tonal combinations are transitions from sequences of High to sequences of Low tones. Hence, there are no tonal conflicts. Transitions between tones similar to the melodic direction are enhanced (indicated by arrows). There is reason to distinguish between an early and a late downslope or upslope in the melody (upslope is dealt with below). In the upper plot, there is a late downslope, and the melody is kept high with no enhanced transitions until the H + L tone sequence. Melodic downslope is aligned with this sequence and enhances the contrast between the two tones. In the bottom plot, there is an early downslope. Lexical tones are realized in such non-conflicting combinations of tones and melody.

Example 66 Illustration of phrases without conflicts between tones, but with conflict between tones and melody.

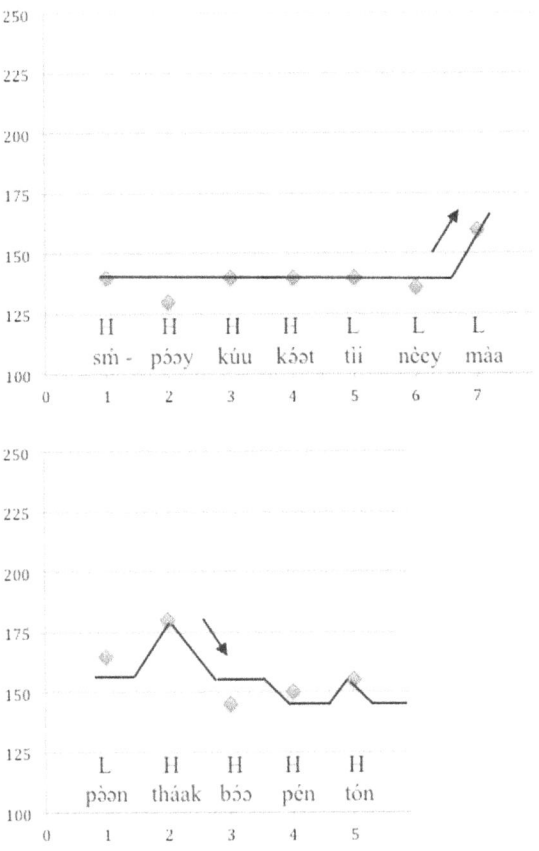

There are many tonal movements within syllables. Lexical tones are preserved by different techniques. For example, a rising movement may occur in the sonorant coda of a Low tone word while the Low lexical tone is preserved on the vowel. The relation between melody and lexical tones is therefore very similar to that found in speech. In principle, melody/intonation is leading unless it conflicts with lexical tones. In *krùu*, the High tone in the combination L+H+L in the rising contour boosts the High tone so that it dominates over the melodic contour. Furthermore, a final Low tone is realized higher when the line is the last one in a thematic episode. A thematic episode is normally marked by a high boundary tone that influences the realization of a final Low lexical tone by raising it. The same pattern is found in speech: intonational marking of boundaries (by high phrase boundary tones) influences the realization of lexical tones.

In the upper plot of Example 66, the melody is rising and conflicts with the final Low tones. The transition from High to Low in *kɔ́ɔt tìi* is not enhanced. This transition conflicts with the rising contour of the melody. Transitions between tones are suppressed and the melody does not rise until at the end, somewhat jeopardizing the identity of the last Low tone. Tones are neutralized and melody is prioritized. In this case, the phrase is tied together with the following phrase (not in the illustration), so there is no actual ending of the musical phrase in the example. The melody is rising on the last Low syllable because the first syllable of the following phrase is High and will be intoned high. In the bottom plot, the melody falls and conflicts with the final High tones. The transition from Low to High in *pɔ̀ɔn tháak* is suppressed as it directly conflicts with the falling contour, and the fall of the melody is aligned with the High–High sequence *tháak bɔ́ɔ* where it does not conflict so much with tonal identities.

Example 67 Illustrations of phrases with conflicts between tones (i.e. sequences with intervening opposite tones) and no conflicts between tones and melody. The dotted arrows show High tones for final syllables intoned with a downward sliding motion.

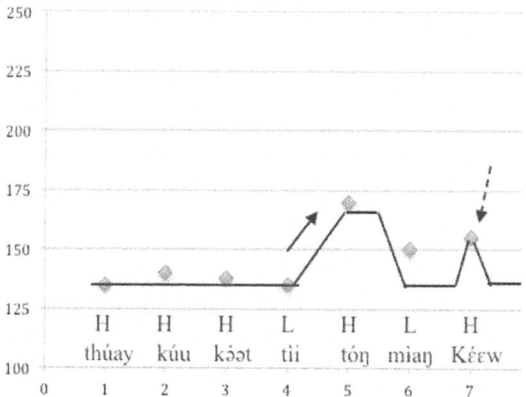

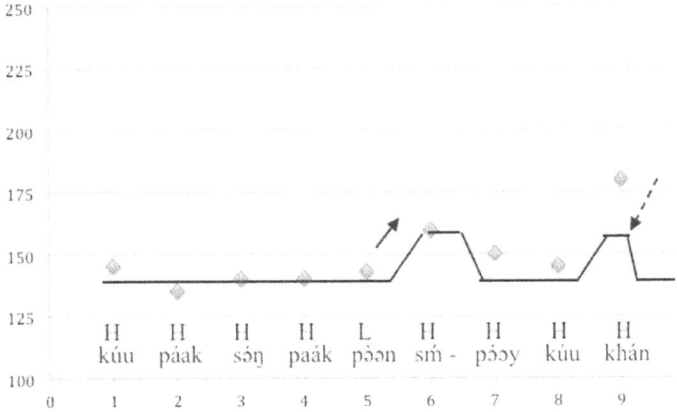

In the plots in Example 67, the conflict with the final High tones is of a different kind. This rising pattern is realized by suppressing High tones at the beginning of the phrases, and the first combination of tones Low–High (which goes in the same direction as the rising melody) is enhanced. Transitions of High–Low combinations are suppressed. At a faster tempo with too many conflicts between adjacent tones, transitions between tones are levelled, and there are no enhancements. The High tone of the last syllable is realized with a falling movement to the lowest pitch. The most common ending of a musical phrase is low, and this pattern dominates over the lexical tone. In this genre, however, the last musical phrase of a section ends with a high pitch (Example 68).

Example 68 Illustration of a phrase with many conflicts between lexical tones, performed at a rapid tempo.

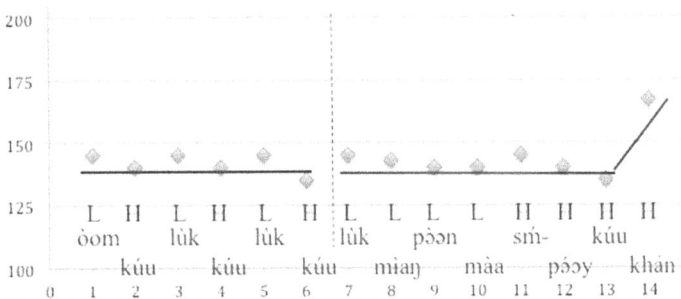

Kammu vocal genres (Laos)

It seems to be a common technique for Kammu genres that transitions between lexical tones are levelled in conflicting situations, so that High and Low are realized on the same level (usually within a somewhat lower pitch range). We do not find 'wrong' tonal transitions (e.g. falling pitch) between Low and High tones. The only exceptions are phrases in a very rapid tempo.

The *krùu* performance template

Melody
- Short melodic phrases with a tonal centre (see Example 61).
- Melodic range: 3–7 semitones.

Rhythm
- Regular pulse.
- Syllabic.

Form
- Litany: the same musical phrase repeated with variations.
- There are one or more sections performed in one breath and finished with 'clearing the throat' ('*hrm*').
- The tempo often increases with each new section.

Phrasing
- The prosodic phrases are organized as phrase-pairs: as question and answer, or antithetically.
- A number of prosodic phrases form a thematic episode.
- Verbal phrasing dominates (a 7-syllable line is two tone durations longer than a 5-syllable line, etc.)
- For most of a performance, prosodic and musical phrases are aligned.
- Musical phrases may be prolonged and incorporate two or more prosodic phrases.

Initial/final formulae
- Many *krùu* have an initial formula, generally with non-lexical words, performed to a variant of the basic musical phrase.
- There may be two or more tones at a low pitch in the beginning of a phrase. This is interpreted as an initial formula.
- Final syllables are performed 3⇒1 or 1. This may be considered a final formula in which lexical tone does not matter.

Word variations
- Same tone duration for long and short vowels, minor and major syllables.
- Reduplication occurs, but is rather infrequent.

- Schwa vowels (normally ə) have the same duration as all other vowels that are performed as short.

Lexical tones
- Basically melody-centred.
- Low lexical tones are generally 1 (but may be higher) or falling (3⇒1).
- High lexical tones are realized at 2, 3, or 4, often gliding to or from these pitches upwards: 1⇒3, 2⇒3, 2⇒3, 3⇒4, or downwards: 2⇒1, 3⇒1.
- The 4th and following syllables of the 2nd phrase of a phrase-pair are generally low, independently of lexical tones.
- In longer combinations, all or most syllables of the second line may be low (1) with no contrary motion in such a passage.

Kammu summary

In the investigation of ten genres of Kammu vocal expressions, musicological approaches and linguistic approaches were combined. We investigated how phonological features are phonetically implemented in performance. The main questions were if, how, and to what degree those phonological features exist in these vocal genres, and whether we would find features that do not occur in speech. We also studied how melody is built up in different genres, that is, whether the melody is primarily built up of lexical tones or if there is a tonal contour to which tones are accommodated.

The syllable was chosen as the domain for comparison. The following phonetic features were compared between genres: lengthening within syllables (whether onset, nucleus, or coda is lengthened in some positions), reduplication of syllables, tonal movements within syllables in terms of the number of tonal turning points and the direction of movement (e.g. tonal movement up–down, up–down–up, etc.), and the alignment of tonal movements within syllables (if the tonal movement starts at the onset or later).

This chapter has shown how performance templates are constructed and how one particular person realizes lexical tones in different genres while also performing vocal expressions in which lexical tones are realized differently. The main characteristics of these genres are listed in Table 4.

Three types of genre-dependent relationships between tones and melody occur in Kammu vocal expressions: tone-centred, melody-centred, and tone- and melody-centred genres. In tone-centred genres,

Table 4 Characteristics of different Kammu genres of vocal expressions

Genre	Melody-centred parts	Tone-centred parts	Initial and final formulae	Syllabic reduplication	Coda prolongation	Lexical tones less pronounced	Realization of lexical tones	Local movement in lexical tones	High or Low final tone
1. Lɨ̀ɔŋ narratives		X					Relative		High
2. Kàm à-thí-tháan, prayer		X	X				Relative (less pronounced)		High or low
3. Ɔ̀ɔc	X					X			High
4. Hrlii	X	X	X				3 pitch levels		–
5. Hruvə̀	X	X	X	X	X	Often	Relational	X	Low
6. Húuwə̀	X	X		X	X		Relative	X	Low
7. Yảam	X	X	X	X	X		Onset of base syllables	X	Low
8a. Yùun tiiŋ dance	X	X		X	X		3 pitch levels		Low
8b. Yùun tiiŋ	X	X		X		X			Low
9. Tə̀əm	X	X	X	X	X		3 pitch levels	X	Low
10. Krúu	X	X	X	Rare	X		Relative	X	High

the melody is built up by the lexical tones. In melody-centred genres, lexical tones adjust to a fixed melodic contour. Performance templates may have initial and final formulae with rather fixed pitches, sometimes also fixed words (melody-centred sections), and variation mainly occurs in the middle part (tone-centred sections). Those genres are tone- and melody-centred. In Table 4, the vocal expressions have been grouped in accordance with the existence of melody-centred, tone-centred, and mixed melody and tone-centred sections.

- *Tone-centred:* These genres are performed at pitches that are close to speech intonation (Analyses 1–2, 4). They do not have the character of fixed melodies, and lexical tones are realized. They can be adapted to poetical lines of varying lengths.
- *Melody-centred:* These genres may be experienced as having fixed melodies, and in two cases this really applies, since they afford little scope for realizing lexical tones (Analyses 3, 8), while lexical tones are realized in other cases (Analyses 5–7). On the other hand, they can all be adapted to poetical lines of varying lengths, which makes them function as performance templates.
- *Melody-centred and tone-centred parts:* These genres have shorter or longer initial and final formulae with rather fixed pitches (the melody-centred parts), and most of the remainder of the performance is dominated by lexical tones (the tone-centred parts) (Analyses 9–10). They also have their respective rhythmical metres and permit the lengthening or shortening of poetic lines.

Typically, vocal expressions that can be explained by performance templates are open to variation and improvisation. The templates include practices which enable the performance of longer or shorter poetical lines. In the majority of cases, prolongation occurs in the middle of the vocal expression, while initial and final formulae remain relatively unchanged. Existing lines can also be prolonged by putting in additional words at the end of a line by prolongation (the musical phrase is simply prolonged) or contraction (several syllables are squeezed into the musical phrase without changing its length). The rhythm patterns and poetic metre of the templates vary between different genres. Some genres make use of non-lexical words or 'song-words'. These are integrated parts of the performance templates, and one of their functions is to mark the genre.

Some words are pronounced differently as compared with ordinary speech. In most of the genres no distinction is made between long and short vowels; the schwa vowels in minor syllables are pronounced with the same duration as phonemic vowels (vowels occurring in major syllables), and sometimes they are even prolonged. Otherwise, prolongation of syllables generally occurs in the coda. Reduplication of syllables is common. Embellishments such as vibrato and other fast tonal movements are normally realized on the final part of the base syllable, or on the reduplicant.

The two lexical tones are realized in most genres, but in different ways. In melody-centred sections, lexical tones are not necessarily realized in the initial or final formulae. Shorter or longer passages occur where syllables are performed low, regardless of lexical tones. In tone-centred parts, the Low and High lexical tones are realized in performance, at either relational or fixed pitch levels. Lexical tone is realized in the initial part of the vowel, and tonal movements in the reduplicant and coda are independent of the lexical tones. Some genres have complex tonal contours in the base syllable, for instance *húuwə̀* (Analysis 6), while in other genres, such as *tə́əm* (Analysis 9), complex tonal movements occur only in reduplicants.

Prosodic phrases are often paired and linked to each other by parallelism and rhyme. In the case of the orally transmitted *trnə̀əm* poem, parallelism and rhyme are extended to form pairs of stanzas that are performed in various vocal genres depending on time, location, age, and gender (Analysis 4–9). Prosodic and musical phrases generally coincide. The musical metre tends to depend on the prosodic phrasing in terms of length and verbal metre, but there are also cases where a musical phrase includes more than one prosodic phrase.

In many cases, the melodic contour is descending, starting at a high pitch and ending lower. The final tone is low and sometimes ends by sliding further downwards. One exception is *hrlìi* (Analysis 4), which apart from an initial formula has no melodic movement or speech intonation at all, only a high and a low pitch relating to lexical tones. The influence of speech intonation is noted in prayers (Analysis 2) and in vocal genres where the final tone is high, which is similar to speech intonation (Analyses 1, 3, 10). The majority of the vocal genres have a tonal centre and a regular rhythm (Analyses 3–11).

Most of the Kammu vocal repertoire can thus be understood as based on performance templates. This means that it is possible to analyse a quantitatively extensive material by combining the use of performance templates with graphic transcriptions, and then to actually analyse large parts only by hearing. Musical and linguistic methods of analysis complement each other by producing overall interpretations on the one hand and exact measurements on the other.

3
Athabascan vocal genres in Interior Alaska

Siri G. Tuttle and Håkan Lundström

The community of Minto lies about 130 miles north-west of Fairbanks, Alaska. This village is known as 'New Minto' because it was created, and moved to, in response to repeated flooding of the historical Tanana River site of the village (Menhti), now called 'Old Minto' (Map 3). The indigenous name of the site of New Minto is Menok'oget, 'face gets chapped', for the sharp winds that blow on the bluff.

The people of Minto are Alaskan Athabascans. Their indigenous culture is characterized by a complex kinship system and seasonal subsistence activities including hunting of moose, caribou, small game and birds, salmon and whitefish fishing, and berry gathering. The people of Minto have been in contact with people of European heritage since the late nineteenth century, when steamboats began to work the Tanana, serving settlers and prospectors during the Alaska gold rush.

Robert Charlie recalls an occasion that proves the importance of composition in Athabascan tradition. He is speaking about his father, Moses Charlie:

> [H]e started singing the song. And people know it was a new song they never heard before. And all the people in that village, must be about maybe four or five hundred people came on to the riverbank to watch my dad. And other people comin' in from Minto area. But my dad was a leader.
> So he was singing this song. He was coming closer and the people start coming down to the riverbank. And there were such many people. There were lots of snow and stuff on the river, and when they sing that song and start dancing they tramped all that snow down. That's what you call really tramping the snow for a memorial potlatch. That's how my dad made this song.[1]

---

1 Robert Charlie, interviewed 6 June 2013.

Map 3 Map of Alaska, including places and rivers occurring in the text. Note that Tanana has three usages: the Tanana river, the Tanana town and the Tanana language.

As fewer people learn the local language and the traditional customs, many elders are increasingly engaged in preserving their heritage. Robert's brother Neal Charlie was a traditional chief of the village, and he knew his culture very well. He was of the opinion that singing was a key for preservation; and at a 2005 workshop, he urged researchers to take up the task of music research:

> I'm going to get back to some of our native ways. These are the things that used to be important. Let young people know about their grandfathers' songs. It's not our songs, it's way back. Little Peter died way before some of you was born, but we still remember the song that he made. The sad part of it is that we're forgetting a lot of it because we never use it, and we're forgetting it. Every day we're

forgetting something of our native ways, because we don't use them no more. And that's too bad there. I think that our native ways, like our languages and our songs, I think is very important to our people, and should be very important to the young people right now.[2]

Alaskan Athabascan language and vocal expressions[3]

Though there are some studies of Athabascan language and music, there was very little, initially in our research, about the interrelation between the two. It was known, however, that the vocal expressions that are studied here were composed. Even though the individual compositions are formulaic to a certain extent, it was not certain whether performances would be useful in the analysis. For this reason, a primary objective in this chapter is to try out how the possible performance templates are constructed, and whether new knowledge can be achieved by using them. Since so little was known about the object of study, the transcription models used are graphs and music notations.

Athabascan languages are spoken in Alaska and also include Navajo and Apache, as well as certain languages of the west coast of North America.[4] All the eleven Athabascan languages spoken in Alaska are endangered, though two languages, Koyukon and Gwich'in, have more adult speakers than the others. Koyukon is spoken in 15 villages in the western part of Alaska. The Gwich'in people live in and near the Brooks Range and sections of the Cordillera, and also in the valleys of the middle Yukon and lower Mackenzie.[5] The Gwich'in village Venetie is on the Chandalar River,

---

2 Summarized from Tuttle 2011: 82–83.
3 The authors gratefully acknowledge the help of Athabascan cultural experts, including Eliza Jones, Norman Carlo, Susan Paskvan, and Allan Hayton; and some who are no longer living: Evelyn Alexander, Neal Charlie, Geraldine Charlie, Bergman and Sarah Silas, Susie Charlie, and Dorothy Titus. Language learners and workers, David Engles, Bertina Titus, and Norman Carlo, have kindly shared their experience and expertise with us. Work with these experts has been supported in part by a grant from the National Endowment for the Humanities (NEH HD-50298-08).
4 Nowadays the term *Athabascan*, an exonym of Cree origin, is frequently replaced by *Dene*, an endonym reflecting the cognate word for 'people' in the languages of the family. In this chapter, we retain the older term in the form recognized by the Tanana Chiefs Conference and adopted by the Alaska Native Language Center.
5 Slobodin 1981.

a tributary to the Yukon. The Tanana people live on the middle stretch of the Tanana River, which flows into the Yukon. The last surviving dialect of Tanana, Minto (Lower Tanana), is spoken in the village of Minto. There are estimated to be 150 speakers in Koyukon and 25 in Lower Tanana,[6] but these estimates may be over-generous, since all three languages continue to suffer significant loss of elders. Gwich'in (Venetie), Tanana (Minto dialect), and Koyukon are all considered to be part of the Central Alaska-Yukon sub-group of Northern Athabascan.[7]

As elsewhere in the western part of the United States, many speakers of Alaska's indigenous languages were relocated as children to boarding schools, where the use of their native languages was strongly discouraged. This assimilative practice continued into the 1970s, when bilingual education was introduced as a new approach.[8] Speakers of Alaska's Native languages were recruited to work in bilingual programmes, though these programmes still had the goal of maximizing the use and learning of English, and not of promoting bilingualism in students. Time was set aside in some schools, making

Figure 3 Elders listen to, and comment on, archival recordings at Neal and Geraldine Charlie's house in Minto. Left to right: Bergman Silas, Sarah Silas, Geraldine Charlie and Neal Charlie. August 2010.

---

6 Internet reference: Alaska Native Language Center.
7 Mithun 1999: 346.
8 Barnhardt 2001.

use of semi-volunteer speakers, to provide support for students who came to school with limited English.

As the Native languages became less used, owing to attrition in the older generations and stigmatization in the majority-language community, the focus in schools has shifted to support for language learning by children whose first language is English. In some areas, speakers of Alaska Native languages have succeeded in gaining educational certification and are able to work with young bilinguals and English speakers alike. In other areas, partly because of the small size of individual language communities, there is minimal representation by speakers in standard certified teacher positions. A number of Athabascan speech communities are of this type.

Old ideas about bilingualism die hard. Many teachers and parents believe that students will not speak English well, and hence will not be successful, if they also speak their Native language (or any other language besides English). Bialystok refers to a 'folk wisdom of childhood bilingualism', which causes fears that acquiring more than one language in childhood could cause linguistic confusion or even general cognitive difficulty.[9] In her studies, she finds a cognitive benefit to childhood bilingualism, beyond the obvious one of knowing more ways of talking about things. Balanced bilinguals, people with equal proficiency in two or more languages, seemed to be better at metalinguistic tasks. Whether this would be considered an important benefit by teachers and parents in Alaskan villages depends on how much they value metalinguistic ability – the ability to observe and analyse patterns in language or, basically, to understand grammar. Bialystok makes it clear that situations where bilingualism is not balanced may not provide any such benefit, even as regards awareness of language.[10] In many Athabascan families in Alaska's interior, some knowledge of and exposure to the heritage language can be heavily outweighed by constant and insistent exposure to English.

For young Athabascans in Alaska's interior, the result is a varied landscape of language opportunities, only a few of which might result in strong proficiency in the structure and pragmatics of the heritage language, and only one or two of which could be available for a particular child. In the experience of the authors, the young people who become most successful in learning their heritage language do so outside the setting of formal education. They achieve this by actively apprenticing themselves to elders who, in turn, take on the

---

9 Bialystok 2001: xi.
10 Bialystok 2001: 144, 150.

responsibility of providing the input the learners need by keeping to their native language when they are in their apprentice's company.

There is another context that seems to result in proficiency, at least for people with a strong passive knowledge of a related language from their childhood. Teaching a language one does not really speak, with constant reference to and study with an elder, seems to bring some people to a high level of proficiency. Again, it is time with the language and an ambition to participate in it that makes the difference – although for teachers, attaining literacy in the language may also facilitate metalinguistic awareness and improve their ability to notice patterns.

It should not surprise anyone that a person can be hired to teach a language they do not really speak. It is not uncommon in US schools for non-native speakers to teach (at some level) a language they learnt in college. In the context of Alaska Native languages, a desire to provide local language content in class produces the most able and willing volunteer, who may well be a certified teacher in some other field or a dedicated learner of a highly endangered language.

Northern Athabascans and music

Northern Athabascans today are in contact with a multitude of musical styles.[11] Among those that have been incorporated over a long period of time are Christian hymns that were given texts in Athabascan languages in the early decades of the twentieth century and are still being used by the elderly. Besides, there is old-time-style fiddling, especially strong in the Gwich'in community, and another strong component is country music. This is often performed in English, and also in Athabascan and other Alaska Native languages. The transmission of oral traditions in Athabascan communities in Alaska – including speaking and writing in the heritage language – is sometimes supported by explicit instruction in school programmes. Child-directed classroom songs with Athabascan lyrics, set to common Euro-American melodies (mainly nursery rhymes), are used in language classes with students of all ages. There are projects that have produced learning materials in the form of traditional songbooks, with cultural information sometimes combined with recordings of performances.[12] These materials

---

11 See further Fast 2002.
12 Johnston 1993, Johnston, Solomon, Jones, and Pulu 1978.

are mainly accessed by those involved in documentation, but sometimes language and music learners find them useful too.

Music and dance are sometimes included in after-school programmes. In the Minto village, for example, students have participated for decades in an active after-school programme led by two generations of fluent elders who were also song-leaders and song-makers. While indigenous vocal expressions are rarely part of the formal curriculum of the Minto School, dancing and singing practice has been nearly as prominent as basketball as an extra-curricular activity. The Minto Dancers have participated in the University of Alaska's Festival of Native Arts for many years, demonstrating the power of their local music tradition.

Tanana (Minto dialect) and Gwich'in (Venetie dialect) have developed differently with respect to music and dance, following contact with white cultures. The Gwich'in encountered Europeans (French and English speakers) in the nineteenth century and developed their own Western musical styles, adding violin and guitars to their traditional vocal and drum tradition.[13] Their older traditional music is less practised today than that of the Tanana, which has retained a strong native musical tradition until the current generation. The recently active generation of elders in Minto has now been nearly completely depleted, as the majority of the group has passed away, and the remaining elders are either ill or inactive in cultural revitalization. Younger people, generally speaking, are not acquiring the language as children, although they are studying the musical tradition.

Gwich'in consulted for this study say that they have not heard much traditional singing, but there are more young speakers of Gwich'in than of Tanana. Accordingly, data for Tanana include recordings made in 2005–12, while the Gwich'in data was recorded in 1972 and archived at the University of Alaska Library as a part of a 'Songs and Legends' collection.

The above summary may suggest that interior Athabascan language, culture, and musical traditions are in danger of disappearing with nearly only archived materials left behind. This is not really the case, though it is not clear yet just how successful current language and culture revitalization efforts will prove. A series of ambitious projects conducted by the Doyon Foundation, which represents most of the Athabascan languages in Alaska, has resulted in increased activity in language learning, teaching, and materials creation. Other

---

13 Mischler 1993, Honigmann 1981: 732.

political developments, especially among Alaska Natives interested in reforming the educational system, may also contribute to more active transmission of language and culture in these communities.

Traditional Northern Athabascan music is predominantly vocal, with or without rhythm accompaniment on drums or on other instruments. This music plays an important role in the festivities called *potlatch*, including, but not limited to, funeral and memorial potlatches. On these occasions people from different villages, or even from different language areas, meet and take part in the singing and dancing. This is one situation in which vocal expressions are learnt and spread.

A memorial potlatch will normally include a *dratakh ch'elik*, 'mourning song', recently made in honour of the person who passed away.[14] A *dratakh ch'elik* performed by the potlatch host is referred to as the *khwtitl ch'elik*, 'potlatch song', and has a special status. Certain older memorial *dratakh ch'elik* that are remembered will be performed as well, some dating back to the early 1900s. The potlatch will then continue with dancing and the performance of *ch'edzes ch'elik*, 'dance songs', to drum accompaniment. In many places, like Minto or other Tanana River villages such as Tanacross, the potlatches provide a context where these kinds of vocal expressions are required. This function has resulted in their being actively used and – not least importantly – newly composed.

The Minto-Nenana dialect and music

The Tanana Athabascan language of Alaska is today represented by the Minto-Nenana dialect, spoken only by people from Minto (Menhti), a village 200 kilometres from Fairbanks, Alaska. Minto is a Northern Athabascan language, closely related to Koyukon and Ahtna, among others. The Minto people are Athabascan Indians. Their traditional economy is based on hunting game, fishing, and gathering berries. Vocal expressions remain an important part of the cultural life of Minto, and the elders are actively engaged in composition and documentation.

Athabascan languages, including Minto, are typologically unusual in structure and known for the complexity of their verb morphology. As polysynthetic languages, they are characterized by long words that may contain multiple word roots and affixes that would occur

---

14 Tanana words are presented in practical orthography, as published in Tuttle 2009.

as separate words in more isolating languages, such as English or Chinese. Many are also tonal languages, with different levels of density of tone. Minto has a sparse and variable low tone from historical vowel laryngealization, and a high-rising tone associated with negative utterances and with certain morphemes. All other pitches in conversational language are provided by intonational patterns that are similar to those observed in many languages of the world: unit-final lowering, pitch and duration changes related to emphasis, and intentional use of pauses.

Linguistic tone in the Athabascan languages of Alaska varies in its realization. Minto Tanana has relatively few low-toned syllables and some high tones, while Gwich'in syllables are more stable in both low and high tones. Some tonal syllables are heard in dialects of Koyukon, but the language as a whole is not classed as tonal. In both Minto Tanana and Koyukon, intonation provides most of the pitch patterns in speech.

Minto has a stress pattern in spoken language that makes word roots and certain vowels more prominent: in musical settings, the rhythm of words is sometimes subordinated to the musical rhythm. However, this depends on the genre. In those we will examine in this chapter, most words carry the rhythm you would hear if they were spoken. However, certain important words are elongated and performed with a special voice quality, a throbbing glottal pulse that keeps very clear time with the beat of the rhythm.

The intonational system of Minto Tanana is characterized by final lowering at intonational phrase boundaries, often but not always with a measurable pause. Intonational low tones are lower than low lexical tones,[15] usually registering the lowest pitch within an intonational phrase. Utterance types (such as questions) are marked by particles and affixes, with intonation playing a secondary role. Emphasis may be expressed with high pitch, and this type of intonational effect can also override the expression of lexical tone. Intonational domains that are smaller than the intonational phrase have not been demonstrated for this language, but are likely to exist, given findings for the closely related Dena'ina.[16]

The interaction between lexical and intonational tone patterns in Minto Tanana makes lexical tone challenging to hear and to learn. Moreover, because of rich inflectional morphology and grammatical patterns, lexical tone bears almost no functional load; it is

---

15 Tuttle 1998.
16 Lovick and Tuttle 2012.

simply part of the pronunciation of words. However, we find that lexical tones are recognized in more speech-like forms of music, as will be shown below.

The traditional music of Minto is vocal and often accompanied by an even drumbeat. The vocal expressions vary in style between different genres, ranging from those using words that express a feeling to those for dancing made up entirely of vocables with no lexical meaning. Similarly, the music ranges from slow and mournful melodies to up-tempo strophic forms with a distinct melodic contour: starting high, descending stepwise, and ending with a tone repetition at a low pitch. The Minto tradition shows many similarities with other Athabascan music and with Native American music in general, but it also has its particular character.[17] Categories of vocal expression have been defined on the basis of interviews with native speakers and practitioners of vocal art, and these categories are reflected in terminology within the language (Table 5).

The English translations reflect the structure of the word *ch'elik*, which is formed from the verb 'to sing', as in *ch'edelik*, 'she or he is singing'. Since all the people are English-speaking, the English forms are also used in the indigenous culture. This means that terms such as *dance song*, *potlatch song* are also seen as indigenous, as well as the names of specific vocal expressions, like *Raven song* or *Caribou song*.

Table 5 Vocal expressions and native vocabulary in Minto (Lower Tanana)

Minto Tanana	English	Literal gloss	Function
dratakh ch'elik	mourning song, sorry song, sad song	mourning song	dedicated to the memory of an individual; used at funerals, memorial potlatches and teaching
khwtitl ch'elik	potlatch song	potlatch song	in the form of *dratakh ch'elik*; performed solo by a potlatch host
ch'edzes ch'elik	dance song	dance song	used to accompany dancing
deyenenh ch'elik, senh ch'elik	shaman's song, medicine song	shaman's song, medicine song	used for healing or some other spiritual purpose

17 Lundström 1980, Pearce 1985, Johnston 1993, Coray 2007.

The structure of Tanana words for vocal expressions ranges from relatively prose-like to strictly metred, depending on the function and situation. *Dratakh ch'elik* for mourning displays prose-like qualities, with melody following tone and intonation to a greater or lesser degree, while *ch'edzes ch'elik* for dancing is highly rhythmic, and the speech tone and intonation are not expressed directly.

A *dratakh ch'elik* basically consists of two parts, the first of which contains key words expressing relationship (like 'my father', 'my child') in combination with vocables. The second part contains words honouring the deceased which are repeated three or more times with much parallelism, ending with vocables. The *ch'edzes ch'elik* have fewer words with lexical meaning, often one or two words that appear at the very beginning of a stanza and are followed by longer passages of vocables, while the melody is usually falling and ends on a tone repetition on a low tone. This stanza will then be repeated a number of times without changes of words or vocables.

Though there are few words with lexical meaning in *dratakh ch'elik*, the words are extremely important and carefully thought out. The combination of the initial key words and music is also significant: usually a short but poignant melodic and rhythmic motif that is often repeated before the performance continues. There are examples of the same word in different musical settings, so even though there is a fairly close relationship between speech and language in vocal performances, there are big differences as well. That is to say that melodic shape is not driven by word prosody, such as lexical tone or morphological stress, although there is an interaction between music and prosody.[18] The parts of the performance that are totally based on vocables tend to be more formulaic, while still unique for the specific vocal expression.

The musical traditions of the Athabascan people have endured through centuries of contact with European cultures in all the geographical regions where this family of languages is spoken. Vocal expressions are performed using Athabascan languages even where the language is no longer transmitted to the new generation. In the context of extended, intensive contact with Euro-American language and culture, the health of the Minto vocal tradition is particularly notable. While there have clearly been many talented composers and performers in Minto in the twentieth century, we believe that this strong tradition also rests on structural components

---

18 Karlsson, Lundström, Svantesson, and Tuttle 2014.

in composition and lyrics. Describing the important aspects of this system may serve to help support a continuation of the tradition.

Our concern with this music has been strongly encouraged by Minto elders, particularly the late Neal Charlie, who believed that composition and performance could help young people to learn the spoken language. In particular, Mr Charlie believed it was important to work with *dratakh ch'elik*, because their words contained important advice for living a good life – expressed, of course, in the Minto language. Neal and his wife, Geraldine, along with fellow Minto elders Bergman and Sarah Silas, contributed greatly to the documentation and maintenance of the Minto vocal traditions, and they worked with us in this project. All of them have now passed away.

Our linguistic analysis starts with the translation of words with these elders who knew them and understood the context of the composition. The words are transcribed, and the phrases and words are analysed and compared with the idiomatic translation and meanings as explained by the elders. Pitch, rhythm, and duration in spoken words are compared with the realization of the words in performance.[19]

---

19 Thanks are due to the late Neal and Geraldine Charlie, Sarah and Bergman Silas, Susie Charlie, and to Hishinlai' Peter and Allan Hayton for their help with translations and explanation. References used in lyric translation include Jetté and Jones 2000, Kari 1994, Tuttle 2009, and Tuttle's field notes 2005–14.

Analysis 11 Raven song

Narratives frequently include vocal expressions. Though they are often referred to in English as *story songs*, this is not really a clearly defined vocal genre in stylistic terms. Story songs occur in narratives where animals are acting characters and also perform vocal expressions. There are a large number of narratives about the Raven, who plays an important role in Athabascan mythology. In many narratives, the Raven is 'a supreme being [...] and endowed with godlike power. (His wishes come true, he creates Alaska, his paddle strokes create islands)[.] He can make people's wishes come true and is often partly human or [anthropomorphic].'[20] People also make offerings to Raven.

Vocal expressions of Raven that belong to narratives are normally referred to as *Raven songs*. They are usually very short and often end with an onomatopoeic imitation of Raven's call or of animals referred to in the tale.[21] Like other story songs, they may also be performed separately from the story for entertainment or – since the raven is also a bird of omen – in relation to certain activities, like for instance hunting.[22]

The *Raven song* performed by Neal Charlie belongs to a narrative, but it was performed separately and there is no summary of the narrative. It lasts less than 6 seconds and consists of two parts: the first part describes a location and the second part consists of two words that are repeated once (Example 69).

Example 69 *Raven song* performed by Neal Charlie, Minto.

Yodo K'oschaget khwts'enh
down at Crossjacket

łi yettha, łi yettha
dogs are barking, dogs are barking

The words *łi yettha* literally translate as 'dogs are barking'; but since it is Raven who sings, they are performed as an imitation of Raven. As can be seen in Example 70, the first section does not

---

20 Rooth 1976: 70. See also Nelson 1983: 79–84.
21 See Lundström 1980: 131–132 and 142 for *Raven songs* from Minto and from Nondalton, Dena'ina area.
22 Nelson 1983: 3.

have a distinct pitch or rhythm pattern, but it is close to speech intonation. The pitch range is, however, wider than normal for the speaker, making it more chant-like. The whole expression forms one phrase, and the final repetition gives it a distinct shape.

Example 70 Melodyne graph of *Raven song* performed by Neal Charlie, Minto. • *14 Raven song*

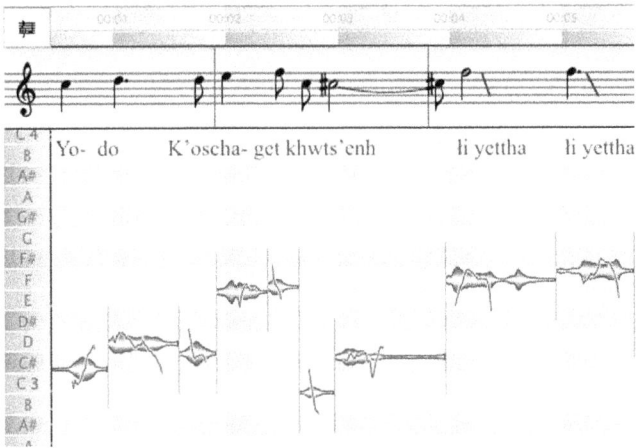

Characteristics of the *Raven song*

There are no variations to the segmental structure of the words, and the sentence does not include any lexical low or high tones.

Melody
- Speech intonation with increased pitch range.

Rhythm
- Slightly slowed speech rhythm, with strong syllables emphasized.

Form
- Binary: A–B, where B is a Raven imitation.

Phrasing
- Prosodic.

Analysis 12 *Caribou song* (Tanana)

The *Caribou song* is one of a set of *senh ch'eliga'*, *medicine songs*, recorded by the highly respected elder Peter John with an unidentified interviewer.[23] This recording is not dated, but it is likely to have been made in the 1970s. It is also an *animal song*, a term used by George Herzog, who counted them as belonging to an old layer of oral traditions.[24] Many pedagogical or etiological tales or myths are about animals, who do things related to such activities as successful hunting or healing. In many of these tales, an animal performs a vocal expression that could, in another context, be used for magical purposes.[25] The *Caribou song* belongs to a well-known teaching story about truthfulness and obedience which explains its meaning. It was recorded by the late Neal Charlie in 2008, and other elders, including Neal's brother Robert, know and repeat the story. Neal Charlie summarized the tale in English as follows:

> They sent a young man up. It was snow, too much snow. Couldn't break trail no more, so they send that young man up, to see if there's any [caribou] track up ahead. He went up there and he come back and he say: 'I don't see no track, not one track'. That night, medicine man wake up with this song:
> You told me that there were none;
> there were none, you told me.
> They say he call that boy over, the boy they sent up. He start to sing this song for him, and he tell him that 'You lied to us'. And that boy, he change his story, he say, 'Didn't I tell you I see one track up there?'

The song, given to the shaman by the caribou themselves, restores the proper relationship between the people and the caribou, after the boy's violation of that relationship with his lie.

The free sharing of this material contrasts with a general caution regarding *senh ch'elik* on the part of the remaining elders of Minto. Since the introduction of Christianity in the Tanana Valley by missionaries in the late nineteenth and early twentieth centuries, expressions of Native Athabascan spirituality have been handled very discreetly in this area. Neal Charlie expressed his feelings about

---

23 TN27, Alaska Native Language Center ANLC2549.
24 Herzog 1935.
25 There are several myths of this kind in Rooth 1971.

this music in the interview in which the story was recorded: he stated that *medicine songs* and other spiritual material could be misused if they were shared without full understanding of their proper application. For this reason, he was not willing to discuss many of those recorded and archived by Peter John. This was an exception, owing to its relationship with the teaching story.

Example 71 Words and translation of the *Caribou song*.

Do sełdini chu
And you tell me

Bekwlá sełdini chu
There are none, you tell me

The *senh ch'elik*, or *animal songs*, are often short. This one resembles Peter John's other examples in being more speech-like than musical. It consists of two sets of words making up a stanza. The binary poetical form is obvious, since the text is performed twice (Example 71). In the first section, *Do sełdini chu* is given 8 beats and *Bekwlá sełdini chu* 10 beats (Example 72). This means that the three extra syllables of *Bekwlá* are simply added with one beat for each syllable. Apart from this, the principle is isorhythmic and the first motif serves as a building block. The descending melody line is also obvious. There are no real tone repetitions to finish off the lines, but that is explained by the fact that this is a different vocal genre from the following examples. It should be noted that there are no vocables without lexical meaning. Rather, it is one sentence repeated once isorhythmically in a descending fashion.

The melody and rhythm adhere closely to the rhythm and pitch contour of speech. The highest point in the melody falls on the negative stem in the word *bekwlá* 'there are none' (see the arrows in Example 72). In the Minto dialect of Tanana, the negative and a few other specific words are marked with a high-rising, nasalized tone that is very distinctive in the language's prosody. In this word, the suffix is melded with the stem of the verb 'to be' to create a marked negative stem. The melody reflects the tone on this stem, which is the only tonally marked syllable in the text. Rhythmically, the one beat per syllable does not recognize the two light syllables in the text (*be-* and *kw*) as meriting different, lesser weight. Nor do the lexical stems in the text get special rhythmic treatment; *chu*, a conjunction, is elongated, but *-ni* 'say' gets just one beat, as does the high *-lá*. However, the overall contour, starting higher and finishing lower, with an emphasized negative, closely matches the contour of a Minto intonational unit.

Example 72 *Caribou song* performed by Neal Charlie, Minto, 10 November 2008. Arrows indicate a higher-pitched final syllable which is also a negative stem in the word *bekwlá* 'there are none'. Original pitch: c ≈ 140 Hz. • **15** *Caribou song***, Neal**

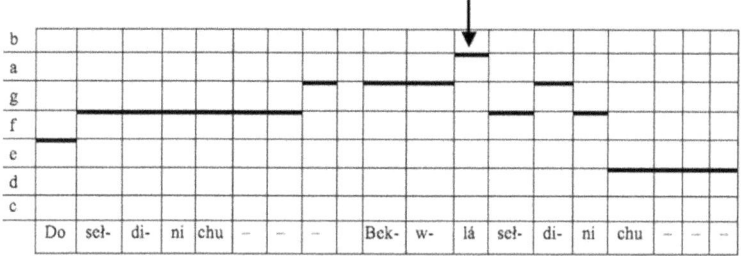

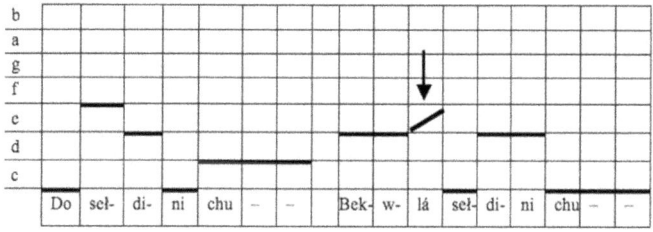

Characteristics of the *Caribou song*

Melody
- Follows the pitch contour of speech closely.
- Descending melody line with a tonal centre.
- Range: 11 semitones.

Rhythm
- Closely follows the rhythm of speech.
- Regular pulse.
- One pulse beat per syllable dominates.
- Isorhythmic organization: the first motif serves as a building block.

Form
- A short binary form made up of one sentence consisting of two sets of words performed twice.

Phrasing
- Verbal metre dominates.

Initial/final formulae
- The final syllable of the phrase (*chu*, a conjunction) elongated to 3–4 pulse beats.

Word variations
- The two light syllables (*be-* and *kw-*) and the lexical stems (*-ni*, *-lá*) in the text have a duration of one beat each.

Lexical tones
- The tone of the negative stem in the word *bekwlá* 'there are none', the only marked syllable in the sentence, is reflected by high pitch.

Dratakh ch'elik

The term *dratakh ch'elik* is a noun compound in which *dratakh* is a noun derived from a verb meaning 'to dance a mourning dance, arms moving up and down'. *Dratakh ch'elik* are made in honour of persons who have passed away and are of particular cultural importance. They would be made by a family member or commissioned from a well-known song-maker. They are performed at ceremonial feasts, particularly the funeral potlatch, and also at memorial potlatches that may occur about a year after the funeral.[26] In some cases, a *dratakh ch'elik* is intended for just one performance, at a memorial potlatch, and is not repeated. These are called *khwtitl ch'elik*, 'potlatch songs'. Those that may be remembered and performed at later funerals and potlatches as well are the *dratakh ch'elik*. Perhaps some *khwtitl ch'elik* can become re-singable *dratakh ch'elik*, but we have not observed this process directly. The Minto repertoire includes *dratakh ch'elik* dating back to the early 1900s, and it is remembered who made them and for whom.

In cases where the *dratakh ch'elik* is composed by a song-maker, the family member determines the verbal content to be included and the composer assists in organizing the lyrics and then sets them to a melody. The melody is not always new, but it must not too closely resemble important melodies that may be in the repertory of the local community or a neighbouring community. New compositions are evaluated by song-leaders and may be revised if they notice errors. Older compositions, especially really beautiful ones, are often performed at funeral potlatches (held just after a death) when there has not been time to create new ones.

---

26 Johnston 1993: 194.

The *dratakh ch'elik* we are working with have been chosen by elders as important for young people to learn, because of their frequent use for funeral and other potlatch occasions, and because they are considered to contain important advice for life. They are shared by Minto elders when they travel to occasions in other Athabascan communities and are thus familiar around Alaska. It is important for the elders that they are recognized as composed by, and for, Minto-Nenana people; and for this reason, composers are explicitly recognized when the *dratakh ch'elik* are discussed.

Analysis 13 Dolo k'adi, 'Missing Dolo'

Dolo k'adi belongs to the type which is called *dratakh ch'elik* in Tanana and is sometimes referred to in English as *sorry songs*. *Dolo k'adi* uses rather complicated 'high' language that is not easy for present-day speakers to translate. It is performed widely at women's funeral potlatches, and is known to members of other language communities in Alaska owing to kinship ties that bring Minto people to potlatches statewide.

Dolo is the name of a woman (Example 73). In most *dratakh ch'elik* examples, only one kinship term is used in the A section (e.g. *en'a* 'mother'). In the case of *Dolo k'adi*, two terms are used, 'mother' and 'sister', which emphasize the great importance of the honouree to her family. This *memorial song* was made by Little Peter in the 1920s for Dolo, who was the eldest daughter of the famous Minto chief Chief Charlie and the mother of Moses Charlie. The performers and translators consulted in this study are her descendants.

Example 73 Words and translation of the *Dolo k'adi*, 'Missing Dolo'.

Vocable/key word part   *Lexical part*

A
O-o-o-o, En'a'ei, O-o-o-o En'a'ei
Oh, mother, oh mother

O-o-o-o, En'a'ei e Soda ya
Oh, my older sister

                                        B
                                        Ekhwdon'a ch'ukat dinot
                                        Just upriver, while out shopping

                                        Logha dit'a khełdi
                                        You are handy, they say

                                        Nelo' dodelu
                                        Your hands [were] praiseworthy

                                        Ye'ał khenino doch'edenoghiloyh yeno
                                        With them you gathered things up

                                        E Soda ya
                                        My older sister

A
O-o-o-o, En'a'ei, O-o-o-o En'a'ei
Oh, mother, oh mother

O-o-o-o, En'a'ei e Soda ya
Oh, my older sister

B'
Ekhwdon'a ch'ukat dinot
Just upriver, while out shopping

Logha dit'a khełdi
You are handy, they say

Nełk'edadheyo
You brought them [people] together

Yełni khw khełdi
As she told him/her, they say

Khenotodoyedenaghiloyh
You brought us together with words

En'a, e soda ya
Mother, older sister

A
O-o-o-o, En'a'ei, O-o-o-o En'a'ei
Oh, mother, oh mother

O-o-o-o, En'a'ei e So-o
Oh, my older sister

The line *Oh-oh-oh-oh En'a'a, oh-oh-oh-oh-oh En'a'a, oh-oh-oh-oh-oh En'a'a Soda* (A in Example 74) appears three times in the performance, with other stanzas in between as a kind of refrain. The overall poetical and musical form will be A–B–A–B'–A. The A part has a binary form, a building block with the words *Oh-oh-oh-oh En'a'a* that is repeated twice in a descending motion, marked with double lines at the bottom of the graph in Example 74. The final word *Soda* is performed as a *pulsating tone*, that is, with a stress coinciding with each beat, a common trait in Native American music, denoted by a shaded line in the graph. It is phonetically marked by a glottal constriction at the onset of each beat. The descending A section thus ends with a tone repetition on one of the lowest pitches that serves as a tonal centre. This *dratakh ch'elik* is performed without a drum, and in the sections in which a few syllables are stretched over a number of beats, glottal pulses serve to underline the beat.

Example 74 Stanza A from *Dolo k'adi* with tone repetitions on vocables at the end. Performed by Neal and Geraldine Charlie, Minto, 5 June 2010. Original pitch: g ≈ 200 Hz. • **16 *Dolo k'adi***

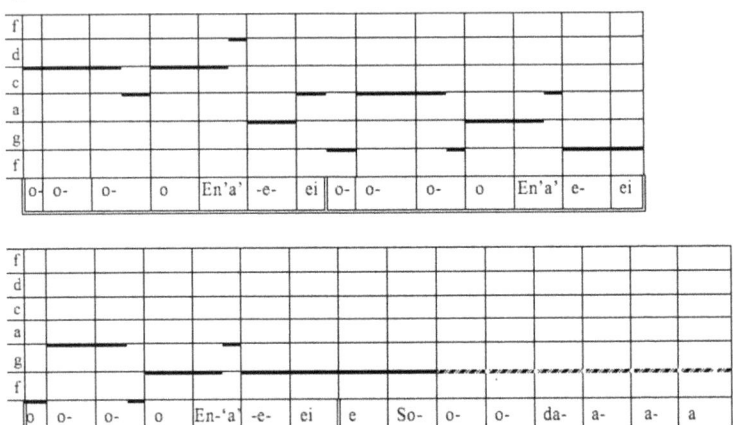

The stanzas B (Example 75) and B' (not transcribed) have no vocables but consist of words with lexical meaning praising the departed. Some *dratakh ch'elik* have four or more stanzas. In this version of *Dolo k'adi*, two were recorded. Minto elders have suggested that three is a proper number for stanzas in such compositions, and that they may focus on the feelings of the composer, on the important virtues of the departed, and, lastly, on something that the departed person enjoyed doing. Examples of older *dratakh ch'elik* recorded today may include fewer verses than were originally composed because not all the words were remembered.

Stanza B starts high and descends before it finishes on a pulsating tone repetition. It is longer than A and contains more words. Basically, this section can be seen as an extended variation of A with motifs that are slightly similar to stanza A in the descending section. It will take further research and comparisons between versions and with other examples of *dratakh ch'elik* in order to establish whether this is a common composition technique.

The B and B' sections have far more linguistic content than the A sections. In most cases, low lexical tone is not represented in the melody. However, morphologically prominent verb and noun stems

Athabascan vocal genres in Interior Alaska

have a tendency to be stressed and are more likely to be lengthened or fall on a new pitch (see arrows in Example 75). This reflects the phonetic prominence of stem morphemes in speech, and probably also aids parsing by listeners.

Example 75 *Dolo k'adi*. Arrows mark stressed morphologically prominent verb and noun stems. Stanzas B. Original pitch: g ≈ 200 Hz.

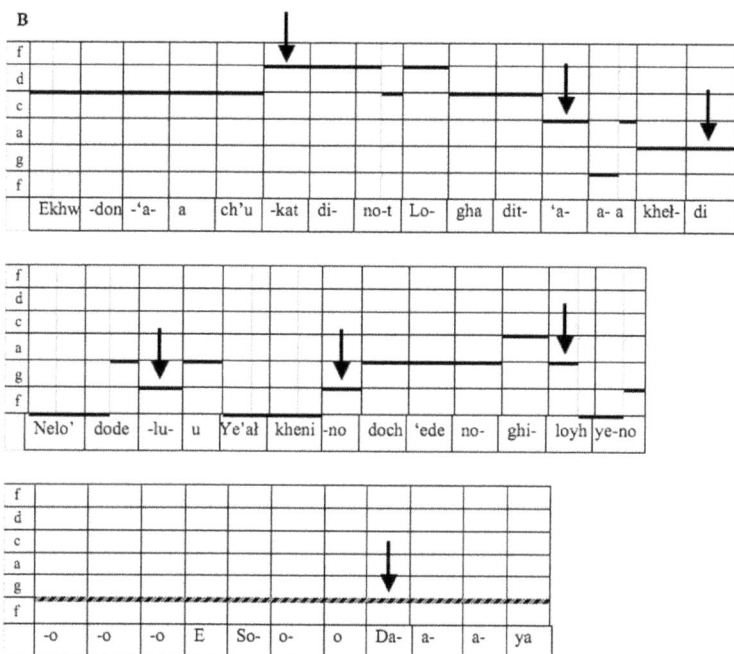

Characteristics of *Dolo k'adi*

Melody
- Descending motion with a tonal centre.
- Range: 12 semitones.

Rhythm
- Regular pulse.
- The pattern short–long, where the long is stressed, dominates.
- Isorhythmic organization: the first motif serves as a building block.

Form
- The overall form is A–B–A–B'–A.
- A consists of vocables and one key word with lexical meaning.
- B and B' consist of words with lexical meaning

Phrasing
- Both A and B end with tone repetitions.
- Prominent verb and noun stems tend to be stressed, lengthened and/or fall on a new pitch, which reflects speech.

Initial/final formulae
- Ends with a tone repetition on the tonal centre; the very last vocable of the performance is short and stressed.

Word variations
- Vocables prominent.

Lexical tones
- In most cases, low lexical tone is not represented in the melody.

Analysis 14 *Segoya* (Bettis, Nenana)

Segoya means 'my baby', 'my child'. This *dratakh ch'elik* was made by Julius Bettis, Nenana, for a son who died as a child. It was performed by Geraldine Charlie, Minto, and the transcription is based on her performance in an interview situation, recorded on 17 May 2013 (Example 76). In the following texts and translations, the parts dominated by vocables are in the left-hand column and parts dominated by words with lexical meaning are in the right-hand column.

Example 76 Words and translation of *Segoya* (Bettis, Nenana).

Vocable/key word part	Lexical part
Hei-ho, Segoya	
Hei-ho, Segoya	
Sedena'	
Ihooo hoo hoooo	
Segoya	
	Ch'eghwtsen' k'alogha
	Seghw notinotoł udesni t'anh
	Do'ił'an'?
Sedena'	
Ihooo hoo hoooo	
Segoya	

Translation:

Hei-ho, My baby	
Hei-ho, My baby	
My child	
Ihooo hoo hoooo	
My baby	
	All the love he had
	I know it will be missed
	Why?
My child	
Ihooo hoo hoooo	
My baby	

The words

The translation in Example 76 cannot easily be derived directly from the words.[27] The language used is elliptical, differing from spoken language by the inclusion of formulaic phrases and varying pronunciations of common words. One word has occasioned some discussion with the elders. *Do'ił'an'* is a word found in other Minto *dratakh ch'elik*, and the elders frequently translate it as 'why?' In spoken language, it would be interpreted as 'What are you doing?' An elder tells us that the addressee of this question is probably not the person who has passed away but, rather, God – hence perhaps the more general translation 'why?' In performance, the word is variously pronounced as *do'ił'ani, do'ił'ana,* or *do'ił'ini*.

The vocables, words without lexical meaning, enclose the meaningful words – they precede them and follow them. A sequence containing vocables, perhaps including a kin term as at the beginning, is called *bent'aya'*, which the elders translate as 'chorus'. Vocables in Minto vocal expressions can contain vowels that are not found in spoken language, such as the diphthong *ei/ey*.[28] In this case, the vowels in the vocables are low- or mid-level in quality. While our sample is still too small to make a strong claim, we believe that the *dratakh ch'elik* uses fewer high- and mid-level vowels than *ch'edzes ch'elik*.

Both vocable syllables and meaningful syllables are elongated on moving sequences of notes. In the case of the meaningful syllables, the moving sequence most frequently corresponds to a morphological stem, but it does not always: *udes<u>ni</u>, t'a<u>nh</u>, do'il'<u>an</u>'*, and of course *se<u>dena</u>* all have a moving sequence on a verb or noun stem. However, the movement on *seghw* occurs on both the prefix and the postpositional stem.

Another type of elongation occurs on the last repetition of *segoya*. This type of augmentation consists of the prolongation of a vowel over many beats with the same pitch, divided by glottal pulses. This type of lengthening of a syllable or syllables of lexical words or vocables is used only in the performance of vocal expressions. It may occur both at the beginning and at the end, in this case only at the end.

---

27 The translation is based on the elders' comments and on similar translations by James Kari 1994.
28 For vocables see further Tuttle 2019.

The music

The performer is sitting down and uses a fairly soft voice relating to the rather intimate situation of the recording session. She accentuates the even beat strongly and rocks slightly forward and back with the rhythm, sometimes in combination with hand movements. *Segoya* is repeated once later on in the interview session and this repetition is identical with the first one, apart from minor variations in pitches that do not change the main outline of the melody.

Segoya starts with vocables on a rising minor third and with short–short–long tones (A in Example 77). This short motif is immediately repeated with the first word, *segoya*. The rhythm short–short–long (with minor variations) recurs many times during the performance, as indicated by brackets in the transcription. It functions as an isorhythmic motif and can be regarded as a building block.[29]

When the highest pitch is reached, it continues with vocables while descending stepwise in a triadic fashion (B, B' and C, indicated by a dashed arrow). It ends on a tone repetition at the lowest pitch (C, indicated by a dashed line). Here the vocables, while poetically amplifying the vowel sounds, musically serve to bring the melody to an end. The tone repetitions consist of vowels prolonged by a series of glottal attacks. This marks the ends of the stanza: A–B–C.

The second stanza is based on a repetition of this melody, but now with words that carry lexical meaning, and it is prolonged for 8 beats at the highest pitch (A', marked with an arrow) before it continues with a minor variation on the melody (B'), and finally ends with the same phrase as the first stanza (C). The order of the phrases is A–B–C–A'–B'–C.

---

29 Nettl 1974.

Example 77 Transcription of *Segoya* (Bettis, Nenana). Performed by Geraldine Charlie, Minto, 17 May 2013. Original pitch: final tone f ≈ 170 Hz.

- 17 *Segoya*, **Bettis**

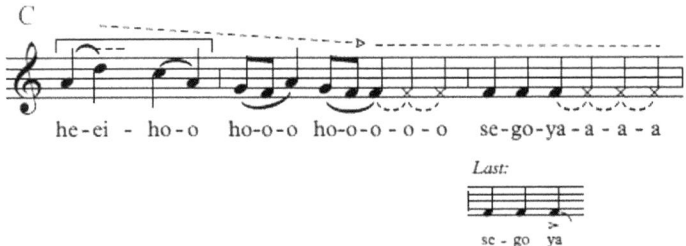

Characteristics of *Segoya* (Bettis)

Melody
- Starts low and rises. After the highest pitch it descends stepwise in a triadic fashion with a tonal centre.
- Range: 12 semitones.

Rhythm
- Regular pulse.
- One pulse beat per syllable dominates.

- The rhythm short–short–long (1–1–2 beats) functions as an isorhythmic motif and as a building block.

Form
- Overall form: A–B–C–A'–B'–C.
- A, B, and C consist of vocables and one lexical key word.
- A' and B' have words with lexical meaning at a high pitch level.

Phrasing
- Phrases end on a tone repetition.
- In the case of the meaningful syllables, the isorhythmic motif often corresponds to a morphological stem.

Initial/final formulae
- Ends with a tone repetition on the tonal centre. The very last vocable of the performance is short and stressed.

Word variations
- Vocables prominent.
- Both vocable syllables and meaningful syllables are elongated at the end of the isorhythmic motif.
- The last syllable of a tone repetition is elongated over several beats.

Analysis 15 Segoya (Titus John)

Another *dratakh ch'elik* for a child was made by Titus John, probably in the 1920s. It was performed by Neal and Geraldine Charlie, Minto, and the transcription is based on their performance in the interview situation on 17 May 2013.

Poetics

The words display a structure which is found in a number of *dratakh ch'elik* and which the elders specifically point to when teaching them. Three specific words *ch'eghwtsen* 'love', *chononi* 'hunting luck', and *gholiyo* 'wealth, good fortune' (*gholiyi* in singing), are inserted into a line of poetry that is otherwise repeated in three separate verses performed with the same music. The verses occur in this order, and we have no examples of deviations from that order. Elders translate the repeated line as something like '[I thought] there would be back and forth downriver' (Example 78).

These three important words are often found in *dratakh ch'elik* composed in honour of adult men. In this case, part of the poignancy comes from the presence of the adult words about someone who will not become an adult, and therefore will not have the opportunity to enjoy the love, luck, and wealth mentioned in the verses.

The verb *k'ets'enilno* is not exemplified in prose examples in our corpus, but because verbs have so many possible forms in Athabascan languages, this does not define it as a purely poetic word. *Do'il'ini* is a different form of *do'il'an'*, found in the Bettis' *Segoya* (Analysis 14), and is translated as 'why?' though the relationship of the meaning to the morphological composition is not clear.

Vocables and words

The vocables are very restricted in vowel quality, comprising only [ei] and [o]. *Segoya*, 'my baby', is lengthened using both changed pitches, in the second measure, and glottal pulses, in the extensions in verses 2 and 6 (see Example 79). Otherwise, 4-syllable sequences are being created, with vocable syllables added where a word does not end in a vowel. So, we have *ch'eghwtsen' ei*, with an added syllable, treated in much the same way as *k'ets'enilno*, which has the same number of syllables and ends with a vowel. The four

Example 78 Words and translation of *Segoya* (Titus John). Words that are changed when a phrase is repeated are underlined.

Vocable/key word part	Lexical part
O-ho-ho-ho-o, ei, Segoya', o, Segoya',	
Ei go ho, o, Segoya', Ei go ho, o, Segoya'	
Ei o-ho-ho-ho,	
O-ho-ho-ho-o, ei, Segoya, o Segoya	Ch'eghwtsen' ei k'ets'eniłno ghedze yodo (2x)
	Do'ił'ini
O-ho-ho-ho-o, ei, Segoya, o Segoya	<u>Chononi</u> k'ets'eniłno ghedze yodo (2x)
	Do'ił'ani
O-ho-ho-ho-o, ei, Segoya, o Segoya	<u>Gholiyi</u> k'ets'eniłno ghedze yodo (2x)
	Do'ił'ani
O-ho-ho-ho-o, ei, Segoya, o Sego	

Translation:

O-ho-ho-ho-o, ei, My baby, o my baby	I thought there would be <u>love</u> moving back and forth downriver (2x)
	Why
O-ho-ho-ho-o, ei, My baby, o my baby	I thought there'd be <u>hunting</u> back and forth downriver (2x)
	Why
O-ho-ho-ho-o, ei, My baby, o my baby	I thought there'd be <u>prosperity</u> moving back and forth downriver (2x)
	Why
O-ho-ho-ho-o, ei, My baby, o my ba[by]	

4-syllable sequences *ch'eghwtsen' ei, k'ets'eniłno, ghets'e yodo* and *do'ił'ini* carry the same metrical weight and have a similar rhythmic pattern. *Chononi* and *gholiyi* do not have 4 syllables, however, and are not augmented by a vocable – they are just spread over the same number of beats as the other sequences. Overall, however, there is an impression that the meaningful words are delivered one syllable to a beat, an emphatic and highly recognizable pattern found in many performances of this type.

Some vowels are specific to vocables and do not occur in spoken language in the Minto dialect. In order to transcribe the vocables, it is sometimes necessary to employ spectrograms. For this reason, a solo performance is needed, since sounds are often blurred in communal situations. Many performances in our material were recorded in communal situations. Therefore, two types of transcription are used in this text: one after detailed analysis, the other (more approximate) by ear using the letters u [u], i [i], o [ɔ], a [ɑ], ey [ɛj], dz [ts], b [p], h [h].

In *do'il'ini*, it is not obvious whether the final open syllable is an added vocable or a meaningful piece of morphology, since the question marker in this language contains the same vowel. This morpheme is glottal final [-iʔ-], but in Minto, the vocal expression's final glottal stop is often not realized. Given the narrow range of vowel qualities in the other vocables, we have chosen to translate it with 'why'.

Example 79 *Segoya* (Titus John), performed by Neal and Geraldine Charlie, Minto. Original pitch: final tone c ≈ 115 Hz for the male voice.

Music

This *Segoya* also starts with a rhythmic combination of vocables and a key word that serves as a building block (A, marked with a horizontal line). The key word *segoya* that follows immediately is performed in a descending motion, so that the final syllable is the lowest. The second time the building block occurs (B), the descending movement, in triads, is prolonged; and in the third repetition, it is further prolonged before ending with a tone repetition at the lowest pitch, followed by a short section at a high pitch which is based on vocables (marked with an X). The B phrase is repeated in a varied form (B') and prolonged so as to fit the words. Each time it ends with a short high-pitched and descending figure (Y), which is a variation on the ending of section B (X), after which A is repeated. This pattern (B'–A) is repeated three times, one for each line of words. The total poetical and musical form is A–B–A–B'–A–B'–A–B'–A. As is often the case, the very last word of the performance is cut short: *sego* instead of *segoya*, with a heavy stress on the syllable *go*.

Characteristics of *Segoya* (Titus John)

Melody
- Descending melody with a tonal centre.
- Range: 14 semitones.

Rhythm
- Regular pulse.
- Isorhythmic organization: the first motif serves as a building block.
- Words with lexical meaning are often grouped in 4-syllable units corresponding to 4 pulse beats.

Form
- Starts with a motif with vocables and a lexical key word that serves as a building block.
- The last phrase of the first part is repeated in a varied form and prolonged so as to fit the lexical words.

Phrasing
- The last syllable of a phrase is lengthened.

Initial/final formulae
- Ends with a tone repetition on the tonal centre.

Word variations
- The vocables are restricted in vowel quality, comprising only [ei] and [o].
- When a word is not vowel-final, vowel syllables are added: *ch'eghwtsen'* becomes *ch'eghwtsen' ei* and is treated in a comparable manner to *k'ets'enihno*. Each 4-syllable unit carries the same metrical weight.
- In other cases, words are elongated to fit the 4-beat pattern: *chononi* and *gholiyi* are not augmented by a vocable but are simply spread over the same number of beats.

Structural framework of *dratakh ch'elik*

The different aspects of the two *dratakh ch'elik* that have been treated separately here are, of course, fully integrated in performance. It is quite obvious that both are built on a framework that is presented in the first stanza ('A' in the examples) and then repeated in the following stanza(s) with variation ('B').

This framework starts with a *key word section* consisting of the musical setting of the main word (*segoya*) that is echoed musically and/or rhythmically with vocables which, in these cases, precede the main word. This is a very poignant motif which serves as a building block for the rest of the framework. Obviously, the originality of the musical setting of the main word and its 'sonoric double' in vocables is of great importance for the originality of the composition. The vocables, in combination with pitch and tone-lengths, also appear to have a poetic function in that they help to accentuate the main word. They also introduce syllables with consonants, and particularly vowels that will be used throughout the melody and thus colour it with a unified sonoric form.

Once the key word section is over, the framework continues with a descending unit with vocables, which descends in rather large, mainly triadic steps. This brings the melody to its tonal centre with a final unit consisting of a tone repetition on the last vowel of the main word that ends the stanza (Table 6).

The repetition of the stanza contains words with meaning and could be called a lexical unit. It consists of one sentence that is constructed so that it can be repeated with only one word changed. The principle thus involves parallelism (see Example 78). The words are performed to the melody of the framework, which is flexible enough to be prolonged so as to comprise a full sentence.

The result is that of a very tightly knit vocal expression in which the structural and aesthetic functions of the music and the language are present simultaneously, and all these elements are integrated and interdependent in the organic whole (Table 6). A comparison with some other Athabascan *dratakh ch'elik* shows that two examples from Minto share similar characteristics.[30] Examples from other places have similar structures with regard to the parallelism of the

---

30 Chief Charlie's memorial song for his elder brother who died 1923 sung by Moses Charlie (Lundström 1980: 137–138); Moses Charlie's song for his mother (Lundström 1980: 138–139).

Table 6 Structural outline of *dratakh ch'elik*

Dratakh ch'elik	Verbal content	Realization
1st stanza		
Key word unit	vocables + key word	– key word combined with poignant musical motif – key word motif mirrored in vocables – becomes isorhythmic pattern
Melodic development	vocables	– based on the isorhythmic pattern – normally descending
Final unit	vocables + key word	– normally tone repetition on lowest pitch
2nd stanza: extended variation(s) of 1st stanza		
Lexical unit	words with lexical meaning	– lexical words to the melody of stanza 1 – melody prolonged as necessary
Melodic unit	vocables	– variation of stanza 1 with vocables
Final unit	vocables + key word	– normally tone repetition on lowest pitch

texts and its content, but differ as regards the musical framework.[31]

Vocables have been widely discussed in the literature on Native American vocal practices, and while their origin is still disputed, there is evidence that vocables should be understood as having many different functions, some of which have been touched upon here. The fact that they are so intimately tied to a musical form and to aesthetic content is probably one reason why vocables in vocal expressions tend to be repeated without change in each new performance, and also why the vocables can be remembered. Concerning Navajo ceremonial vocal expressions, Frisbie says:

> I suspect that the vocables that occur at the beginning of songs, the chorus-verse link, and the ending of the song are the functional

---

31 Memorial song for Chief Simeon Chickalusion 1880–1957 composed by Shem Pete (Kari and Fall 2003: 59–61); Dena'ina Memorial song for a young man who drowned near Nondalton in December 1953 (Coray 2007: 55–60); Dena'ina Memorial song (The mountain range extends, Coray 2007: 61–62).

equivalents of the formulas, conventional transitions, phrase connectors, and other devices used in reciting myths.[32]

This may indeed be so in certain vocal genres. In the particular case of *dratakh ch'elik*, the poetical form is more fixed than a myth would generally be. Frisbie's reflection is still relevant, though, when it comes to memorability. This study of two *dratakh ch'elik* has shown that when the vocables are seen as an integrated part of the total linguistic–musical–poetic framework, there are many cues that serve to increase memorability. This may also explain why the performer first searches for the initial building block when she is trying to remember a specific *dratakh ch'elik*. When she has found it, the *dratakh ch'elik* unfolds.

The structure of the *dratakh ch'elik* thus serves as a performance template that facilitates the creation and re-creation of specific vocal expressions. In this performance template matters like parallelism and vocables – in which musical and linguistic factors are integrated – play a significant role.

The *dratakh ch'elik* performance template

Melody
- Often, but not always, stepwise descending melody with a tonal centre (see Example 74).
- Range: 8–14 semitones.

Rhythm
- Regular pulse.
- One pulse beat per syllable dominates.
- Isorhythmic organization common: the first motif serves as a building block.

Form
- Strophic.
- Section A consists of vocables and one key word with lexical meaning denoting kinship.
- Other parts consist of words with lexical meaning praising the deceased: one line that is repeated with each repetition constructed so that one important word can be exchanged for each repetition (see Example 73).

---

32 Frisbie 1980: 376.

Phrasing
- Phrases end on a tone repetition.
- A–B with variations.
- Both A and B end with tone repetitions.
- A contains vocables and a lexical key word, B (and repetitions) contains lexical words.
- The words with a lexical meaning are delivered over 4 beats.
- In the case of the meaningful syllables, the isorhythmic motif often corresponds to a morphological stem.
- Prominent verb and noun stems tend to be stressed, lengthened and/or fall on a new pitch, which reflects speech.

Initial/final formulae
- Ends with a tone repetition on the tonal centre; the very last vocable of the performance is often short and stressed.

Word variations
- Vocables prominent and restricted in vowel quality, comprising only [ei] and [o].
- Both vocable syllables and meaningful syllables are elongated at the end of the isorhythmic motif.
- When a word is not vowel-final, vowel syllables may be added: *ch'eghwtsen'* becomes *ch'eghwtsen' ei* and is treated in the same way as *k'ets'enihno*. Each 4-syllable units carries the same metrical weight.

Ch'edzes ch'elik

Ch'edzes ch'elik are performed with dancing at gatherings of all types, including formal feasts – potlatches – in honour of deceased or living persons. They may also be performed for audiences. The Tanana expression literally means 'dance song', which is a compound of two nouns. It is the term used by elders when designating this type of music. The dance is led by performers and drummers, and many people can join in. Some dances are choreographed – like *Minto crow dance* or *Back and forth* – while others may be free, dancers moving individually or in a row. The *ch'edzes ch'elik* themselves are rather short and usually strophic, consisting of one stanza that is repeated several times. They make abundant use of vocables; some have no words with lexical meaning at all, but consist entirely of vocables.

The Minto Dance and Song Group was formed in the early 1960s. It was one of the first groups in a revitalization movement of Athabascan music through the organization of village dance teams.

Sometimes such an initiative was taken by a single dedicated individual.[33] Among prominent early members in the Minto Dancers were the late Peter Jimmie – who was a dance leader and also composed many *ch'edzes ch'elik* and dances that are still performed – and, over the years, song-leaders such as the late Evelyn Alexander, the late Dorothy Titus who was also a famous song-maker, and Sarah Silas. The Minto Dancers still exist and have performed at pow-wows and on stage at various celebrations. The dance group also serves as a learning opportunity outside the school.

There are some early recordings of the Minto Dancers. One contains 11 *ch'edzes ch'elik* originally recorded – probably in 1963 – by Gordon Olson, who was then a missionary in Old Minto.[34] They were copied by the Swedish folklorist Anna Birgitta Rooth, who recorded a great number of myths and tales, together with some vocal performances, during fieldwork in Alaska in 1966. The Rooth collection also includes some 30 *ch'edzes ch'elik* recorded at a potlatch in Tanacross.[35]

In 2009, Tuttle interviewed some of the elders in Minto about the *ch'edzes ch'elik* in this particular sample, including Neal and Geraldine Charlie and Bergman and Sarah Silas. This provided some new information and, in several cases, also new recordings made by those elders who were present, with better sound quality than the original. The enhanced quality made it possible to transcribe vocables with greater precision. There are also recordings of the Minto Dancers from 1967 in the Alaska Native Language Archive, Fairbanks. Another collection of *ch'edzes ch'elik* was used by Tony Scott Pearce for his master's thesis.[36] These recordings include about 100 examples recorded in Minto (1972–73), Nenana (1974), and Fairbanks (1983).

The *ch'edzes ch'elik* are normally accompanied by drumming, using a frame drum. The drumming coincides with the pulse of the

---

33 Johnston 1993: 216.
34 In 1969 the Minto village was moved to its present location because of flooding.
35 Rooth 1971 and Lundström 1980. Here follows a list of the *ch'edzes ch'elik* linked to the numbering in Lundström 1980. D1: *Entrance song* (also called *Walk in*), D2: *Gee Haw*, D3: *Old time dancing song*, D4: *Dance song*, D5: *Twist* [or *Athabascan twist*], D6: *Minto Crow song*, D7: *Dance song*, D8: *He to he*, D9: *Take it easy* [?], D10: *Back and forth* (also called *Welcome song*), D11: *Back and forth #2*. Of these D2, D5, and D8 were composed by Peter Jimmie.
36 Pearce 1985.

vocal performance, but there are small variations in the form of pauses for one beat, double speed, or more complex rhythms. There are no cases of final formulae, but *ch'edzes ch'elik* normally end with one short and stressed tone that coincides with one strong drumbeat. There are three cases of tertiary division (notated 3/8) with drumbeats on 1 and 3.

The most common overall musical forms of the Minto *ch'edzes ch'elik* can be described as A–A–A–A, A–B, A–B–B' or A–B–C, but paired phrasing (A–A–B–B) is rare. Usually the B-part of an A–B *ch'edzes ch'elik* will be dominated by vocables. The A-part may consist of vocables + lexical words or of vocables only. Phrase endings have tone repetitions, mainly using vocables.

The melodic contour is dominated by downward motion: starting high and ending low. An undulating motion around a central tone is also common. Downward passages make use of sequences, i.e. a series of repetitions of a short motif in a stepwise downward motion so that each repetition starts on a lower pitch than the preceding one. Occasionally, this also occurs in an upward motion. Sequences are especially common in the B section. It is common for sequences to be performed in half as long tones, notated as quavers, while the drum keeps on with the quarter notes. This has the effect of speed doubling and makes the music swing. The variants shown in Example 80 (starting at the arrows) could be characterized as a) consecutive downward, b) pendulum upwards and c) interlocking. This is especially common close to the final tone repetition.

Example 80 Rhythmic sequences in the endings of *ch'edzes ch'elik*, particularly in Minto (from Lundström 1980: a = E2, b = D5, c = E10).

The Rooth and Pearce samples mentioned above contain *ch'edzes ch'elik* from Minto, Nenana, Tanacross, and Fairbanks. With many traits in common, they represent a North Athabascan style. It is also possible to distinguish some local traits, for instance a short final tone common in Minto, or paired phrasing which is much more common in the Tanacross material. Comparison between different local traditions is difficult, however. Until the mid-1950s people were seasonal nomads. Even after people began to settle in more permanent villages, there were still many contacts between villages, not least in connection with potlatch feasts when people from several villages gather and take part in the celebrations. Another factor is that, as in most modern societies, young people move away for education or for work. So local practices have spread and mixed in many ways. On the other hand, since people often remember who produced a certain composition, why it was made, and when it was introduced at a potlatch, they also keep track of which local style it represents by comments such as 'that is a Nenana song', 'that song was first introduced in Tanacross', etc. Sometimes an attribution of origin is made on the basis of stylistic features.

Analysis 16 *Joni ło'o,* 'Here it is!' (Tanana)

In this *ch'edzes ch'elik* the words are limited to one sentence (Example 81; see also Example 82 for the melodic outline). The *ganhok* is a tall dance staff. *Joni ło'o* is said to have been composed on the occasion of the introduction of the *ganhok* to the Tanana people – the word is of uncertain origin, though there is speculation that the staff was introduced through Tlingit contact.[37] While the recording here was made by a small group of elders, normally it would be performed by a hall full of people all shouting together.

In this case, the melody and rhythm overwhelm the words, and all the meaningful syllables are given the same weight: one strong beat. Phrase-final vocable syllables are lengthened over several beats. There are no tonal syllables. There are 8 meaningful syllables, arranged in two groups of 4 (Examples 81 and 82). The following vocable sequences also form patterns in groups of 4. All the syllables are heavy, in accordance with the Tanana stress system, in which full vowels and closed syllables count as heavy. A sequence of 4 heavy syllables would not be impossible in speech, but such a sentence is usually broken up by light syllables (CV, where V is a schwa) in the normal composition of sentences.

Example 81 Words and translation of *Joni ło'o* 'Here it is!'

Joni ło'o Ganhok tolał
Here, this will be the Ganhok

Iyaho'ey, iyaho'ey, iyaho'ey
[Vocables]

The first half of the text (A, *Joni ło'o*) is performed as three short tones and one long, and the same rhythm is repeated for the second half (*Ganhok tolał*, Example 82). The final tone of these words finalizes the first section and functions as its tonal centre. The second section (B) is built on the same rhythm, which is repeated twice, but with vocables with no lexical meaning (*Iya ho'ey*). For the third repetition, these syllables are performed at the same pitch, which stresses the tonal centre of the section.

---

37 Jeff Leer, personal communication.

Athabascan vocal genres in Interior Alaska

Example 82 Graphic representation of the melodic movement in the dance song *Joni ło'o*. The vertical axis shows the pitches. For the most part, there is one syllable per drumbeat; but at the end of each phrase, each syllable is held for two beat-pulses with a glottal stop or a dip for each new beat. Performed by Neal and Geraldine Charlie, Minto, 14 May 2009. Original pitch: g ≈ 200 Hz.

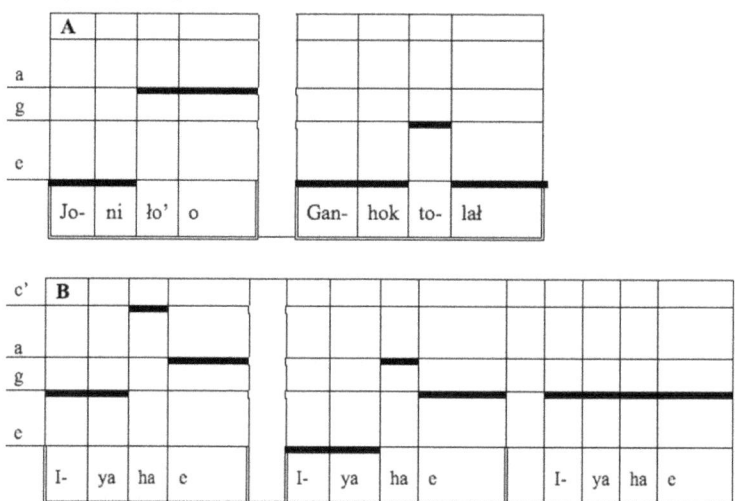

Several characteristics are common in Native American music in general: it is strophic (the diagram in Example 82 shows one stanza that is then repeated with minor changes); it is isorhythmic (that is, built on one rhythmic idea throughout); it has a stepwise downwards or falling motion (the second section of the stanza); and it ends on a tone repetition at one of the lowest pitches that serves as a tonal centre (denoted with a wave-line in the graph).

In his study, Pearce concludes that the overall musical form in this genre is usually binary, i.e. there are two distinct sections within each stanza. He also finds that they are often built around one melodic/rhythmic motif that is repeated at consecutively lower pitches, a pattern which, in a musicological term, is called sequences. Pearce sees this motif as a building block around which the melody is built (denoted by a double bottom line in the graph).[38]

Joni ło'o may represent a category that starts out with a poignant melodic/rhythmic setting of a verbal phrase. That phrase then becomes the nucleus, whereupon it comes to serve as a building block. It is

---

38 Pearce 1985.

combined with vocables, sequences in a downward motion, and ends with a tone repetition.

Characteristics of *Joni ło'o*

Melody
- Stepwise descending melody, with a tonal centre.
- Range: 8 semitones.

Rhythm
- Regular pulse.
- One pulse beat per syllable dominates.
- Isorhythmic: the first motif serves as a building block.
- All meaningful 8 syllables arranged in two groups of 4.

Form
- Strophic.
- Binary form A–B: A has words with lexical meaning, B consists of vocables.

Phrasing
- Vocable sequence patterns in groups of 4.
- Phrases end with tone repetitions.

Initial/final formulae
- Ends with tone repetitions: phrase-final vocable syllables are lengthened over several beats.

Word variations
- Vocables.
- All meaningful syllables are heavy and given the same weight: one strong beat. In speech they would normally be followed by light schwa vowels.

Analysis 17 Christmas tree

Compositions in traditional style with words in both Athabascan languages and English became common in the twentieth century, and are some of the most popular ones; their composers are often remembered. The Minto *Airplane song* is a perennial favourite and has been popularized in a video – in this case the airplane is a positive force, a ride to the potlatch.[39] Another Minto *dance song* inserts English words such as *whiskey* in the framework *enu'ey!* 'Away with it!' In this case, the influence of white outsiders is disapproved of.

Christmas tree was composed by the late Dorothy Titus, who was a widely respected song-maker. She was known for her ability to compose on the spot. This is the recollection of Geraldine Charlie, who performed the version recorded here:

> We used to have Christmas tree, and we make ornaments out of paper, different … and we make chains and hang it all over that tree. Just icicles, no light, no nothing. It was our Christmas tree. Make star out of tinfoil, we'd wrap that tinfoil over that, make star. But one night she went to the hall, and lights come on and off and on, you know. That was *new* to her. It was *exciting* to her. So first thing came to her mind was that: [starts singing]. (Geraldine Charlie, Minto, recorded 17 May 2013)

There are only two words with lexical meaning: *Christmas* and *tree* (Example 83). All the other words are non-lexical syllables or vocables:

Example 83 The words of *Christmas tree*.

Heey ha, 'eey, Christmas tree

Heey ha, 'eey, Christmas tree

Heey ha, 'eey 'eey hiyaheey

'Eey, eey haa

'Eey heey hiya

Ghiha 'ee'e'eey 'oo

---

[39] See www.youtube.com/watch?v=0aZybHWyCvE for a video of this song in staged performance.

As is common in the *ch'edzes ch'elik*, the lexical contents come in the first phrase as words, not a full sentence. In this case, the first phrase is repeated (Example 84). The vocable part of the first phrase mirrors the lexical part, which makes this quite an original start. The general contour is a stepwise falling: phrase 1: c'–g, phrase 2: g–c and phrase 3: e–c. The two final phrases end with tone repetitions, and the vocable ending is of the *hiya*-type. It marks the end of the stanza, and before the tone repetitions there is a typical rhythmic sequence. It is a very tight composition, and this is probably a quality that helped to make it remembered. While performing it, Geraldine Charlie made hand movements depicting a Christmas tree.

Example 84 *Christmas tree.* Performed by Geraldine Charlie, Minto, 17 May 2013. Brackets show tone repetitions at the end of phrases. Original pitch: final tone c ≈ 240 Hz.

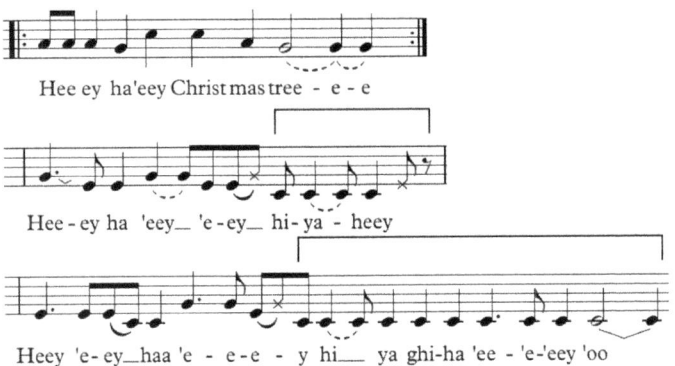

Characteristics of *Christmas tree*

Melody
- Falling melody contour in a series of sequences with a tonal centre.
- Range: 12 semitones.

Rhythm
- Regular pulse.
- Many beats subdivided into two (8th notes); dotted rhythms occur.
- Isorhythmic organization prominent.

Form
- Form: A–A–B–B'.
- A consists of vocables and one lexical key word in a melodic motif.
- B and B' consist of vocables.

Initial/final formulae
- Ends with a tone repetition on the tonal centre; the very last vocable of the performance is short and stressed.

Word variations
- Vocables dominate.

Athabascan leadership and composing

The maintenance and revitalization of highly endangered languages require a supportive context. While language documentation can create reference materials in the form of resources, and classroom teaching can begin the process of initiating new speakers, these activities do not provide the most important component: a reason to speak in the target language. And without this component, neither maintenance nor revitalization can be achieved;[40] there will be no viable place for the language outside the classroom.

Reasons to speak come in the form of situations in which the language must be spoken. Political leaders and public cultural representatives for indigenous groups in the United States must often demonstrate fluency in a particular language. Ceremonial contexts may also require proficiency in languages that are otherwise being replaced by more politically powerful codes. A third context is public performance, where the performers serve as cultural representatives of their own communities or of their language community as a whole.

For some members of minority language communities, these three situations become conflated: political leadership may require demonstrations of language proficiency in ceremonial and performance situations as well as in communications with fluent peers or elders. In the interior of Alaska, young people who are moving into leadership positions now face these challenges. This section examines some of the strategies they are using to develop their linguistic proficiency.

Conversation with several young leaders from the lower Tanana River area (Minto and Tanana) suggests that learners develop innovative strategies to carry out their goals, including methods that draw on academic documentation, indigenous learning and teaching, and also digital media sharing. Art and leadership develop together, providing an instructive example for supporters of language revitalization.

The *dratakh ch'elik* and the *ch'edzes ch'elik* are well suited to communal performance. The prominent setting of the key words stands out and is 'catchy', while the vocable parts contain comparatively common musical material that is fairly easy to learn at the first hearing, particularly if the vocal expression is performed several

---

40 Hinton 2010.

times in a row. Children can learn them at potlatches by listening, and gradually take a more active part in the performance and dancing.

Communal performance may, at best, keep the vocal expressions in mind; but, if a musical culture is to be alive, there must also be individuals who relate to the music by learning, adapting, and transmitting it. In Northern Athabascan culture, this includes composition, which requires the composition of lyrics in combination with vocables and the handling of the interaction between the lyrics and the music.

The tradition seems to be that composing is something you do alone; but even experienced elders will seek the judgement or advice of other experienced persons, particularly in the case of *dratakh ch'elik* that have a formal character. There is no evidence of a tradition of more formalized teaching situations.

Learners become involved with the older repertoire and try to create their own vocal expressions. They may seek out elders for counselling concerning the proper use of language, and for advice concerning the quality of the vocal expression and its originality. They will also consult other friends with a good knowledge of the field. In addition, they contact linguists to help them with transcription, and to learn interview techniques to help them access the history of specific vocal expressions. Counsellors, both indigenous and non-indigenous, are seen as resources and colleagues, and learner confidence grows with each achievement.

Community leadership and song-leading go together in Interior Athabascan communities. In Minto, for instance, the late Neal and Geraldine Charlie were both community leaders and song-leaders, and Neal was also a song-maker. The path to leadership in tribal politics or ceremony is not provided for at school. Instead, leadership develops along with verbal and artistic skill when students themselves take on the goals of mastering language or verbal art. These younger leaders are independently carrying out a programme that elders have frequently advocated: using vocal expressions to learn language.

While the idea of learning language through vocal expressions is appealing, it has not been easy to see how to apply it in classroom teaching. *Ch'edzes ch'elik* contain very few words, though these words are of great cultural importance (e.g. Tanana *ch'eghwtsen'* 'love', *gholiyo* 'prosperity, right living'). In addition, the pronunciation of these words may differ from spoken pronunciation, making them hard to understand in the strong shouting register of group performance. The child-directed classroom songs, with Athabascan words used in language class, also contain little language, and have the additional disadvantage of further adapting the rhythm of Athabascan words to fit into English metrics. Other types of vocal expressions, such as the *dratakh ch'elik* used at potlatches, contain a considerable amount of text, but the text is often complex and poetic, much too difficult for beginners or intermediate learners to parse. These vocal expressions are often also off-limits outside their ceremonial context.

What we observe is that language learning through vocal expressions involves taking on a role other than that of classroom student. That is, the learners who make progress are those who decide that they want to create vocal expressions, or be song-leaders. These choices require understanding and use of a language that is culturally appropriate and functional, though it may be minimal in lexical coverage.

To understand what it means to dedicate oneself to community learning, it is helpful to consider examples. Norman Carlo, a young man whose family roots are in the village of Tanana, is one such example. In the following section, we document some of the choices he has made in order to gain sufficient language proficiency to compose songs that are acceptable in the linked communities of Tanana, Minto, and Tanacross.

Norman Carlo's learning project

Norman Carlo holds an associate science degree in process technology from the University of Alaska Fairbanks. Born in the village of Tanana in 1988, he has now joined the International Brotherhood of Electrical Workers and works on the Alaska Pipeline. He also has a major project: to make a comprehensive set of compositions for his native village, where traditions have lapsed since the older generation passed away. He wants to teach them to the people of Tanana and help them to develop the repertory so that they can present them as their own when visiting potlatches.

Geographical and language names can be confusing here. Tanana, originally a Native village situated at the confluence of the Tanana and Yukon rivers, has been heavily impacted by contact with non-natives due to its location on the rivers and the fact that rail lines run through it. The language native to the area is Upper Koyukon, a dialect of Koyukon that shares many phonological and lexical features with the Lower Tanana language spoken in Minto. Language shift has moved more quickly in Tanana than in Minto. Minto is now on the road system, but the village was moved there from a place on the Tanana River in 1969, owing to repeated flooding.

Partly because of this historical difference, more Athabascan elders who have stayed active in song-making and song-leading remain in Minto. Until very recently, elders have been able to lead performances and to assist with the composition of *dratakh ch'elik*. This has not been the case in Tanana. The result is that far fewer vocal expressions from the area have been represented in potlatches in recent years, and fewer older ones are remembered and performed. Norman says:

> You know, like one day, I do want to share these songs with my fellow other villagers, and sing it with them, but my vision of it is for my home town to learn them first ... And so people know that this song is Tanana's song, but other people, you know, if they want to sing it down the road, like I sing a lot of songs from other villages, they'll know where it comes from, and give credit, you know, that the song is from Tanana. (Norman Carlo, interviewed 17 February, 2015)

Norman's process in developing these compositions has drawn on the talents and mentorship of both Athabascan elders and University contacts. He attends all possible occasions for dancing and vocalizing in the presence of knowledgeable elders; and he has studied old videos to observe conservative styles of performance.[41] These videos feature performances and other activities carried out by Lower Tanana elders from Minto. In addition, he has worked on Koyukon literacy with Tuttle in an independent study where his goal was to create lyrics in this language. As he began to build his collection, Norman recorded each composition in a laboratory environment with Tuttle at the Alaska Native Language Center, providing copies of the material and allowing us to keep track of his progress and talk about it.

The potlatch functions as a context for language and music. Before starting to compose, Norman had learnt vocal performance, drumming, and dancing in situations like potlatches and other celebrations, both as an observer and as a participant. While he gradually acquired these performance skills, he noticed that people watched him and listened to him. This gave him confidence to continue. He learnt about structures from listening to older recordings and present

---

41 Madison, Pearce, Kamerling, Frank, and Russell 1985 and Madison, Charlie, and Titus 2011.

performances, but he had not acquired the local language as he was growing up; so, in order to compose he needed to develop his language proficiency. In this case, after acquiring performance skill at potlatches, Norman found a reason to learn the language of his home village – and what is more, something of neighbouring languages as well. Hence, musical activity and the potlatch as a functioning context led to language learning. An important element in Norman's story is the continued vitality of the Minto Dance and Song Group. Without this continuing strand of language-infused culture, Norman's quest to become a song-maker and leader might not have been realized. (Figure 4)

The crucial context for language use, as demonstrated by Norman's journey, is the potlatch, a domain where outsiders have no significant role. As Hinton demonstrates, no strategy for language revitalization that requires motivation or organization from outside the speech community can persuade people to learn and use a language.[42] Those who take on the challenge of learning and using a fragile minority language need internal motivation. However, the roles that Hinton identifies for external helpers (help with literacy and documentation) are exactly those that Norman chooses for his academic supporters.

Which language is he learning? Norman's lyrics often use forms that could belong to several different languages of the Athabascan family, since the languages are distinguished by relatively few consonant contrasts and the vowel systems are very similar. However, his lexical choices reflect the content of the lyrics, extending across languages. For example, in a composition he prepared for a Tanacross elder, he included both Koyukon and Tanacross language in the lyrics in order to honour this mentor from upriver (Tanacross is the Athabascan language spoken east of Fairbanks; the name refers to 'Tanana crossing'). This Athabascan language is phonologically and lexically more different from Upper Koyukon than Tanana; so, to translate to it, Norman consulted speakers from Tanacross. Morphology, syntax, and spoken phonology are hard for him in all the languages. Even so, distinguishing between the three, and working with important concepts and words from each of them, is something he expects and indeed *needs* to do.

It may seem strange to approach three languages as opposed to just one when all three are highly endangered. However, the people

---

42 Hinton 2010.

Athabascan vocal genres in Interior Alaska

Figure 4 Norman Carlo dancing at the *Alaska Federation of Natives Convention* in Anchorage, in the autumn of 2015.

of the Tanana River have always lived in a multilingual environment. Being comfortable with language differences (which Athabascans often refer to as dialect differences) is part of their cultural heritage. Norman's language learning is still developing, but he does not seem to be at all confused by learning from people who speak different languages; instead, he seems free from a common problem among language learners: the need to learn 'my grandmother's language' and no other. This hang-up about locality may cause severe problems for language learners when mentors are scarce. Therefore, Norman's approach may have a great deal to recommend it.

Norman, along with other Alaskan Athabascans, is developing the skills he needs to move into a changed world: one where the village is no longer limited to physical locality, but is defined by blood and marriage relationships and shared history. In order to get his lyrics and melodies out to the stakeholders he wishes to contact, Norman created a closed Facebook group into which the lab videos of his performances are linked. This strategy allows him to obtain feedback from a fairly widespread, discontinuous village. His revised *Caribou song*, a composition for his mother – one part related to sobriety, and one inviting his friends to dance – is linked to this page. This web development is relatively new, and it is not clear exactly how the feedback will develop. Participation on Facebook is high among Alaska natives in all except the oldest generations, and its interactive format may provide a way for other learners to comment more freely than they might do in a formal, local context.

Analysis 18 *Caribou people* version 2 by Norman Carlo

Norman Carlo has created a set of compositions that he continues to revise and refine as he receives feedback from people he considers stakeholders. He recently changed the melody of one of them (originally *Caribou song* in honour of his clan, not to be confused with the *Caribou song* (Analysis 12)), to make it easier to distinguish it from the work of another, older song-maker, Robert Charlie, whose musical experience includes the heritage of his father, Moses Charlie, and his grandfather Chief Charlie. The revised version is transcribed in Examples 85–86. This version was questioned again for lyrical content when an elder remarked that it is boastful to speak about one's clan. Norman revised the lyrics accordingly, the result being *The people's song*, which is both more inclusive and more culturally appropriate.

The genre is that of *ch'edzes ch'elik*. There are three words with lexical meaning. They are:

Example 85 Words of *Caribou people* version 2.

	In singing	In speech	Meaning
Deneey	[tɛnɛj]	[tɛnæ]	'people'
Bedzeey	[pədzi, pədzij]	[pədziɛ]	'caribou'
Haaliyaa	[holiya]	[ɣɔlijɔ]	'wealth, luck'

Example 86 Musical transcription of *Caribou people* version 2. Performed by Norman Carlo, 17 February 2015.

Most of the discussion and revision have centred on the introductory words and their musical realization. Example 87 shows how the original phrase a) was quite similar to that of an existing *dance song* b), while that of the revised version is quite different c). The second part, consisting mainly of vocables, was not altered at all; see Example 88 (one exception is the first tones of c) which are higher in order to link the first high-pitched phrase with the second phrase). Apparently, considerations of meaning, originality, and

Example 87 The initial phrase of a) *Caribou people* version 1, and b) a *dance song* by Robert Charlie performed by Norman Carlo • **18 *Caribou people*, v1 1st phrase a and b** and c) the final phrase of the first stanza of *Caribou people* version 2. Performed by Norman Carlo. Original pitch: final tone f ≈ 188 Hz. • **19 *Caribou people*, v2 1st phrase**

Example 88 The second (and final) phrase of a) *Caribou people* version 1, b) a *dance song* by Robert Charlie performed by Norman Carlo, and c) *Caribou people* version 2 performed by Norman Carlo. • **20 *Caribou people*, v2 2nd phrase**

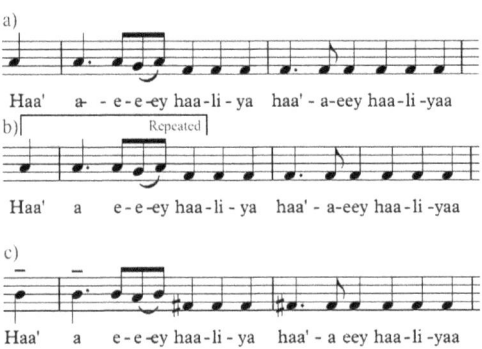

aesthetics focus on the initial part of the vocal expression, whereas the longer falling phrases tend to be more common or formulaic in nature. This pattern explains how *ch'edzes ch'elik* have the capacity to combine the unique with the everyday, a capacity which enables the composition of new songs as well as communal performance and learning. The same pattern accounts for the memorability of these songs and their inclusion in the general repertory.

Characteristics of *Caribou people* 2

Melody
- The overall contour is falling with a tonal centre.
- Range: 6 semitones.

Rhythm
- Regular pulse.
- Syllabic except in tone repetitions.
- One pulse beat per syllable dominates.
- The first part (A) is isorhythmic.

Form
- Form: A–A–B–B'.
- The initial part, A, contains vocables and key words with lexical meaning.
- The final part, B and B', consists of vocables and a song-word.

Phrasing
- The final syllable of a phrase is lengthened.

Initial/final formulae
- Ends with a tone repetition on the tonal centre; the very last vocable of the performance is short and stressed.

Word variations
- Vocables dominate.
- Lexical words are pronounced differently from ordinary speech.
- Final tone repetitions consist of vocables and one lexical word, *haaliyaa*, that functions as a song-word in this context.

Ch'edzes ch'elik endings or 'refrains'

Norman Carlo presented some twenty *ch'edzes ch'elik* in two recording sessions, most of which he had not presented before (30 August 2016 and 8 September 2016). He used recordings he had made on his cell-phone in order to recall them. Norman does not verbalize much on the process of composition, except in connection with revision. Usually he says that it 'just came to me'; but he has said that 'usually when I start off, I start with the tune and then I think of words to put in there'. Most of the *ch'edzes ch'elik* in these recording sessions had not yet been tried out in actual dancing situations. Some of them may never be used; but it is just as likely that some will be used and become part of Norman's regular repertory, and also be learnt by others.

The musical form is similar to *ch'edzes ch'elik* in general, and A–B, A–A–B, A–B–B or A–B–C dominate. Some of the newer ones were longer and had more sections repeated: A–A–B–B'–C–C' or A–A'–A"–B–A'''–B'. Perhaps this shows a progression in his composing. Some have key words with lexical meaning, while some consist of vocables only. The majority have the same *haaliyaa*-type ending as *Caribou people* (Example 89). *Haaliyaa* (*gholiyo* in speech) means prosperity and right living. Usually further vocables are added, for instance *e-e-ey haaliya h-o-o-hey ho* or *e-e-ey haaliya hi-hey-ho-o-hey-ho* (Example 90). Sometimes the last vocables in the chain are

Example 89 Final vocable refrain *Eey haaliyaa hiheyho heyho ooho*. Prolonged *haaliya*-type. Vertical: pitch, horizontal: time (1 column = 1 second). Performed by Norman Carlo, 2016.

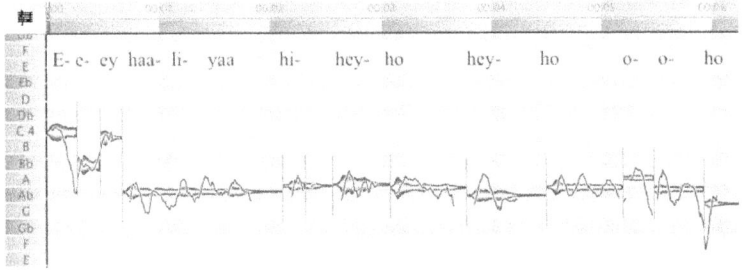

Example 90 Final vocable refrain *Hiya hooheyho* using the vocable *hiya*. Performed by Norman Carlo, 2016.

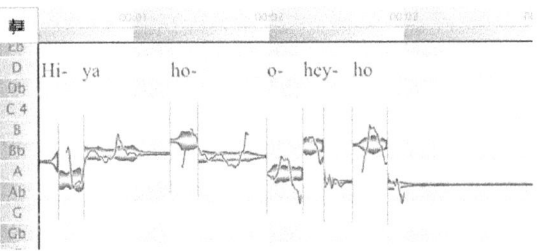

Example 91 Long final vocable refrain with the vocables *ho* and *ha* dominating. Performed by Norman Carlo, 2016.

performed one octave higher. Such octave doubling is common in the very last refrain of Athabascan *ch'edzes ch'elik*, and Evelyn Alexander of the Minto Dancers was particularly well known for octave doubling.

A couple of his *ch'edzes ch'elik* have the ending *Hiya ho-o-hey-ho* or *Hey hiya ho-o-hey ho*. There is also a long ending, dominated by the vocables *ho* and *ha* (Example 91).

The first part of the *ch'edzes ch'elik*, consisting entirely of vowels, is less formulaic. This is – as seen above – the section that characterizes a composition by the combination of the key word(s) and a pregnant or original melodic or rhythmic motif (Example 92).

Example 92 Initial melodic motif. Performed by Norman Carlo, 2016.

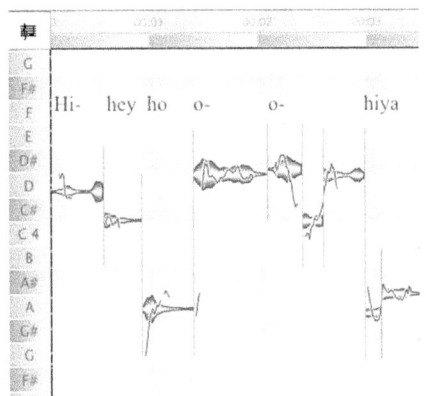

There are two main types of motifs for the beginning:

- a melodic motif with much (often mainly descending) movement between pitches (Example 93; compare for instance Example 84, *Christmas tree*), and
- a flat motif at a high pitch with little melodic movement, usually at one interval and/or micro-intervals (Example 94; compare for instance Example 86, *Caribou people* 2).

Musical form

Though there is much variation in detail, there is also a good deal of repetition of material, particularly in the final vocable parts. This can be illustrated as follows. The basic form A–B may start with either a melodic motif or a flat motif. Both A and B may

Athabascan vocal genres in Interior Alaska

Example 93 An initial melodic motif is often repeated, resulting in 'paired phrases': a–a, marked with a vertical line. Performed by Norman Carlo, 2016.

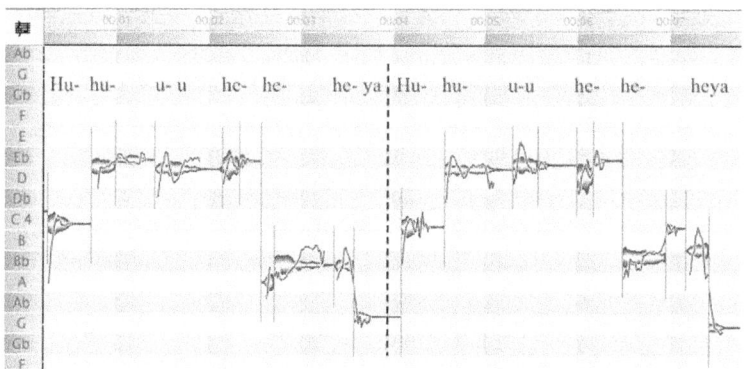

continue as low final vocables or as high (Example 95). The A section may contain lexical words (usually one or two), vocables only, or a combination of both.

A *ch'edzes ch'elik* may be made longer by means of repetition of the motif in A, either identical or with minor variation, resulting in an A–A–B form (Example 96).

Prolongation may be achieved by descending more slowly and inserting an intermediate vocable section (Example 97). This is usually called an A–B–C form; but since the B and C parts are usually quite similar, A–B–B' would also be a possible description.

There are many ways to vary a composition of this type, for example by combining and repeating the form components in various ways.

Performance templates and composition

Among the vocal expressions, *dratakh ch'elik* are composed for specific memorial situations, and they are sometimes commissioned from people known to be skilled song-makers. The *dratakh ch'elik* studied here are old and rather well known, but others are still being composed in the Minto tradition. The framework that has been described here combines comparatively set patterns with flexibility and shares many characteristics with improvised musical styles.[43] This is not an improvisatory genre per se, but the

---

43 Cf. Nettl 1974, Lundström 2010.

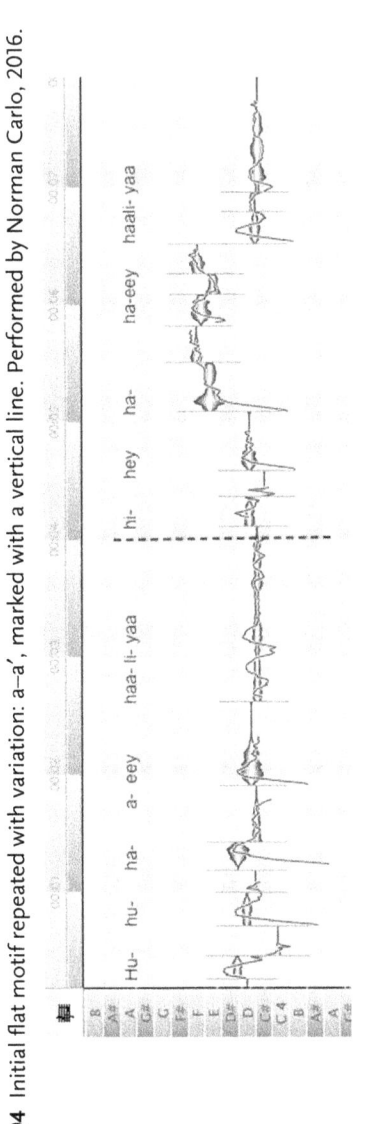

Example 94 Initial flat motif repeated with variation: a–a', marked with a vertical line. Performed by Norman Carlo, 2016.

Athabascan vocal genres in Interior Alaska 185

Example 95 Main outline of the A–B form of composition.

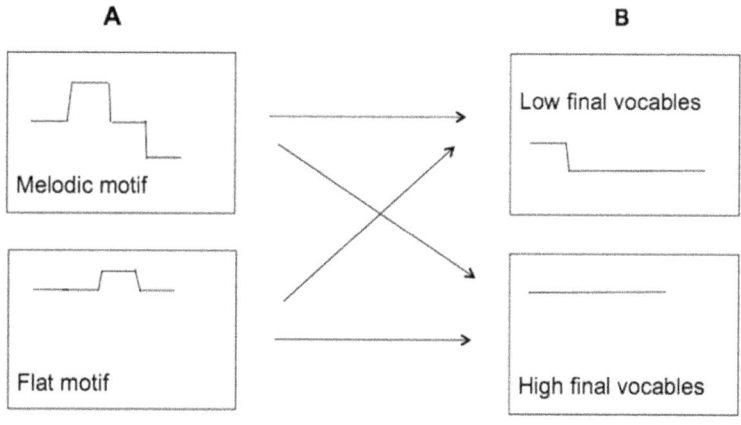

Example 96 Main outline of an A–A–B form of composition.

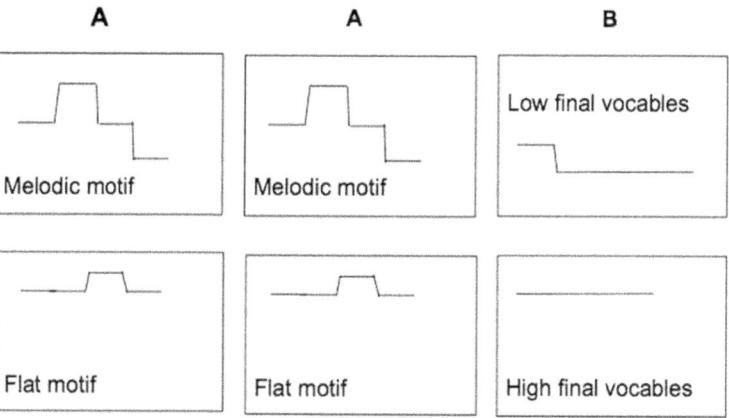

process of composition and that of improvisation have much in common.

It seems to be the linguistic–musical–poetic framework that makes it possible to compose a stylistically satisfactory *ch'edzes ch'elik* in rather a short time. This framework thus has the basic function of a performance template. Coupled with the fact that *ch'edzes ch'elik* are collectively performed and heard in potlatches, the existence and efficiency of this method of composition are likely to play an important part in the survival of this Minto tradition, as well as for the transmission of Minto culture and language to younger generations.

Example 97 Main outline of the A–B–C form of composition.

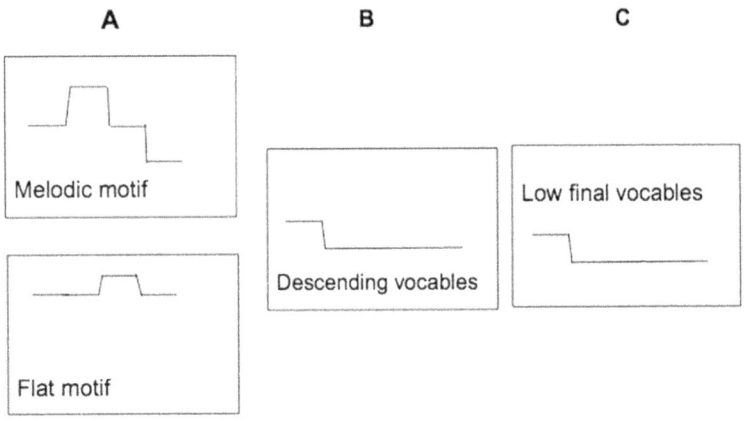

Ch'edzes ch'elik for the dancing situation are composed either *ex tempore* on sudden inspiration, or by developing a basic idea by trying it out on others, privately or in the dancing situation. Most *ch'edzes ch'elik* share a similar basic structure and are made up of a few words with lexical meaning at the beginning, while vocables make up the remainder; there are also some that consist entirely of vocables. The most original part is the very beginning, where the words with meaning are combined with a melodic/rhythmic motif. The latter part tends to be more formulaic, and the same or slightly varied endings may be used for many different *ch'edzes ch'elik*. However, these parts also tend to become stable once a composition is fixed.

One may look on the process of composition as a form of improvisation that differs from *ex tempore* improvisation in that it will be further perfected until – as in Athabascan practice – it achieves a final form, which is then retained basically without changes each time it is performed. If this position is taken, it is relevant to use the concept of a performance template in this case as well. What has been outlined in the analysis is the approximate basic character of such templates. It should be noted that there are other vocal genres in the Athabascan tradition, such as the *senh ch'eliga'*, 'medicine song' (Analysis 12), which have a completely different form and are more closely related to intonation, with neither vocables nor tone repetition. There is no evidence to the effect that vocal expressions of this genre are ever newly composed.

By way of conclusion, the Athabascan vocal genres *dratakh ch'elik* and *ch'edzes ch'elik* may be approached via performance templates, and this approach leads to an understanding of them as vocal expressions in which language and music are one. One important function of the vocables proves to be that of making composition of these genres possible, even composition of *ch'edzes ch'elik* completely made up of non-lexical words, which are then repeated identically each time the composition is performed. Yet another function on the part of the vocables in Athabascan tradition has been demonstrated: they form the basis of the performance template that facilitates composition. Perhaps this was what Geraldine Charlie meant in an interview when she said that 'the vocables are there to keep the words in place'.[44]

The *ch'edzes ch'elik* performance template

Melody
- Melody generally descending stepwise in a sequential manner and with a tonal centre (see Examples 84, 86).
- Range: 6–16 semitones.

Rhythm
- Regular pulse.
- One pulse beat per syllable dominates.
- Pulse beats may be subdivided into two; dotted rhythms occur.
- Isorhythmic organization prominent.
- Vocable sequence patterns often arranged in groups of 4 beats.

Form
- Strophic.
- Binary form A–B or A–B–C with variations: A has vocables and key word(s) with lexical meaning, other sections consist of vocables (see Examples 95–97).
- In A, the key word and 'corresponding' vocables form a poignant musical motif or 'building block'.

Phrasing
- The final syllable of a phrase is lengthened, and phrases end with tone repetitions.

Initial/final formulae
- Ends with a tone repetition (often on the tonal centre); the very last vocable of the performance is short and stressed.

---

44 17 May 2013.

Word variations
- Vocables dominate.
- Lexical words may be pronounced differently from ordinary speech.
- Final tone repetitions consist of vocables only, sometimes with one lexical word (*haaliyaa*) that functions as a 'song-word'.

4
Seediq canonic imitation (Taiwan)

Arthur Holmer and Håkan Lundström

There are several ethnic groups in Taiwan belonging to the Austronesian language family. Their musical traditions are characterized by various forms of canon performances, which are often polyphonic. There is a high degree of improvisation, and the main performer will be followed by the rest of the participants when they recognize the words or when there are recurring refrains. Vocables – or non-lexical words – are very common. They may occur in combination with lexical words, but entire performances may be made up of vocables that are rather fixed in each case.[1]

The Seediq are one of the most recent groups to be officially recognized as one of Taiwan's indigenous groups, in 2008. They were previously classified as a sub-group of the Atayal, together with the closely related Truku or Taroko people, who were recognized as an independent tribe in 2004 (Map 4). The Seediq language is spoken to the north-east of Puli in Central Taiwan, past Wushe and the valleys to the east and north-east, and across the Central Range to the Taroko Gorge and the Pacific coast. It belongs to the Atayalic group of languages, which, in addition to Seediq, comprises Squliq and Ci'uli (both often referred to as dialects of Atayal). Linguistically, Seediq is divided into three dialects: Truku or Taroko, spoken in Hualien County (and today officially recognized as the separate language of the independent Taroko tribe); Toda, spoken in a couple of villages in the north-eastern parts of Nantou County; and Tgdaya, spoken between Puli and Wushe, and in and around Wushe itself. The data analysed here are from the Tgdaya dialect as spoken in Chingliu, and Chungyuan in the Guoxing valley north of Puli.

---

1 Loh 1982, Tan 2012.

190   In the borderland between song and speech

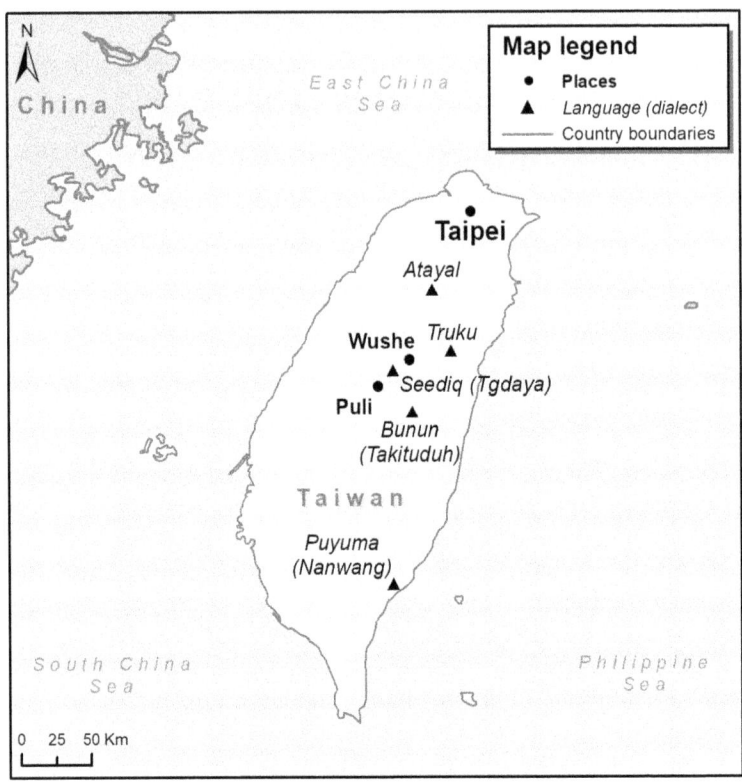

Map 4   Map of Taiwan with the approximate location of Seediq and other ethnic groups mentioned in the text.

An example of Seediq canonical singing is included in the movie *Warriors of the Rainbow: Seediq Bale*, released in 2011. It is a historical drama built on the Wushe Rebellion, which began in October 1930 and formed an uprising against the Japanese forces in Japanese Taiwan.[2]

The Seediq language and vocal expressions

Though there are some studies of the music of ethnic groups in Taiwan, and some of those incorporate linguistic aspects, there are

---

2   Internet reference: *Seediq Bale song*. For more information and controversy regarding historical representation, see https://en.wikipedia.org/wiki/Warriors_of_the_Rainbow:_Seediq_Bale.

very few descriptions of the music of Seediq. Our main objective has been to study vocal expressions of the form that contains repetitions of phrases, in order to see to what extent the concept of the performance template is relevant as an approach to analysis. This was done by transcribing the verbal phrases performed into notation, and by investigating relationships between them.

Two Seediq performances will be discussed here. They are similar, forming dialogues about a maiden and a man meeting in the forest to go together and work in the swidden fields. Two females perform them together: Uma Watan and Lubi Mahung, both from the village of Gluban (Chingliu 清流 in Mandarin). Translation is complicated by the fact that some words are archaic, and by the presence of vocables – the most common ones being *wa*, *e*, *ewa*, *siyo*. The exact boundary between what is a vocable and what is an archaism may be hard to establish. One possible criterion might be that if an expression does not appear to obey the phonotactic patterns of Seediq, it can safely be viewed as a vocable; but, given that phonotactic patterns may change, this is not entirely reliable either. One such phonotactic pattern concerns vowel realization. In Tgdaya Seediq, stress is on the penultimate syllable. Vowels preceding the stressed syllable are systematically elided, and the resulting underlying sequences of consonants are re-syllabified with epenthetic vowels where necessary. In speech, these epenthetic vowels are usually realized as [u], although this is not always very clear, as they are unstressed. In vocal expressions, however, they may surface in a stressed position, because the stress patterns of the lyrics and the melody do not necessarily match. When this happens, the vowel quality [u] is very clear. Furthermore, cases like these show that the morphophonemic changes in Seediq are not just an automatic question of the realization, but have become phonological.

For both performances, very rough translations of the lexical items or phrases that are clear have been added. This serves to give a general picture of the meaning. More detailed surveys of the lyrics become quite difficult, given the preponderance of archaisms and vocables mixed with the lyrics, as well as single interspersed lexical items.

Analysis 19 Uuyas obio, 'The obio song'

Obio is a vocable, and *uuyas* is a manner of performing a vocal expression that is usually translated as 'song'. This is a dialogue about a maiden and a man meeting in the forest and going to work together in the swidden fields. It has five sections (Example 98 A–E) which consist of phrases performed to short musical motifs. There are two persons who perform in unison, and each phrase is repeated once (in the transcription of the words, though, the poetic phrases are written out only once, while the first phrase is written out with the repetition in the notated example that starts each section):

o- yo- su na o- yos   o- yo- su na o- yos ...

The repetition is either identical or with slight changes in pitch, particularly on the final tone, so that the final tone is lower in the repetition. The effect is that of an echo, and musically the second part mirrors the first so that the two phrases sound like a unit. For each section (A–E), the notated introductory unit is repeated throughout, with minor variations.

Each section functions as a stanza held together by sound rhymes (vowel rhymes, consonant rhymes), repetition, and parallelism. Each stanza has its own metre. Exclamations (section A) and questions (section B) parallel spoken language fairly clearly, and speech rhythm and intonation may play important parts in the rhythmic and tonal characteristics of the corresponding musical motifs.

In the following, the lyrics will be presented, as far as they can be identified, without differentiating between actual words, vocables, and possible archaisms which we have not identified as actual words. Epenthetic vowels that are added in speech but are almost inaudible are clearly audible in performance, and they are written in italics (normally the vowel *u*). Rough translations are provided, not so much to give the exact meaning of each line, but to convey the general meaning of the entire stanza. It follows that the lyrics have not been glossed.

Seediq canonic imitation (Taiwan)   193

Example 98 A–E *Obio*. Original pitch: f# ≈ 203 Hz. • **21 *Obio***

Section A (0:0)
9 syllables: (2+1+)5+1 (⌣ ⌣ —) ⌣ – ⌣ – ⌣ —

o-	bi-yo!		
ya-	hi ku	sumba-	rux
e-	wa de	musa-	re
sa-	re yo	sa-	re
o-	bi-yo!		
ya-	hi ku	sunter-	ung
ce-	ka be	qute-	lun
sa-	re yo	sa-	re

Obio! Come to work the fields with me. ... maiden ...
Obio! Come and meet me
in the middle of the forest path ...

Section B (0:26)
6 syllables: 5+1 ⌣ – ⌣ – ⌣ —

o-	yosu		na o-	yos
i-	ma si		mae-	kan
pa	diyax su-		nara	ki
o-	yosu		na o-	yos

Who will eat?

Section C (0:48)
5 syllables: 4+1 ⌣ – ⌣ – —

i-	ma ngayan	su?
nga-	yan mu l-	buy
i-	ma su i-	su?
mu-	lawa ba-	kan

194 In the borderland between song and speech

```
i-      ma ku ya-    ku?
Nu-     harung Ba-   so
```

what is your name?
I am Ibuy, I am Ibuy, Who are you?
bakan calls
who am I
Harung, son of Baso (or possibly Baso is Harung's)

Section D (1:19)
6 syllables: 5+1 ᴗ – ᴗ – ᴗ —

```
li-     xo rumading   wa
e-      wa kisoring   ni
tu-     lame texan    ho
n       Tado Robo     ni
```

let us leave off beginning
let us try once
Robo is Tado's

Section E (1:39)
7 syllables: 2+1+4 ᴗ ᴗ — ᴗ ᴗ ᴗ

```
suwa-   e ta da-   ki ni
n-ni-   ta nii     da ho
```

farewell, let us part

Seediq canonic imitation (Taiwan)

Analysis 20 Meeting and working in the fields

In this performance, the content resembles *Uuyas obio*, and some of the words are the same or similar. It is performed in the form of canonic imitation, a way of constructing music that is well known in what is possibly its most basic form in Seediq practice.[3] The canonic imitation works like this: the lead performer starts a phrase and repeats it just as in the previous performance, whereupon the second performer repeats the same phrase twice, with a delay. In this case the delay is generally arranged so that the main beats coincide, but in some longer phrases the rhythmic relationship is more complex. In principle, then, each performer repeats each phrase twice, i.e. it is performed four times before the next phrase starts:

e- nu- gu a- gu- uh e- nu- gu a- gu- uh ...
e- nu- gu a- gu- uh. e- nu- gu a- gu- uh ...

There are seven sections (Example 99 F–L). Each section has its own motif which is coordinated with the number of syllables in the line and with different distributions of stressed and unstressed syllables. A very similar construction of a 'Tayal song' (i.e. a performance from the closely related Atayal group) has six sections with similar rhythmic motifs.[4] A further similarity is that longer lines are performed slowly, resulting in more complex rhythmical relationships between the parts of the two performers.

---

3 Loh 1982: 315–316. The Atayal and the Seediq are closely related both linguistically and culturally.
4 Loh 1982: 249–50.

Example 99 F–L Meeting and working in the fields. Original pitch; f# 185 Hz. • **22 Working in the fields**

Section F (0:0)
5 syllables: 4+1 ᴗ – ᴗ ᴗ —

e-	nugu	agu-	uh
hai-	ta ru-	meno-	o
e	wa mu-	sare-	e
tu-	lame	texa-	an
sa	malu	exa-	an
ka	pera-	dinga-	an
wa	kesing	na we-	e

Let us play round, maiden*
let us try once,
the beginning

Note: * *Msare* is glossed by consultants as meaning the same as *weewa* 'maiden, young woman'. It is actually attested only in song lyrics, however, and only as a form of address, or possibly an exclamation, suggesting that it is not necessarily a form that could be used syntactically as a noun.

Section G (0:35)
5 syllables: 1+3+1 — ᴗ – ᴗ —

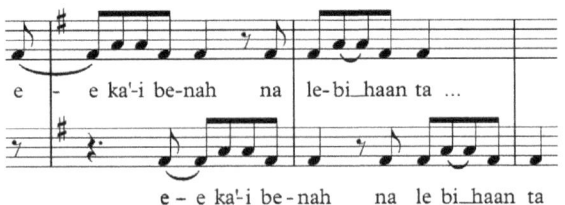

| e- | e ka'- | i be- | nah |
| na | lebi | i haan | ta |

Seediq canonic imitation (Taiwan)

Section H (0:46)
6 syllables: 5+1 ᴗ – ᴗ – ᴗ —

li-	xo ru-	mading	wa
e-	wa mu-	sare	ni
te-	lame	texan	ho
na	pera-	ding	han ho
e-	wa	mu-	sare ni

let us leave off beginning
maiden
let us try once
the beginning

Section I (1:10)
4 syllables: 2+1+1 ᴗ ᴗ — —

n-na beno mi
5 syllables: 3+1+1 ᴗ ᴗ ᴗ — —

...

sino qu-leng-	un
sino ma Te-	mi
hai be tuma-	ra
ceka qu-te-	lun
e n nami	nii

wine is necessary
wine and Temi*
go really and wait
in the middle of the forest path

Note: * This line may have been added spontaneously as a joke, since one of the listeners present is called Temi.

Section J (1:46)
6 syllables: 2+2+2 – ᴗ – ᴗ – ᴗ

...

a su*mpu** sum-	barux
a kedi ku-	hayan
a riso su-	lawa
tu-lame ta	texan
o nawe ta-	wa so

work in the fields together
young man,
let us try once

Note: * This word is sung as [sumpu] in this recording but is presumably intended as *suupu* 'together', in which case it occupies the correct position in the phrase *suupu sumbarux* 'work in the fields together'.

Section K (2:13)
5 syllables: 4+1 ᴗ ᴗ ᴗ ᴗ —

...

siyo, siyo,	si-i[yo]
rumeno wa	so-o

Seediq canonic imitation (Taiwan)

mutara hi- ya-a
ewa musa- re-e

play around
wait there
maiden

Section L (2:34)
6 syllables: 5+1 ⌣ – ⌣ – ⌣ –

...

nio tu   di tan-   da
lixo ru- mading   wa
ewa ki   so ring- wi
tulame   texan   ho
nu Tado Rabo   ni

let us leave off beginning
let us try once
Rabo is Tado's

...

Figure 5 Wet-fields in the Seediq village of Gluban, central Taiwan, in August 2006.

Poetry, metre, and rhythm

Generally speaking, a section forms a stanza and a stanza stands out as a poetic unit based on parallelism, repetitions, and rhymes. In the following discussion, references are made to Analysis 19 (Example 98, sections A–E) and Analysis 20 (Example 99, sections F–L). In Analysis 19 section A, two lines are repeated (*obio* and *sare yo sare*), a beginning of a line is repeated (*yahi ku*...), there are rhymes built on similarity of sound (*sumbarux* / *sunterung* / *qutelu'*) and final rhyme (*musare / sare*), which can also be seen as a chain rhyme where one of the last words in a line rhymes with one of the first in the following line (*musare / sare yo*). Vowel and consonant rhymes are also numerous.

> obio
> yahi ku sumbarux
> ewa de musare,
> sare yo sare
> obio
> yahi ku sunterung
> ceka be qutelun
> sare yo sare

Similar techniques are found, for instance, in sections B and H for repeated lines, and in C and J for repeated words at the beginning of lines. In other stanzas, a final rhyme or a vowel rhyme dominates. In this manner the stanzas are firmly tied together while, in turn, they sometimes have their own distinctive metres. The dominating poetic metres of the two performances are listed in Table 7. There are some variations among them, and there are a few cases of lines prolonged with one syllable within a stanza. In such a case, an extra syllable is then added to the short ones in the metre within the same time slot.

Lines of 5–6 syllables are the most common, and the iambic pattern dominates. The most common way to perform an iambic 6-syllable line starts with an upbeat: - | - - - - ——. A 5-syllable line may just tie the two last tones together: - | - - - ——. In this rhythmic pattern, it is essential that the epenthetic vowel [u], which otherwise occurs in unstressed positions only, is given the same length as other vowels, and this differs from speech. Interestingly, the 5-syllable line (C) has a different pattern: ᴜ – ᴜ – — realized - | - - - ——. This may be because most of the words themselves are fairly short, and they do not (with the exception of *m[u]-lawa* and *n[u]-harung*) contain

Seediq canonic imitation (Taiwan)

Table 7 Metres and their realization in the sections of the two performances. The transcription in the Rhythm column uses bar-lines: |, short unstressed note : -, short stressed note: –, and long note: —

Section	Words	Syllables	Performed	Metre	Rhythm
A	yahi ku sumbarux	6	5+1	ᴗ – ᴗ – ᴗ —	- | - - - - —
B	oyosu na oyos	6	5+1	ᴗ – ᴗ – ᴗ —	- | - - - - —
D	lixo rumading wa	6	5+1	ᴗ – ᴗ – ᴗ —	- | - - - - —
G	e-e ka'i benah	6	5+1	ᴗ – ᴗ – ᴗ —	- | - - - - —
H	lixo rumading wa	6	5+1	ᴗ – ᴗ – ᴗ —	- | - - - - —
L	nio tu di tanda	6	5+1	ᴗ – ᴗ – ᴗ –	- | - - - - -
F	enugu aguuh	5	4+1	ᴗ – ᴗ ᴗ —	- | - - - ——
C	ima ngayan su?	5	4+1	ᴗ – ᴗ - —	- | - - - —
J	a sumpu sumbarux	6	6	– ᴗ – ᴗ – ᴗ	- - - - - -
K	siyo, siyo, si	5	4+1	ᴗᴗᴗᴗ —	- - - - —
A	obio	3	2+1	ᴗ ᴗ —	- - | —
E	suwae tadaki ni	7	2+1+4	ᴗ ᴗ — ᴗ ᴗ ᴗ ᴗ	- - | —- - - -
I	sino qulengun	5	3+2	ᴗ ᴗ ᴗ — —	- - — | —

any underlying consonant clusters which could be syllabified into pre-stress vowels. Alternatively, given that several lines in (C) are questions, it might reflect speech intonation.

Trochee patterns (J, K) are musically performed in the same rhythm by discarding the upbeat; 6 syllables: – – – – – –, and 5 syllables: – – – – —.

There are some sections that begin with an anapest: - - | —. One of them is the vocable *obio* (A), while others are longer. These sections are performed more slowly, and the stresses fall differently. One of them was transcribed as 5/4 beat rhythm, but whether these lines should be interpreted as an instance of triple metre (3/4) might also be discussed. These sections stand out in the performance by having a contrasting slow rhythm, compared to the generally fast 4-beat delivery that dominates the other sectors. It is also connected with words that are emotional in content, like the pleading *obio! come to work the fields with me. ... maiden ...* (A) *and go really and wait, in the middle of the forest path* (I). It also occurs in the final sections of the first performance, which is a farewell: *farewell, let us part* (E).

In performance, then, the tightly woven poetry of the stanzas is combined with strict metres and rather fixed rhythmical patterns. While this sets up a number of criteria that open the field for improvisation of new words, it would also make existing lines or stanzas more stable. This may explain the use of unchanged vocables as well as the use of archaic words which may have lost most or all of their meaning.

The Seediq imitation performance template

Melody
- Built on short melodic motifs of less than 4 beats, with a tonal centre (see Examples 98, 99).
- Speech rhythm and intonation affect the tonal realization.
- Range: 7 semitones.

Rhythm
- Regular pulse.
- Speech rhythm affects the rhythmic realization.
- Prosodic phrases are performed to variants of: - | - - - - —, where the first tone in the bar and the last long one are stressed.

Form
- Litany: dialogue divided into sections or stanzas.
- A stanza is held together by sound rhymes (vowel rhymes, consonant rhymes), repetition, and parallelism.
- A stanza starts with a line that has a different number of syllables from the preceding one, as well as a new variant of the short rhythmic/melodic motif.
- In imitation style, the performer (or performers in unison) repeats each line using the same rhythmic/melodic motif.
- In canonic imitation, performer 1 starts with one phrase while performer 2 repeats the same words and melody. The performers thus repeat each other with a time delay.

Phrasing
- The last syllable of a prosodic phrase is generally lengthened, and often at a low pitch.
- There is one example of the lengthening of the last syllable of an interrogative phrase, and at a high pitch that might reflect speech intonation.

Word variations
- Vocables occur.
- Schwa vowels (normally *u*) have the same duration as all other vowels.

Seediq canonic imitation (Taiwan)

The two Seediq performances demonstrate many characteristics similar to other vocal expressions that are studied here. They can be understood as performance templates that give performers the possibility to vary the words or to add words, or to improvise new words *ex tempore*. In this case, the metre of the words changes from one stanza to another. It seems as though each new stanza or section is made up of a new phrase and that new lines are made up in the same metre for the remainder of that stanza, until a new phrase of a different metre commences. The realization of these lines of different metres is basically of two kinds: (1) a short motif in a rather fast pattern dominated by short tones in an iambic beat and ending with a long tone, and (2) slightly longer and slower phrases, including a long tone on the third syllable. These motifs and corresponding words are repeated in pairs. These pairs may be performed by two performers interlocked in a canonic imitation, so that the second performer starts later than the first, and this delay will last until the end of the performance.

5
An Akha shaman performance (Thailand)

Inga-Lill Hansson and Håkan Lundström

The Akha people live in the border areas of China, Burma, Thailand, Laos, and Vietnam. Most of them live in the southwestern part of the Yunnan province of China, forming part of the Hani nationality, and in adjacent areas in Burma. In Thailand, they are reported to have arrived from Burma at the beginning of the twentieth century. In Akha tradition, long texts are transmitted in the death ritual performed by priests, *phirma*, and in the rituals of the shamans, *nyirpaq*. The recording of a seance by Sjhá-gàw, the shaman employed here, was made in the Saensuk Akha village in north-western Thailand, in the Chiengrai province close to the Burmese border (Map 5); the priest Àbáw-Gaw assisted with the translation.

The shaman texts are said to be personal to each shaman, and to vary from one performance to the next. The shaman, male or female, makes a spiritual journey to find the reason for sickness. While on the journey, the shaman recites or chants everything she encounters. Inga-Lill Hansson went to one shaman twice just to see if her texts were the same; there was a seven-year gap between these visits. The texts are not identical, but they are very similar. Certain parts of the shaman's journey, which goes from the house, out of the village, to the borderline dividing humans and spirits, continues to the ancestors, where a rope leading back to the shaman's house is kept. This process is the same, and is described in more or less the same words. Other parts of the journey seem to be specific to each shaman and to each journey.

> The shamans grow up listening to both the priests' and the shamans' reciting, thereby learning the rhythms and many of the stock phrases. They then build on this and express their own personal visions, drawing from others' texts and adding their new experiences which are modelled on what they have learned by listening. I believe that the shamans, to a certain extent, reformulate themselves at each

An Akha shaman performance (Thailand)

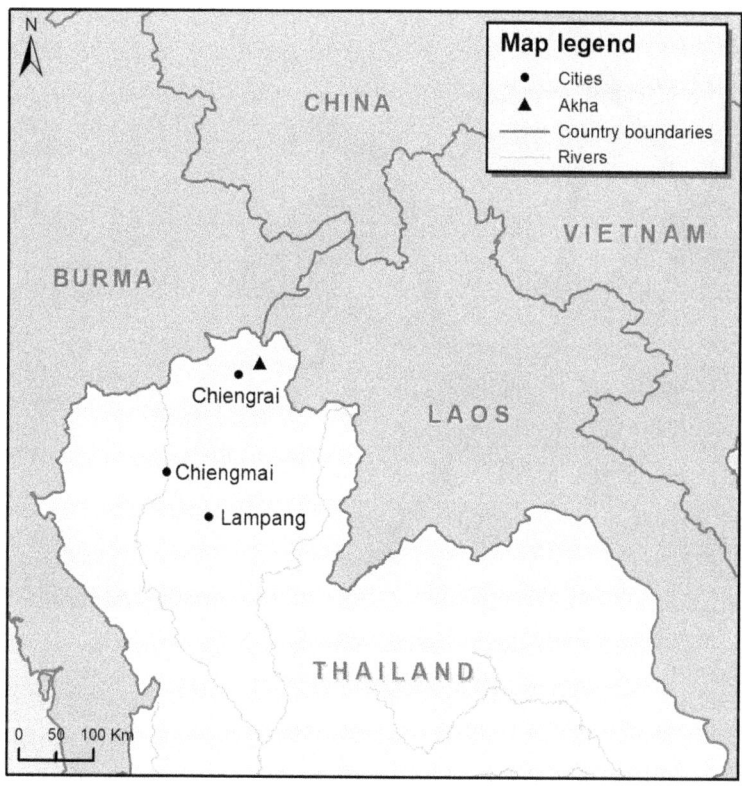

Map 5 Map of northern Thailand, with the approximate location of the Akha population and the village of Saensuk.

'performance'; thus, for instance, their visions may occur in a different order. The performance probably also involves a moment of creation and depends on what the shaman sees on this particular journey. The recitations are, however, expressed and moulded according to a given pattern that appears to be shared by all shamans.

Akha ritual texts are organized into lines based on iambic feet with a degenerate final foot. Briefly, it may be said that each line is built upon what I call a *rhythm pair*, i.e. two syllables with the second one more stressed. Each line contains a row of such pairs + one last syllable, making each line in slow recitation consist of an odd number of syllables.[1]

---

1 Summarized from Hansson 1994: 26–27.

Figure 6 The swing festival in the Akha village of Saensuk, northwestern Thailand.

Akha language and the shaman's vocal expression

The words of Akha shaman performances have been studied to some extent but, to our knowledge, there has been no previous study of the relationship between the linguistic and musical aspects of the performances. It was rather obvious that the long vocal expressions, based on a fundamental recurring melodic formula and variation, would be suitable for analysis from the performance-template perspective. Since Akha is a tone language, it was also obvious that relationships between lexical tones and pitches would play an important role. The main objective of this chapter is to analyse the way that musical phrases are modified – lengthened or shortened – in the realization of the prosodic phrases. This was done purely by use of Melodyne graphs, which are well suited for comparisons as they permit simultaneous aural and visual observations.

The Akha language belongs to the Tibeto-Burman sub-group of the Sino-Tibetan language family. It is closely related to the Hani language in China. There are three lexical tones: High (H), Mid

An Akha shaman performance (Thailand)

(M), and Low (L). They are marked with accents over the vowel, for example *á* (High) and *à* (Low); the Mid tone is unmarked. Traditionally, Akha has no writing system; but during recent decades different writing systems, mainly based on Latin letters, have been introduced in Burma, Thailand, and China. The recording of a seance by the shaman Sjhá-gàw was made by Hansson in the Akha village of Saensuk in north-western Thailand, close to the Burmese border, in December 1983.[2] The materials used for this study consisted of a cassette tape-recording and Hansson's typewritten field notes consisting of glossed transcriptions of the words with lexical tones.

General starting points

- A section of approximately 13 minutes of the recording was digitized by means of the free Audacity audio software and saved as a wav. file.
- The field notes had been organized into lines, numbered for each page in the document, so that each page starts with the number 1. For this study, the lines were coded 'page: number', so that, for example, 166:7 refers to line number 7 on page 166.
- The starting points of the 68 lines corresponding to the recording were tagged in Audacity.
- The wav.file was transferred into Melodyne for analysis.
- It was found that the recording could be divided into 3 sections:
  - Section 1 (approximately 166:6–168:13): The shaman speaks about beating bamboo on the way to the spirit village (so that the spirits would hear the shaman coming).
  - Section 2 (approximately 168:14–169:9): The shaman is in the spirit village, but is not able to tell everything.
  - Section 3 (approximately 169:10–171:7): The shaman returns to the human world.
- Each of these sections contains sub-sections marked by the repetition of certain lines.
- Some of the lines and the corresponding musical phrases are performed in pairs. The second musical phrase of a pair is often

---

[2] Hansson conducted extensive fieldwork among the Akha in northern Thailand in several periods. She stayed two years there in 1977–78, about two months per year in 1981–91, and paid shorter visits more or less yearly until 2013, when one of the main informants passed away. The shaman, Sjhá-gàw, and the priest Àbáw-gàw, who assisted with the translation, both passed away in 1984.

more compact, i.e. performed in a shorter time, and usually at a lower pitch. There may also be relatively long passages in which more lines are grouped together in this manner.
- It is possible to distinguish some identical or nearly identical lines that appear during the performance, usually only within the same main section. These provide possible material for analysing the performance manner. Some lines have identical words. Some lines contain syllables that are identical – or fixed – and syllables that are varied. Therefore, lines can be used for measuring consistency as well as variation in performance, particularly concerning lexical tones.
- A number of lines with obvious similarities were made into separate wav.files and were run through the Melodyne software with the aim of looking for regularities or irregularities with regard to musical phrases and the realization of lexical tones.

The performance

The performance tells a story at a rather slow tempo. The initial line starts with a very long tone (Example 100). Line 2 in the example contains words presented at a fairly slow tempo, alternating between a couple of pitches. The third line is a compressed line with many syllables delivered rather fast. The section ends with a long tone that appears as the tonal centre. The performer uses a creaky voice quality so that a rather steady pitch one octave below the notated 'c' is clearly audible, almost like a drone.

An Akha shaman performance (Thailand)

Example 100 The first line of the section discussed in this chapter (166:6). Stressed tones are marked with >. The arrow shows a long final tone performed in a creaky voice. Performed by Sjhá-gàw, Saensuk village, north-western Thailand in December 1983. Original pitch: c ≈ 130 Hz. Pulse ≈ 60 b/s. For translation and Melodyne graph, see Example 106.
- **23 Sjhá-gàw 166:6**.

Analysis 21 Realization of lexical tones in identical lines

Comparison 1

Lines 166:8–9 and 167:8a–8b are both pairs of phrases. The pairs contain identical words and lexical tones.[3]

166:8 and 167:8a ŋà da làq-bŏ-shɛ́-há í gà ɛ́ xhɔ̀ xhə á là
166:9 and 167:8b da lɔ̀ làq- bŏ-shɛ́-há gà ɛ́ xhɔ̀ xhə
  beating to let my spirit father làq- bŏ-shɛ́-há hear it

In performance, there are restrictions on what types of grammatical forms can be in which position within a rhyme-pair. For example, the negation can only be in the first position, and noun and verb particles only in the second. Any problem with regard to ensuring the correct placing of the words may be resolved by means of, for instance, prefixes or suffixes. The filler syllable *lɔ̀* is frequently used to fill an otherwise empty second position, exemplified by *da lɔ̀* in line 166:9 above.[4]

In both cases, the first part (166:8 and 167:8a) starts high and ends low around G, below the tonic C, while most of the second part is lower than, or at most a second (2 semitones) above, the tonic.

The graphs in Example 101, which all used Melodyne, show that the pitches in the two versions of this linguistic phrase are nearly identical, and so it is possible to see how lexical tones are realized:

- The initial 5 syllables LMLHH are performed L<u>HH</u>L<u></u>H (aberrations underlined).

In the remainder of the phrase:

- The High lexical tones are performed a fourth to a fifth (or 5–7 semitones) above the final tone, but in two cases a sixth to a seventh (7–11 semitones above). They are often falling.

---

3 Actually, 166:9 has 3 additional syllables at the end that are disregarded here since the initial 10 syllables are identical to 167:8b.
4 Hansson 2014: 283–285. See Hansson 1991 for a detailed description of these factors in a death-ritual text.

An Akha shaman performance (Thailand)   211

Example 101 Melodyne graphs of a) 166:8 (top) • **24 Sjhá-gàw 166:8** and b) 167:8a (bottom) • **25 Sjhá-gàw 167:8a**. Vertical: pitch, horizontal: time (1 column = 1 second). Syllable numbers and lexical tones (L, M, H) are given with the words.

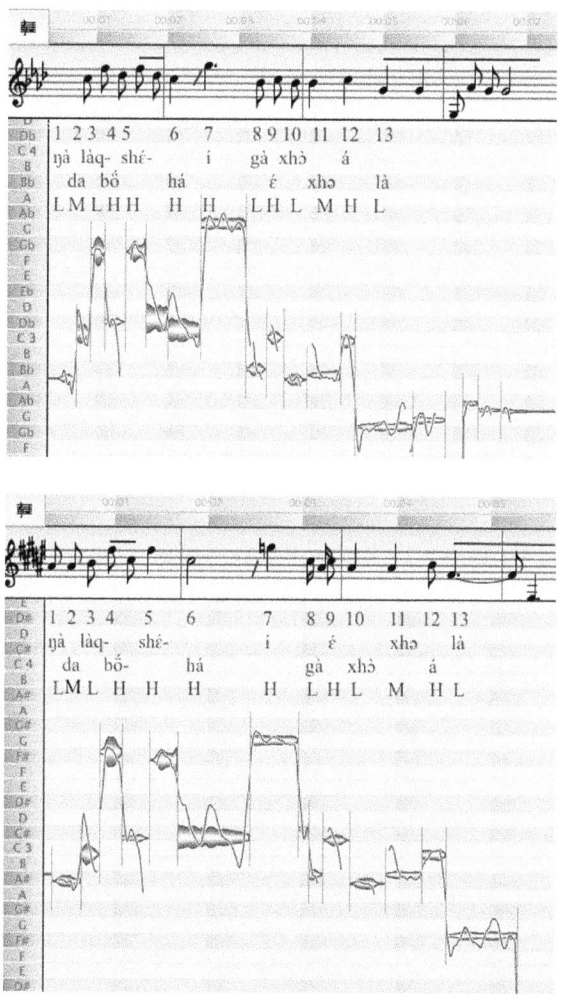

212　　　　　　　　　　　In the borderland between song and speech

- The Low lexical tones are performed a second (2 semitones) above the final tone, or a second below (in the phrase ending).
- In both examples, only one Mid lexical tone (syllable 11) is performed higher than the previous Low and lower than the following High.

Example 102 Melodyne graphs of 166:9 (top) and 167:8b (bottom).

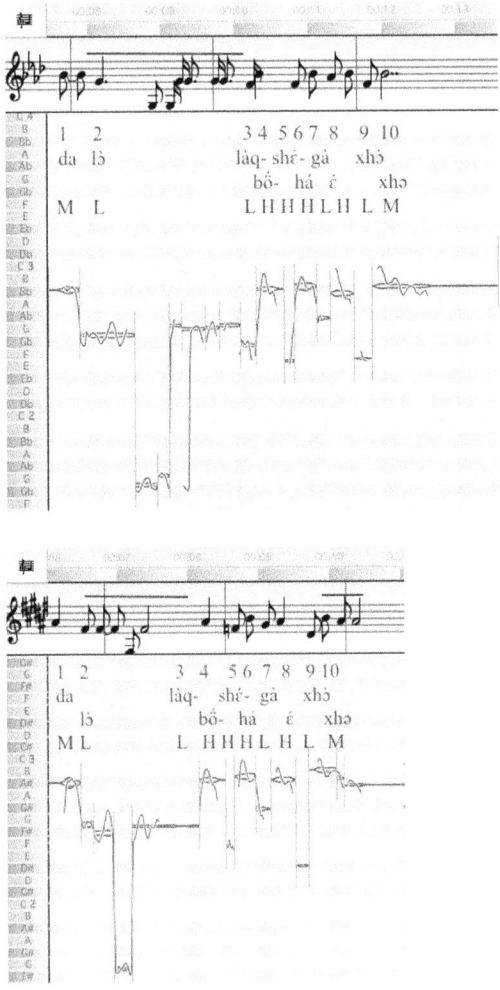

The graphs in Example 102 show that the two performances of this linguistic phrase are quite similar to the previous one:

- The first Mid tone syllable is performed higher than the following Low, albeit relatively high in pitch.

An Akha shaman performance (Thailand)

- Syllables 3–10 are performed in a quick pendulum movement, the tones being short–long or unstressed–stressed. If the unstressed syllables are written with lower-case letters: l, m, h, and the stressed ones with capitals, this section is performed: lHlHlHlH, though the lexical tones are LH<u>H</u>HLHL<u>M</u> (aberrations underlined). This may be a case of melodic dominance over lexical tones.

Comparison 2

166:11, 167:4, and 167:11, which are nearly identical, are compared.

166:11   já pyq já né [le] bɔ̀ áŋ shḿ làq xhɔ̀ xhə lé la é
167:4   já pyq já né gàŋ áŋ shḿ làq xhɔ̀ xhə lé la é
167:11   já pyq já né gàŋ áŋ shḿ làq xhɔ̀ xhə lé la
            beating three times on the burnt field, the soil becomes red

There are some differences at the very ends of the phrases in Examples 103–105, but generally:

- High lexical tones are the same as the tonal centre (C or B♭ respectively) or higher. Syllable 7 in Example 103 and syllable 6 in Example 104 (both *áŋ*) are slightly lower than the tonic, but higher than the preceding Low.
- Low lexical tones are a second to a fourth (2–5 semitones) lower than the tonal centre.
- Mid lexical tones are at the tonic level or lower.
- One word's lexical tone is uncertain (syllable 5, *le*, interpreted as Mid in Example 103).

Example 103 Melodyne graph of 166:11.

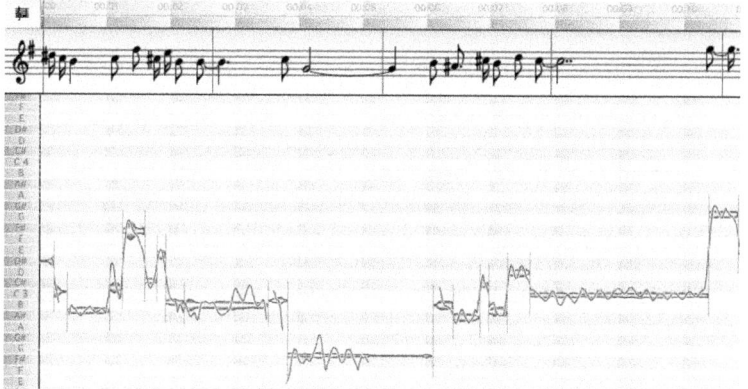

Example 104 Melodyne graph of 167:4.

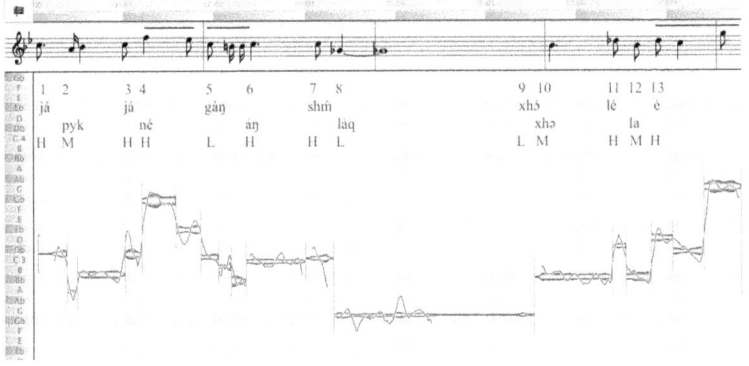

Example 105 Melodyne graph of 167:11.

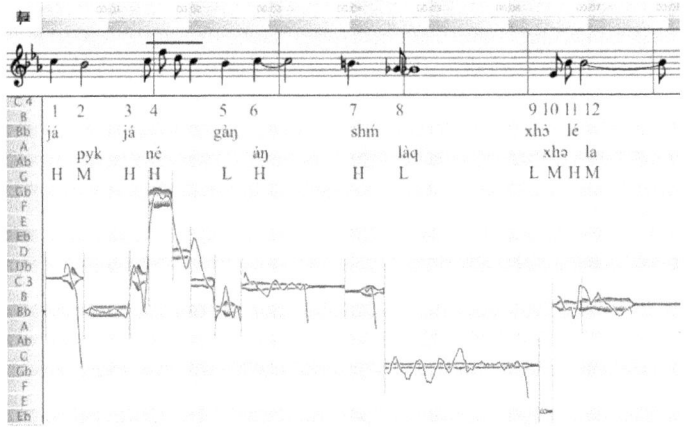

Characteristics of the Akha shaman performance

- Lexical tones are realized.
- High lexical tones: higher than the tonal centre, normally from a second to a fifth (2–7 semitones).
- Mid lexical tones: at the level of the tonal centre, or slightly lower.
- Low lexical tones: between a second (2 semitones) below the tonal centre, or a second (2 semitones) above.
- Exceptions: There are some aberrations in one case of introductory movement and one case of fast pendulum movement.

An Akha shaman performance (Thailand)   215

Analysis 22 Performance of line-pairs

The performance is, for the most part, carried out with lines/ linguistic phrases that constitute pairs, semantically and musically. Normally, the first line of a pair is slow and performed in long tones, whereas the second part is faster and compressed.

The lines 166:6 and 166:7 form a pair in which the first (6) is performed in long tones and the second (7) is compressed and shorter, while the number of syllables is almost the same.

166:6
 zàq mja də làq xhɔ̀ xhə làq ó xhɔ̀ xhə làq í / xhɔ̀ xhə làq í ò xhɔ̀ xhə làq hí xhɔ̀ í xhə
 beating on the zàq-mja bamboo də làq ó, beating làq í / beating làq í, beating làq hí

166:7
 zàq mja də làq xhɔ̀ xhə làq í ò xhɔ̀ xhə làq / xhɔ̀ xhə lɔ́ í hí xhɔ̀ xhə làq xhɔ̀ xhə lɔ́ hí
 beating on the zàq-mja bamboo də làq, beating làq í, beating làq ò / beating là í hí, beating làq, beating lɔ́ hí

Example 106 Melodyne graph of 166:6. • **23 Sjhá-gàw 166:6**

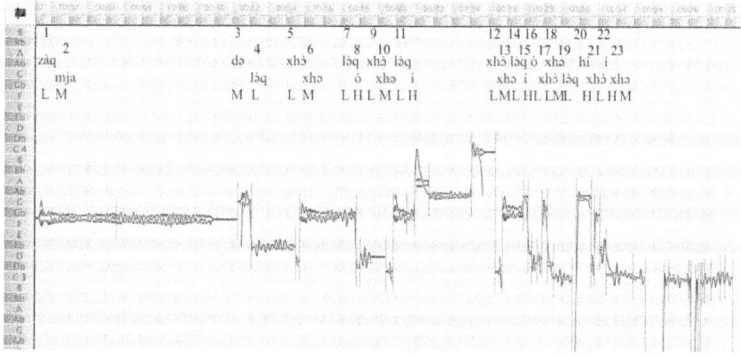

166:6 in Example 106 is basically built on the combination short + long (of varying lengths). Normally it is 1 short + 1 long, but in two cases extra syllables are squeezed in: 3 short + 1 long. The two lines are about the same length, 23 and 24 syllables, respectively. While 166:6 is performed in 37 seconds (Example 106), the second line of the pair, 166:7, lasts for only 22 seconds (Example 107).

Example 107 Melodyne graph of 166:7. The number of syllables is indicated. The jump to the low octave on syllable 23 (*là*) is the result of a creaky voice on the last long tone of the phrase. • **26 Sjhá-gàw 166:7**

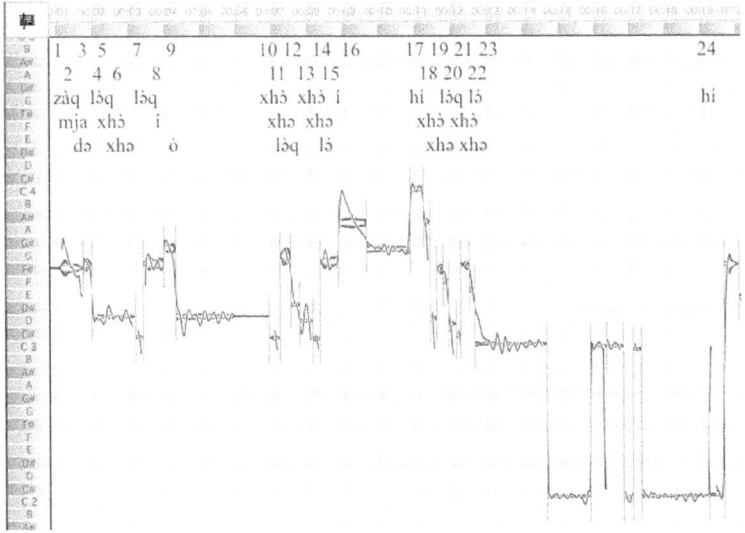

The extent of contraction increases in the second line. More syllables are performed with very short durations, there are fewer long syllables, and those long syllables that do occur become shorter. This can be seen when corresponding phrases are compared (long syllables are marked with lines).

166:6 (Example 106): zàq mja də làq———
166:7 (Example 107): zàq mja də làq
166:6 (Example 106): xhɔ̀ xhə——— làq ó———
166:7 (Example 107): xhɔ̀ xhə làq í ò—

Several syllables are squeezed in, the effect being that the words are pronounced in shorter time. At the end of the second line, 6–7 syllables are squeezed in between the longer ones.

166:7 (Example 107): xhə làq xhɔ̀ xhə lɔ̀——— hí
xhɔ̀ xhə làq xhɔ̀ xhə lɔ̀ í——— hí

Characteristics

- Mid lexical tones are principally about a fourth to a fifth (5–7 semitones) above the tonal centre (c).
- High lexical tones are principally a fifth to a seventh (7–11 semitones) above.
- Low lexical tones are principally a second to a fourth (2–5 semitones) above.
- The long *í* in the middle of the line is performed high with a dip.
- The initial melodic pattern is falling G#–F#–D (Example 107).

Exceptions

- The first syllable is Low, but performed slightly high. That might be explained as a starting pattern.
- Syllable 8 (*ó*) is performed low between two Low syllables (Example 106).
- Syllable 11 (*làq*) is performed high (glissando or upward-sliding movement). This might be explained by the movement up to the following High syllable. Similarly, syllable 13 (*xhò*) is performed high, while the melody falls from a preceding high pitch (Example 106).
- Syllable 6 (*xhə*) is Mid but performed low, possibly because it is preceded and followed by Low syllables (Example 107).

Analysis 23 Performance of the final part

In the latter part of the performance, section 3, the performance changes character and becomes more melodious. The words here are about the shaman's soul returning from the spirit world to the human world. The sub-sections start with *hɔə* (169:6, 10; 170:2, 5, 7, 12; 171:4, not transcribed; see, however, Example 110).

169:6
 lo ma lɛq áŋ mɔ́ le mɛ́ nɔ̀ hɛ̀ lo / ma àmjàŋ lɛq áŋ mɔ́ le mɛ́ i
 seeing the big stone on the market, seeing the big stone on the market making us look like fools [for sitting on it even though it isn't allowed].

169:10
 àda nèq yòq zá poq zá poq yòq dm̀ dzɛ[?] í mía hɛ̀ ɛ́
 I'm going home on the spirits road

170:2
 zɔ́ za mì màq tjhɔ̀ bɔ zɔ́ thé gà là mía hɛ̀ ɛ́
 longing for the voice of the child-maker, who accompanies me

Example 108 Melodyne graph of 169:6. • **27 Sjhá-gàw 169:6**

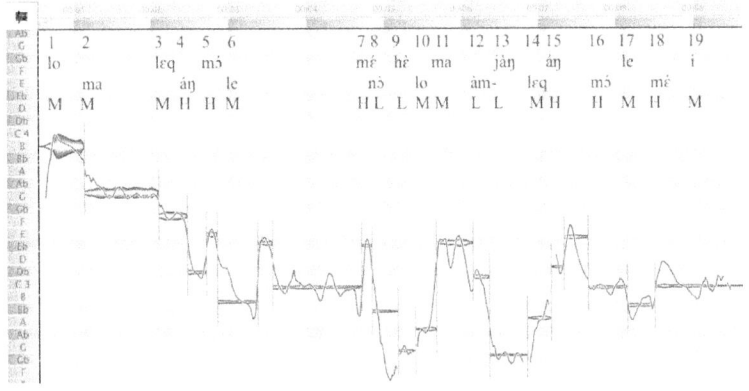

Characteristics of 169:6 (Example 108)

- The performance starts with a long *hɔə* in a high position (about 200 Hz, not included in Example 108).
- The final tone is about a fifth (7 semitones) lower and feels like a tonic (128 Hz).

An Akha shaman performance (Thailand)

- Syllables 1–3 (disregarding the initial *həə*) are Mid-tone syllables, performed high and gradually lower.
- High syllables (4, 5, 7, 15) are in all cases performed higher than the tonic, approximately a third higher (3–4 semitones, 155–165 Hz), but they may be performed rising or falling.
- Syllables 16 and 18, both High, are performed at the tonic; this is the ending of the musical phrase.
- Low syllables (8, 9, 12, 13) are performed approximately one fourth lower (5 semitones, around 95 Hz) than the tonic (but sometimes start much higher and slide down). One exception is syllable 12. It is the first of two consecutive Low lexical tones, preceded by a Mid-tone syllable performed as if High. Hence, it is performed at a lower pitch than the preceding syllable, and the pitch continues falling for the next Low.
- Mid syllables (1, 2, 3, 6, 10, 11, 14, 17, 19):
  - Syllables 1–3 seem to be part of the initial formula at high pitches. Syllable 6 is between two High syllables and performed lower (at the tonic pitch).
  - Syllables 10–11 are between two Low syllables; syllable 10 is performed higher than the preceding Low and syllable 11 higher than the following Low (same level as a High syllable).
  - Syllable 14 is between a Low and a High syllable, and the pitch is in between.
  - Syllable 17 is between two High syllables performed at the tonic pitch. Syllable 17 is performed lower.
  - Syllable 19 is performed at the tonic or final pitch, as part of the final formula.

Example 109 Melodyne graph of 169:10.

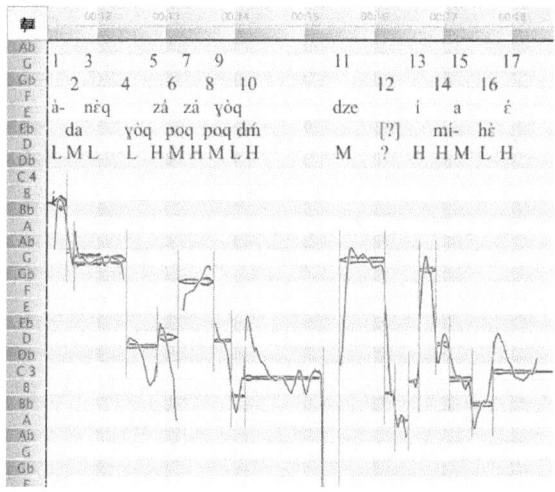

Characteristics of 169:10 (Example 109)

- The performance starts with a long *hɔə* in a high position (c. 200 Hz, not shown in Example 109). The final tone is about a fifth lower and feels like a tonic (7 semitones, 131 Hz).
- Syllables 1–4 are part of the initial formula; they are performed high and gradually lower. In this case, syllables 1, 3, and 4 are Low and 2 is Mid.
- Syllables 5, 7, 10, 13, and 14 are High. They are performed about a second higher than the tonic (2 semitones, 144–148 Hz), but the maxima are higher. Syllable 13 is really high, nearly a fifth (7 semitones, about 195 Hz).
- The last syllable (17) is High. It ends approximately on the tonic but starts as a high.
- Syllable 9 is Low at 119 Hz and 16 is Low at 116 Hz.
- Syllables 6, 8, and 11 are Mid. Syllables 6 and 11 are placed between two Highs and performed still higher than those (180 and 195 Hz, respectively). Syllable 8 is located between a High and a Low.

Characteristics of 170:2 (Example 110)

- Main outline as above (169:6 and 10).
- Syllable 8 is High. It is preceded by a High and followed by a Low. The preceding and following syllables are performed as high and low, but syllable 8 is relatively low (tonic pitch). This may be because of a downward movement.

Example 110 Melodyne graph of 170:2.

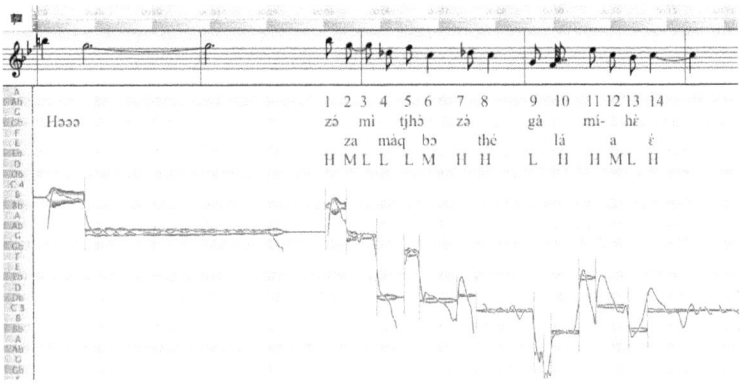

Analysis 24 Variation

The basic delivery of the words is iambic and consists of a number of rhythm pairs, i.e. short + long, and a final long tone.[5] This conclusion is based on performances by priests and shamans. The priest appears to have learnt the words by heart and repeats them fairly consistently from one performance to another, whereas the shaman performances are personal and open to changes from time to time, even during the same performance. This is evident in the section analysed here. The rhythm pairs are certainly there, but there is also a high degree of variation.

Example 111 Melodyne graph of rhythm pairs in the beginning of 166:6. Arrows indicate the short initial syllable of a rhythm pair consisting of 2 syllables.

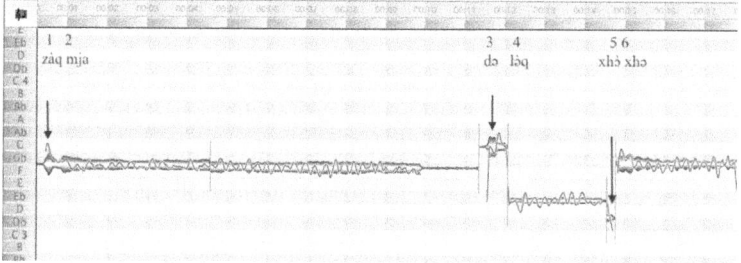

Example 111 shows three rhythm pairs from the very first line of the digitized part of the performance. The short initial syllables of each pair are marked by arrows. It may be noted that even the first long tone (which occurs in some lines) contains a rhyme-pair: it is the second syllable of the line that is really long. Apart from such an exceptional long tone, the length of the second syllable in a pair is not constant, whereas there is not so much room for varying the length of the first short syllable. The tones are rising or falling, mainly – but not exclusively – being determined by the lexical tones.

When the speed increases, a line is compressed into a shorter time space, the differences in time between short and long become marginal, and the syllables are mainly distinguished by pitch and stress, sometimes – it would seem – disregarding lexical tones. In Example 112,

---

5 Hansson 2014: 284.

the word *shé* is performed as if it had a Low lexical tone. In cases like this, it may be that the iambic pattern dominates over the lexical tones. This can be regarded as 'condensed rhythm pairs'.

Example 112 Melodyne graph of condensed rhythm pairs in 166:9. Arrows show first syllables of condensed word-pairs.

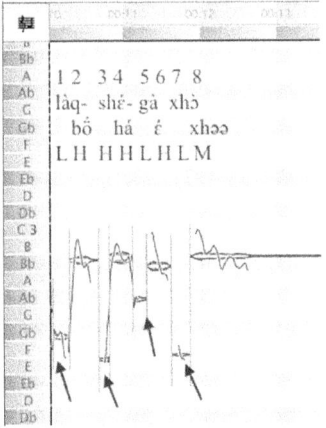

Another way of performing more syllables in the same time slot is to squeeze in 2, 3, or even 4 short syllables before the long one (Example 113). Occasionally, the long syllable is divided as well.

Example 113 Melodyne graph of compressed rhythm pairs in 166:7. Boxes show short syllables squeezed into the first slot of two word-pairs (3 syllables in the first and 4 in the second). Lines show long syllables.

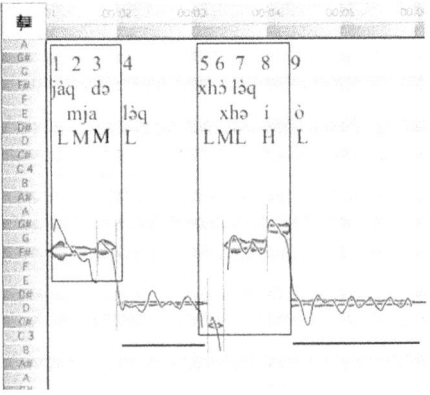

An Akha shaman performance (Thailand)

Sometimes a compressed rhythm pair is organized in a falling pattern, as is the first rhythm pair in Example 113 (*zàq mja də làq*). In the very last section (section 3) of the performance, this falling pattern takes on a more 'song-like' form, perhaps signalling the return of the shaman's spirit to the human world (Example 114).

170:5
Həə, thḿ lé mí màq dɔ̀ dáŋ mà dö tjhő ə
Həə, talking, but I can't tell all the words to the end

Example 114 Melodyne graph of 170:5. The arrow shows stepwise downward melodic movement.

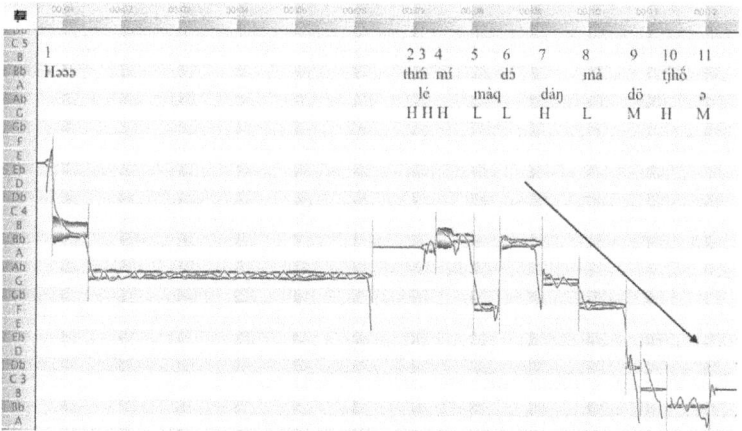

The Akha shaman performance template

Melody
- Undulating, with much downward motion and a tonal centre (see Examples 100, 110).
- After a couple of short syllables of prosodic phrasing, the melody moves to high and falls gradually, a pattern which generally lasts for two rhyme-pairs and is repeated within the same phrase.
- Range: 20 semitones.

Rhythm
- Slow regular pulse.
- An iambic pattern dominates: iambic rhythmic pairs consisting of two syllables with the second one more stressed.

Form
- Litany with sections.

Phrasing
- Prosodic phrases built on iambic rhythmic pairs with variations.
- The prosodic phrases are organized in pairs in which the first is generally slow and long, while the second is faster and shorter. Such a pair may be continued with further parallel phrases.
- The musical phrases are organized in pairs, the first generally being slow and long whereas the second is faster and shorter.
- Contraction occurs: musical phrases are made shorter by squeezing several syllables into one space.
- Final syllables are lengthened.

Initial/final formulae
- The initial formula of a section consists of an initial long, high-pitched tone (*Həə*) and falls stepwise with the very first syllables.
- The initial formula of a sub-section consists of a lengthened syllable in the mid pitch area.
- In a final formula, the pitches level out at the tonic.

Word variations
- Certain grammatical forms can be located only in certain positions within the rhythm pair, e.g. a negation can only be in the first position, noun and verb particles only in the second.
- This location pattern is realized by the use of, for example, prefixes, suffixes, and filler syllables [lɔ].

Lexical tones
- High lexical tones are generally performed above the tonic, a second (about 145 Hz) or a third (about 175 Hz), sometimes much higher.

- Low lexical tones are performed significantly lower, often lower than the tonic, about a second to a fourth below the tonic, at about 95–115 Hz.
- The pitches may be approached by an upward or left by a downward sliding motion.
- Mid lexical tones tend to be between the High and the Low in cases where the lexical tone is realized.
- In other cases, such syllables with Mid lexical tone are used in order to separate consecutive identical lexical word tones: for example, High–Mid–High or Low–Mid–Low can be performed high–higher–high or low–high–low.

It can be concluded that the description of this vocal expression may be considered as a performance template – or rather as performance templates, since it consists of different sections. There are melody-centred parts in initial and final formulae and certain other parts, like a fast pendulum movement, and there are also tone-centred parts. The basic structure is that of line-pairs with rhyme-pairs within the lines. Lines may be performed slow or fast and, in the latter case, short syllables are apt to be inserted. The general movement is from a high pitch to a low one. Lexical tones are realized, except when musical or rhythmical movement dominates.

6
Waka and ryūka performances (Japan/Ryukyu)

Yasuko Nagano-Madsen and Håkan Lundström

Waka and *ryūka* are short poems originating in Japan and the Ryukyu Islands, respectively. *Waka* has a very long history and flourished during the Heian period, which began around the year AD 800. The *waka* studied here belong to *Ogura Hyakunin Isshu*, a collection of 100 *waka* compiled around the first half of the thirteenth century, and the *karuta* game based on it. *Waka* – nowadays often referred to as *tanka* – is widely used in contemporary Japan, from the New Year recital at the Imperial court to popular *tanka* magazines and newspaper columns to which anybody can submit their poems. Though they have existed in writing for centuries, the oral aspect of *waka/tanka* is still strong, both with regard to how they are conceived and how they are orally presented.

Ryūka is known from the seventeenth century onwards. It originated in the higher strata of society as poems with separate melodies that were accompanied on the three-stringed long-necked lute, *sanshin*. The genre spread to other social contexts, and perhaps the best-known *ryūka* poetess was Onna Nabii, who lived in a village in the eighteenth century (Map 6). At that time, Japanese society was under feudal constraints; but her poems were free, sometimes sarcastic about politicians, and sometimes filled with amorous passion. A film has been made about her life.[1] *Ryūka* are performed orally with or without instrumental accompaniment, using a basic melodic formula.

The Ryukyu Kingdom was an independent country before it was integrated into Japan in 1879. Owing to the integration policy of the Japanese government, particularly after the Second World War, the Ryukyuan languages have been severely suppressed, and the vast majority of people on the Ryukyu Islands are monolingual – in Japanese. There has been debate about whether Ryukyuan should

---

1 Internet reference: *Onna Nabii*.

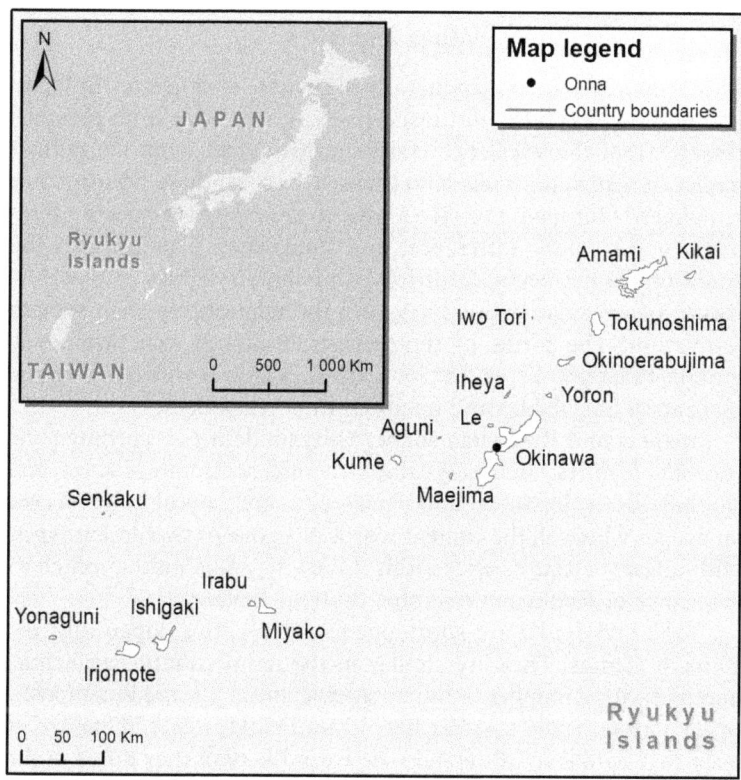

Map 6 Map of the Ryukyu Islands, with the village Onna on the main island of Okinawa.

be considered as an independent language, forming a language family with Japanese, or as a dialect of Japanese. It is widely agreed that they are related, and that Ryukyuan resembles Old Japanese more than Modern Japanese. Here we will use the terms Japanese and Ryukyuan, as these terms are commonly used in Western literature. Because of differences with regard to phonology, grammar, and lexicon, Japanese and Ryukyuan are not mutually intelligible.

Since Ryukyuan is a severely endangered language, *ryūka* is also under threat. Today, it is more common for people in the Ryukyu Islands to compose *waka* than *ryūka*, since only the older generation can speak genuine Ryukyuan, whereas the younger generation speak Japanese only.[2]

---

2 Partly summarized from Nagano-Madsen 2011: 178–179.

Waka and ryūka

The terms *waka* and *ryūka* literally mean *uta*, 'song/poem', in Japan and in the Ryukyu Islands, respectively. It was clear from previous research that the vocal expressions which result from the performance of *waka* and *ryūka* lend themselves to study as performance templates.[3] Our main objectives were to describe the respective templates and to study differences and similarities. This includes the study of the performance of long and short syllables, the performance of irregular poetic lines, and the relationship with spoken intonation. The forms of representation chosen were Melodyne graphs, Praat graphs, and graphic transcription with a focus on the realization of syllables and on approximative pitches.

Japanese and Ryukyuan share major similarities regarding their prosodic features, such as syllable structure, accent, intonation, and rhythm. Both Japanese and Ryukyuan are lexical pitch-accent languages where all the content words have one of two accent types, with a few dialects as exceptions. Likewise, some intonation characteristics of Ryukyuan resemble those of Japanese.[4]

Waka and *ryūka* are short poems representing Japan and the Ryukyu Islands. They are similar in the mora counting principle, and in the total number of morae (metric units): a *waka* is composed of 31 morae, while a *ryūka* has 30 morae. However, there are at least two significant differences between the two: they differ in the number of phrases and in their respective compositions. *Waka* are based on an odd number of morae divided into five phrases: 5–7–5–7–7 morae, while *ryūka* are based on an even number: 8–8–8–6 morae, consisting of four phrases. Another way to express this is that the metrical form of *waka* terminates by lengthening (5⇒7 morae), whereas that of *ryūka* terminates by shortening (8⇒6 morae). It is interesting to note that both final lengthening and final shortening are commonly observed in human speech to indicate terminality.

Waka and *ryūka* also differ with regard to music. While *ryūka* developed along with the accompanying musical instrument, *sanshin*, and with a number of fixed melodies, *waka* have less often been connected with fixed melodies. Both, however, have a 'recitation-like' form of performance, and it is this form that will be analysed here.

---

3 For information about the poetry and its use in music, see Gillan 2012: 29–30.
4 See Nagano-Madsen 2015.

Analysis 25 Two *waka* performances

Waka (*tanka*) is a traditional form of Japanese short poetry that is still often performed orally. *Karuta* is a memory game, in which cards displaying one half of a *waka* are distributed with the reverse side up and the players compete by combining the first and the last parts of the *waka* correctly. In this process the *waka* are normally read out aloud, and the material consists of two complete collections of such readings on a cassette tape, by males in both collections.[5]

Naniwazu is a *waka* poem which is not included in the collection itself but is used to start the *karuta* game (Example 115). In the two recordings, it is read without interruptions (the other 100 *waka* have a pause in the middle, long enough for the listener to fill in the second half before the correct continuation follows).

Example 115 The *waka* poem *Naniwazu*.

naniwazu ni	at Naniwa Bay
sakuya kono hana	the flowers are in bloom
fuyugomori	after winter's rest
ima o harube to	spring is now arriving
sakuya kono hana	the flowers are in bloom

When *waka*/*tanka* are printed in Japanese, they are usually written in one line. There are exceptions, though, such as the three-line *tanka* of the poet Ishikawa Takuboku (1886–1912). In translation into Western languages, they are commonly written in five lines of 5-7-5-7-7 morae, but before about 1950 usually in four lines. These are, however, matters of typography. The usual way of defining a musical phrase in orally transmitted vocal expressions is that of a metric unit that has a recognizable ending, usually recurring more than once, consisting of, for instance, a long tone and/or a pause. In the performances studied here, these musical phrases

---

5 *Naniwazu* 1: *Ogura Hyakunin Isshu Rōei kasetto tēpu* (Chanting cassette tape of Ogura Anthology of 'One Hundred Tanka by One Hundred Poets'). Rōei (chanting): Yamada Akira. *Kabushiki gaisha Daiwa* (Daiwa Co. Ltd.): TBS *Sābisu* (TBS Service), n.d. *Naniwazu* 2: Internet reference: *Sixtieth Karuta Meijin (Master) Match 2014*.

coincide with each of the five lines. There is also a fairly long break after the first three lines so that, in the *karuta* game, they are divided into 5-7-5 and 7-7. In this case, the five lines also coincide with linguistic phrases. Linguistic phrases will simply be referred to as phrases, whereas musical phrases will be specified where this is deemed necessary. In Example 116, the *waka Naniwazu* is divided into five phrases and the morae are numbered.

Example 116 The *waka Naniwazu* divided into lines and morae.

na -	ni -	wa -	zu	ni		
1	2	3	4	5		
sa -	ku -	ya	ko -	no	ha -	na
1	2	3	4	5	6	7
fu -	yu -	go -	mo -	ri		
1	2	3	4	5		
i -	ma	o	ha -	ru -	be	to
1	2	3	4	5	6	7
sa -	ku -	ya	ko -	no	ha -	na
1	2	3	4	5	6	7

Naniwazu 1

Characteristics:

- Total length ≈ 18 seconds.
- *1st part* equalling 5 + 7 + 5 morae: ≈ 9 seconds.
- Dominating pitch C4 ≈ 259–263 Hz.
- Lowest pitch (starting pitch) B2 ≈ 124 H.
- *2nd part* equalling 7 + 7 morae ≈ 6.5 seconds.
- Dominating pitch C4 ≈ 258–263 Hz.
- Lowest pitch (starting pitch) E3 ≈ 163 Hz.

There are two musical phrases, A and B. Actually, both are mainly performed at the same pitch, with interspersed shorter morae performed at a lower pitch. It is also clear that some morae are performed long and some much shorter. This is demonstrated in Examples 117–118. The distribution of short and long morae in lines of different length serves to give the performance a certain musical metre. It has been suggested that in performance, *waka* of

Example 117 Melodyne graph for *waka Naniwazu* 1 by a male performer. The vertical lines show ends of lines (metric units). Vertical: pitch, horizontal: time (1 column = 1 second). • **28 *Waka Naniwazu* 1**

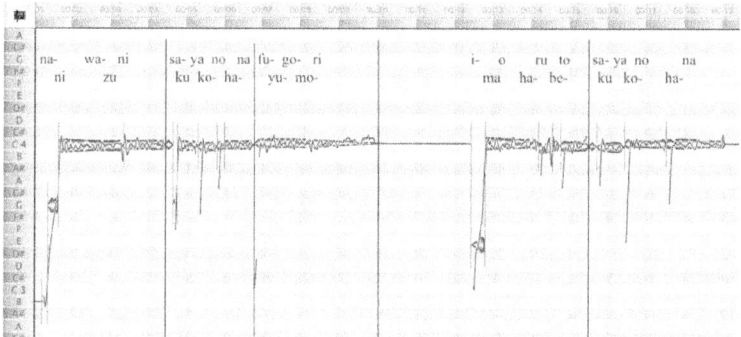

5- and 7-morae lines fall into 4-beat measures.[6] In Example 118, stressed morae are preceded by vertical lines that serve as bar-lines. Whether or not this creates 4-beat measures is hard to say, but there is definitely a slow and steady pulse.

Example 118 Morae performed long and short in *Naniwazu 1*. Vertical lines in the graphic description approximately denote 4-beat measures, i.e. an even musical metre. Vertical lines in the text denote breaks between poetic lines.

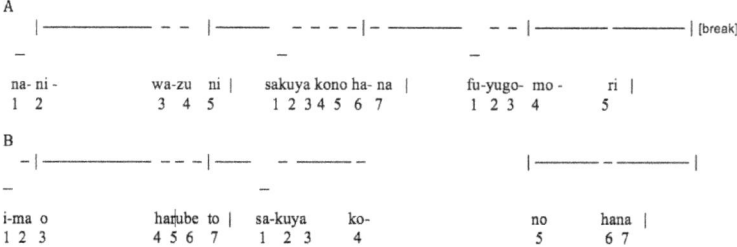

- The first musical phrase A consists of the first 3 lines of the *waka* (5–7–5), and B of the final two lines (7–7).
- The first parts of A and B are nearly identical; but while the first part of A corresponds to a line of 5 morae, a line of 7 morae is compressed into what is basically the same time-frame in B. This is achieved by squeezing two morae into the space of one, or three morae into the space of two.

---

6 Kawakami 1973.

- The second and third lines (7 + 5) in A are performed one unit (= bar) longer than the second line in B (7). In both musical phrases, 5 morae are performed long. They are distributed as follows:

<u>Long morae:</u>

A)
Line 1: 2nd and 5th
Line 2: 7th
Line 3: 4th and 5th

B)
Line 4: 3rd and 5th
Line 5: 3rd, 5th and 7th

The combination of pitches and rhythm is assumed to constitute the performance template in this style of *waka* performance. This means that all *waka* will follow the same basic pattern when performed in this style. A preliminary listening test supports this interpretation. Still, there may be variations depending on which sounds occur in various *waka*. This involves factors like long vowels and morae consisting of a single sonorant consonant (the 'moraic nasal' N). If speech intonation plays a part, it is not obvious. Furthermore, there are *waka* that differ from the norm regarding the number of morae in a line.

Naniwazu 2

Characteristics:

- Total length ≈ 15.5 seconds.
- *1st part* equalling 5 + 7 + 5 morae: ≈ 7 seconds.
- Dominating pitch B♭3 ≈ 231–235 Hz.
- Lowest pitch (starting pitch) E♭3 ≈ 154 Hz.
- *2nd part* equalling 7 + 7 morae ≈ 7.5 seconds.
- Dominating pitch B♭3 ≈ 233–237 Hz.
- Lowest pitch (starting pitch) D♭3 ≈ 139 Hz.

The Melodyne graph clearly shows the two parts (Example 119). In this case, the initial phrase has a shorter long tone on *ni*; and the very last mora of the second part, *-na*, is held for a relatively longer duration. Apart from this, the structure is similar: the pitch is rather stable, and the first mora of each line is performed short and at a low pitch (the graph did not register these for lines 2 and 5, but they are clearly audible). The structural sketch (Example 120) demonstrates how more morae are squeezed in, compared to example 118, while the basic principle is the same.

The combination of pitches and rhythm is taken to constitute the performance template in this style of *waka* performance. This means that all *waka* performed in this style will follow the same basic

Waka and ryūka performances (Japan/Ryukyu)

Example 119 Melodyne graph for *waka Naniwazu* 2 by a male performer. The vertical lines show ends of lines.

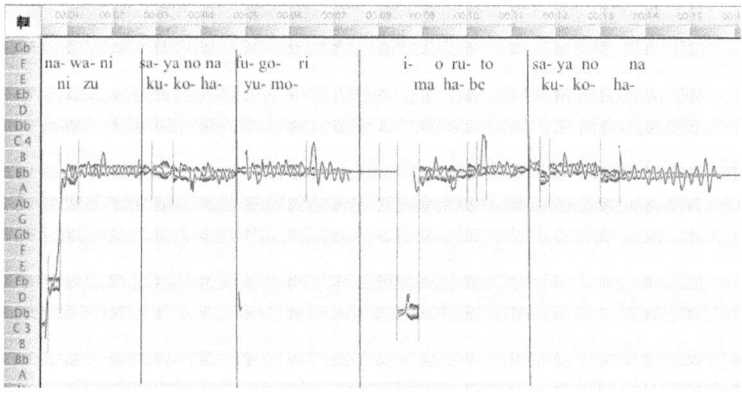

Example 120 Approximate pitches and short and long morae in the *Naniwazu* 2. Sections with several morae squeezed in are underlined.

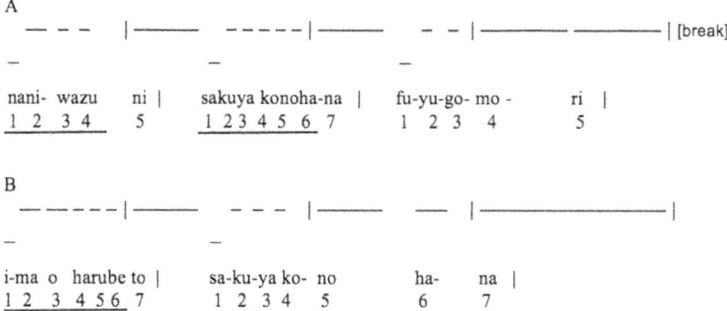

pattern. This interpretation is supported by listening. A comparison with other *waka* performances shows that the sonorant consonant N is treated as one mora while long vowels are treated as two morae. Variations occur in cases of irregular lines, for instance lines with 6 morae instead of 5, or lines with 8 morae instead of 7.

Soundwave, amplitude, and duration of *waka* performance

Example 121 shows the soundwave and amplitude for the *waka* performances. The duration of each phrase is measured from the soundwave (Example 122). The following observations are made:

- Both performances are performed as two phrases of approximately the same loudness (cf. amplitude value in dB). In the performance in Example 121: top, the first musical phrase ends with decreasing loudness, while in Example 121: bottom, it is the second musical phrase that ends with decreasing loudness.
- The duration of phrases does not reflect the number of morae as speech does. Japanese is a mora-timed language for which each mora takes about the same time in speech, so that, for instance, a phrase containing 7 morae has a longer duration in speech than a phrase with 5 morae. This contrasts with stress-timed speech rhythm, where stress is isochronous. Germanic languages such as English and German are examples of stress-timed languages.[7]

Example 121 The soundwave, transcription, and amplitude for the *waka Naniwazu* 1 (top) and *waka Naniwazu* 2 (bottom) by male speakers. The vertical lines indicate the division between 5–7–5–7–7. The arrow A indicates decrease of amplitude.

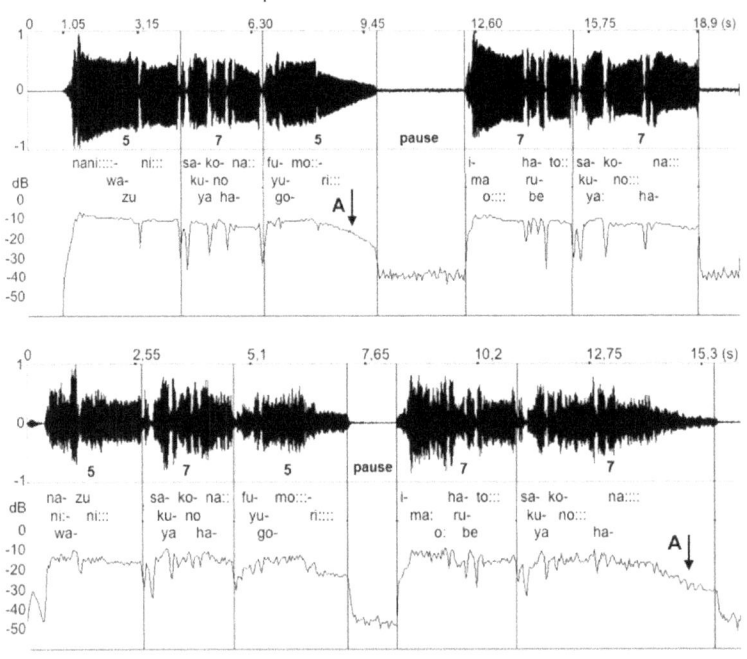

---

7 Cf. Nagano-Madsen 1992.

The duration of each phrase is shown graphically in Example 122. For the speaker of *Naniwazu* 2, the durations of 5- and 7-mora lines are nearly equal in the two pairs 5–7 and 5–7, while the last 7-mora line is much longer. In order to accommodate this, words in 7-mora lines are compressed while words (vowels) in 5-mora lines are lengthened. The two speakers (*Naniwazu* 1 and 2) differ slightly as to exactly which vowels are lengthened.

Example 122 The duration in milliseconds for each 5 and 7 phrases/lines for the two *waka* performances. N1 = *Naniwazu* 1 and N2 = *Naniwazu* 2.

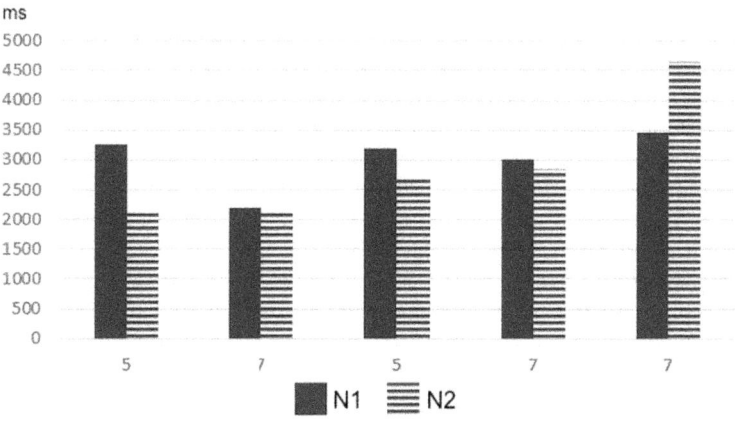

The *waka* performance template

Melody
- Level melody without speech intonation, but with a tonal centre (see Example 117).
- One dominating high pitch.

Rhythm
- Regular pulse.
- Even musical metre.

Form
- Short (15–18 seconds).
- Binary: Two musical phrases divided by a pause.

Phrasing
- Prosodic and musical phrases are aligned.
- Musical phrases end on lengthened morae (but other morae are also lengthened).

- A line of 7 morae is compressed into the same time-frame as a line of 5 morae. This is done by contraction: squeezing two morae into the slot of one, or three morae into the slot of two.
- Variations occur in cases of lines of irregular length.

Initial/final formulae
- Lines start with a glissando from a lower pitch on the first mora.

Analysis 26 Three *ryūka* performances

This analysis builds on performances of three *ryūka* attributed to the eighteenth-century *ryūka* poetess Onna Nabii, who lived in a village on Okinawa (Figure 7). *Ryūka* performance appears to be based on morae rhythm and does not show a clear metric pattern.

Ryūka kanjaganu

This *ryūka* follows the general pattern of four lines of 8–8–8–6 morae.[8] It should be observed that in Ryukyuan, the moraic nasal N counts as one mora (Example 123).

A Melodyne graph of the *Ryūka kanjaganu* performance shows two clear sections: A of 8–8 morae and B of 8–6 morae (Example 124). The melodic phrases A and B have different pitches, with B significantly lower than A. The melodic phrases start with a rising interval

Figure 7 A scene from the movie about Onna Nabii, showing the recitation of *Ryūka Unnadaki* and a transliteration with Japanese characters.

---

8 Female performer. Internet reference: *Kyoko Gushiken*.

Example 123 *Ryūka kanjaganu*, translation and morae.

kaNjaganu mijiya	well water
chubire iNnayui	makes people communicate
kamaraganu mijimu	spring water
nuyakutachuga	is useful for people

Morae (N = moraic nasal):

ka-N-ja-ga-nu mi-ji-ya | chu-bi-re i-N-na-yu-i ||
ka-ma-ra-ga-nu mi-ji-mu | nu-ya-ku-ta-chu-ga

and end with a falling interval, and they have a short final tone. There are many small intervals in the course of a performance; these small intervals are not recorded in detail. The distribution of morae and approximate pitches is shown in Examples 124–125.

Example 124 Melodyne graph for *Ryūka kanjaganu* by a female performer, Kyoko Gushiken. The vertical lines show ends of lines.

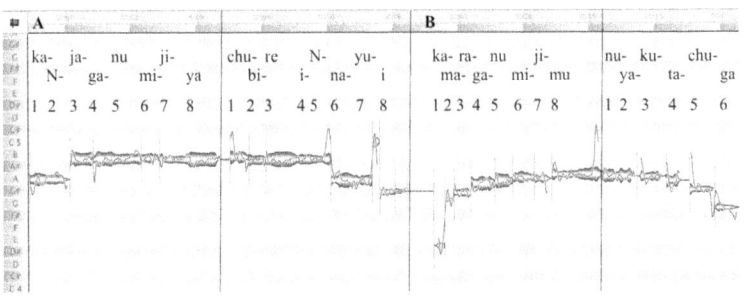

Example 125 Distribution of morae in the *Ryūka kanjaganu*. Double vertical lines show the beginnings of major sections (preceded by upbeats), whereas single vertical lines show the ends of poetic lines.

Ryūka Unnadaki

This *ryūka* by Onna Nabii is featured in a film about her life (Examples 126–127).[9]

Example 126 *Ryūka Unnadaki*, translation and morae.

uNnadaki agata	behind the mountain UNna
satugaNmarijima	is the village my love is born
muruNushinukiti	by pushing the mountain aside
kugatanasana	I will draw it to me

Morae (N = moraic nasal):

u-N-na-da-ki a-ga-ta | sa-tu-ga-N-ma-ri-ji-ma ||
mu-ru-N-u-shi-nu-ki-ti | ku-ga-ta-na-sa-na

Characteristics:

- Total length ≈ 10 seconds (9.9).
- *1st part* equalling 8 + 8 morae: ≈ 5 seconds (5.1).
- Initial pitch ≈ A#4: 461 Hz.
- Dominating pitch C5: 529 Hz – C#5: 545 Hz – C5: 529 Hz.
- The performance starts and ends on approximately the same pitch.
- *2nd part* equalling 8 + 6 morae ≈ 4.5 seconds (4.6).
- Initial pitch ≈ F#4: 370 Hz.
- Dominating pitch A#4: 471 Hz – B4: 508 Hz – A4: 444 Hz.
- The performance pitch is where the first half starts and ends about a semitone lower.
- The penultimate mora comes out one octave too high in the graph, i.e. twice the frequency: A#5: 909 / 2 Hz = A#: 454 Hz (marked with an arrow).
- Two other high pitches in that line start high and drop down, but this is not shown in the graph (appoggiatura, marked with arrows in the graph of Example 127).

The basic structure of this performance is similar to that of the previous one (*Ryūka kanjaganu*). However, the first melodic phrase ends at the starting pitch instead of going down (A in Example 128). As in *Ryūka kanjaganu*, there is a tendency towards a very small pitch difference in the last two morae in a line. In this case, however, the pitch rises slightly instead of falling.

---

[9] The authors are grateful for permission to use the recitations contained in the film *Onna Nabii*. Internet reference: *Onna Nabii*.

240   In the borderland between song and speech

Example 127 Melodyne graph for *Ryūka Unnadaki* by a female performer. Arrows mark registrations that came out wrong in the graph (compare Example 128). The vertical lines show ends of lines.

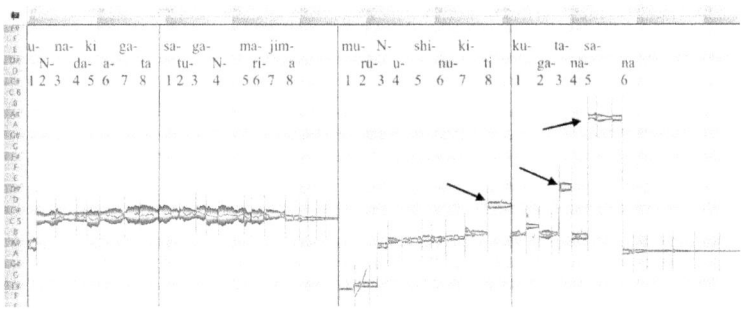

Example 128 Distribution of pitches and morae in *Ryūka Unnadaki*. Double vertical lines indicate the beginnings of major sections (preceded by upbeats); single vertical lines signal the ends of poetic lines.

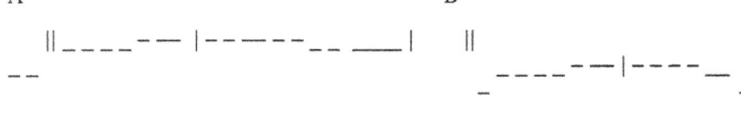

Ryūka Unnamachi

This *ryūka* by Onna Nabii is featured in the same film (Example 129).[10]

Characteristics:

- Total length ≈ 9 seconds.
- *1st part* equalling 8 + 8 morae: ≈ 5 seconds.
- Initial pitch ≈ A4: 444 Hz (rising).
- Dominating pitch C5: 517 Hz – C#5: 545 Hz – C5 535 Hz.
- The performance starts and ends at approximately the same pitch.
- The pitch on the last two morae falls to ≈ A4: 452 Hz.

---

10 Internet reference: *Onna Nabii*.

Waka and *ryūka* performances (Japan/Ryukyu)   241

Example 129 *Ryūka Unnamachi*, translation and morae.

uNnamachishichani	under the pine tree in UNna
chijinuhuetachusu	a monument of ban is placed
kuishinubumadiN	but it does not ban the hidden love
chijiyanesami	between man and woman

Morae (N = moraic nasal):

u-N-na-ma-chi-shi-cha-ni | chi-ji-nu-hu-e-ta-chu-su ||
ku-i-shi-nu-bu-ma-di-N | chi-ji-ya-ne-sa-mi

- *2nd part* equalling 8 + 6 morae ≈ 4 seconds.
- Initial pitch ≈ F#4: 360 Hz.
- Dominating pitch A4 452 Hz – B4 483 Hz – falls to G#4 425 Hz at the end.
- The performance pitch is approximately where the first mora of the first half is performed, and ends about a semitone lower.

The basic outline agrees with the previous *ryūka*. The last two morae in the first and third lines are performed at a slightly higher pitch (Examples 130–131). As in the other performances, the

Example 130 Melodyne graph for *Ryūka Unnamachi* by a female performer (the same as for *Ryūka Unnadaki*). The vertical lines show ends of lines (metric units). • **29** *Ryūka Unnamachi*

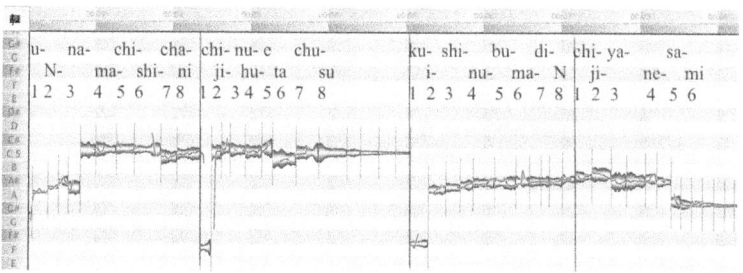

Example 131 Distribution of pitches and morae in *Ryūka Unnamachi*. Double vertical lines indicate the beginnings of major sections (preceded by upbeats); single vertical lines show the ends of poetic lines.

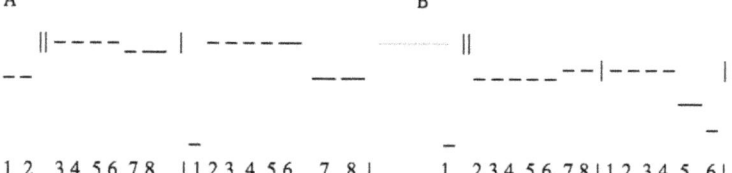

second musical phrase starts at a low pitch, but in this case the second line also starts low on the first short mora (*chi* in *chijinu-*).

Soundwave, amplitude, and duration of *ryūka* performance

Example 132a–b shows the soundwave and amplitude for the *ryūka* performances of *Ryūka Unnadaki* and *Ryūka kanjaganu*. The duration of each phrase/line is measured from the soundwave.

Example 132 Soundwave, transcription, and amplitude curve for two *ryūka* performances. a) *Ryūka kanjaganu*: the vertical lines indicate the division between 8–8–8–5. The arrow A indicates amplitude decrease. b) *Ryūka Unnadaki*: the vertical lines indicate the division between 8–8–8–6. The arrows A and B indicate amplitude decrease.

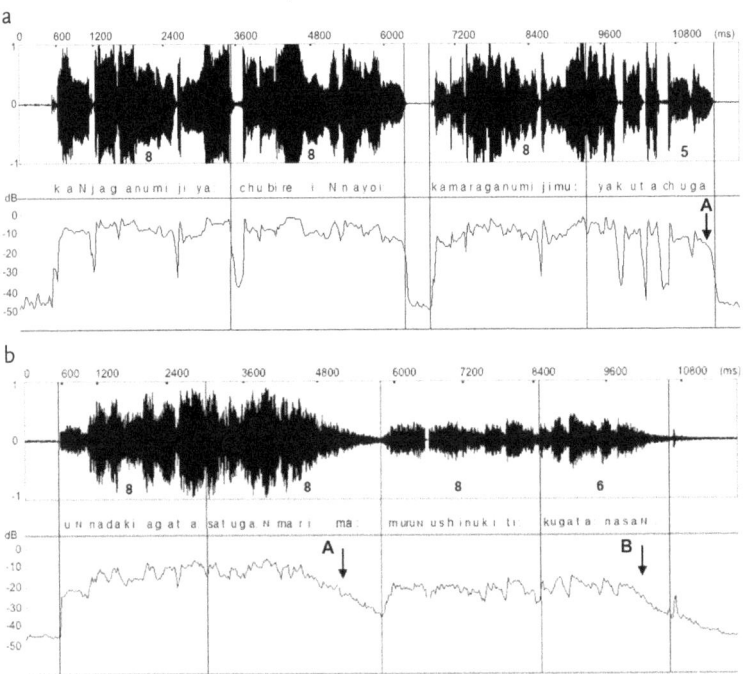

In performance a), there is some amplitude decrease (amplitude value in dB) in the second group of 8 morae and a more pronounced decrease at the very end of the performance. In performance b), the total melody is clearly divided into two musical phrases that differ in loudness. Difference with regard to loudness is also seen in the width of the soundwave. The first part is much louder than the second. Each musical phrase is performed with rapidly decreasing loudness for the last sonorant, here a prolonged [m:] indicated by the arrow A and [N:] indicated by the arrow B.

The decrease in amplitude is paralleled by a decrease in duration. In Example 133, the performances of *Ryūka Unnamachi* and *Ryūka kanjaganu* are compared in this respect. It shows that the duration decreased in the second half of the performances.

Example 133 The duration in milliseconds for each 8 and 6 phrases/lines for the two *ryūka* performances. uN = *Ryūka Unnamachi*, kaN = *Ryūka kanjaganu*.

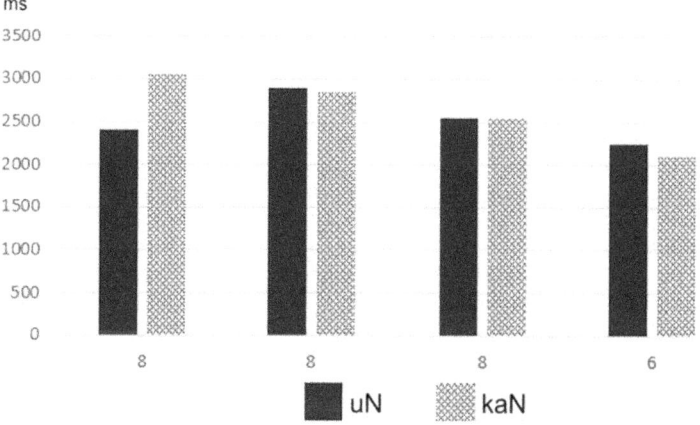

The *ryūka* performance template

Melody
- Two musical phrases, of which the second is lower than the first, corresponding to downstep in speech intonation (see Example 124).
- Speech intonation is present in the rising start of musical phrases and in the falling endings.

Rhythm
- Each phrase constitutes one (slow) pulse.
- There is no regular rhythmic subdivision within a phrase.

Form
- Short (9–12 seconds).
- Binary: Two musical phrases divided by a pause, corresponding to lines of 8 + 8 and 8 + 6 morae, respectively.

Phrasing
- Musical phrases end on shortened morae and with decreasing amplitude.

Initial/final formulae
- Musical phrases start with a glissando from a lower pitch on the first or second morae.
- Musical phrases generally end with a falling interval, and with the final mora short and unstressed.

Word variations
- The moraic nasal N has the duration of one mora.

Speech and vocal expression

The performances of *waka* and *ryūka* display some notable differences compared to the spoken forms of Japanese and Ryukyuan as regards rhythm and intonation. *Waka* performances deviate from speech, both in rhythm and in intonation.

Rhythm

In performance, the number of morae in the phrases/lines is not reflected in duration, as is usually the case in speech. As seen in Examples 121–122, the entire sequence of 5–7–5–7–7 phrases is divided into 5–7 | 5–7 | 7, each line with an increasing duration. Segmental durations in 7-mora phrases are shorter than those in 5-mora phrases. The *waka* verse form itself is a short–long verse:

short (5 morae) – long (7), short (5) – long (7), long (7). When performed, this pattern is further reinforced by the distribution of short and long tones. There are some cases in which the second mora of a bi-moraic foot is lengthened, as argued by Poser: *nani:* (line 1), *kono:* and *hana:* (both in line 5) and there are no examples of lengthening of the first mora pair.[11]

In contrast, the *ryūka* verse form is composed of a long (8) – long (8), long (8) – short (6) pattern. This seems to be reinforced in the performance by a subdivision of the two musical phrases that coincides with the poetic lines, as shown in Example 128. *Ryūka* employs shortening to mark finality, whereas *waka* employs lengthening for finality. In *ryūka*, the lengthening tends to be on the last vowel or on a moraic nasal of the musical phrase.

A notable difference between *waka* and *ryūka* performances is seen in their pitch patterns, as demonstrated in the Melodyne graphs (Examples 117 and 119 for *waka*, Examples 124, 127, and 130 for *ryūka*). Although both *waka* and *ryūka* performances have two musical phrases, which are separated by a pause, there is a difference in the way they are arranged. In *waka* performance, the two musical phrases are produced at the same pitch register, while in *ryūka* performance the second musical phrase is produced at a lower pitch register than the first. One of the characteristics of Japanese and Ryukyuan intonation is placing a final group of words at a lower pitch register. Furthermore, each musical phrase starts with a pitch rise and terminates with a pitch fall in *ryūka*, exactly as in Ryukyuan intonation. The onset pitch rise is also present in Japanese intonation, but it is not reflected in *waka* performances. Example 134 shows the intonation contour for the sentence *Manamigaru naafankaija ichura*, 'Manami goes to Naha', as spoken by a male speaker of the Shuri dialect. The utterance can be seen to be divided into three intonation units that descend gradually in pitch register. Each unit starts with a pitch rise and ends with a pitch fall. Furthermore, the rapid pitch fall with disappearing tone found in the *ryūka* citation is also a reflection of Ryukyuan intonation. Note that this final weakening is not reported for Japanese intonation.[12]

Other acoustic features such as loudness (shown in the amplitude) were not found to be consistent for *ryūka*. In one speaker's *ryūka* (see Example 132b), the second musical phrase was consistently

---

11 Poser 1990.
12 Details of the intonation in Shuri Ryukyuan are reported in Nagano-Madsen 2015.

Example 134 The spoken phrase meaning 'Manami goes to Naha' (male speaker, Shuri dialect). Three intonation units are separated by the vertical lines and numbered 1–3. Each unit starts with a pitch rise and ends with a pitch fall. (Adapted from Nagano-Madsen 2015)

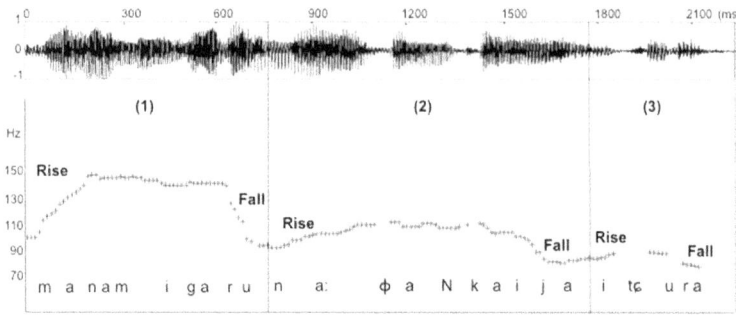

performed with lower amplitude; but this was not found in a *ryūka* performed by another female speaker (Example 132a).

Waka and *ryūka* summary

The characteristics of *waka* and *ryūka* performances are summarized in Table 8.

Performances of traditional poems in Japan and the Ryukyu Islands, *waka* and *ryūka*, were compared for their melodic patterns, rhythmic patterns (duration), and amplitude. The *waka* performances

Table 8 Summary of comparison between *waka* and *ryūka* performances

Waka	Ryūka
Organized in an even-beat metre (many morae are short and squeezed in)	Syllable-counting (morae are not squeezed in to create metre)
Basically on one high pitch	One pitch level for the first section, a lower for the second
Starts with a very short, almost spoken tone	Rising interval at the start of musical phrases
Musical phrases end on a high pitch	Musical phrases generally end with a falling interval
A long final tone	A shorter 'fading' final tone
Stable high pitches, or low for short morae	Many (micro-)intervals

revealed a total deviation from Japanese speech rhythm and intonation. The melody of *waka* performance has a high-level pitch in the same pitch register throughout, with an extreme final lengthening for the two sections. Mora-timed rhythm, reflecting the number of morae in an utterance, was not observed.

As for the melody of *ryūka* performance, a high level pitch register, as observed for *waka*, was also present. However, the melody of *ryūka* also exhibits some similarities to the phrase- and sentence-level intonation in Ryukuan speech. Since Ryukyuan (and also Japanese) is a lexical pitch-accent language in which each content word has its own accent, it is not possible to formulate a melody that fits all the *ryūka*. However, the components of Ryukyuan intonation at the phrase and sentence levels are uniform, regardless of the pitch-accent components of each word. These phrase and sentence-level components of intonation are copied in the performance of *ryūka*. They are: 1) an initial pitch rise for each musical phrase of *ryūka*, 2) a final pitch fall found at the end of a musical phrase, 3) the second unit of *ryūka* is produced at a lower pitch register, and 4) a rapid pitch fall and intensity decrease at the end of *ryūka*. All the four components are found in corresponding intonation units of Ryukyuan. Though the first three characteristics are equally present in the intonation of Japanese, they are not reflected in the *waka* performance.

7
Performance templates: method, results, and implications

Håkan Lundström and Jan-Olof Svantesson

Our research has focused on vocal expressions in the area where speaking and singing overlap. Our ultimate interest has been neither the description of performance practices nor their relation to possible 'culture areas', no matter how interesting these things may be, but how those principles that make vocal expressions possible are constructed. Therefore, the cultures under study have been chosen not for reasons of comparison, but for their suitability in studying the borderland between song and speech, and on the basis of the participating researchers' special interests. We have found that in all these cultures – cultures which, with the exception of Alaska, are concentrated in East and South-East Asia – there are vocal expressions that can be understood as being made from performance templates. These practices have some basic functions in common, functions that make the following features possible:

- variation, re-creation, and creation of vocal expressions;
- specific vocal expressions for situations involving social or communal interaction;
- specific vocal expressions for situations involving the spiritual world.

This is demonstrated by the Kammu material, which contains a number of genres of vocal expressions, each related to a specific spiritual context, a specific social context, a specific time and/or a specific geographical context such as a village, fields, or a forest [3–10].[1] The very general nature of these functions indicates that instantaneous re-creation of vocal expressions is as fundamental to human nature as speech, and can indeed be understood as a different mode of speech.

Obviously, different ways of using vocal expressions for these basic needs of human society have evolved in their separate cultural

---

1 In the following, references to analysis numbers are placed in square brackets.

contexts. The vocal expressions appear to be the result of parallel developments in language and music, and this accounts for similarities as well as differences in the material under study here. The performance templates serve to organize the vocal expression of words in accordance with the principles of several parameters labelled melody, rhythm, form, phrasing, initial/final formulae, word variations, and lexical tones. It has been shown that the contexts studied all have principles for organizing these and other parameters; but each context does it in its own unique way – it is, for instance, easy to tell a Kammu vocal expression from an Athabascan one merely by hearing, while telling it apart from an Akha vocal expression takes a little more experience of the styles. Seediq canonic imitation is unique in the material studied here, but those vocal expressions can still be explained by the use of performance templates [19–20].

We have focused on certain musical and linguistic parameters and have not considered others – for instance gesture, movement, body posture, or musical scales – and we have related this to social or cultural context only in certain cases. These areas could generate additional relevant parameters for the description of performance templates. With these delimitations, we have found that the performance templates have a common feature in that they combine and integrate musical and linguistic parameters in certain ways.

The descriptions of performance templates may appear to be similar to descriptions of musical style in general. The difference is that the relevant parameters are central to how musical and linguistic parameters coexist and are integrated. The template is more than a description in that it aims at capturing what the performer does when applying these principles in performance, which in some cases is done more or less instinctively, in others through strategic planning. This is, in turn, different from a 'deep structure' of the kind used in generative grammar in order to explain an underlying general principle for performances.

Performance template as method

Approaching vocal expressions from the perspective of performance templates has certain advantages. The alternative musicological way of studying vocal expressions would be to transcribe variants of expressions and use comparative analysis to find one or more lowest common denominators: a basic or 'original' melody. Using performance templates works in the opposite way: one performance – or a few – is/are analysed. If a performance template can be extracted, it will be tested on a few similar performances; and if it meets the test requirements, it has been proven. Since a performance template is basically a set of principles, it can be further refined when and if further study demands more details in some respects. In reality, then, the researcher starts out with the hypothesis that a performance can be explained by a performance template, which is then defined, tested, and – if necessary – further refined.

In many cases when ordinary methods of analysis yield no special results, the use of a performance template as a method produces new knowledge. Performances that may otherwise be disregarded as 'recitations', or nothing but 'heightened speech', may provide a basis for new knowledge and an explanation of factors inherent in vocal expressions and in the relationship between music and language. What is gained is that (1) the knowledge produced is of a generic kind that says something about how the vocal expression is constructed and how the performer handles the principles of the template in performance, and that (2) qualitative knowledge can be gained from a large amount of material within a comparatively limited time.

For instance, detailed transcription and analysis of some 200 or more vocal expressions in the repertoire of one Kammu singer is time consuming; and the information gained about the expressions is, in principle, limited to the description of melodic and rhythmic movement and comparisons of variants. Defining relevant performance templates from a handful of performances or segments of long performances does not take much time. The information gained gives a fairly deep insight into what the performer is actually doing and affords an understanding of the reasons for some variations between performances that might otherwise have been left unexplained. Once this is done, a researcher could, if necessary, continue studying details of the performance, individual variation, intonation, tonality, and so on.

The most time-consuming task for us has been to explore *if* and *how* performance templates can be applied to the Kammu and Athabascan material. In the case studies of the Akha, Seediq, and Ryukyuan/Japanese material, in which the performance template as a method is merely tested, it was easy to see that the method would be useful and could produce knowledge.

This method makes certain demands of the source material. Apart from audio or audio-visual documentation, the words of each performance should be transcribed with the systematic use of symbols employed by linguists, and preferably also glossed word-for-word.

In the case of tone languages, the lexical tones need to be included in the transcriptions.[2] Though a specialist in a particular language may do this long after the recordings have been made, ideally it should be done when the material is collected in the course of fieldwork, while the researcher has the possibility of discussing words and their meanings and other aspects of the performance with the performer or other persons who know the language well.

The performance template as an approach appears to be particularly useful for analysing and describing large samples of vocal expressions and extremely long performances. The largest of the samples used in this study are those of Kammu and Akha, but on-going digitization shows that there are many similar samples in archives of various kinds, samples that still await analysis.[3] The method is probably most useful for genres that are improvisatory or involve much variation, while being rather less useful for more determined musicopoetical forms for which other methodologies already exist. However, it did prove relevant to the study of those Athabascan vocal expressions that are composed beforehand and are rather settled in form [13–18]. No sharp borders were found between the processes of re-creation carried out in the performance situation and composition prepared beforehand. The differences between the two are perhaps better defined by the individual's aim for the activity. A Kammu performer's aim would be to re-create a vocal expression and vary it so that the result would be more or less different every time. An Athabascan performer, who is also a composer, would aim at creating the vocal expression and refine it until it has acquired a definite form, and would then expect it to be performed more or less in the same way every time. The use of a performance template in the analysis yields insights into the creative stage in both cases.

The interdisciplinary combination of linguistics and ethnomusicology with the concept of the performance template has proved useful for continued studies of samples of vocal expressions in the borderland between song and speech which – as for instance the Akha material used here – include all the necessary information. This paves the way for research on recent documentation, as well as on many as yet unstudied samples stored away in archives that could increase

---

2 Compare the wishlist presented by Barwick 2006.
3 This is our experience from the collaboration with the ongoing research project 'Rwaai: Digital Multimedia Archive of Austroasiatic Intangible Heritage' at Lund University, Sweden, led by Niclas Burenhult.

our knowledge of the relationship between music and language, and of the role of vocal expressions in human life.

Parameters in performance templates

This summary and discussion is organized in accordance with the parameters used in the analyses and in the same order: melody, rhythm, form, phrasing, initial/final formulae, word variations, and lexical tones. The parameters have been divided into sub-sections. While the previous chapters have focused on each separate cultural context, this section is based on a comparative perspective, applied in relation to existing research.

Melody

The melody parameter in our material spans from intonation and melody with a tonal centre to monotone (Table 9). In speech melody, the intonation of ordinary speech dominates the melodic movement, and pitches are not very fixed. In melody with a tonal centre pitches are more fixed, and the basic melodic shape is dominated by the relationship between the various pitches and the tonal centre. Since descending motion is dominant, the tonal centre is also often the lowest pitch. In the monotones, the speech intonation is flattened and the fixed pitch – or pitches, where lexical tones are realized – functions as a tonal centre. This pattern occurs in the Kammu prayers [2], which is not unexpected, since 'leveling speech prosody on a flat, monotone, contour ... is usually associated with transcendental speech as in prayers and magic spells'.[4] It is also found in the *hrlïi* Kammu genre [4] and in the performance of Japanese *waka* [25].

In the Athabascan material, the overall contour of the *Caribou song* [12] – starting higher, finishing lower, and with the negative emphasized – closely matches the contour of a Minto intonational unit. *Dratakh ch'elik*, performed at memorial feasts (potlatches), also display prose-like qualities in wordy sections, with the melody following tone and intonation to a greater or lesser extent. There are examples, though, of one and the same word in different musical settings, so even though the music and prosody interact, melodic shape is not only driven by word prosody, such as lexical tone or morphological stress. *Ch'edzes ch'elik* are highly rhythmic and the

---

4 Banti and Giannattasio 2006: 196.

Table 9 The *melody* parameter summarized from all performance templates (Analyses 1–26) and ordered in sub-categories (analysis numbers in square brackets)

Speech melody
- Closely follows pitch contour of speech [11–12].
- Melodic movement with relatively fixed pitches and no tonal centre [1–2].
- Musical phrase pairs: the second is lower than the first, corresponding to downstep [1, 26].
- Speech intonation is present in a rising start and a falling ending [26].

Melody with a tonal centre
- Short melodic phrase(s) [3, 7, 10, 19–20].
- Descending [5–6, 8–9, 12–18, 26].
- Initially rising, then descending [14, 21–24].
- Undulating with much downward motion [21–24].
- Successive lowering of pitches within each prosodic group [5–6].

Monotone
- Level contour without speech intonation but with a tonal centre [4, 25].
- Two pitch levels reflecting lexical tones but without speech intonation [4].

---

speech tone and intonation are not expressed directly, but melodic patterns dominate. In Seediq, speech rhythm and intonation seem to play important roles for the rhythmic and tonal characteristics of the corresponding musical motifs. Exclamations [19 section A] and questions [19 section B] parallel spoken language rather closely.

The *waka* performances reveal a deviation from Japanese speech intonation. The melody of *waka* performance has a high-level pitch in the same pitch register throughout. *Ryūka* performance, however, exhibits some similarities to the intonation of the Ryukyuan language: 1) initial pitch rise, 2) final pitch fall for the two sections, as well as a lower pitch register in the second section, 3) the last intonation unit becomes lower in pitch register. Though these three characteristics are equally present in the intonation of Japanese, this is not reflected in the *waka* performance. In the *ryūka* performance, a rapid reduction of amplitude occurs, in combination with a lowering of pitch in the final section, which is also a characteristic of Ryukyuan intonation.

In Kammu, lexical tones restrict the use of intonation, which is otherwise the same in both tonal and non-tonal dialects of spoken Kammu. In the case of some melody-centred genres, we found that the relationship between lexical tones and melodic pitches is very similar to that in speech. In both cases, melody/intonation is dominant until it conflicts with lexical tones. The separate sections of the *krùu* spells are marked by a higher and louder ending [10], much like the narrative style [1] and the *Ɔɔc* [3], so the endings of the melodic contour are dominated by the intonation. A thematic episode is marked by a High boundary tone that influences the realization of a final Low lexical tone by raising it. The same pattern is found in speech: intonational marking of boundaries by high-phrase boundary tones influences the realization of lexical tones.[5]

When all the studied vocal expressions are taken into account, it appears relevant to consider those vocal expressions that permit the incorporation of speech intonation as made up of music-centred and language-centred parts. The role of prosody in the relationship between music and language – or, more precisely, singing and speaking – is important and complex. Ivan Chow and Steven Brown have presented a method for using musical notation in order to obtain a more detailed understanding of speech intonation.[6] Our approach, in which we combine musicological and linguistic methods in the study of vocal expressions as totalities with both musical and linguistic ingredients, was also found useful in the study of genres that are close to speech [1–2]. This is partly because certain aspects in the performances, such as the degree of regularity in pitches and rhythm, become more obvious in notation, and partly because the approach supplies a basis for comparison with other genres.

Rhythm

Rhythm is recognized in both language and music, and in vocal expressions the two interact in various ways. Aniruddh Patel formulated a definition of rhythm that was intended to cover both language and music contexts:

> [rhythm] denotes periodicity, in other words, a pattern repeating regularly in time … Although all periodic patterns are rhythmic, not all rhythmic patterns are periodic. That is, periodicity is but one type of rhythmic organization … I will define rhythm as the systematic patterning of sound in terms of timing, accent, and grouping.[7]

---

5 Ewald 2013 found similar templates in spontaneous narratives in the Austroasiatic languages Jahai and Mah Meri, Malaysia.
6 Chow and Brown 2018.
7 Patel 2008: 96.

Performance templates

The presence of a regular beat is often referred to in characterizing music as different from spoken language. In a discussion about what Alan Lomax calls *parlando rubato*, 'in which no regularly recurring beat can be distinguished', he characterized it as 'often close to speech in general effect; accents and rhythmic patterns are grouped in meaningful ways, but without reference to a regular division of time into steady beats'.[8] Sometimes the concepts beat and pulse are understood as synonyms.[9] Here, pulse refers to the slower rhythm made up of units of beats that correspond to the musical concept of 'measures'.

In each of the cultural contexts that our sample stems from, there are examples of a strong presence of speech rhythm in the vocal expressions (Table 10). The majority of the vocal expressions have

Table 10 The *rhythm* parameter summarized from all performance templates (Analyses 1–26) and ordered in sub-categories (analysis numbers in square brackets)

Speech rhythm
- Rhythmic movement in rather uniform repeated patterns [1–2, 26].
- Rhythmic movement, basically created by the lengthening of final syllables in prosodic phrases [2].
- Closely adheres to rhythm of speech [11–12].
- Words are grouped in four-syllable units corresponding to four pulse beats [15–16].
- Isorhythmic motif corresponds to a morphological stem [14].
- Certain grammatical forms can only be in certain positions within a rhythm pair, which is achieved by the use of e.g. prefixes, suffixes, and filler syllables [21–24].
- Speech rhythm plays a role for the rhythmic realization [19–20].

Steady rhythm/beat
- Regular pulse [3–10, 12–25].
- [Mainly] syllabic [3, 4, 10, 12–14, 18].
- One tone duration dominates [4–6, 12, 15, 16, 18].
- Iambic movement dominates [7–9, 13, 21–24].
- Dotted rhythms occur [17].
- Isorhythmic organization [12–18].
- Prosodic phrases are performed to variants of: - | - - - - — where the first tone in the bar and the last long one are stressed [19–20].
- Even metre, generally 4-beat units [25].

---

8 Lomax 1968: 49.
9 Fabb 1997: 97.

a regular steady rhythm or beat that is closer to music than to speech. Some are syllabic and may be dominated by one tone duration. Iambic rhythms are comparatively common. Even though some may be said to have an even metre, generally 4-beat units, there is no case in which the wider metrical level is regular, consisting of sections of, for instance, 4, 8, or 12 units or measures. Instead, sections are of varying length, even if there is an even metre. This is, in its turn, closely related to phrasing (see below).

Form

There is a close relationship between poetical form and musical form (Table 11). Several vocal expressions from Kammu, Seediq, and Akha are of the litany type, by which is meant a continuous repetition of phrases in groups of two or more that are linked by parallelism and/or rhymes and are performed to one or two musical phrases that are also repeated throughout.[10] Two of these are organized as call-and-response between two or more performers [1, 20].

Binary form, described as A–B, is present in a great many cases, particularly in the Athabascan material [11–18]. The pairing principle is a fundamental formal concept that can be varied and developed in many ways, also as extended variants. Many of the Athabascan vocal expressions are strophic, and stanzas are often built on the A–B pattern. In Kammu *tə́əm*, one may speak of two separate binary forms: a linguistic poetical form spanning over two stanzas and a musical form spanning over one stanza [9]. There are also cases in which the linguistic binary form is not paralleled in the music, which then consists of a short phrase repeated with minor variations. This occurs in some cases where Kammu *trnə́əm* poems are performed in other genres than *tə́əm* [4–7]. The pairing principle will be further discussed in connection with phrasing.

In a study of the music of ethnic groups in Taiwan, particularly Ami and Puyuma, I-to Loh found litany in its different variations to be a common form of performance. He relates form to function and manner of performance:

> A Shaman's ritual conducted with assistants is performed first in responsorial manner; the leader sings phrase a and the assistants

---

10 The term 'litany' in connection with musical form was introduced and defined in Lomax 1968: 58–61.

Table 11 The *form* parameter summarized from all performance templates (Analyses 1–26) and ordered in sub-categories (analysis numbers in square brackets)

Litany
- Consecutive prosodic phrase pairs connected by repeated word(s)/rhymes [1–3, 10].
- A number of consecutive prosodic phrases form a thematic episode [1, 10].
- Divided into sections of various lengths [10, 19–24].
- A performer repeats each line using the same rhythmic/melodic motif [19–20].

Call/response
- Call (higher pitch level) and response (lower pitch level) [1].
- Performer 1 starts with one phrase, while performer 2 repeats the same words and melody with a time delay [19–20].

Binary
- One prosodic phrase performed twice [12].
- A–B [15–18, 21–26].

Extended
- A–A–B–B' [17, 18].
- A–B–A–B'–A [13].
- A–B–C–A'–B'–C [14].

Strophic
- Strophic [4–9, 16].
- A stanza is held together by sound repetition, parallelism, and rhymes [19–20].
- The initial part of a stanza contains vocables and key words with lexical meaning [13–15, 17–18].

---

sing phrase b. After the second statement, the music becomes antiphonal between the two groups, each repeating its own phrase with little or no variation ... The Shaman's ritualistic action is repeated over and over again, and the words of exorcism, cursing or healing may last a long time. After repetitive singing of the same formula, they may go into a trance in order to attain maximum magic power for executing the rite. This may have accounted for this particular form.[11]

---

11 Loh 1982: 230.

Binary organization also occurs abundantly in most of our material in word-pairs, rhyme-pairs, paired phrases, etc. At the micro-level, this feature is fundamental for the construction of both prosodic and melodic phrases.

Phrasing

In the vocal expressions studied here, language and music are closely integrated and interdependent with regard to phrasing. In the discussion, there has been reason to look at prosodic phrasing and musical phrasing as two aspects of the totality (Table 12). Generally, though, the performances are dominated by verbal phrasing, which, in principle, means that when prosodic phrases are prolonged, the musical phrases are prolonged as well. There is also the technique of squeezing more syllables into a musical phrase by means of placing two or more syllables in the space designated for one syllable, a technique called contraction. In Kammu *tɔ̀əm*, this results in increased prominence of musical phrasing [9]. *Tɔ̀əm* performances may thus oscillate between primarily verbal phrasing and primarily musical. The Athabascan material [11–18] is an exception, partly owing to the dominance of vocables and partly because of the isorhythmic organization and the basic four-syllable pattern (compare Table 10).

The length of a prosodic phrase is normally marked by a distinct ending which may be intonational by using boundary pitches [1–2] or prolongation. The latter is commonly the case in musical phrases in each of the cultures studied. Since musical phrases depend on the prosodic phrases for their length, the two are normally aligned, so that beginnings and endings coincide. There are some exceptions, however, particularly where musical phrases are extended to include two or more prosodic phrases, which sometimes occurs in the Kammu material when speed is increased [9–10].

Without exception, the vocal expressions that were analysed are based on parallel pairs. In many cases, the parallel phrases create A–B forms that coincide at the musical and linguistic levels (compare Table 11). Parallel pairs occur on every level:

- word-pairs, sometimes rhyme-pairs (Kammu, Akha, Seediq);
- linguistic phrase-pairs: anaphors that repeat the previous phrase (Kammu), mirrored phrases (Kammu, Seediq);
- stanza-pairs (actually linguistic phrase-pairs on a more extensive level, Kammu);

- musical phrase-pairs: musical phrases repeated, often so that the second musical phrase is lower than the first (Akha, Athabascan, Seediq, Kammu, Ryukyuan/Japanese);
- musical paired phrasing: the repetition of a musical phrase and the corresponding words (Athabascan, Seediq).

A similar practice is described as an organizing principle in Antoinet Schimmelpenninck's study of the *shan'ge* traditions in southern Jiangsu:

Table 12 The *phrasing* parameter summarized from all performance templates (Analyses 1–26) and ordered in sub-categories (analysis numbers in square brackets)

Prosodic phrasing
- Successive right-edged phrase boundary tones, with the highest boundary tone coinciding with the end of each episode [1].
- A high boundary tone coincides with the end of a phrase [3].
- Small syntactic groups end on a high boundary tone, with a lengthening of the final syllable [2].
- Prosodic phrases are organized as phrase pairs as repetition, antithetically or as question-and-answer [1–3, 10, 21–24].
- Prosodic phrases are based on iambic rhythm pairs with variations [21–24].
- Prosodic phrases may be prolonged by words or additional phrases [8–9].
- Creakiness occurs at the end of a prosodic group and might signal a phrase boundary [5–6].
- Verbal phrasing dominates (a 7-syllable line is two tone durations longer than a 5-syllable line, etc.) [3–10, 12, 21–25].

Musical phrasing
- Prosodic and musical phrases are generally aligned [3–10, 19–25].
- The last word of a phrase is (normally) prolonged [2, 5–7, 15, 18–25].
- Musical phrases end with tone repetitions: phrase-final vocable syllables are lengthened over several beats [14–16].
- Musical phrases end on shortened morae and lowered amplitude [26].
- Musical phrases are organized in pairs, where the first phrase is generally slow and long while the second is faster and shorter [21–24].
- Prosodic phrases are divided into prosodic groups marked by a higher first lexical tone [5].
- In verbal metre, musical phrases are either prolonged or contracted [9–10, 21–25].

One such organizing principle is antithesis, the combination of parallel or opposed images ... Many dialogue songs in the Wu area are antithetical, with one phrase (or a pair of lines or a stanza) contrasting with the next.[12]

There is a rich literature on parallel pairs, from word-pairs to parallel phrases or stanzas.[13] Word-pairs are common in the vocal form *lam* which occurs in Laos and north-eastern Thailand.[14] Nguyen Van Huyen saw word-pairs as a fundamental organizational principle in the poetry of Vietnamese alternating songs.[15] Emeneau built his analysis of Toda song poetry, India, on 'three-syllable song-units from which are built the longer syntactic structures and the paired parallel units and sentences', especially by the construction of parallel pairs.[16] From micro to macro level, binary form is sufficiently widespread to be considered as universal in vocal expressions in the borderland between song and speech.

The relationship between phrasing and metre is complex. By analysing a large number of performances, it is, for instance, possible to create basic or underlying forms of the *trnə̀əm* poetry used for Kammu *tə́əm* performance. Poetic lines and stanzas can be defined by phrasing and phrase endings. Lines will usually have 5 or 7 syllables [4: Example 27]. In performance, though, they may be combined with new words, and often two or more *trnə̀əm* are superimposed on one another.[17] From our study of the Kammu performance templates, it is evident that in most cases a 7-syllable line is simply longer than a 5-syllable line [4, 8]. In more complex performances, there are lines with slots for 5, 7, 9, and 11 syllables to permit the prolongation of lines [8: Example 46]. A similar technique is used in the Seediq performances, but here each section has its individual number of syllables [20: Example 99]. Prolongation of a similar kind occurs in Chinese practice as well:

---

12 Schimmelpenninck 1997: 197.
13 Here, the typology of parallelism presented in Fabb 1997 and the parallelism of Toda songs, India, should be mentioned, as described together with differences between spoken and sung language in Emeneau 1966.
14 Compton 1979, Miller 1985.
15 Nguyen 1954.
16 Emeneau 1971: 15.
17 For basic forms and transcriptions of words in such combined performances, see Lundström and Tayanin 2006: 33–199 and 201–206.

How can a singer produce such a line without crippling the basic structure of his melody? The answer is that, during the course of this prolonged phrase, he stays within the realm of one or two intervals of the melody. He freely repeats these intervals until he reaches the end of the line, and then continues with the rest of the melody.[18]

When even more words are performed in a Kammu *tɔ́ɔm*, some slots are divided to contain the extra syllables.[19] This kind of contraction also occurs in the Akha shaman performance [24: Examples 112–113] and in the Japanese *waka* [25: Example 118]. Only in the case of *waka* is there a clear adjustment of poetical metre to musical metre [25: Example 118]. In other cases, it seems more relevant to refer to a word-based metre in which poetical and musical metre are treated as one. This also happens in the North Athabascan *dratakh ch'elik*, while musical phrasing dominates the *ch'edzes ch'elik* that have very few words with lexical meaning.

There are many examples of similar techniques, especially in East and South-East Asia. Thus 'added phrases that result in the lengthening of the melodic line are common in the narrative songs in northern China, such as the *Peking drumsong* and *Shandong drumsong*'.[20] As regards *Beijing opera*, Elizabeth Wichmann reports a similar practice:

> The insertion of padding written-characters increases the number of written-characters in a seven-written-character line to as many as sixteen ... they extend the line beyond its standard length to clarify its meaning.[21]

From these descriptions and from the musical notations, it is obvious that both prolongation and contraction occur in Beijing opera. In studies of the music of Chinese music drama, notations are generally in regular 2- or 4-beat measures, so apparently alterations of syllables or words in performance must relate to a musical metre. Bell Yung identifies seven speech types in *Cantonese opera*.[22] Considering the many levels of speech (or 'song') and the line lengthening practice, some of these forms of oral delivery are

---

18 Schimmelpenninck 1997: 192.
19 This is summarized in Lundström 2010: 76–77. The concepts of contraction and prolongation approximately correspond to the embedding and conjoining of Feld 1990: 253.
20 Yung 1989: 94–95.
21 Wichmann 1991: 34.
22 Yung 1989: 57.

probably suitable for analysis by means of performance templates. Such analysis might reveal more parallels with the vocal expressions in our research.

Poetical and musical metre on the one hand and word-based phrasing on the other are not total opposites; but it seems reasonable to conclude that re-creation based on orally learnt performance templates permits a flexible relation to metre, in many cases.

Initial/final formulae

Many vocal expressions have beginnings or endings that stand out from the main part of the performance (Table 13). They often consist of a few syllables that are performed at a pitch or duration that contrasts with the main part of the performance.

Certain initial formulae are relatively long and start with a long vocative at a high pitch that descends while the first syllables of the meaningful words begin. Such a beginning marks the start of a prayer [2] and a shaman's performance [10, 21–24], calling attention to the vocal expression and signalling a genre. This, too, is the case

Table 13 The *initial/final formulae* parameter summarized from all performance templates (Analyses 1–26) and ordered in sub-categories (analysis numbers in square brackets)

Initial formulae
- Initial vocative phrase (with lengthened syllables) starting at a high pitch and descending [2, 9, 21–24].
- An initial formula at the very beginning of the performance [3].
- The first syllable(s) of a phrase is/are performed low [4, 6].
- Lines start with a glissando from a lower pitch on the first syllable [25–26].

Final formulae
- In a final formula, the pitches level out at the tonic [21–24].
- The final syllable of the phrase elongated to 3–4 pulse beats [12].
- Ends with a tone repetition, mainly on the tonal centre [14–18].
- The penultimate syllable of a line is lengthened [3–4].
- The penultimate syllable of a phrase and the very last syllable of a stanza are longer and form a final formula [4].
- A short final formula in each phrase [3].

Initial and final formulae
- Both initial and final formulae [8–10].

in social forms of vocal communication such as the Kammu *tɔ́ɔm*, which also has an initial formula for later phrases in a stanza and a final formula, as well as being highly distinct as regards the genre [9]. In most cases, a final formula signals the end of a phrase or a section of a performance.

Initial and final formulae may be purely musical, using pitches or a pattern that deviates from the main part of the performance while using the words that belong to the prosodic phrase or poetic line in question [4]. In many cases, the formulae combine musical and linguistic factors that make them stand out as formulae. One characteristic type consists of an initial high-pitched *hɔɔɔy* (or similar) followed by a descending movement on the part of the first prosodic phrase [2, 9, 21–25]. This is common in vocal expressions among South-East Asian ethnic groups. Another variant that combines musical and linguistic factors is initial formulae in the form of shortened musical phrases with words that may be non-lexical or lexical [3: Example 23; 10: Example 62], or a full phrase [10: Example 63]. In such cases, the vocal expressions tend to be aimed at a listener or listeners: human as in the case of social feasting, and both human and spiritual in the case of prayers and spells. In his description of musical litany form, Alan Lomax notes that a simple litany consists of '[o]ne or two phrases repeated over and over again in the same order with little or no variation: A A A A or AB AB AB AB ... even when such a form is preceded by one or two phrases of introduction'.[23]

Hans Oesch characterized final formulae in the Yao tradition, Thailand, as 'musical culminations where music often dominates'.[24] Final formulae normally mark the end of musical phrases and coincide with the end of prosodic phrases – sometimes by a lengthening of the last syllable [10], as is often the case in normal speech, sometimes in a manner different from speech, for example by lengthening the penultimate syllable [3], or by a specific musical motif [9].

In the Athabascan tradition, most vocal expressions start with a poignant rhythmic/musical motif, but this functions as a first section of a performance rather than as an initial formula. Endings of phrases or stanzas, however, are very prolonged, with characteristic tone repetitions, often using vocables [13–18]. These are particularly important to the musical form.

---

23 Lomax 1968: 58.
24 Oesch 1979: 18–19.

Word variations

There are differences in the use and pronunciation of words in many of the vocal expressions studied, in comparison with everyday speech (Table 14). They also include words that are not used in speech, or that acquire a special organizational function in the performances.

Vocables are words without lexical meaning. They occur in several examples in our sample, but are particularly dominant in the North Athabascan performances. This is a common phenomenon in Native American vocal expressions, where performances may consist purely of vocables. Vocables have many functions, including a structural dimension.[25] This structural dimension becomes obvious when looking at the vocal genres in performance templates: vocables are indispensable parts of the performance templates, and they play a vital structural role in the composition process.

In *Beijing opera*, vocables are referred to as 'empty words'.[26] Vocables are common among all ethnic groups in Taiwan, including Seediq, where they are often fixed in each vocal expression. There are also vocal expressions made up entirely of vocables, much like the North Athabascan genres.[27]

Some vocal expressions have lexical meaning but are not generally used in daily speech. They are pronounced differently or appear not to belong to the poetry that is being performed. These are generally known as 'song-words'. Among the Dyirbal, a population of hunter-gatherers in Australia, about 300 song-words were identified, explained as 'words used only in poetic diction and never in ordinary communication ... they made up almost one third of the occurring words'.[28] We found that song-words, just like non-lexical words, may be constituent factors in performance templates (Athabascan; Kammu: [9: Example 48]).

In many cases, no distinction is made between long and short vowels, even though vowel length changes the meaning of a word. Reduplication of syllables is common in Kammu vocal expressions. Hans Oesch has published a transcription of a Yao song, from Thailand, with a phenomenon similar to reduplication. In this case, the syllable *a* is pronounced with the final consonant of a word,

---

25 Mulder 1994 and O'Keeffe 2007: 57.
26 Wichmann 1991: 151.
27 Loh 1982: 202–206.
28 Dixon and Koch 1996 quoted in Banti and Giannattasio 2006: 306.

Table 14 The *word variations* parameter summarized from all performance templates (Analyses 1–26) and ordered in sub-categories (analysis numbers in square brackets)

Vocables
- Vocables [13–20].
- The vocables are restricted in vowel quality, comprising only [ei] and [o] [15].

Song-words
- A word without lexical meaning at the end of each line: *ís* [3].
- Song-words with lexical meaning [8–9, 18].
- Vocative song-words (*Həəəy, Həə, Eee*) [9, 23: Example 110].
- An auxiliary word *sáh*, 'I say', at the start of phrases, performed very short [4, 9].
- Lexical words are pronounced in ways that differ from ordinary speech [14, 18].

Vowel length
- Same tone duration for long and short vowels, minor and major syllables [3–9].
- The moraic nasal N is treated as one mora [25–26].
- The two light syllables (*be-* and *kw-*) and the lexical stems (*-ni, -lá*) in the text have the duration of one beat each [12].
- Coda prolongation is frequent [5–7, 9].

Syllabic reduplication
- Syllabic reduplication is frequent [5–9].

Schwa vowels
- Schwa vowels have the same duration as all other vowels that are performed as short [3–7, 10, 19–20].
- All vowels, including schwa (ə), are of approximately the same duration. In addition, schwa are long when falling on the second long tone of an iambic unit [8–9].
- Schwa vowels are not audible [1].
- Schwa vowels are very short and hardly audible [2].
- When a word is not vowel-final, vowel syllables are added [15].

regardless of which vowel preceded it. There are other syllables without meaning, too.[29]

Syllables whose vowels are more or less inaudible in speech, referred to as schwa or epenthetic vowels, are often of the same

---

29 Oesch 1979: 16–17.

duration as other vowels in performance templates, pronounced ə in Kammu or *u* in Seediq.[30] This also occurs elsewhere, as demonstrated by François Dell in connection with Tashlhiyt Berber, which he calls 'a language that allows vowel-less syllables':

> [S]chwas do not play any role in the phonology of the language (e.g. in syllable structure) nor in versification. In text-to-tune alignment, however, schwas acts as carriers for pitch, exactly like *bona fide* vowels[.][31]

In two of the Kammu genres [8, 9], however, schwa (ə) will be performed as long when it is reduplicated or when it falls on the second long tone of an iambic unit.

John D. Smith found three versions in the Rajasthani *Epic of Pâbûjî*: a nuclear or unembellished underlying text, a sung text, and a declaimed spoken text. Particularly at the beginning of lines and before cadences in the sung version, 'particles, vocatives, pronouns, and similar redundant sentence-fillers, together with repeated key words' were added. He concluded that these additional embellishments were made in order to fit the poetry to the demands of different melodies, thereby obscuring the metre.[32]

Words that appear to be 'added' or 'extra' are often referred to as padding syllables that have the function of coordinating poetical and musical metre. This is the case in the Akha shaman performance [21–24], where the syllable *lɔ̀* is used to create a rhyme-pair of a monosyllabic word and where prefixes or suffixes are used to fill 'empty' spaces in pairs where a syllable must have a certain position within the pair. Similarly, in the Athabascan material, words are adapted to fit 4-word units [15–16]. Syllable reduplication in certain iambic Kammu vocal genres can also be partly explained along similar lines [5–9].

This is not the only function of such words, however. In relation to *Cantonese opera*, Bell Yung defines six types of padding syllables used in performances:

1 added phrase;
2 phrase leader syllable: syllables moved from a stressed beat to an upbeat;

---

30 This factor is so strong in Kammu *hrlii* that it was used as additional proof of the existence of schwa vowels in so-called minor syllables; Lundström and Svantesson 2008: 124–125.
31 Dell 2011: 182–183.
32 Smith 1979 and 1991: 27 ff.

Performance templates 267

3 multiplets: squeezing several syllables into a slot (the contraction mentioned above);
4 interlude filler: words are sung to an instrumental interlude;
5 tail syllables: grammatical particles added to the end of a line;
6 nonsense syllables: vocables added after a regular syllable.[33]

Evidently, padding syllables can be many things, and they are common in performances in which the performer re-creates the vocal expression. The words *həəəy*, approximately 'hey', which is used at the beginning of a Kammu *tə́əm* performance, and *kàay sáh*, approximately 'I say', used at the end of the last line of a stanza, may appear to be rather arbitrary fillers. They coincide with the initial and final formulae of *tə́əm*. Like the vocables in North Athabascan vocal expressions, they are indispensable for the structure of the performance and are thus integrated into the performance template. Apart from this, they are also important genre markers. They signal that the performance is of the *tə́əm* variety, and they signal that the performer comes from the Yùan dialect area in northern Laos. Other Kammu dialects in the area around Yùan use different words to start and finish lines in their performance templates, words that are typical for each dialect.[34] Similarly, concerning *shan'ge* in southern Jiangsu, China, Antoinet Schimmelpenninck noted: 'Some non-semantic syllables are apparently associated with specific songs or specific song regions.'[35] Analysing performances from the perspective of a performance template has made it possible to understand meanings of words or syllables that have sometimes been seen as arbitrary ornamentation.

Lexical tones

Tonal languages add the factor of lexical tones (Table 15). In the Kammu language, with two lexical tones, lexical tones are realized in all the different vocal genres performed by the same person [1–10], though there are genres in which the lexical tones are not systematically produced in the performance [8], or where the melodic formula is rather fixed and limits the possibility of realizing lexical tones [3]. Tones are realized on the original syllable

---

33 Yung 1989: 94–98.
34 See Lundström 2010: 86, 213–17 for four other dialect templates and transcriptions.
35 Schimmelpenninck 1997: 195.

Table 15 The *lexical tones* parameter summarized from all performance templates (Analyses 1–26, analysis numbers in square brackets)

Exact pitch
- High and low pitch levels correspond to lexical tones [4].
- Lexical tones are realized at three pitch levels, and a neutral pitch or medium pitch is often used both for High and Low lexical tones [8–9].
- High lexical tones are generally performed above the tonic, Low lexical tones are performed significantly lower, and Mid lexical tones tend to be between the High and the Low in cases where the lexical tone is realized [21–24].
- Low lexical tones are generally 1 (but may be higher) or falling (3⇒1) [10].

Relative
- The realization of tones is relative: a High tone is higher than a preceding Low tone, and a Low tone is lower than a preceding High tone [6].
- Owing to melodic declination, a High tone can start lower than a preceding Low tone in the same prosodic group [5].
- The high tone of the negative stem in the word *bekwlá* 'there are none' is reflected by a high pitch [12].

Tonal movement
- Lexical tones are realized at the onset of base syllables [7–9].
- The melodic movement within syllables is flat or falling [2].
- There is tonal movement in almost every base syllable (pitch goes up or down, or up–down, down–up) [7].
- High lexical tones start at a high pitch level, or occasionally at a medium pitch level, in which case the high pitch occurs within the vowel [7].
- High lexical tones are performed with a sliding upward motion when approached from a lower pitch; a High lexical tone followed by a Low is performed with a sliding downward movement [4, 10, 21–24].
- A 'neutral' pitch (n) is often used for both High and Low lexical tones, but Low and High may be realized by sliding from the initial pitch: Low may be performed l–n or n–h, High may be performed h–n [8, 9].
- There is very little movement in words with Low lexical tones that are realized as low, while there is movement in words with High tone [4].
- Low lexical tone may make the High boundary tone at the end of an episode low [1].

Lexical tones not prominent
- Lexical tones are not very pronounced [2].
- Lexical tones are often ignored. When realized, lexical tones are relative [5].

Performance templates

Table 15 (Continued)

- Lexical tones are not realized in a systematic manner, but contrary movement is rare [3].
- Reduplicants ignore lexical tones [6–7].
- In long combinations of phrases, all or most syllables of the second line may be low with no contrary motion in such a passage [9–10].
- Movement contrary to lexical tones is common [2].

(near the vowel onset or throughout the vowel, depending on the genre), while reduplicants ignore tones. In some genres there is tonal movement in each syllable, which implies a different technique for realizing tones, in comparison with genres that have a level tone on each syllable. It also shows that a performer can shift between genres that require lexical tones to be treated differently in performance. The most consistent pattern proved to be the combination of melody-centred parts, mainly at the beginning and end of phrases where melodic movement dominates over lexical tones, and in tone-centred parts where lexical tones dominate over melodic movement.[36] The Akha shaman recitation with three lexical tones evinced a similar order.[37]

There are genres where lexical tones are realized by fixed pitch, which means that a High lexical tone is performed at a higher pitch-level than a Mid level, which is higher than a Low. In other genres, the realization is relative and similar to spoken language, a High tone being higher than a preceding Low tone and a Low tone lower than a preceding High tone [6]. Because of melodic declination, a High tone may start lower than a preceding Low tone in the same prosodic group [5]. In some Kammu genres, there is also a neutral pitch level that may be used for both High and Low tones. Within syllables the pitch is more or less level, or slides up or down. There may also be sections within the performance of consecutive syllables at the lowest pitch level regardless of lexical tone [9–10], which is due to performance practice when many syllables are repeated rather fast in order for the performer not to run out of breath.

Many languages in China and South-East Asia are tonal, both among the majority populations and in ethnic minorities. There are many tonal languages in Africa, and there are Native American

---

36 See Table 4 on p. 119.
37 See the Akha shaman performance template, p. 224.

tonal languages as well. Consequently, the relationship between music and lexical tones has been well studied. In the relevant literature, the process of combining lexical tone and melodic pitch is generally called text-setting, a term that also includes the combination of poetic and musical phrasing. Robert Ladd and James Kirby regard text-setting as a concept that is primarily useful in the context of Western-influenced music – such as Cantonese pop songs and Vietnamese *tân nhạc* or 'new music' – that differs from tone/melody correspondence in more performance-based styles:

> Correspondences between tone and melody in traditional art forms such as Cantonese opera [are] also well studied …, but the problem of matching tune and text in these cases is to some extent a matter of performance practices rather than text-setting. Roughly speaking, in the acculturated (i.e. Western-influenced) musics of much of East and Southeast Asia, melodies are relatively fixed and texts must be chosen to fit, whereas in many 'traditional' forms the melodies are fairly abstract templates and may be modified in performance to achieve optimal tone-melody correspondence with a particular text. This issue also arises in the analysis of tone-melody correspondence in a number of Southeast Asian vocal traditions …[38]

The concept of text-setting has a history in the study of Western 'written music'; but it does not fit in equally well with the process when lexical tones and musical pitches are combined in vocal expressions re-created in accordance with a performance template. In this context, they are combined simultaneously with all other stylistic factors in a manner that seems to be as instinctive as intonation or lexical tones in ordinary speech. François Dell expresses a similar view:

> A song is a composite object with two components, a linguistic object, the 'text', and a musical object, the 'melody'. The two objects have structures that are independent of one another, and each can be realized in the absence of the other. An essential feature of singing is that the text and the melody are produced simultaneously by the same machinery, i.e. the mind and the vocal apparatus of the same person.[39]

In our approach, however, we do not see the words and melodies as two separate objects. For instance, Kammu *trnɔ̀ɔm* – i.e. the words –

---

38 Ladd and Kirby 2020: 678–679, note 1.
39 Dell 2011: 173.

Performance templates

and the melody associated with those templates that may be used for performing *trnə̀əm* seldom if ever appear alone. Nevertheless, in practice, researchers sometimes use these concepts to discuss the same things as in our research. Thus, the outcome of the analysis of differences in handling lexical tones in a number of Kammu performances supports Teresa Proto's comment that 'textsetting should be studied while simultaneously taking into account multiple levels of interaction between both the musical and the prosodic structures in a given piece'.[40]

Ladd and Kirby define four ways in which lexical tones and pitches can be combined. This is illustrated by a disyllabic word consisting of a Low and a High lexical tone (L – H) and different combinations of low and high pitch (l, h): contrary = h – l, similar = l – h, oblique = l – l or h – h. All these combinations occur in the Kammu material. In the *tə́əm* performance, there are also examples of L – L being performed h – l. This is caused by a 'neutral' pitch (n) between high and low, which means that L – L may be performed n – l and H – L may be performed h – l or n – l. In languages with several lexical tones, and perhaps especially in art music forms, the relationship between lexical tone and musical pitch is sometimes very complex. In Thai court song, it has been shown that certain combinations of lexical tones may result in longer sequences of pitches.[41]

George List used graphic transcriptions in the form of spectrograms in his studies of speech and song in central Thailand.[42] Modern technology and software like Praat or Melodyne made detailed studies and experimental studies more feasible.[43] In our study of the realization of lexical tones in Kammu vocal expressions, the technology made it possible not only to see the general outline of pitch movements but also to measure factors of tonal movement within single syllables/pitches, and to study where in the syllable a tone is realized. It has also made it possible to discern detailed movements related to lexical tones in passages in which melodic movement is fairly dominant.

---

40 Proto 2015: 126.
41 Tanese-Ito 1988.
42 List 1961 and 1963.
43 See for example Morey and Schöpf 2011, Crupi 2014, Schellenberg 2014, and Pooley 2018.

Implications

The above section summarizes the factors we encountered in the borderland between song and speech. Comparisons with other research show that our results are not limited to the cultures, languages, or language families represented in our material. In the following discussion, our results will be considered in relation to wider research areas.

The continuum from speech to song

The borderland between song and speech was conceived as a segment of a broader continuum from speech to song, or in a still wider perspective: from language to music. This view of a continuum is shared by a number of researchers, especially, perhaps, in ethnomusicology. In Chapter 2 on Kammu vocal genres, that aspect was exemplified in a table of a continuum of poetic complexity (Table 1). In Table 16, the other parameters have been added in order to see how they relate to one another. Generally, the different parameters appear to change gradually with the genres, and basically in a similar fashion. This finding supports the assumed continuum.

Of the other cultures represented in our material, only the Athabascan has more than one genre. The *Caribou song* (*senh ch'eliga'*) closely adheres to the pitch contour and rhythm of speech while having a regular pulse and a tonal centre. This would place it to the left of the middle in the continuum in Table 16. The *dratakh ch'elik* performed at memorial feasts are strophic, with distinct melodic movement and strong musical phrasing, while prosodic rhythm is prominent in sections consisting of words with lexical meaning. It is located further to the right on the spectrum. The *ch'edzes ch'elik* used for dancing is on the far right of the spectrum. The Athabascan material does not contradict the Kammu continuum.

Two parameters behave slightly differently, though. The initial/final formulae are lacking in Analyses 5 and 7. This might not be one of the most important parameters and it should be noted that there is a floating border between phrase endings and final formulae. More important is the fact that the assumed continuum from speech melody to musical melody is disrupted by the monotone. The monotone includes vocal expressions that lack speech intonation, and it is based on one pitch or – in the case of Kammu with two lexical tones – on two pitches (initial formula disregarded). Since monotonic scale is recognized, one may speak of a tonal centre in a case of monotone. This is definitely the case with *hrlïi* [4]. It could be seen as only partly monotonic; but this would not solve the problem of the continuum if, for instance, *waka* performances are considered [25]. With regard to rhythm, *waka* with a musical metre belongs rather far to the right in the spectrum, disrupting the melody continuum.

In his classification of a continuum from speech to song, George List sees two routes between the two phenomena: one goes via expansion of intonation and stability of pitch, the other via negation of intonation and expansion of scalar structure.[44] In the latter case, List places the monotone as the extreme. List's model has the advantage of including the monotone, and it is sometimes used in order to place vocal expressions somewhere on a scale; but since it builds on a presupposed idea of evolution, it also has limitations.

It is notable that certain factors in the continuum in Table 16 coincide: tonal centre, fixed pitches, and regular beat coincide with word variation, namely same tone-duration for long and short vowels and the same duration for schwa vowels and song-words. Hence, it seems that the combination of regular rhythm and tonality provides the basis for durational variations of words. Similarly, the combination of tonality and iambic rhythm and increased prominence of musical phrasing coincide with syllabic reduplication. These particular word variations are language-specific, or specific to languages that are similar to Kammu in these respects. Nevertheless, the observation that tonality and regular beat coincide and may, in their turn, generate other changes could be more general. That also goes for the addition of a higher proportion of musical phrasing.

In all essential respects, our material supports the idea of a continuum. The exceptions seem to indicate that one cannot expect a continuum that runs parallel in all possible parameters; rather, it needs to be envisioned as a multi-dimensional system.

Vocal expressions and genres

In Chapter 3 on North Athabascan music, two genres were discussed in detail. There are structural similarities between them, for instance the use of tone repetitions at the end of a phrase; but they

---

44 List 1963: 9.

Table 16 Kammu vocal genres in the speech–song continuum with regard to poetic techniques, word variations, rhythm, and melody

← SPEECH   SONG →

	Lɔ̀ɔŋ (narratives)	Kàm à-thítháan (prayers)	Ceremonial expressions (Ɔ̀ɔc, etc.)	Krùu (spells)	Hrlii	Hrwà, Húuwà	Yàam	Yùun tíiŋ	Tə̀əm
	Analysis 1	Analysis 2	Analyses 3, 8a	Analysis 10	Analysis 4	Analyses 5–6	Analysis 7	Analysis 8b	Analysis 9
Word variations									
	Schwa barely audible								
			Schwa same duration as all other vowels that are performed as short						
			Same tone duration for long and short vowels						
						Song-words			
						Syllabic reduplication			
								Schwa can be long Schwa can be reduplicated	
Initial/final formulae									
		Initial		Initial and final				Initial and final	
Form									
	Litany Prosodic phrase pairs					Strophic			

← SPEECH							SONG →
Làɔŋ (narratives)	Kàm à-thí-tháan (prayers)	Ceremonial expressions (Ɔ̀ɔc, etc.)	Krìɑu (spells)	Hrlìi	Hrwà, Húuwà	Yàam	Yùun tíiŋ	Tə̂əm
Analysis 1	Analysis 2	Analyses 3, 8a	Analysis 10	Analysis 4	Analyses 5–6	Analysis 7	Analysis 8b	Analysis 9
Phrasing								
Prosodic		Prosodic and musical phrasing aligned Verbal phrasing dominates			Musical phrasing gradually more prominent			
Rhythm								
Speech rhythm		Regular beat One-beat rhythm				Iambic rhythm		
Melody								
Speech melody		Tonal centre, fixed pitches		(Monotone)				

also differ, particularly in the use of words with or without lexical meaning. Both are performed at potlatch feasts, but they have different functions there. *Dratakh ch'elik* serve the purpose of honouring the deceased, whereas *ch'edzes ch'elik* belong to the feasting that follows this ceremonial part. The genres are deeply linked with cultural and social practice.

The vocal expressions analysed in the Kammu chapter represent several different genres, in most cases performed by the same person. These genres range from mainly language-centred performances to mainly music-centred ones. Several of the genres are distinctly different in the handling of the studied parameters. In Kammu culture, these genres are deeply embedded in cultural practice. The vocal expressions have their different time, place, and function. Kammu music activity, as a whole, is closely tied to different periods in the life cycle and to different stages of the farming year. Its formal characteristics also signal the situation to which they belong. In the case of the music of the farming year, that function is integrated into other practical and ceremonial activities, thus serving as a calendar.[45]

The fact that cultural context produces different genres is not unique for North Athabascan and Kammu culture; indeed, as exemplified by a number of studies, it is the norm rather than the exception. In his study of the music of the Venda culture in northern Transvaal, John Blacking presents a graph that shows 'the relationship between the performance of communal music and the seasonal cycle'.[46] Similarly, concerning Aka, on the border between the Central African Republic and the Democratic Republic of the Congo, Susanne Fürniss lists genres, situations, voice, and instruments in a graphic representation called 'the musical universe of the Aka'.[47] Writing about the Kalankira in the Bolivian Andes, with chapters dealing with 'Orchestrating the year: Seasonal alternation, calendars and powers' and 'The music of a year', Henry Stobart says:

> Musical knowledge, discourse and practices in Kalankira are not neatly separated from other spheres, but they are deeply integrated into more general ideas about 'production' ... The 'Poetics of production' in this book's title aims to stress the mutual independence of musical and socio-economic production ...[48]

---

45 This is summarized in Lundström and Tayanin 1982: 132–135, Table 1.
46 Blacking 1965: 30, Fig. 2.
47 Fürniss 2006: 166, Fig. 5.1.
48 Stobart 2006: 5.

This demonstrates the social importance of vocal expressions in human culture; and since many of these exist in the borderland between song and speech, there is good reason to include them in the study of music and language.

The mono-melodic principle

The mono-melodic, sometimes called mono-thematic, phenomenon refers to a practice in which one melodic framework is used for a number of sets of words. In the Yùan dialect area of Kammu culture, for example, the Yùan *tə́əm* performance template is used for practically all social singing on festive occasions. One collection contains about 150 *trnə̀əm* performed in accordance with the same Yùan template.[49] The mono-melodic organization of vocal genres in Kammu culture is a special case in which a number of different mono-melodic genres are used in very specific contexts, and one and the same *trnə̀əm* may – at least in theory – be performed in accordance with either genre's performance template [4–9].

Mono-melodic practices are widespread in southern China and South-East Asia, on islands as well as on the mainland, not least in the cultures of the numerous ethnic groups in that part of Asia, and they are closely related to alternating singing.[50] For instance, a mono-melodic system is reported by Antoinet Schimmelpenninck concerning the *shan'ge* traditions in southern Jiangsu:

> Every village in the Wu area appears to have its own tune or its own local variant of a regionally popular tune. Within every village, every singer appears to have his own, personal interpretation of such a tune. This 'monothematism' of the performance is one of the most remarkable aspects of *shan'ge* singing in the area ... This leaves me with the need to define the notion of a 'melodic framework' ... No doubt several other 'monothematic' regions exist in the Wu area.[51]

As in Chinese narrative genres, one can also see the 'fixed tunes' or 'tune types' in Chinese music dramas as examples of mono-melodic systems.[52] Similarly, lullabies in South-East Asia and elsewhere often use a particular melodic framework. This is the case in Thailand:

---

49 Lundström and Tayanin 2006.
50 See Lundström 2018: 989–991.
51 Schimmelpenninck 1997: 224, 226, 267.
52 Yung 1989: 128–137, Pian 1993.

lullabies are generally sung to a short melodic formula which is repeated over and over with more or less variation. In some cases many short nursery rhymes are strung together which results in longer performances ... Though the melodies of the different regions differ ... they do have a core of tonal material in common.[53]

Lullabies are often tied together into very long performances built on the same melodic formula. This is due to the function of lullabies as explained by Johannes Kneutgen, who found, by measuring a child's breathing rhythm, that an Argentine lullaby needed 14 repetitions before the child was asleep.[54] In Swedish tradition, a common melodic formula for lullabies is called 'The fishing ground tune'. Carl-Allan Moberg studied about 100 variants of the tune from different music genres in order to find its origin.[55] The 19 lullaby variants show examples of prolonging and contraction, discussed above under 'phrasing'. This is an example of an approach from the perspective of vocal expression and performance template that might place the focus on things other than – in this case – the perspective of the original and variants. The example also indicates that even though we have studied vocal expressions in a few cultural contexts in East and South-East Asia and Alaska, the method is likely to be useful in all parts of the world.

The cross-cultural aspect

The present study is cross-cultural, since it is based on material from five distinct cultural contexts. We were looking for diversity and richness of vocal expressions rather than similarities, so the comparative perspective has not been in the foreground. Comparative musicology – in German 'vergleichende Musikwissenschaft' – was a branch of musicology from the very beginning of the discipline in the late nineteenth century. The extensive material that was collected was analysed, compared, and ordered in accordance with the *Kulturkreis* school, i.e. Darwin's theory of evolution applied to human culture and music. Researchers took an interest in basic vocal expressions because they fitted the assumption that everything had developed from the primitive to the advanced, rather than for their role as vehicles for expression and communication. In the case

---

53 Stone and Lundström 2000.
54 Kneutgen 1970.
55 In Swedish: 'Fiskeskärsmelodin'. Moberg 1950.

of vocal expressions, the factors that were measured were primarily pitches, the number of tones in scales, types of scales, and rhythmic organization. Another aspect of comparative musicology was diffusionism, according to which all things had a common origin and had spread from one place to another. Comparative musicology was thus much occupied with evolution and history and went hand in hand with racial biology.[56]

After the Second World War, these views were no longer viable. One critique within the developing field of ethnomusicology was that comparative musicology had built on generalizations concerning music that had been taken out of the musical context and then analysed from an ethnocentric Western perspective. Ethnomusicology instead focused on the study of music in cultures, which was the focus of Alan P. Merriam's anthropology of music.[57] There is now a rich material of studies of music in its cultural contexts in all parts of the world. On the other hand, there is no complete overview of music on a global scale. Linguistics has developed differently and seems to have escaped this dichotomy of views. One reason may be the early influence of structuralist theory, which made it possible to develop a generally accepted set of theoretical parameters for the study of languages.

Against this background, it is not surprising that new theoretical possibilities for cross-cultural studies are now developing in interdisciplinary research. Patrick E. Savage and Steven Brown are aiming at a new comparative musicology:

> As with its sister discipline of comparative linguistics, comparative musicology seeks to classify the musics of the world into stylistic families, describe the geographic distribution of these styles, elucidate universal trends in musics across cultures, and understand the causes and mechanisms shaping the biological and cultural evolution of music.[58]

This field is not seen as a 'replacement for ethnomusicology or historical musicology but as a specific stream within the overall umbrella of musicology'. Savage and Brown attempt to bridge the dichotomy of between-culture and within-culture facets of cultural diversity by considering the two simultaneously, using methodology developed in the study of genetic diversity in population genetics (analysis of

---

56 See Brabec de Mori 2017: 116–119 for a summary of this research method.
57 Merriam 1964.
58 Savage and Brown 2013: 148.

molecular variance, AMOVA). Using music samples from a number of Austronesian-speaking peoples in Taiwan and the Philippines, they find that

> [t]he multi-dimensional scaling plot clearly demonstrates the high level of internal heterogeneity in each population's musical repertoire and the high degree of overlap between populations ... This validates and quantifies the critiques of ethnomusicologists that Cantometrics' cross-cultural approach underestimated the diversity of musical repertoires within each culture.[59]

One of the critiques against Alan Lomax's worldwide mapping of folk-song styles, carried out by way of the application of his Cantometrics system, has concerned a number of parameters that were to be coded by the researcher and therefore risked being subjective.[60] The use of samples that were sometimes small and gathered under varying circumstances was criticized, too. While Cantometrics focused on the social setting of performances, the coded parameters in the new CantoScore focus totally on musical theory.[61] In a sense, this limitation is a return to the old comparative musicology, though a much larger number of parameters are now involved. The problem with limited samples and subjectivity in the coding process remains; but another factor constitutes a new problem, namely that the musical transcriptions that play a key role were made by different researchers, at different times, and with different aims.[62]

The study of the music of Austronesian ethnic groups on Taiwan and in the Philippines may be regarded as a pilot study.[63] The results do not contradict our two Seediq performances, and further research may make it clear whether the use of new methodologies for classifying and mapping intra- and cross-cultural variation will compensate for some of the limitations of the method. In another article, the speech/language continuum is discussed in relation to cross-cultural research:

> A truly universal approach cannot exclude 'nonmusical' vocalizations but must accommodate any type of vocalization sitting along the

---

59 Rzeszutek, Savage, and Brown 2011: 1608.
60 Lomax 1968.
61 Savage, Merritt, Rzeszutek, and Brown 2012.
62 The method CantoCore and the practical coding are presented in Savage, Merritt, Rzeszutek, and Brown 2012. The limitations of the method are discussed in Savage and Brown 2013: 149–151.
63 Savage and Brown 2013.

musilinguistic spectrum of communicative forms from speech, to songs, to everything in between.[64]

In our research, we have attempted to steer clear of the dichotomy between music and language. The concepts 'vocal expression' and 'performance-template methodology' have proved useful in that respect. This approach should have the potential to contribute to comparative cross-cultural research by making the dichotomy of language/music less problematic, by increasing knowledge of the degree and nature of variation in vocal expressions, and by isolating further key parameters for cross-cultural study. The approach might, in turn, also be used for validation of the statistical or mathematical methodologies that are employed in research along such lines.

Universals and evolution

Five principal research issues are listed in the description of the new comparative musicology: classification, cultural evolution, human history, universals, and biological evolution.[65] In our study, we have viewed the performances and vocal genres as the contemporary practices they are, and have not touched upon matters of origin or evolution. It could be noted, however, that some results – for example the image of a continuum from speech to song (Tables 4 and 16) – coincidentally show similarities to Steven Brown's 'Musilanguage' model, which was used to illustrate a theory of common origins for language and song.[66]

In the field of (ethno)musicology, the attitude to evolution and universals has mainly been one of suspicion. This may to some extent be explained by the fact that these terms were burdened by the way they had been used in connection with the pre-Second World War comparative musicology described above. A different focus is adopted by Steven Brown and Joseph Jordania in an attempt to focus on a positive approach to possible universals rather than conduct a meta-critique about the concept as such. They provide a list of possible universals in music, divided into four main groups at a fairly high degree of generalization.

> Regardless of the type of category or system analyzed, there will be *varying degrees of generality* for any component when performing

---

64 Savage, Merritt, Rzeszutek, and Brown 2012: 89.
65 Savage and Brown 2013: 150.
66 See Brown 2000: 274 ff.

a cross-cultural comparison, as based on the frequency of appearance of that trait in the world's musics. In other words, there will be a *gradient of universality* for the family of components, some components being more prevalent than others. This gradient should vary from complete universality to complete culture-uniqueness.[67]

When considering that vocal expressions in the borderland between song and speech would be as universal as music and language, their characteristics are likely to contain traits that could add to the list of possible universals and, as a result, contribute to a wider base for cross-cultural or comparative studies. This is definitely the case if potential universals are viewed as factors that could vary from complete universality to complete culture-uniqueness. Some recurring aspects of our material could easily be listed: binary form, the existence of vocables, the existence of 'song-words', initial and final formulae, prolongation, contraction, melody-centration, and word-centration, to mention just a few.

The Music Lab at Harvard University does broadly interdisciplinary research on music within the 'The Natural History of Song' (NHS) project, aiming at 'a systematic investigation of the world's vocal music'.[68] Their comparative research is based on two representative corpora, one composed of ethnographic descriptions of song performances and one composed of field recordings. The aim is to conduct 'systematic analysis of the features of musical behaviour and structure across cultures, using scientific standards of objectivity, representativeness, quantification of variability, and controls for data integrity'.[69] The Music Lab scholars study four song types – dance, lullaby, healing, and love – through 'automatic music information retrieval, annotations from expert listeners, annotations from naive listeners, and staff notation transcriptions (from which annotations are automatically generated)' as well as a number of statistical operations, including reliability tests.

> Our analyses of the NHS Discography show that four common song types, distinguished by their contexts and goals, have distinctive musical qualities worldwide. These results suggest that universal features of human psychology lead people to produce and enjoy songs with certain kinds of rhythmic or melodic patterning that naturally go with certain moods, desires, and themes. These patterns

---

67 Brown and Jordania 2011: 233.
68 Department of Psychology, Harvard University, www.themusiclab.org/.
69 Mehr and Singh 2018: 2.

do not consist of concrete acoustic features, such as a specific melody or rhythm, but rather of relational properties like accent, meter, and interval structure.[70]

The results were clearest for the lullaby and dance categories. Inevitably, the research includes many approximations and generalizations. The approximations may be based on Western music theory (major and minor third as approximations of a number of intervals that in many cases are not stable, even if thus perceived) or views, such as the approximation of 'single vowel' for 'vocalization' in the case of the CantoScore, to mention a couple of examples. From the point of view of our research, which is basically intracultural, it is natural to question what cumulative effects a series of similar approximations in the basic data may have on the outcome.

In the material used for our present study, there are no lullabies, but it contains several vocal expressions that involve healing situations and dancing. These differ in character from the other vocal expressions. However, in Kammu *tɔ́əm* there are performances that deal with love, praising, criticizing, birds or nature, etc. All such different themes may occur in the same festive situations, although some cases are specific situations for love themes.[71] This example shows that the functions of vocal expressions are not necessarily linked with differences in the music or performance. Future research may show whether Kammu is an exception, or perhaps whether lullaby and dance are exceptions as 'universal archetypes'.

Endangerment and transmission

Since vocal expressions in the borderland between song and speech demand language knowledge – in some cases very deep knowledge – they are endangered to the same degree as the language in question. This circumstance is expressed as follows by Allan Marett and Linda Barwick with regard to Australian native tradition:

> It is widely reported in Australia and elsewhere that songs are considered by culture bearers to be the 'crown jewels' of endangered cultural heritages whose knowledge systems have hitherto been maintained without the aid of writing. It is precisely these specialised repertoires of our intangible cultural heritage that are most endangered, even in a comparatively healthy language. Only the older members

---

70 Mehr and Singh 2018: 2.
71 See Lundström and Tayanin 2006.

of the community tend to have full command of the poetics of song, even in cases where the language continues to be spoken by younger people.[72]

The Athabascan situation in interior Alaska is an example of this. Vocal expressions occur mainly at special feasts, some of which are related to a funeral or memorial. Very few elders are still living who know how to compose, while younger persons who start composing must struggle with the language. This has actually led to a situation in which music supports language revitalization in the potlatch feast context.[73] The music and dance revival has also included staged performances; and the Minto dancers have taken part in pow-wows, where native musics are staged in the context of music and dance contests in meetings organized and run by Native Americans, basically as an internal activity.

In a study from a sociolinguistic perspective of two Alaskan Eskimo communities, Hiroko Ikuta reports a situation similar to the Athabascan in that 'the heritage languages – Yupik on St Lawrence Island and Iñupiaq in Barrow on the Northern shore of Alaska – have secured a continued existence in the context of song-and-dance performances'.[74] Ikuta continues:

> It is the withdrawal of language and cultural performance, away from globalisation processes that have moved English in a dominant position, that has created a safe space for the use of the heritage language, be it that in this process the heritage language has been reduced to emblematic forms ... I suggest that practice of Eskimo dancing and singing that local people value as an important linguistic resource can be considered as a de-globalised sociolinguistic phenomenon, a process of performance and localisation in which people construct a particular linguistic repertoire withdrawn from globalisable circulation in multilingualism.[75]

This is an example in which music, dance, and language in combination give those that do not speak the 'heritage language' an ethnolinguistic identity and the feeling of cultural continuity. The places – the arenas for performance, the potlatch in the Athabascan case – are of central importance for this form of language and music continuity.

---

72 Marett and Barwick 2001: 144.
73 See Sleeper 2018: 83–88 for music in language revitalization.
74 Ikuta 2010: 172.
75 Ikuta 2010: 171–172.

The close relationship between language and music has led Catherine Grant to suggest that approaches relating to the maintenance of endangered languages can assist ways of supporting endangered music genres. She does this by developing 'the Music Vitality and Endangerment Framework (MVEF), for identifying and measuring music endangerment, based on a framework developed by UNESCO for identifying and measuring language endangerment'.[76] Similarly, Neil R. Coulter has demonstrated that GIDS (Graded Intergenerational Disruption Scale), which he adapted into GDMS (Graded Music Shift Scale), can be used to give a nuanced picture of music shift with regard to genres and generations among the Alamblak in Papua New Guinea.[77] This approach makes it possible to express the degree of endangerment of a kind of music, or of specific music genres, in processes of change.

In many cases, change is brought about by national cultural policies. A common method, especially in the socialist cultural policies of China and Vietnam, is the staging of certain music styles and dancing. Staging usually means recontextualization of music in the sense that the music has moved to another place or a new social or cultural setting and has taken new roots there.[78] Certain vocal or instrumental music and/or dances then become representative of individual ethnic groups. The music is often rearranged to fit the current national style, and it may be performed by individuals who do not belong to the ethnic groups in question, as in the Vietnamese 'neotraditional music'. There may be a whole spectrum of contexts, from performances in the ethnic village on the one hand, to the music becoming part of a totally different context as an aspect of a politically created repertoire at the other extreme. This principle has been described by Sue Tuohy in relation to China.[79] The consequences for music genres and for the people who perform them have been described by Ó Briain concerning Hmong in Vietnam.[80] Catherine Ingram presents an account of the staging of *dage*, 'big song singing', of the Kam (or Dongzu) population in the Guizhou Province in southern China:

---

76 Grant 2014.
77 Coulter 2011.
78 Schippers 2010: 121.
79 Tuohy 2001.
80 Ó Briain 2018.

[A]s a result of the social and political restrictions in Kam villages during the Cultural Revolution ... the singers involved in staged big song performances from the 1980s onwards began to include many Kam people with no experience in village big song singing. The 1980s also marked the beginning of Kam song classes in tertiary institutes specifically for training Kam professional performers. In the 1990s, staged performances increased in popularity and began to feature in televised broadcasts ... Kam people refer to the staged performance of Kam songs, including big song, as cha tai dor ga – literally, 'going onstage to sing songs'. The various features of staged big song singing that allow Kam people to distinguish it from big song singing occurring in the village context have remained virtually static over the last sixty years.[81]

There are no reports as yet about Kammu in the Yùan area in northern Laos, or the Akha of northern Thailand, becoming involved in a similar change. Thomas Turino speaks of cultural nationalism in Latin America and in colonial and post-colonial Zimbabwe.[82] Cultural nationalism occurs everywhere and these processes are not limited to socialist countries, though methods may vary. In Taiwan, there are archives containing recordings of the music of ethnic groups, and revival movements are also going on among the Seediq.[83]

Sustainability is a sensitive matter and researchers are divided in this respect: some want to preserve local traditions, while others are prepared to accept recontextualization as one way for a music and its function for individual cultural or social identity to survive. This view was taken in a project led by Huib Schippers, in which matters of endangerment and sustainability were studied in 11 different contexts in different parts of the world; Schippers employed the same set of parameters, which included relationships with national states and the media. The result was an overview of similarities and diversity in sustainability processes.[84] The point is that the relationship or tension between village (or local) music culture and national cultural policy is present everywhere:

> The Vietnamese example demonstrates that the music culture of an ethnic minority group or village cannot only be seen as a separate unit but also must be seen in relation to the national music culture

---

81 Ingram 2012: 439–440.
82 Turino 2003 and 2008: 145 ff.
83 The movie *Warriors of the Rainbow: Seediq Bale (2012)* actually includes a Seediq canonic imitation performance. Internet reference: *Seediq Bale song*.
84 Schippers and Grant 2016.

of which it is a part and to the processes going on there. This is crucial when thinking of the future of this music.[85]

Likewise, the transmission of musical and linguistic knowledge depends on national educational policies. Kathryn Marsh has studied children's game songs in a global perspective.[86] She found that the formulaic character of some children's game songs means that the children know how to use the formulae for varying the songs and for inventing new ones. This phenomenon could be described in terms of vocal expressions in the borderland between song and speech, and be studied by means of performance templates. Marsh points out that this fact is generally not recognized when children start school, which sometimes leads to 'deskilling'.[87]

> Teachers are thus in the position to show an acceptance of children's musical traditions and the varied sources on which they draw. From this position of acceptance, they can then broaden children's musical perspectives by providing a wide range of music for performance, listening and as a basis for creation … Classroom musical activities can thus contribute to, rather than be antithetical to, the continued flourishing of multiple traditions of children's musical play.[88]

The role that music education in school plays for the transmission of cultural knowledge is often underestimated, especially in view of the fact that Western school-music education is one of the most globalized musical activities, a process that started in the mid-nineteenth century.[89] Awareness of children's knowledge in creation, re-creation, and transmission of vocal expressions has increased as a result of research in ethnomusicology and music education. The fact that children also learn a structure for language expression is of relevance for literacy education and the communication arts, as exemplified by Akosua Addo concerning Ghana.[90] In her study of 'Miskitu children's speech and song on the Atlantic coast of Nicaragua', Amanda Minks has shown how the communicative competencies children possess, and have developed, are used in an intercultural context to create social identity.[91]

---

85 Lundström 2018: 1001.
86 Marsh 2008.
87 Marsh 2008: 314.
88 Marsh 2008: 317.
89 See Cox and Stevens 2010.
90 Addo 2013.
91 Minks 2013.

Transmission of vocal expressions is not limited to words and melodies; above all, it is a matter of the ability to relate to vocal expressions by learning, adapting, and transmitting.[92] When traditional vocal expressions are recontextualized in the case of stage performance, or when taught in school, they usually appear in a normalized stable form that is learnt and then repeated. If children – or adults, for that matter – are not 'deskilled' from their ability to create and re-create vocal expressions, they become more receptive to the transmission of vocal expressions. Our research has shown that it is not enough to transmit the performance: knowledge of how to re-create vocal expressions in performance needs to be transmitted, too. This, in turn, calls for a certain level of music and language proficiency.

In our research, we have combined ethnomusicology with different specializations within linguistics in order to study vocal expressions as neutral objects – neither song nor speech, but both. There is a tradition of combining methodologies of musicology and linguistics, more perhaps for the study of music than for the study of linguistics. The term *musicolinguistics* that has been used by Steven Feld and Aaron Fox – and even by some in our own group – has recently been incorporated in the title of a study by Morgan Sleeper.[93] This term may be useful as a label of interdisciplinary research involving musicology and linguistics as a sub-area within the two disciplines.

Written 'MusiCoLinguistics', the same term is used for language, music, and cognition research by Rie Asano at the University of Cologne.[94] Cognition is an area that we have barely touched upon in this discussion. While we have collaborated in trying to use our specializations in musicology and different fields of linguistics, and also in bridging the gaps between them, it may be observed that there is still a gap between researchers in the humanities and those who use scientific methods, partly because of different perspectives, methods, and languages. In Aniruddh Patel's words:[95]

> The music–language relations is one area in which scientific and humanistic studies can meaningfully intertwine, and in which interactions across traditional boundaries can bear fruit in the form of new

---

92 See further Lundström 2012: 654–656.
93 Feld and Fox 1994, Lundström and Svantesson 1996, and Sleeper 2018.
94 Internet reference: MusiCoLinguistics.
95 Patel 2008: 417.

ideas and discoveries that neither side can accomplish alone. Studies that unify scientific and humanistic knowledge are still uncommon ...

Scientific and humanistic knowledge cannot be unified until both kinds of research – the scientific and the humanistic – can understand and evaluate each other's results. There is a large gap between them in this respect – a gap that may be bridged only in interdisciplinary collaborations which provide contexts for learning to communicate these matters.

Our research is a step in that direction. While linguists often define music in terms of pitches and rhythm, most ethnomusicologists avoid definitions and go by feeling to search for, as Ian Cross puts it, 'something like music'.[96] In our case, we chose to focus on a borderland between song and speech. This choice has made definitions of music, language, or the difference between them unnecessary, thereby paving the way for collaboration.

We have found that it is possible to recognize forms of human communication that can be described as vocal expressions in the borderland between song and speech, and that it is also possible to design a method for studying them that leads to new knowledge of this borderland. It is a fairly distinct yet loosely defined category that – in addition to general knowledge of one's own cultural context – calls for knowledge of the language and of the performance templates that are necessary for realizing these forms of human communication. We have also shown that it is possible to speak of a continuum from speech to song, even though it may not always be as clear cut as is often depicted.

It is not obvious where this borderland ends. A pragmatic view would be to say that it ends where the method does not produce results and cannot be replaced by a different method that works. While we have necessarily had to restrict our studies to a limited number of vocal expressions, they are widely disseminated and hence relevant to many – if not most – areas of musicological and linguistic research, as the preceding paragraphs have demonstrated. Examinations of these vocal expressions consequently add to the state of knowledge in all those areas.

---

96 Cross 2012: 317.

Appendix 1
Software used

In the process of analysis various software packages have been used, often in combination with other kinds of graphic transcription or musical notation. Certain types of software are well known to linguists and others to musicologists. Therefore, they are briefly presented here, with a few examples which – in the case of Praat and Melodyne – also serve as guides for understanding the graphs that occur in the text.[1]

Praat

Praat, which is free and developed by Paul Boersma and David Weeninck, is useful for analysis and annotation of short recordings or segments of longer recordings.[2] Example 135 is a screen capture of a whole annotation. On top there is the soundwave, and below it the movement of the fundamental frequency (F0). The grey shading in the same area is the spectrogram in which overtones or timbre can be analysed. Tiers can be added and named according to preference. In this case, syllables were separated (manually) and written into the segments, with pitch measurements in the *mel* scale written into tier 4 below. The pitch measurements can also be annotated in semitones or at different Hertz settings, and they do not look hugely different; but the numbers recorded would of course differ. Other possible tiers could include pitch ranges for a particular section, or some measure of voice quality. Syllable-sized tiers may contain morphological information or other annotations.

Example 136 is a picture exported from the same file in Praat. It shows the pitch range in *mel*s on the left on a more detailed scale,

---

1 For further information, see Sleeper 2018.
2 Version 5.3.68, retrieved 20 March 2014. Internet reference: Praat: doing phonetics by computer.

Example 135 Screen capture of an annotated Praat graph (*Raven song*). There is a segmentation based on phrases in tiers 1–4, segmentation built on syllables in tier 3, and pitch measurements of these in tier 4. The *mel* scale is on the right side (spanning from 83.35 to 170.6). The numbers on the left side denote loudness and Hertz, respectively. These depend on the settings, which can be changed in order to adapt the display to matters under investigation. The vertical dotted line is the playback cursor, and the figure on top of it shows where the cursor is placed in the clip. • **14 Raven song**

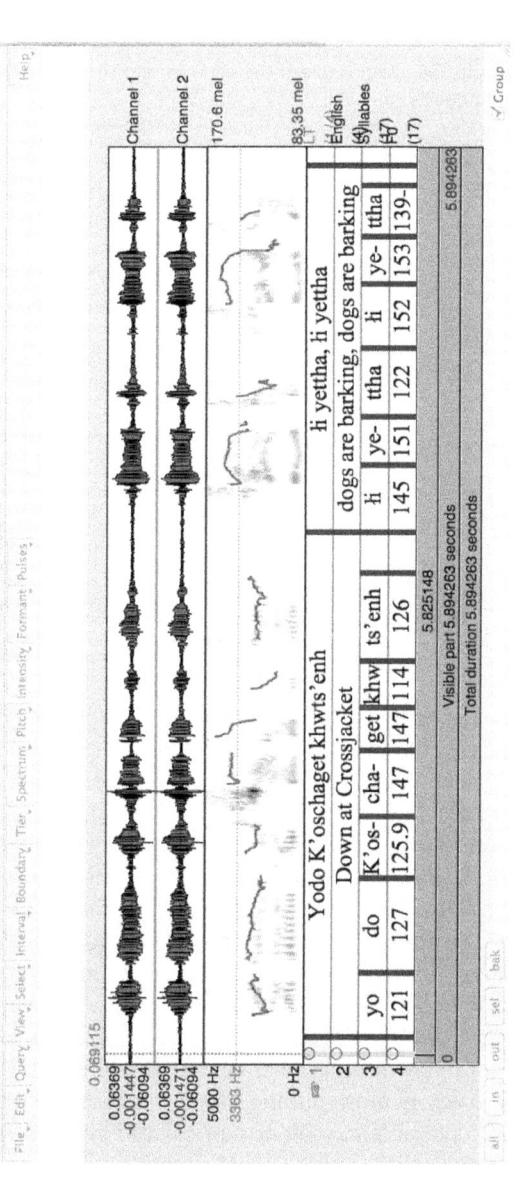

and the annotations below the pitch track. It is a little easier to read in terms of pitch and, since it is basically a line drawing, it is easier to display in print.

Example 136 Exported annotated Praat graph of Example 135 (*Raven song*).
• 14 *Raven song*

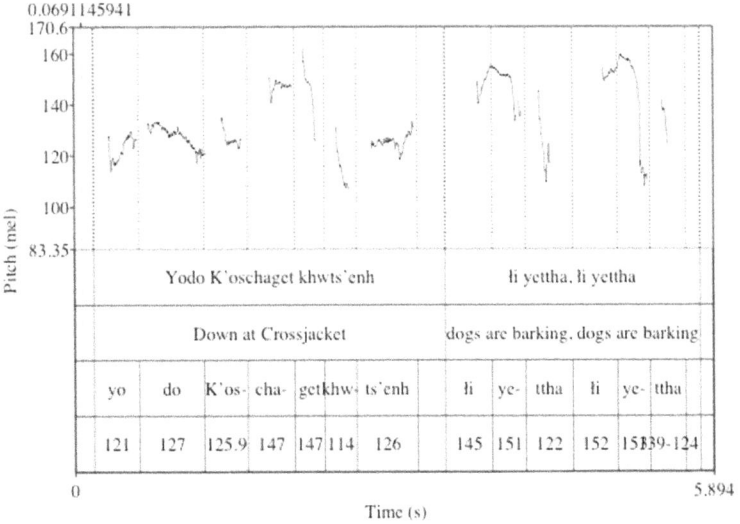

The *mel* scale used for measuring the pitch in Examples 135–136 may be changed to a scale of semitones. The scale is shown on the right (Example 137). The exported version is shown in Example 138. The semitones are numbered in relation to a fixed standard of 100 Hz, showing how many semitones above or below 100 Hz the pitch is. By using settings, it is possible to transpose a melody to a level where, for instance, the tonic is at 100 Hz. Then the indication of semitones will be relevant in relation to the tonic.

Praat was developed for linguistic analysis. As shown here, it is also useful for some musical analysis.[3] It can be used for monophonic music, that is, music consisting of a melody only, without harmony or musical accompaniment. Since most of our material in this study is monophonic, Praat has been useful in this context. It is also possible to look at musical and linguistic factors in the same display.

---

3 See further Wim van der Meer's manual, Internet reference Praat manual (for musicologists).

Example 137 Developments on the same file (*Raven song*) with new tiers showing functions of syllables (tier 5) and durations in milliseconds (tier 6). The pitch is rendered in semitones relative to 100 Hz. • **14 *Raven song***

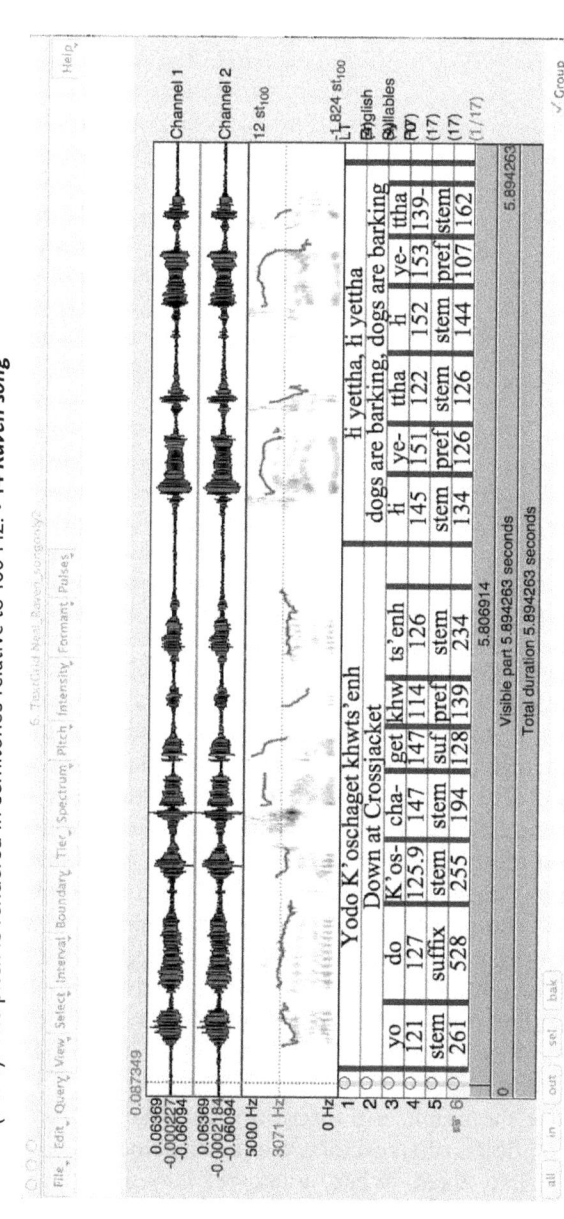

Example 138 Exported Praat graph of Example 136 (*Raven song*)
• **14 *Raven song***

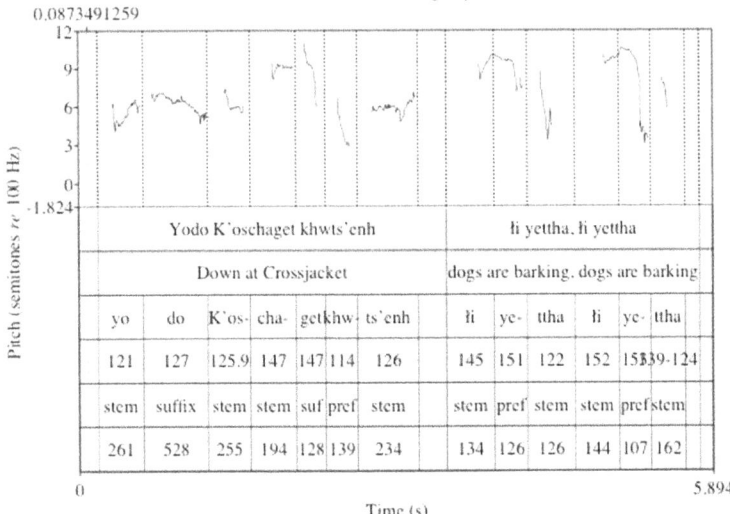

Melodyne

Melodyne was actually constructed for pitch correction.[4] It comprises many possibilities, but here it has been used only for graphic description of performances. Melodyne can take long pieces of performances, and the size (width and height) of the graph can be adjusted. The speed can also be changed for closer listening, for instance at half speed. The pitches are given in semitones in Example 139, but this can be changed to Hertz. Time is measured in seconds on the top scale, and by clicking anywhere in the graph, the pitch in Hertz at that particular moment may be obtained. Since Melodyne is developed particularly for music, the thin line in the graph shows the F0 of the performance. The wider fields – the blobs – partly surrounding this graph show amplitude but also approximate the graph to tone levels, much in the same way as a musicologist does when transcribing.

Above the graph, a transcription in notation may be selected. This notation is often useful when the movement is slow and pitches are relatively fixed. When necessary, horizontal lines (instead of arches) have been added above notes in order to indicate that they

---

4 Internet reference: Melodyne.

are tied together. Other signs that are added are self-explanatory. In more complex performances, manual revision is necessary; this is not possible in Melodyne but has to be accomplished in a separate notation program. The musical notations were made in Sibelius and Scorecloud.[5]

Example 139 The same *Raven song* as in Examples 135–138 in a Melodyne graph, with words added manually. Vertical: pitch, horizontal: time (1 shaded column = 1 second). • **14 *Raven song***

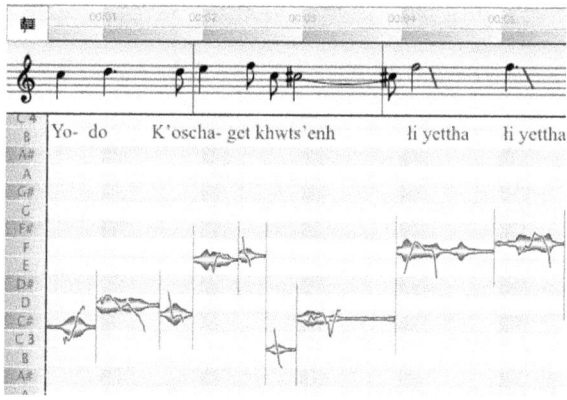

It is not possible to write text in the graph so as to add the words of a performance. A screen capture must be made, and words must be typed into the screen capture. Any other annotation can be achieved in the same manner, of course. When listening to the performance as it moves along the graph, Melodyne produces a very intuitive analysis of the sound, and it can cope with long recordings.

ELAN

ELAN was developed by The Language Archive (TLA) of the Max Planck Institute for Psycholinguistics.[6] It can be used for various kinds of measurements of audio and video files. By adding tiers for various parameters, much information can be inserted and tagged with the audio/video recording. ELAN can handle long, continuous recordings.

---

5 Internet references: Sibelius; Scorecloud.
6 Internet reference: ELAN.

Example 140 A Seediq performance on a video file in ELAN. The tiers used in this case are, from the top: melody, Seediq, gloss, translation, comments, tags.

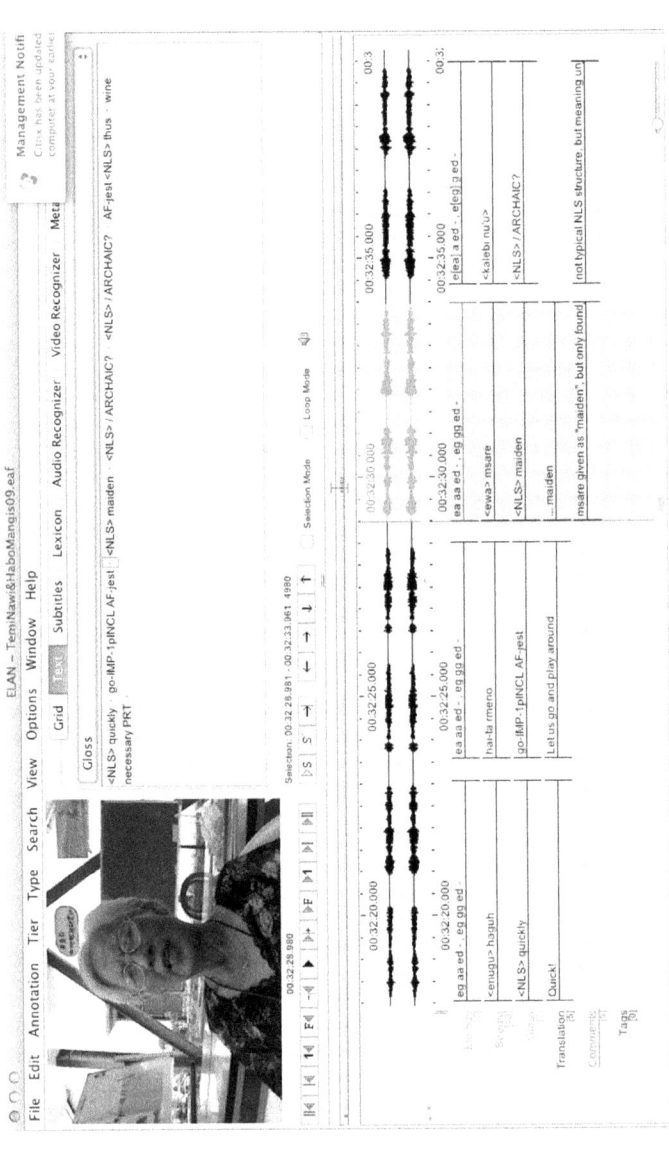

In Example 140, the first tier that starts with 'eg aa ed - ...' is an example of 'letter notation' that can also be used in Praat, although it is not technically possible to use standard music notation. This problem is also recognized by Morgan Sleeper, who uses an ABC notation developed by Christopher Walshaw for including music transcriptions in ELAN.[7]

Letter notation

C D E F G A   c d e f g a b   c' d' e' f' g' a' b'

𝅝   𝅗𝅥   𝅘𝅥   𝅘𝅥𝅮   𝅘𝅥𝅯𝅘𝅥𝅯

c3   c2   c   c̲   c̲c̲

- A punctuated note is reserved for indicating added quaver lengths. When this happens, a following letter note completes the beat. Thus, in c· d, the D is only a quaver completing the second beat, not a crotchet.
- The number notation for length is preserved across bar boundaries, otherwise indicated by:
- A crotchet pause is realized by 0.
- Long silences are lengthened by additional numbers (02 is a minim pause).
- Notes shorter than a crotchet are indicated by two letters written together: each graphic 'word', i.e. a group of letters separated by spaces, corresponds to a crotchet length. Thus, *ab* indicates a quaver A followed by a quaver B, *aba* indicates a triplet, and *ac'ba* indicates four semiquavers.
- Units of different lengths are indicated by grouping the smaller units in square brackets. Thus *e[ge]* indicates a quaver E followed by two semiquavers. For units shorter than a crotchet, punctuation indicates, as in traditional stave notation, the addition of half a length. Thus, the C in *c·d* is a punctuated quaver, while the C in *c·def* is a punctuated semiquaver.
- If the second note of a pair is punctuated, this implies that the preceding note is halved to compensate.

---

7 Sleeper 2018: 19 ff. See further Internet reference: Walshaw 2011 and 2015.

Audacity

Audacity is useful for capturing analogue sound and for converting to .wav or .aiff files.[8] The speed can be changed, and the captured sound file can be edited: cut, amplified, noise-reduced, etc. (Example 141). The factors that can be measured are amplitude and time. Audacity is easy to use for identifying and exporting audio files of, for instance, songs within comparatively long recordings that also include discussion or speech.

Example 141 The same *Raven song* as in Examples 135–138 in Audacity.
• 14 *Raven song*

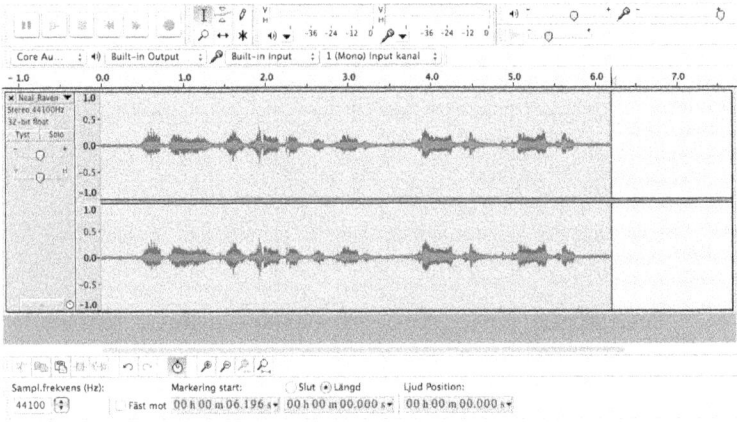

Notation software

There seems to be no notation software that is particularly suitable for musical transcription. The major Sibelius software is very flexible; but, on the other hand, it is quite difficult to use if not used on a regular basis. It is also quite costly.[9] Sibelius has been used for some of the notations. ScoreCloud has also been used for some notations.[10] It is easier to use; but, like several of the free notation software types, it was constructed in order to make the writing of conventional scores easy. For non-metric or metrically complex notations, it is necessary to find ways of neutralizing a

---

8 Internet reference: Audacity.
9 Internet reference: Sibelius.
10 Internet reference: ScoreCloud.

number of automatic functions. Since the number of signs is limited, it is sometimes necessary to add signs manually to the final notation. Adding words is simple, and various phonetic signs can be used. ScoreCloud has a function enabling it to import audio-files for automatic notation. Editing such notations is, however, more time consuming than transcribing the recording manually. While far from perfect, the automatic notation of Melodyne is actually faster and can be used in order to facilitate manual transcription (cf. Example 139).

Appendix 2
Number notation[1]

Octaves:

Number: 1 2 3 4 5 6 7   1 2 3 4 5 6 7   1 2 3 4 5 6 7
Corresponds to   C D E F G A B   c d e f g a b   c' d' e' f' g' a' b'

Comment: The range in our material is normally less than an octave.

Length:

Whole note (semibreve):	𝅝	1 – – –	Dotted whole:	𝅝.	1 – – – – –
Half note (minim):	𝅗𝅥	1 –	Dotted half:	𝅗𝅥.	1 – –
Quarter note (crotchet):	♩	1	Dotted quarter:	♩.	1·
Eighth note (quaver):	♪	<u>1</u>	Dotted eighth:	♪.	<u>1</u>·
Sixteenth note (semiquaver):	𝅘𝅥𝅯	<u>1</u>	Dotted sixteenth:	𝅘𝅥𝅯.	<u>1</u>·

Other signs:

Pause: 0
Raised (by a semitone):   ♯1, ♯2 etc.
Lowered (by a semitone):   ♭1, ♭2 etc.
Returned to normal: ♮1, ♮2 etc.
Slightly higher pitch: $1^+, 2^+$ etc.
Slightly lower pitch: $1^-, 2^-$ etc.
Glissando (sliding between tones):   ⇒

---

1   See further Internet reference: Numbered musical notation.

Original pitch:

Original pitch for 1 in number notation or 'c' in letter notation is presented separately, for example: 1 = 220 Hz or c = 220 Hz.

Appendix 3
Terminology used

Term	Field	Meaning
Affix	Ling.	Prefix or suffix
Anaphor	Ling.	A phrase that refers back to the previous phrase
Aspirated	Ling.	A consonant that is followed by a puff of air
Base (syllable)	Ling.	The original syllable whose vowel is reduplicated; see 'Reduplication'
Boundary tone	Ling.	For instance, rising pitch at the end of questions
Chain-rhyme	Poet.	One of the last words of a line rhymes with one of the first in the following line
Coda	Mus.	An 'extra' musical phrase that ends a piece
	Ling.	The final consonant(s) of a syllable
Contour	Mus.	The graphic form of a melody in pitch and time
Contrastive	Ling.	Speech sounds that distinguish meanings, e.g. *p* and *b* in English (*pill* vs. *bill*)
Crotchet	Mus.	Quarter note. Tone often coinciding with the beat of a tune, notated: ♩
Downstep	Ling.	A lowering of pitch at the end of a phrase
Epenthetic vowel	Ling.	A vowel added in a word to make pronunciation easier
F0	Ling.	Fundamental frequency (first harmonic) of e.g. the sound of a voice
Final formula	Mus.	A distinct and recurring ending
Formulaic	Mus.	Built on often recurring basic formulae
Glissando	Mus.	Sliding between two pitches
Gloss	Ling.	Translation of a word or part of a word
Iambic	Poet.	Poetic foot: short + long

Appendix 3: Terminology used

Term	Field	Meaning
Inflectional morphology	Ling.	Change of the form of a word that has a grammatical function, e.g. addition of the plural marker -s in English
Initial formula	Mus.	A distinct and recurring starting pattern
Interval	Mus.	The distance between two pitches
Intonation	Ling.	Pitch and stress pattern in speech
Isorhythm	Mus.	A rhythm pattern (of a melody) that dominates a tune
Language-centred		Part of vocal expression dominated by linguistic patterns
Laryngeal	Ling.	Sound produced by the larynx, e.g. [h]
Laryngealization	Ling.	Articulation with laryngeal modification
Lexical tone	Ling.	Tones that differentiate words; e.g. tones in Kammu: high (*kláaŋ* 'eagle') vs. low (*klàaŋ* 'stone')
Line	Poet.	In oral tradition, usually defined by a long final syllable and/or a pause
Litany	Mus.	Poetry built on consecutive series of repeated phrases
Long vowel	Ling.	A vowel that has long duration and usually contrasts with a short vowel
Major syllable	Ling.	In e.g. Kammu, an 'ordinary' syllable that contains a vowel; e.g. *mú* in *kmmú* 'human being'
Melody-centred		Part of vocal expression dominated by melody
Minimal pair	Ling.	Pair of words that differ in only one element (e.g. lexical tone); cf. 'contrastive'
Minor syllable	Ling.	In e.g. Kammu, a short unstressed pre-syllable; e.g. *km* in *kmmú* 'human being'
Mono-melodic	Mus.	Music organized so that different sets of words are performed to the same melody or melodic frame
Mora	Ling.	The smallest rhythmical unit in languages like Japanese

(continued)

Term	Field	Meaning
Morphology	Ling.	How words are built from smaller meaningful elements such as prefixes, roots, and suffixes (e.g. *un-load-ed*)
Music-centred		Part of vocal expression dominated by musical patterns
Onset	Ling.	The initial consonant(s) of a syllable
Original	Mus.	A theoretically conceived basic form of an orally transmitted piece of music
Performance template	Mus.	A tool for analysis of a performer's assumed mental image of a vocal expression
Phonotactics	Ling.	How speech sounds can be combined in syllables or words
Phrase	Ling.	A group of words that in some way forms a unit
Pitch	Mus.	Tone height
Pitch level	Mus.	The approximate position of a number of tones
Prefix	Ling.	A meaningful element added at the beginning of a word, e.g. *un-* in *unstable*
Prosody	Ling.	Properties of a word or phrase such as stress, tone, and intonation
Pulsating tones	Mus.	Long tones with rhythmically organized glottal stops common in Native American music
Quaver	Mus.	Eighth-note. Short tone. Half the length of a crotchet. Notated: ♪
Range	Mus.	The interval between the lowest and the highest tones of a performance
Reduplication	Ling.	Repetition of all or part of a word. For example, Kammu *nàaŋ* can be reduplicated as *nàaŋ-a*; *nàaŋ* is called the base and -a the reduplicant
Refrain	Mus.	Recurring musical phrase, often at the end of a stanza
Schwa vowel	Ling.	See 'Epenthetic vowel'
Semiquaver	Mus.	Sixteenth-note. Very short tone. Half as long as a quaver. Notated: ♬

Appendix 3: Terminology used

Term	Field	Meaning
Semitone	Mus.	The smallest interval in the diatonic musical scale, used e.g. in the tuning of pianos
Sequence	Mus.	Short melodic motif repeated in a descending or ascending series
Short vowel	Ling.	See 'Long vowel'
Sonorant	Ling.	A consonant that can be sung, like [m] or [l]
Speech melody	Ling.	Intonation
	Mus.	Melodic movement strongly depending on intonation
Stanza	Poet.	In orally transmitted vocal expressions, a unit of two or more lines with a clear ending
Stop	Ling.	A consonant such as [p] or [t] produced by stopping the airflow
Suffix	Ling.	A meaningful element added at the end of a word, e.g. *-ed* in *followed*
Syllable	Ling.	A part of a word usually consisting of a vowel preceded and followed by consonants. For example, the word *consist* consists of the syllables *con* and *sist*
Tone-centred		Part of vocal expression dominated by lexical tones
Tone duration	Mus.	The length of a musical tone
Tone repetition	Mus.	Series of repeated tones on the same pitch, often occurring at the end of musical phrases in Native American music
Tonic	Mus.	The basic tone, in oral traditions usually the tone that dominates the piece (in time) and often coincides with the final tone
Transposition	Mus.	Moving a melody to a higher or lower position. Here mainly in order to avoid complex notation or to make tunes easily comparable

(continued)

Term	Field	Meaning
Unaspirated	Ling.	A consonant that is not aspirated (not followed by a puff of air)
Undulating	Mus.	Melody progressing in 'wave-form' (cf. 'Contour')
Variant	Mus.	Variations of orally transmitted pieces of music that developed over a period of time, cf. 'Original'
Vocable	Ling.	A syllable or word that is non-lexical, i.e. has no meaning
Vocal expression	Mus.	Those expressions that differ from 'normal speech'
Vocal genre	Mus.	Sub-category of vocal expression
Vowel	Ling.	A speech sound produced with a relatively open vocal tract and vibration of the vocal cords
Vowel onset	Ling.	The beginning of a vowel

References

Addo, Akosua Obuo 2013. 'What's in a singing game? Exploring children's oral literature'. In Asimeng-Boahene, Lewis and Michael Baffoe (eds): *African traditional and oral literature as pedagogical tools in content area classrooms: Pre-K-12*. Charlotte, NC: Information Age Publishing, 21–41.

Banti, Giorgio and Francesco Giannattasio 2006 (2004). 'Poetry'. In Duranti, Alessandro (ed.): *A companion to linguistic anthropology*. Oxford: Blackwell, 290–320.

Barnhardt, Carol 2001. 'A history of schooling for Alaska native people'. *Journal of American Indian Education* 40: 1, 1–30.

Barwick, Linda 2006. 'A musicologist's wishlist: Some issues, practices and practicalities in musical aspects of language documentation'. *Language Documentation and Description* 3, 53–62.

Barwick, Linda, Bruce Birch, and Nicholas Evans 2007. 'Iwaidja Jurtbirrk songs: Bringing language and music together'. *Australian Aboriginal Studies* 2, 6–34.

Baudhuin, R. F. (ed.) 1960. *Selected readings translated from traditions and myths of the Taiwan aborigines: Compiled by Ogawa and Asai, c. 1930*. University of San Francisco: Ricci Institute.

Bengtsson, Ingmar, Per-Arne Tove, and Stig-Magnus Thorsén 1972. 'Sound analysis equipment and rhythm research ideas at the Institute of Musicology in Uppsala'. In Emsheimer, Ernst (ed.): *Studia instrumentorum musicae popularis*, vol. 2. Stockholm: Musikhistoriska museet [Museum of music history], 53–76.

Bialystok, Ellen 2001. *Bilingualism in development: Language, literacy and cognition*. Cambridge: Cambridge University Press.

Blacking, John 1965. 'The role of music in the culture of the Venda of the northern Transvaal'. In Kolinski, Mieczyslaw (ed.): *Studies in ethnomusicology*, vol. 2. New York, NY: Oak Publications, 20–53.

Brabec de Mori, Bernd 2017. 'Musical spirits and powerful voices: On the origins of song'. *Yearbook for Traditional Music* 49, 114–128.

Bracknell, Clint 2017. 'Conceptualizing Noongar song'. *Yearbook for Traditional Music* 49, 92–113.

Brown, Steven 2000. 'The "Musilanguage" model of music evolution'. In Wallin, Nils L., Björn Merker, and Steven Brown (eds): *The origins of music*. Cambridge, MA: The MIT Press, 271–300.

Brown, Steven and Joseph Jordania 2011. 'Universals in the world's musics'. *Psychology of Music* 41: 2, 229–248.

Chafe, Wallace 2001. 'The analysis of discourse flow'. In Schiffrin, Deborah, Deborah Tannen, and Heidi E. Hamilton (eds): *The handbook of discourse analysis*. Oxford: Blackwell, 671–687.

Chow, Ivan and Steven Brown 2018. 'A musical approach to speech melody'. *Frontiers in Psychology* 9: Article 247, 1–17.

Compton, Carol J. 1979. *Courting poetry in Laos: A textual and linguistic analysis*. DeKalb, IL: Northern Illinois University, Center for Southeast Asian Studies.

Coray, Craig 2007. *Dnaghekt'ana qut'ana k'eli ahdelyax (They sing the songs of many peoples): The 1954 Nondalton recordings of John Coray*. Anchorage, AK: Kijik Corporation [with CD].

Coulter, Neil R. 2011. 'Assessing music shift: Adapting EGIDS for a Papua New Guinea community'. *Language Documentation and Description* 10, 61–81.

Cox, Gordon and Robin Stevens (eds) 2010. *The origins and foundations of music education: Cross-cultural historical studies of music in compulsory schooling*. London: Continuum.

Cross, Ian 2012. 'Music as a social and cognitive process'. In Rebuschat, Patrick, Martin Rohrmeier, John A. Hawkins, and Ian Cross (eds): *Language and music as cognitive systems*. Oxford: Oxford University Press, 315–328.

Crupi, Vanna Viola 2014. 'The relationship between language and music in the Bakonzo culture, Uganda'. *Jahrbuch des Phonogrammarchivs der Österreichischen Akademie der Wissenschaften* 4, 63–80.

Dell, François 2011. 'Singing in Tashlhiyt Berber, a language that allows vowel-less syllables'. In Cairn, Charles E. and Eric Raimy (eds): *Handbook of the syllable*. Leiden: Brill, 173–193.

Dixon, Robert M. W. and Grace Koch 1996. *Dyirbal song poetry: The oral literature of an Australian rainforest people*. St Lucia, Queensland: University of Queensland Press.

Emeneau, Murray Barnson 1966. 'Style and meaning in an oral literature'. *Journal of the Linguistic Society of America* 42: 2, 323–345.

—— 1971. *Toda songs*. Oxford: Clarendon Press.

Engelhardt, Jeffers and Estelle Amy de la Bretèque (guest eds) 2017. *Yearbook for Traditional Music* 49.

Engstrand, Lennart, Marie Widén, Björn Widén, Kàm Ràw (Damrong Tayanin), and Jan-Olof Svantesson 2009. 'A checklist of Kammu plant names'. *Mon-Khmer Studies* 38, 223–248.

Évrard, Olivier 2012. 'Following Kàm Ràw's trail'. In Tayanin, Damrong and Kristina Lindell, *Hunting and fishing in a Kammu village: Revisiting a classic study in Southeast Asian ethnography*. Copenhagen: NIAS Press, 1–28.

Ewald, Otto 2013. 'Signaling discourse structure: The marking of discourse topic boundaries in Jahai and Mah Meri spontaneous narratives'. Bachelor's thesis, Lund University, Centre for Languages and Literature. https://www.lunduniversity.lu.se/lup/publication/3410917.

Fabb, Nigel 1997. *Linguistics and literature*. Oxford: Blackwell.

Fast, Phyllis 2002. *Northern Athabascan survival: Women, community, and the future*. Omaha, NE: University of Nebraska Press.

Feld, Steven 1974. 'Linguistic models in ethnomusicology'. *Ethnomusicology* 18: 2, 197–217.

—— 1982. *Sound and sentiment: Birds, weeping, poetics, and song in Kaluli expression*. Philadelphia, PA: University of Pennsylvania Press.

—— 1990. 'Wept thoughts: The voicing of Kaluli memories'. *Oral Tradition* 5: 2–3, 241–266.

Feld, Steven and Aaron A. Fox 1994. 'Music and language'. *Annual Review of Anthropology* 23, 25–53.

Finnegan, Ruth 1988. *Literacy and orality: Studies in the technology of communication*. Oxford: Blackwell.

—— 1992 (1977). *Oral poetry: Its nature, significance and social context*. Bloomington, IN: Indiana University Press.

Frisbie, Charlotte J. 1980. 'Vocables in Navajo ceremonial music'. *Ethnomusicology* 24: 3, 347–392.

Fürniss, Susanne 2006. 'Aka polyphony: Music, theory, back and forth'. In Tenzer, Michael (ed.): *Analytical studies in world music*. Oxford: Oxford University Press, 163–204.

Gillan, Matt 2012. *Songs from the edge of Japan: Music-making in Yaeyama and Okinawa*. Farnham: Ashgate Publishing.

Grant, Catherine 2014. *Music endangerment: How language maintenance can help*. Oxford: Oxford University Press.

Gussenhoven, Carlos 2004. *The phonology of tone and intonation*. Cambridge: Cambridge University Press.

Hansson, Inga-Lill 1983. 'Death in an Akha village'. In McKinnon, John and Wanat Bhruksasri (eds): *Highlanders of Thailand*. Kuala Lumpur: Oxford University Press, 279–290.

—— 1991. 'The language of Akha ritual texts'. *Linguistics of the Tibeto-Burman Area* 14: 2, 155–167.

—— 1994. 'The wonderful words of Akha'. In Lauritzson, Gun (ed.): *Cooperation East and West – continued: Ten years with the Programme for East and Southeast Asian Studies*. Lund: Lund University Programme for East and Southeast Asian Studies, 18–30.

—— 2014. 'Grammatical aesthetics of ritual texts in Akha'. In Williams, Jeffrey P. (ed.): *The aesthetics of grammar: Sound and meaning in the languages of mainland Southeast Asia*. Cambridge: Cambridge University Press, 280–288.

―― 2017. 'Akha'. In Thurgood, Graham and Randy J. LaPolla (eds): *The Sino-Tibetan languages* (2nd edn). London: Routledge, 885–900. [Originally published in 2003.]

Herzog, George 1935. 'Special song types in North American Indian music'. *Zeitschrift für vergleichende Musikwissenschaft* 3, 22–33.

Hinton, Leanne 2010. 'Language revitalization in North America and the new direction of linguistics'. *Transforming Anthropology* 18: 1, 35–41.

Holmer, Arthur 1996. *A parametric grammar of Seediq*. Lund: Lund University Press.

―― 2005. 'Verb serialization in Kammu'. *Working Papers* (Lund University, Department of Linguistics) 51, 65–84.

Honigmann, John J. 1981. 'Expressive aspects of Subarctic Indian culture'. In Helm, June (ed.): *Handbook of North American Indians*. Washington, DC: Smithsonian Institution, 718–738.

Hsu, Tsang-Houei and Shui-Cheng Cheng 1992. *Musique de Taiwan*. Paris: Maisnie-Trédaniel.

Ikuta, Hiroko 2010. 'Eskimo language and Eskimo song in Alaska: A sociolinguistics of deglobalisation in endangered language'. *Pragmatics* 20: 2, 171–189.

Ingram, Catherine 2012. 'Tradition and divergence in Southwestern China: Kam Big Song singing in the village and on stage'. *The Asia Pacific Journal of Anthropology* 13: 5, 434–453.

Jakobson, Roman 1987. 'Linguistics and poetics'. In Pomorska, Krystyna and Stephen Rudy (eds): *Language in literature*. Cambridge, MA: The Belknap Press, 62–94. [Originally published in 1960.]

Jetté, Jules and Eliza Jones 2000. *Koyukon Athabaskan dictionary*. Fairbanks, AK: Alaska Native Language Center.

Johnston, Thomas F. 1993. 'The social role of Alaska Athabascan potlatch dancing'. *Dance: Current selected research*, vol. 3, 183–226 [Reprinted in *Alaskan Indian dance*. Fairbanks, AK: University of Alaska 1994.]

Johnston, Thomas F., Madeline Solomon, Eliza Jones, and Tupou Pulu 1978. *Koyukon Athabascan dance songs*. Anchorage, AK: National Bilingual Materials Development Center.

Kari, James 1994. Lower Tanana Athabaskan dictionary. Unpublished manuscript.

Kari, James and James A. Fall 2003. *Shem Pete's Alaska*. Fairbanks, AK: University of Alaska Press. (First edition 1987).

Karlsson, Anastasia, David House, and Jan-Olof Svantesson 2012. 'Intonation adapts to lexical tone: The case of Kammu'. *Phonetica* 69: 1–2, 28–47.

―― 2015. 'Prosodic signaling of information and discourse structure from a typological perspective'. In The Scottish Consortium for ICPhS 2015 (ed.): *Proceedings of the 18th International Congress of Phonetic Sciences*. Glasgow: the University of Glasgow, paper number 0013.

Karlsson, Anastasia, Håkan Lundström, and Jan-Olof Svantesson 2018. 'Coordination between lexical tones and melody in traditional Kammu singing'. *Journal of the Phonetic Society of Japan* 22, 30–41.

Karlsson, Anastasia, Håkan Lundström, Jan-Olof Svantesson, and Siri Tuttle 2014. 'Speech and song: investigating the borderland'. *Jahrbuch des Phonogrammarchivs der Österreichischen Akademie der Wissenschaften* 4, 142–179.

Karlsson, Anastasia, Jan-Olof Svantesson, and David House 2013. 'Multi-functionality of prosodic boundaries in spontaneous narratives in Kammu'. In Mertens, Piet and Anne Catherine Simon (eds): *Proceedings of the Prosody–Discourse Interface Conference 2013*. Leuven: University of Leuven, 45–49.

Karlsson, Anastasia, Jan-Olof Svantesson, and Håkan Lundström 2018. 'Phonetic and phonological approaches to the study of singing'. *Journal of the Phonetic Society of Japan* 22: 3, 29.

Kawakami, Shin 1973. 'Nihongo onsuuritu no saikentoo' [Re-examination of the rhythm of Japanese verse]. In *Onisi hakusi kiju kinen onseigaku seikai ronbunshu* [Worldwide anthology of papers in phonetics in honor of Dr Onishi's seventy-seventh birthday]. Tokyo: Phonetic Society of Japan, 665–671.

Kneutgen, Johannes 1970. 'Eine Musikform und ihre biologische Funktion: über die Wirkungsweise der Wiegenlieder [The biological function of a category of music: on the effect of lullabies]'. *Zeitschrift für experimentelle angewandte Psychologie* 17: 2, 245–265.

Ladd, D. Robert and James P. Kirby 2020. 'Tone–melody matching in tone language singing'. In Gussenhoven, Carlos and Aoju Chen (eds): *The Oxford handbook of language prosody*. Oxford University Press, 676–688.

Lawson, Francesca R. Sborgi 2011. *The narrative arts of Tianjin: Between music and language*. Farnham: Ashgate Publishing.

Lindell, Kristina 1988. 'Rhyme-pivot sayings in northern Kammu'. In Littrup, Leif (ed.): *Analecta Hafniensia: 25 years of East Asian studies in Copenhagen*. London: Curzon Press, 88–99.

Lindell, Kristina, Håkan Lundström, Jan-Olof Svantesson, and Damrong Tayanin 1982. *The Kammu year: Its lore and music*. London: Curzon Press.

Lindell, Kristina, Jan-Öjvind Swahn, and Damrong Tayanin 1977. *A Kammu story-listener's tales*. London: Curzon Press.

—— 1980. *Folk tales from Kammu II: A story-teller's tales*. London: Curzon Press.

—— 1984. *Folk tales from Kammu III: Pearls of Kammu literature*. London: Curzon Press.

—— 1989. *Folk tales from Kammu IV: A master-teller's tales*. London: Curzon Press.

—— 1995. *Folk tales from Kammu V: A young story-teller's tales*. London: Curzon Press.

—— 1998. *Folk tales from Kammu VI: A teller's last tales*. London: Curzon Press.

List, George 1961. 'Speech melody and song melody in central Thailand'. *Ethnomusicology* 5: 1, 16–32.
—— 1963. 'The boundaries of speech and song'. *Ethnomusicology* 7: 1, 1–16.
—— 1974. 'The reliability of transcription'. *Ethnomusicology* 18: 3, 353–404.
Loh, I-to 1982. 'Tribal music of Taiwan: With special reference to the Ami and Puyuma styles'. PhD Diss., University of California, Los Angeles.
Lomax, Alan (ed.) 1968. *Folk song style and culture*. Washington, DC: American Association for the Advancement of Science.
Lord, Albert B. 1960. *The singer of tales*. Cambridge, MA: Harvard University Press.
Lovick, Olga and Siri Tuttle 2012. 'Prosody of Dena'ina narrative discourse'. *International Journal of American Linguistics* 78: 3, 293–334.
Lundström, Håkan 1980. 'North Athabascan story songs and dance songs'. In Rooth, Anna Birgitta (ed.): *The Alaska seminar*. Stockholm: Almqvist and Wiksell, 126–164.
—— 2010. *I will send my song: Kammu vocal genres in the singing of Kam Raw*. Copenhagen: NIAS Press [with CD].
—— 2012. 'Music education from a slightly different perspective'. In McPherson, Gary E. and Graham F. Welch (eds): *The Oxford handbook of music education, Vol. II*. Oxford: Oxford University Press, 651–656.
—— 2014. 'Beautifying techniques in Kammu vocal genres'. In Williams, Jeffrey P. (ed.): *The aesthetics of grammar: Sound and meaning in the languages of mainland Southeast Asia*. Cambridge: Cambridge University Press, 118–132.
—— 2018. 'Music among ethnic minorities in Southeast Asia'. In Bader, Rolf (ed.): *Springer handbook of systematic musicology*. Berlin: Springer-Verlag, 987–1004.
Lundström, Håkan and Jan-Olof Svantesson 1996. 'Features of Kammu music terminology – a musico-linguistic study'. In *Pan-Asiatic Linguistics. Proceedings of the Fourth International Symposium on Language and Linguistics, January 8–10, 1996*. Bangkok: Institute of Language and Culture for Rural Development, Mahidol University at Salaya, vol. IV, 1528–1534.
—— 2005. 'Kammu som tonspråk [Kammu as a tonal language]'. In Lundström and Svantesson (eds) 2005, 131–140.
—— 2008. 'Hrlïi singing and word-tones in Kammu'. *Working Papers* (Lund University, Department of Linguistics) 53, 117–131.
Lundström, Håkan and Jan-Olof Svantesson (eds) 2005. *Kammu: om ett folk i Laos* [Kammu: about a people in Laos]. Lund: Lunds universitetshistoriska sällskap.
Lundström, Håkan and Damrong Tayanin 1982. 'Music in the fields'. In Lindell, Lundström, Svantesson, and Tayanin 1982, 60–160, 169–171.

—— 2006. *Kammu songs: The songs of Kam Raw*. Copenhagen: NIAS Press.
Madison, Curt, Neal Charlie, and Charlie Titus 2011. *Hitting sticks, healing hearts*. DVD produced by River Tracks productions and KUAC-TV, Fairbanks, Alaska.
Madison, Curt, Tony Scott Pearce, Leonard Kamerling, Carlos Frank, and Garry Russell 1985. *Songs in Minto life*. VHS video produced by Kyuk Video Productions, Bethel, Alaska.
Marett, Allan and Linda Barwick. 2001. 'Endangered songs and endangered languages'. In Blythe, Joe and R. McKenna Brown (eds): *Maintaining the links: Language identity and the land: Seventh conference of the Foundation for Endangered Languages*. Bath: Foundation for Endangered Languages, 144–151.
Marett, Allan and Linda Barwick (eds) 2007. *Studies in Aboriginal song*. (*Australian Aboriginal Studies* 2007: 2).
Marsh, Kathryn 2008. *The musical playground: Global tradition and change in children's songs and games*. Oxford: Oxford University Press.
Mehr, Samuel A. and Manvir Singh 2018. 'A natural history of song'. Working paper. www.themusiclab.org/ [accessed 3 April 2019].
Merriam, Alan P. 1964. *The anthropology of music*. Evanston, IL: Northwestern University Press.
Miller, Terry E. 1985. *Traditional music of the Lao: Kaen playing and mawlum singing in northeast Thailand*. Westport, CT: Greenwood Press.
Minks, Amanda 2013. *Voices of play: Miskitu children's speech and song on the Atlantic coast of Nicaragua*. Tucson, AZ: The University of Arizona Press.
Mischler, Craig 1993. *The crooked stovepipe: Athapaskan fiddle music and square dancing in Northeast Alaska and Northwest Canada*. Champaign, IL: University of Illinois Press.
Mithen, Steven 2007. *The singing Neanderthals: The origins of music, language, mind, and body*. Cambridge, MA: Harvard University Press.
Mithun, Marianne 1999. *The languages of Native North America*. Cambridge: Cambridge University Press.
Moberg, Carl-Allan 1950. 'Två kapitel om svensk folkmusik: 2. Ro, ro till fiskeskär'. *Swedish Journal of Musicology* 32, 25–49 [In German: 'Ro, ro till fiskeskär' in *Studien zur schwedischen Volksmusik*. Uppsala: *Studia musicologica Upsaliensia*. Nova Series 5, 1971.]
Morey, Stephen and Jürgen Schöpf 2011. 'Tone in speech and singing: A field experiment to research their relation in endangered languages of North East India'. *Language Documentation and Description* 10, 37–60.
Mulder, Jean 1994. 'Structural organization in Coast Tsimshian music'. *Ethnomusicology* 38: 1, 81–125.
Nagano-Madsen, Yasuko 1992. *Mora and prosodic coordination: A phonetic study of Japanese, Eskimo, and Yoruba*. Lund: Lund University Press.

—— 2011. 'Intonation in Ryukyuan: With reference to modality, syntax, and focus'. *Language Documentation and Description* 10, 177–207.

—— 2015. 'Intonation in Okinawan'. In Heinrich, Patrick, Shinsho Miyara, and Michinori Shimoji (eds): *Handbook of the Ryukyuan languages*. Berlin: De Gruyter Mouton, 199–225.

—— 2016. 'Lexical H*+L pitch accent in Ryukyuan: diversities in phonological patterning and phonetic manifestation', in Barnes, Jon, Alejna Brugos, Stefanie Shattuck-Hufnagel, and Nanette Veilleux (eds): *Speech Prosody 2016: Proceedings of the 8th International Conference on Speech Prosody, Boston University*. Baixas: International Speech Communication Association, 455–458.

Nelson, Richard K. 1983. *Make prayers to the Raven: A Koyukon view of the northern forest*. Chicago, IL: Chicago University Press.

Nettl, Bruno 1974. 'Thoughts on improvisation: A comparative approach'. *The Musical Quarterly* 40: 1, 1–19.

Nguyen Van Huyen 1954. *Les chants alternés des garçons et des filles en Annam*. Paris: Paul Geuthner.

Ó Briain, Lonán 2018. *Musical minorities: The sounds of Hmong ethnicity in Northern Vietnam*. New York, NY: Oxford University Press.

Oesch, Hans 1979. 'The music of the hilltribes in Northern Thailand'. *Journal of the National Research Council of Thailand* 11: 2, 1–26.

Ogura Hyakunin Isshu Rôei kasetto têpu [Chanting cassette tape of Ogura Anthology of 'One Hundred Tanka by One Hundred Poets'] n.d. Rôei [chanting]: Yamada Akira. Kabushiki gaisha Daiwa [Daiwa Co. Ltd.]: TBS Sābisu [TBS Service].

O'Keeffe, Isabel 2007. 'Sung and spoken: An analysis of two different versions of a Kun-barlang love song'. *Australian Aboriginal Studies* 2007: 2, 46–62.

—— 2017. 'Multilingual manyardi: manifestations of multilingualism in the manyardi/kun-borrk song traditions of Western Arnhem Land'. PhD diss., University of Melbourne.

Ostler, Nicolas and Brenda W. Lintinger (eds) 2015. *The music of endangered languages, FEL XIX–NOLA, New Orleans, October 7–9*. Hungerford, England: Foundation for Endangered Languages.

Patel, Aniruddh 2008. *Music, language, and the brain*. Oxford: Oxford University Press.

Pearce, Tony Scott 1985. 'Musical characteristics of Tanana Athabascan dance songs'. Master's thesis, University of Alaska, Fairbanks. [With sound recordings].

Pian, Rulan Chao 1993. 'Text setting and the use of tune types in Chinese dramatic and narrative music'. In Wade, Bonnie C. (ed.): *Text, tone, and tune: Parameters of music in multicultural perspective*. New Delhi: Oxford and IBH Publishing, 201–234.

Pooley, Thomas M. 2018. 'Depressing melodies: Consonants and tone in Zulu song'. *Journal of the Phonetic Society of Japan* 22: 3, 42–49.

Poser, William J. 1990. 'Foot structure in Japanese'. *Language* 66: 1, 78–105.
Proschan, Frank 1989. 'Kmhmu verbal art in America: The poetics of Kmhmu verse'. PhD diss., University of Texas at Austin. [UMI no. 9016959].
Proto, Teresa 2015. 'Prosody, melody and rhythm in vocal music: The problem of textsetting in a linguistic perspective'. *Linguistics in the Netherlands* 32: 1, 116–129.
Rooth, Anna Birgitta 1971. *The Alaska expedition 1966*. Lund: Lund University.
—— 1976. *The importance of storytelling*. Uppsala: Uppsala University.
Rooth, Anna Birgitta (ed.) 1980. *The Alaska seminar*. Stockholm: Almqvist and Wiksell.
Rzeszutek, Tom, Patrick E. Savage, and Steven Brown 2011. 'The structure of crosscultural musical diversity'. *Proceedings of The Royal Society B: Biological Sciences* 279: 1733, 1606–1612.
Savage, Patrick E. and Steven Brown 2013. 'Toward a new comparative musicology'. *Analytical Approaches to World Music* 2: 2.
Savage, Patrick E., Emily Merritt, Tom Rzeszutek, and Steven Brown 2012. 'CantoCore: A new cross-cultural song classification scheme'. *Analytical Approaches to World Music* 2: 1, 87–137.
Schellenberg, Murray 2014. 'Studying tone and singing in the laboratory'. *Jahrbuch des Phonogrammarchivs der Österreichischen Akademie der Wissenschaften* 4, 195–208.
—— 2017. 'Music, notation and the representation of lexical tone'. Helsinki Second International Workshop on the history of Speech Communication Research. www.researchgate.net/publication/324485021_Music_notation_and_the_representation_of_lexical_tone.
Schimmelpenninck, Antoinet 1997. *Chinese folk songs and folk singers: Shan'ge traditions in southern Jiangsu*. Leiden: Chime Foundation.
Schippers, Huib 2010. *Facing the music: Shaping music education from a global perspective*. New York, NY: Oxford University Press.
Schippers, Huib and Catherine Grant (eds) 2016. *Sustainable futures for music cultures: An ecological perspective*. New York, NY: Oxford University Press.
Schöpf, Jürgen (guest ed.) 2014. *Jahrbuch 4 des Phonogrammarchivs der Österreichischen Akademie der Wissenschaften*. Göttingen: Cuvillier Verlag.
Seeger, Anthony 1987. *Why Suyá sing: A musical anthropology of an Amazonian people*. Cambridge: Cambridge University Press.
Seeger, Charles (moderator) 1964. 'Symposium on transcription and analysis: A Hukwe song with musical bow'. *Ethnomusicology* 8: 3, 223–277.
Sleeper, Morgan Thomas 2018. 'Musicolinguistics: New methodologies for integrating musical and linguistic data'. PhD diss., University of California, Santa Barbara.
Slobodin, Richard 1981. 'Kutchin'. In Helm, June (ed.): *Handbook of North American Indians*. Washington, DC: Smithsonian Institution, 514–532.

Smith, John D. 1979. 'Metre and text in Western India'. *Bulletin of the School of African and Oriental Studies* 42: 2, 347–357.
—— 1991. *The epic of Pâbûjî: A study, transcription and translation.* Cambridge: Cambridge University Press.
Stobart, Henry 2006. *Music and the poetics of production in the Bolivian Andes.* Farnham: Ashgate Publishing.
Stone, Achara J. and Håkan Lundström 2000. *Sleep, close your two eyes ... Thai lullabies and nursery rhymes collected by Achara Jaiyaqam Stone.* Malmö: Malmö Academy of Music, Lund University, Sweden MMHCD 2008 [CD and booklet].
Svantesson, Jan-Olof 1983. *Kammu phonology and morphology.* Lund: Gleerup.
—— 2011. 'The representation of Tai onsets in Kammu loanwords'. *Linguistics of the Tibeto-Burman Area* 34, 27–84.
Svantesson, Jan-Olof, Niclas Burenhult, Arthur Holmer, Anastasia Karlsson, and Håkan Lundström (eds) 2011. *Language Documentation and Description*, vol. 10. London: School of Oriental and Asian Studies.
Svantesson, Jan-Olof and Arthur Holmer 2014. 'Kammu'. In Jenny, Mathias and Paul Sidwell (eds): *The handbook of Austroasiatic languages.* Leiden: Brill, 955–1002.
Svantesson, Jan-Olof and David House 2006. 'Tone production, tone perception and Kammu tonogenesis'. *Phonology* 23, 309–333.
Svantesson, Jan-Olof and Anastasia Karlsson 2004. 'Minor syllable tones in Kammu'. In Bel, Bernard and Isabelle Marlien (eds): *Proceedings, International Symposium on Tonal Aspects of Languages (TAL2004).* Beijing: Chinese Academy of Social Sciences, 177–180.
Svantesson, Jan-Olof, Kàm Ràw (Damrong Tayanin), Kristina Lindell, and Håkan Lundström 2014. *Dictionary of Kammu Yùan language and culture.* Copenhagen: NIAS Press.
Tan, Shzr Ee 2012. *Beyond 'innocence': Amis aboriginal song in Taiwan as an ecosystem.* Farnham: Ashgate.
Tanese-Ito, Yoko 1988. 'The relationship between speech-tones and vocal melody in Thai court song'. *Musica Asiatica* 5, 109–139.
Tayanin, Damrong (Kam Raw) 1994. *Being Kammu: My village, my life.* Ithaca, NY: Cornell University.
—— 2006. *Where do our souls go after death? Kammu traditions, rituals and ceremonies.* [Printed in Thailand].
Tayanin, Damrong (Kam Raw) and Kristina Lindell 2012. *Hunting and fishing in a Kammu village: Revisiting a classic study in Southeast Asian ethnography.* Copenhagen: NIAS Press. [Originally published in 1991.]
Tenenbaum, Joan M. 2006. *Dena'ina sukdu'a: Traditional stories of the Tanaina Athabascans.* Fairbanks, AK: Alaska Native Language Center, University of Alaska.

Tuohy, Sue 2001. 'The sonic dimensions of nationalism in modern China: Musical representation and transformation'. *Ethnomusicology* 45: 1, 107–131.
Turino, Thomas 2003. 'Nationalism and Latin American music: Selected case studies and theoretical considerations'. *Latin American Music Review* 24: 2, 169–209.
—— 2008. *Music as social life: The politics of participation*. Chicago: The University of Chicago Press.
Turpin, Myfany 2011. 'Song-poetry of Central Australia: Sustaining traditions'. *Language Documentation and Description* 10, 15–36.
Tuttle, Siri G. 1998. 'Metrical and tonal structure in Tanana Athabaskan'. PhD diss., University of Washington.
—— 2009. *Benhti Kokht'ana Kenaga', Lower Tanana pocket dictionary*. Fairbanks: Alaska Native Language Center.
—— 2011. 'Language and music in the songs of Minto, Alaska'. *Language documentation and description* 10, 82–112.
—— 2019. 'Vowels and vocables in Lower Tanana Athabascan.' *Journal of the Phonetic Society of Japan* 22: 3, 50–60.
Wichmann, Elizabeth 1991. *Listening to theatre: The aural dimension of the Beijing Opera*. Honolulu, HI: University of Hawai'i Press.
Yung, Bell 1989. *Cantonese Opera: Performance as a creative process*. Cambridge: Cambridge University Press.
Zon, Bennett 2007. *Representing non-Western music in nineteenth-century Britain*. Rochester, NY: University of Rochester Press.

Internet references (accessed 2011–19)

Alaska Native Language Center. www.uaf.edu/anlc/
Audacity. www.audacityteam.org/
ELAN. https://tla.mpi.nl/tools/tla-tools/elan/
Kyoko Gushiken. www.youtube.com/watch?v=nXAxtptLKTI
Melodyne. www.celemony.com/en/start
MusiCoLinguistics. www.musicolinguistics.de/
Numbered musical notation. https://en.wikipedia.org/wiki/Numberedmusicalnotation
Onna Nabii produced by Onna Village Chamber of Commerce and Industry. www.youtube.com/watch?v=169oH6LBLDE
Praat: doing phonetics by computer; Boersma, Paul and David Weenink. www.praat.org/
Praat manual (for musicologists); van der Meer, Wim. https://culturalmusicology.org/uncategorized/praat-manual-for-musicologists/
Rwaai. http://projekt.ht.lu.se/rwaai
ScoreCloud. https://scorecloud.com/
Seediq Bale song. www.youtube.com/watch?v=OH0BZU4v8S0
Sibelius. www.avid.com/sibelius

Sixtieth Karuta Meijin (Master) Match 2014. Kyogi-Karuta: www.karuta.or.jp/
The Music Lab at Harvard University. www.themusiclab.org/
Walshaw, Christopher 2011. *The abc music standard 2.1*. http://abcnotation.com/
—— 2015. *The DRAFT abc music standard 2.2*. http://abcnotation.com/wiki/abc:standard:v2.2

Index

When names and concepts that occur in the running text also appear in footnotes, references to the latter have been omitted. The names of this book's authors have not been indexed, nor have – with some exceptions – names and concepts that occur in tables and example texts. Page numbers in italics refer to illustrations.

Àbáw-gàw 204, 207n2
aboriginal music (Australia) 7, 283
  see also Dyirbal
Addo, Akosua 287
Ahtna (language) 130
Akha (language) 1, 13, 15–16, 204–225, 249–251, 256, 258–259, 261, 266, 269, 286
Alamblak (Papua New Guinea) 285
Alexander, Evelyn 125n3, 161, 182
Amis (Ami, Taiwan) 15, 256
amplitude 18, 233–234, 242–246, 253
Amy de la Bretèque, Estelle 7n18
anapest 201
Apache (language) 125
appoggiatura 239
Asai, Susuma 15
Asano, Rie 288
Atayal (language) 189, 195
Athabascan (language family) 1, 12–13, 15–16, 123–188, 249–252, 256, 258–259, 261, 263–264, 266–267, 272–273, 276, 284
Audacity (software) 207, 298–299
Austroasiatic (language family) 1, 12, 23, 254n5

Austronesian (language family) 1, 189, 280
Banti, Giorgio 5, 252n4, 264n28
Barnhardt, Carol 126n8
Barwick, Linda 7, 251n2, 283, 284n72
Baudhuin, R. F. 15n38
Beijing opera 261, 264
Bengtsson, Ingmar 18n42
Bettis, Julius 147–152
Bialystok, Ellen 127
bilingualism 126–127
binary form 136, 138–139, 143, 165–166, 187, 235, 244, 256, 258, 260, 282
Birch, Bruce 7n19
Blacking, John 276
Boersma, Paul 290
boundary tone 25, 31–35, 37–39, 42, 44, 46–48, 53, 115, 254, 258
Brabec de Mori, Bernd 2n2, 279n56
Bracknell, Clint 7n19
Brown, Steven 2n3, 254, 279, 280n59, 280n61–63, 281, 282n67
building block 138, 143, 149, 155, 157, 159, 165–166
Bunun (language) 15

Burenhult, Niclas 1n1, 7n18, 15, 251n3

call-and-response 39–42, 256–257
canonic imitation (Seediq vocal genre) 13, 189–203, 249, 286n83
cantometrics 280
Cantonese opera 261, 266, 270
Cantonese pop songs 270
CantoScore 280, 283
Carlo, Norman 16, 125n3, 172–174, *175*, 176–184
cèem ə̀əy (melody) 79
Chafe, Wallace 35n19
Charlie, Chief 142, 157n30, 177
Charlie, Dolo 142
Charlie, Geraldine 125n3, *126*, 134, 144, 147, 150, 152, 154, 161, 165, 167–168, 171, 187
Charlie, Moses 123, 142, 157n30, 177
Charlie, Neal 124, 125n3, *126*, 134–137, 139, 144, 152, 154, 161, 165, 171, 173n41
Charlie, Robert 123–124, 137, 177–178
Charlie, Susie 125n3, 134n19
ch'edzes ch'elik ('dance songs', Athabascan vocal genre) 130, 132–133, 148, 160–188, 252, 261, 272, 276
Cheng, Shui-Cheng 15n39
Chickalusion, Chief Simeon 158n31
children's game songs 5, 287–288
Chow, Ivan 254
Chungyuan (village) 189
Ci'uli (language) 189
communicative competence 287
comparative musicology 278–281
comparative studies 281–283
composition 2–3, 9
  in Athabascan music 13, 123, 125, 130, 134, 140, 144, 157, 163, 167–168, 171–174, 176–177, 179–188, 228, 251, 264
Compton, Carol J. 260n14

continuum from speech to song 3, 5–6, 28–29, 272–273, 280–281, 289
contraction (of line) 84, 86, 95, 120, 216, 224, 236, 258, 261, 267, 278, 282
Coray, Craig 132n17, 158n31
Coulter, Neil R. 285
Cox, Gordon 287n89
creakiness 66–67, 71, 208
Cross, Ian 289
cross-cultural variation 278–282
Crupi, Vanna Viola 271n43
cultural nationalism 286
Cwàa (Kammu dialect) 79
cymbals 97, 99

dancing 73, 77–79, 123, 129–130, 132–133, 140, 160–161, 164–165, 167, 171, 173–176, 178, 180, 182, 186, 272, 282–285
Darwin, Charles 278
Dell, François 266, 270
Dene (Athabascan) 125n4
deskilling 287–288
dirge 73
Dixon, Robert M. W. 264n28
downstep 244
dratakh ch'elik ('mourning songs', Athabascan vocal genre) 130–134, 140–160, 170–173, 183, 186, 252, 261, 272, 276
drumming 129–130, 132, 143, 160–162, 165, 173, 261
duration
  of morae 232
  of phrases 233–235, 242–244
  of syllables 26, 46, 56, 120–121, 216, 262
  of tone 55–56, 255–256, 273
  of vowels 120–121, 202, 266, 273
  see also schwa
Dyirbal (Australia) 264

Index

education *see* learning
ELAN (software) 17, 19, 295–297
Emeneau, Murray B. 260
endangerment 1, 4, 125, 128, 170, 174, 227, 283–288
Engelhardt, Jeffers 7n18
Engles, David 125n3
Engstrand, Lennart 8n21
Evans, Nicholas 7n19
evolution 2, 273, 278–283
Évrard, Olivier 20n1
Ewald, Otto 254n5
ex tempore 4, 186, 203

Fabb, Nigel 9, 255n9, 260n13
Fairbanks, Alaska 123, 130, 161–162, 174
Fall, James A. 12n30, 15n37, 158n31
farming year 35–36, 43n22, 276
Fast, Phyllis 128n11
Feld, Steven 4, 5n13–14, 7, 261n19, 288
filler syllable 84, 210, 224, 255, 266–267
  see also padding syllable
final formula 10, 53, 59, 64, 77, 84–85, 104, 120–121, 162, 219, 225, 249, 252, 262–263, 267, 272, 282
  see also performance template
Finnegan, Ruth 3, 9
folk narrative 31, 34n18, 135, 165
form 10–11, 55, 143, 180, 182–183, 185, 245, 256–258, 282
  strophic 62, 67, 71, 75, 82, 95, 132, 159–160, 165–166, 187, 256, 272
  syllabic 53, 55–56, 62, 104, 117, 179, 256
  see also performance template
Fox, Aaron A. 5, 288
Frank, Carlos 173n41
Frisbie, Charlotte J. 158–159
fundamental frequency (F0) 18, 26, 66, 100, 239, 290
  see also pitch
Fürniss, Susanne 276

Giannattasio, Francesco 5, 252n4, 264n28
Gillan, Matt 228n3
glottal constriction 143
glottal pulse 131, 144, 148–149, 152
glottal stop 24, 154, 165
Gluban (Chinliu, village) 191, *199*
gong 97, 99
Grant, Catherine 285, 286n84
Gushiken, Kyoko 237n8, 238
Gussenhoven, Carlos 44n25
Gwich'in (language) 125–126, 128–129, 131

haiku (Japanese poem) 9n27
Hani (nationality) 204, 206
Hayton, Allan 125n3, 134n19
Herzog, George 137
Hinton, Leanne 170n40, 174
Hmong (Vietnam) 285
Honigmann, John J. 129n13
House, David 8n21, 24n7, 27n12, 31n15, 34n18, 94n35
hrlìi (Kammu vocal genre) 55–63, 71, 100, 104, 121, 252, 266n30, 273
hrwə̀ (Kammu vocal genre) 64–68
Hsu, Tsang-Houei 15n39
húuwə̀ (Kammu vocal genre) 68–72, 121

iambs 256, 266, 273
  Akha 205, 221–222, 224
  Kammu 75, 78, 80, 82, 84, 86–87, 91, 95–96
  Seediq 200, 203
Ikuta, Hiroko 284
improvisation 2, 4, 10, 13, 120, 185–186, 189, 202
Ingram, Catherine 285, 286n81
initial formula 10, 50, 54, 56, 59–60, 64, 71, 74, 77, 84–85, 93, 96, 104, 106, 117–118, 120–121, 224–225, 262–263, 267, 272–273, 282
  see also performance template

intonation (in speech) 11, 14, 250, 252–254, 258, 270, 272–273
   Athabascan 131, 133, 136, 139, 186
   Kammu 25, 27–28, 47, 55, 62, 98, 110, 114–115, 120–121
   Ryukyuan/Japanese 228, 232, 235, 244–247
   Seediq 192, 201–202
intra-cultural variation 280
Iñupiaq (language) 284
Ishikawa Takuboku 229
isorhythm 138–139, 145, 149, 151, 155, 158–160, 165–166, 168, 179, 187, 258

Jahai (Malaysia) 254n5
Jakobson, Roman 9
Japanese (language) 226–236, 244–247, 250, 252–253, 259, 261
Japonic (language family) 1
Jetté, Jules 134n19
Jimmie, Peter 161
John, Peter 137–138
Johnston, Thomas F. 128n12, 132n17, 140n26, 161n33
Jones, Eliza 125n3, 128n12, 134n19
Jordania, Joseph 281, 282n67

Kaluli (Papua New Guinea) 4
Kam (Dongzu, China) 285–286
kàm à-thí-tháan (prayer, Kammu vocal genre) 43–48, 98, 100
Kàm Mán 21
Kàm Ràw (Damrong Tayanin) 8, 16, 20, *21*, 22n3, 23n6, 29, 35–36, 39–40, 43n22, 45, 47, 51, 55n26, 57, 59, 65, 68, 73–74, 78–80, 86–87, 88n33, 89, 97, 99, 100–102, 106, 111, 260n17, 276n45, 277n49, 283n71
Kamerling, Leonard 173n41
Kammu (language) 1, 3, 10, 12–14, 16, 20–122, 248–253, 256, 258–277, 283, 286

Kari, James 12n30, 15n37, 134n19, 148n27, 158n31
karuta (game) 226, 229–230
Kawakami, Shin 231n6
khwtitl ch'elik ('potlatch songs', Athabascan vocal genre) 130, 140
Kirby, James 270–271
Kneutgen, Johannes 278
Koch, Grace 264n28
Koyukon (language) 125–126, 130–131, 172–174
Kulturkreis school 278
Kwὲεn (Kammu dialect) 38, 68, 84
kymograph 18

Ladd, Robert 270–271
lam (Laos) 260
Lao (language) 97
Lawson, Francesca 9
learning 20–22, 55, 124–131, 134, 141, 161, 170–174, 176, 179–180, 204, 287–289
Leer, Jeff 164n37
lexical tones 1, 10–12, 252–254, 267, 269–271
   Akha 206, 210, 212–213, 221–222, 225
   Athabascan 131–133, 144
   Kammu 23, 25–26, 32–33, 39, 42, 44, 48–51, 53–63, 65–67, 71, 74–86, 89–96, 100–118, 121
   see also performance template; pitch
Lindell, Kristina 8, 23n6, 36n20, 39n21, 43n22, 43n24
Lintinger, Brenda W. 7n18
List, George 5, 7, 17n40, 271, 273
litany 42, 48, 53, 75, 82, 117, 202, 224, 256, 263
Little Peter 124, 142
Loh, I-to 189n1, 195n3–4, 256, 257n11, 264n27
Lomax, Alan, 255, 256n10, 263, 280
lɔɔŋ (narrative, Kammu vocal genre) 31–42, 50, 100
Lord, Albert 3

Index

Lovick, Olga 131n16
Lü (language) 97
Lubi Mahung 191
lullaby 68, 277–278, 282–283

Madison, Curt 173n41
Mah Meri (Malaysia), 254n5
Maori (New Zeeland) 5
Marett, Allan 7n18–19, 283, 284n72
Marsh, Kathryn 287
Mehr, Samuel A. 282n69, 283n70
melodic contour 27, 89–90,
    110–111, 115, 120–121, 132,
    138, 162, 254
    see also phrase, musical
melodic formula 53, 68, 84, 112,
    206, 267, 278
melodic motif 50, 64, 133, 165, 182,
    186
melodic movement 11, 34, 38, 99,
    112, 121, 182, 250, 252–253,
    269, 271–272
melodic pattern 246, 253, 282
melody 3, 5–6, 10, 28, 249, 252–254,
    261, 270–273, 277–278, 283
    Akha 213, 218, 226
    Athabascan 133, 138, 140, 144,
        149, 157, 164, 176–177
    Kammu 47, 49, 69, 73, 77, 79, 84,
        95, 113–116, 118, 120
    Ryukyuan/Japanese 228, 242, 247
    Seediq 191
    see also performance template
melody centration 11, 54, 82, 85, 94,
    96, 112, 118–121, 225, 253,
    269, 282
Melodyne (software) 16, 19, 34–35,
    60, 64, 136, 206–216,
    218–223, 228, 231–233,
    237–238, 240–241, 245, 271,
    290, 294–295, 299
Merriam, Alan P. 279
Merritt, Emily 280n61–62, 281n64
metre 9, 53, 64, 120–121, 133,
    139, 192, 200–203,
    230–231, 235, 246, 256,
    260–262, 266, 273
Microsoft Excel (software) 27

Microsoft PowerPoint (software) 27
Microsoft Word (software) 85
Miller, Terry E. 260n14
Minks, Amanda 287
Minto (village) 16, 123, 126,
    129–142, 144, 147–148, 150,
    152, 153, 157, 160–162, 165,
    167–168, 170–174, 182–183,
    185, 252, 284
Minto Dance and Song Group 129,
    160–161, 174, 182, 284
Minto-Nenana (Tanana dialect)
    130–134, 141
Mischler, Craig 129n13
Miskitu (Nicaragua) 287
Mithen, Steven 2n3
Mithun, Marianne 126n7
Moberg, Carl-Allan 278
Mon-Khmer (language group) 23–24
mono-melodic principle 4, 8,
    277–278
mora 228–242, 244–247
mora-timing 234, 247
Morey, Stephen 271n43
Mulder, Jean 264n25
musicolinguistics 7, 288
Musilanguage 281

narratives 31–46
    antithesis 100, 260, 287
    thematic episode 35–38, 100–101,
        110, 115, 254
    thematics 23, 31
    topic 35–37
    see also folk narratives
nasal, moraic 232, 237–239, 241,
    244–245
Navajo (language) 125, 158
Nelson, Richard K. 135n20, 135n22
Nenana (village) 147, 150, 161–163
Nettl, Bruno 149n29, 183n43
Nguyen Van Huyen 260
number notation 17, 50, 97,
    101–102, 106, 110–111, 297

Ó Briain, Lonán 285
octave doubling 182
Oesch, Hans 263–264, 265n29

Ogawa, Takuji 15
O'Keeffe, Isabel 7n19, 264n25
Okinawa 1, 227, 237
Olson, Gordon 161
Onna (village) 227
Onna Nabii 226, 237–240
ɔ̀ɔc ('wassail', Kammu vocal genre) 49–54, 254
Ostler, Nicolas 7n18

Pâbûjî, Epic of 266
padding syllable 86, 266–267
  see also filler syllable
parallelism 6, 29, 46, 50, 55, 88, 100, 121, 133, 157, 159, 192, 200, 202, 256, 260
parlando rubato 255
Paskvan, Susan 125n3
Patel, Aniruddh 2n4, 254, 288
Pearce, Tony Scott 12n30, 15n37, 132n17, 161–162, 165, 173n41
Peking drumsong 261
performance template 9–10, 12, 13, 17, 23, 31, 84, 112, 120–121, 125, 183–186, 191, 225, 232, 248–289
  Akha 224–245
  Athabascan 159–160, 187–188
  Kammu 41–42, 48, 53–54, 62–63, 67, 71–72, 75–76, 82–83, 95–96, 117–118
  parameters of 10, 27, 249–286
  Ryukyuan/Japanese 235–236, 244
  Seediq 202–203
Pete, Shem 158n31
Peter, Hishinlai' 134n19
phrase 17, 64, 100, 148, 228
  boundary 32, 39, 115, 131, 254
    see also boundary tone
  ending of 89, 105, 111, 162, 164, 213
  linguistic 11, 131, 168, 192, 206
  musical 11, 58, 85, 87, 89–95, 100, 105, 111, 116, 168, 178–179, 206, 237, 239, 247, 258, 263

pairing of 50, 100, 105, 110, 121, 207–208, 215, 258–259
prolongation of 80, 120, 155
prosodic 32–33, 39, 44, 47–48, 100, 105, 110, 121, 131, 206, 258, 263
repetition of 55, 191–192, 195, 256
  see also phrasing
phrasing 5, 27, 40, 46, 110, 113–117, 121, 256, 258–262, 270, 272–273, 278
  musical 162, 273
  prosodic 25, 43–44
  prosodic and musical combined 97, 101–102, 105–106, 111, 115, 121, 210, 215, 228–235, 242–243, 245, 256, 258, 263, 272–273
  see also intonation; performance template; phrase
Pian, Rulan Chao 277n52
pitch 46, 60, 131–132, 134, 136–138, 149, 162, 164, 230, 232, 258, 262–263, 266, 269–273, 279, 289–290
  accent 228, 247
  and final syllable 44, 192
  area 39, 41, 93, 95, 224
  declination of 65–66, 182, 247
  fixed 29, 34, 40, 50, 120, 252, 273
  level 40, 56, 64, 74, 76, 96, 121, 224, 269
  region 26, 28, 63, 71
  register 61, 245, 247, 253
  relative to tone 58, 69, 77, 80, 84, 89–93, 100–101, 104–106, 112, 116–117, 120–121, 210–217, 219, 221, 253–254, 269–271
  see also fundamental frequency (F0); lexical tones; syllables: tonal movement within

poetry 4–5, 9, 84, 100, 149, 152, 157, 172, 229, 260, 264, 266
　form 58, 100, 138, 143, 155, 159, 256
　line 56, 58, 120, 152, 192, 228–242, 245, 260, 263
　metre 120, 200, 261–262, 266
　syllable-counting 10, 14, 49–50, 58, 100, 102, 228
　techniques 29, 272
　word-pairs 73, 258, 260
　see also parallelism; phrasing
Pooley, Thomas M. 271n43
population genetics 279–280
Poser, William J. 245
potlatch 123, 130, 132, 140–142, 160–161, 163, 167, 171–174, 185, 252, 276, 284
pow-wow 161, 284
Praat (software) 17, 19, 27, 228, 271, 290–294, 297
priest (Akha) 204, 207n2, 221
prolongation
　of lines 64, 73, 80, 84, 86–87, 95, 105, 117, 120, 149, 155, 157, 183, 200, 258–261, 263, 278, 282
　of syllables 26–27, 56, 64, 67, 69–71, 75, 87, 93, 95–96, 105, 117, 121, 148–149, 243, 258, 282
Proschan, Frank 79n30
Proto, Teresa 271
Proto-Southwestern Tai (language) 97
Pulu, Tupou 128n12
Puyuma (language) 15, 256

recontextualization 285–288
re-creation 2, 4, 9–10, 159, 248, 251, 262, 267, 270, 287–288
reduplication 23, 26–29, 34, 46, 64–71, 75, 77–78, 82, 87, 93, 96, 105, 117–118, 121, 264–266, 273

repetition 6, 55–56, 88, 100, 136, 148–149, 155, 159–160, 164, 182–183, 191–192, 200, 202, 207, 256, 259, 278
　see also tone repetition
revitalization 1, 129, 160, 170, 174, 284, 286
rhyme 5, 29, 43, 46, 48–50, 53, 55, 73, 88, 121, 192, 200, 202, 256
　of a syllable 26–27
rhyme-pair 88, 210, 221, 224–225, 258, 266
rhythm 3, 5, 10, 228, 232, 234, 237, 244–247, 249–250, 252–256, 263, 272–273, 278–279, 282–283, 289
　Akha 204, 225
　Athabascan 130–131, 133–134, 136, 138, 149, 153, 155, 157, 162, 164, 168, 172, 182
　Kammu 31, 34, 40–41, 44, 47, 49–50, 55, 58, 64, 77, 120–121
　Seediq 192, 195, 200–202
　see also form, isorhythmic; performance template
rhythm pair 205, 221–225
Rmcùal (village) 14, 20, 29, 49, 51, 55, 77
Rɔ̀ɔk (Kammu dialect area) 39–40
Rooth, Anna Birgitta 13n31, 15, 135n20, 137n25, 161–162
Russell, Garry 173n41
ryūka (Ryukyuan poem) 13–14, 226–228, 237–247, 253
Ryukyu Islands 13–14, 226–247
Ryukyuan (language) 1, 16, 226–247, 250, 253, 259
Rzeszutek, Tom 280n59, 280n61–62, 281n64

Saensuk (village) 204–207, *206*, 209
sanshin (lute) 226, 228
Sanskrit 97
Savage, Patrick E. 279, 280n59, 280n61–63, 281n64–65

Schellenberg, Murray 2n5, 18n41, 271n43
Schimmelpenninck, Antoinet 259, 260n12, 261n18, 267, 277
Schippers, Huib 285n78, 286
Schöpf, Jürgen 7n18, 271n43
schwa (epenthetic vowel) 24, 42–43, 48, 50, 54, 56, 63, 67, 71, 75, 78, 80, 82, 96, 118, 120, 164, 166, 191–192, 200, 202, 265–266, 273
   duration 50, 54, 63, 67, 71, 75, 118, 120–121, 202, 273
   long 80, 82, 96, 266
   reduplicated 78, 266
ScoreCloud (software) 295, 298–299
seasonal cycle 36, 77, 123, 276
   see also farming year
Seediq (language) 1, 13, 15–16, 189–203, 249–250, 253, 256, 258–260, 264, 266, 280, 286
Seediq Bale 190, 286n83
Seeger, Anthony 6–7
Seeger, Charles 17n40, 18
Séɛn (shaman) 21
senh ch'elik ('medicine songs', Athabascan vocal genre) 137–138, 186, 272
sequence
   linguistic 113–115, 148, 152–153, 164, 166, 187, 191, 244
   musical 148, 162, 165–166, 168, 271
Sét Mán 39–40
shaman 256–257
   Akha 13, 204–225, 261–262, 266, 269
   Athabascan 137
   Kammu 21–22, 43, 45, 46, 97–99, 110
Shandong drumsong 261
shan'ge (China) 259, 267, 277
Shuri (Ryukyuan dialect) 245–246
Sibelius (software) 295, 298
Silas, Bergman 125n3, *126*, 134, 161
Silas, Sarah, 125n3, *126*, 134, 161

Singh, Manvir 282n69, 283n70
Sino-Tibetan (language family) 1, 206
Sjhá-gàw 204, 207, 209
Skype (software) 10
Sleeper, Morgan 5n14, 7, 8n20, 284n73, 288, 290n1, 297
Slobodin, Richard 125n5
Smith, John D. 266
Solomon, Madeline 128n12
Somswàt Búnkɔ́ət 38
song-leading 129, 140, 161, 171–173
song-making 13, 16, 129, 140, 161, 167, 171, 173–174, 177, 183
song-word 49, 53–54, 82, 86–87, 96, 120, 179, 188, 264, 273, 282
soundwave 233–234, 242, 290
speed doubling 162
spells (*krùu*, Kammu vocal genre) 22n3, 43, 45–47, 97–118, 252, 254, 263
spirits 21–2, 31, 39, 43, 46, 49, 73, 97–110, 207, 210, 218, 223
Squliq (language) 189
staging 285
stanzas 55–56, 58, 60, 63, 68, 73, 85–89, 95–96, 121, 133, 138, 143–144, 149, 157, 160, 165, 168, 192, 200, 202–203, 256–258, 260, 263, 267
Stevens, Robin 287n89
Stobart, Henry 276
Stone, Achara J. 278n53
story songs (Athabascan vocal genre) 135
stress 24, 56, 131, 133, 143, 145, 155, 162, 164, 191, 195, 200, 205, 221, 231, 234, 252, 266
stress-timing 234
sustainability 1, 286
Suyá (Brazil) 6
Swahn, Jan-Öjvind 8n21
syllabification 58

Index

syllables 34, 57–58, 111, 118, 131, 139, 151–152, 157, 195, 202, 228, 258, 260–263, 265, 271
  and rhythmic pulse 138–140, 150, 159, 164, 166, 179, 187
  base syllable 26, 69–70, 74, 76
  coda of 26, 92
  elongation 148, 151, 160, 164, 166, 179, 187
  final 44, 48, 56, 63, 101, 104, 106, 116–117, 140, 151, 154–155, 164, 202, 224, 263
  heavy 136, 164, 166
  initial 46, 60, 63, 71, 96, 217, 220–221, 236
  light 138, 140, 164
  long 228
  major and minor 24, 56, 120–121
  penultimate 53, 63, 191, 263
  second of iambic unit 80
  tonal movement within 17, 26, 46, 48, 61, 66–67, 69–71, 74, 83, 92, 94, 96, 110, 113, 115, 121, 148
  see also boundary tone; duration; lexical tones; poetry; prolongation, reduplication
syntactic groups 43–44, 48

Tá Khám 40
Tan, Shzr Ee 15n39, 189n1
tân nhạc (Vietnam) 270
Tanacross (village and language) 130, 161–163, 172, 174
Tanana (village and language) 1, 123–126, 129–133, 137–139, 142, 160, 164–166, 170–176
Tanese-Ito, Yoko 271n41
Tashlhiyt Berber (language) 266
Tayanin, Damrong *see* Kàm Ràw
tə̀əm (Kammu vocal genre) 55, 84–96, 98, 100, 121, 256, 258, 260, 267
Tenenbaum, Joan M. 15n37
text-setting 7n18, 270–271

Tgdaya (Seediq dialect) 189–191
Thai (language) 97
Thorsén, Stig-Magnus 18n42
Tiānjīn 9
Tibeto-Burman (language group) 206
Titus, Bertina 125n3
Titus, Charlie 173n41
Titus, Dorothy 125n3, 161, 167
Titus, John 152–155
Toda (India) 260
Toda (Seediq dialect) 189
tonal centre 50, 56, 117, 121, 143, 157, 164–165, 208, 213, 252, 272–273
tone repetition 132–133, 138, 143–146, 149, 151, 155, 157, 160, 162, 165–166, 168–169, 186–188, 263, 273
tone-centred 11, 72, 76, 84–85, 90, 94, 96, 120–121
Tove, Per-Arne 18n42
transcription (musical) 2, 11, 15, 16–19, 23–24, 28, 34, 50, 53, 58, 77, 86–87, 92, 97, 121–122, 125, 134, 154, 161, 191, 228, 250, 271, 280, 282, 290, 297–299
transmission 2, 8–9, 13, 15, 55, 84, 88, 121, 128, 130, 133, 171, 185, 204, 229, 283, 283–288
trnə̀əm (Kammu poem) 55–71, 73–75, 79–95, 98, 121, 256, 260, 270–271, 277
Truku (Taroko, Seediq dialect) 189
Tuohy, Sue 285
Turino, Thomas 286
Turpin, Myfany 7n19

Uma Watan 191
universals 260, 279–283
upstep 32
uuyas ('song', Seediq vocal genre) 192, 195

van der Meer, Wim 292n3
Venetie (village) 125–126, 129

vibrato 27–28, 121
vocables 10, 132–133, 138, 142, 144–149, 151–162, 164, 166–171, 178–183, 186–189, 191–192, 201–202, 258, 263–264, 267, 282
vocal expression 1–5, 7–11, 13–16, 248–252, 254–256, 258, 260, 262–264, 267, 270–273, 276–279, 281–284, 287–289
  Akha 206–207, 225
  Athabascan 125, 128–130, 132–133, 135, 137, 148, 154, 157–159, 170–173, 179, 183, 186–187
  Kammu 23, 27, 29, 31, 44, 55, 65, 73, 84, 97–98, 118–120
  Ryukyuan/Japanese 228–229, 244–246
  Seediq 190–192, 203
vocal genre 11–13, 26–29, 58–59, 118, 121, 132, 135, 138, 159, 186–187, 264, 266–267, 272–277, 281
vocative 44, 46, 48, 100, 262, 266
vowel
  length 26, 56, 264
  onset 27, 74, 76, 92
  quality 152, 156, 160, 191, 265

waka (*tanka*, Japanese poem) 13–14, 226–236, 244–247, 252–253, 261, 273
Walshaw, Christopher 297
Weeninck, David 290
whistling 97
Wichmann, Elizabeth 261, 264n26
Widén, Björn 8n21
Widén, Marie 8n21
word structure 24, 130
  sesquisyllabic 24

yàam ('weeping', Kammu vocal genre) 73–76
Yamada, Akira 229n5
Yao (Thailand) 263–264
Yùan (Kammu dialect) 20, 22–23, 39–41, 57–58, 79, 84–87, 94, 267, 277, 286
Yung, Bell 261, 266, 267n33, 277n52
Yupik (language) 284
yùun tìiŋ ('water-tube dance', Kammu vocal genre) 77–83

Zon, Bennett 19n43

EU authorised representative for GPSR:
Easy Access System Europe, Mustamäe tee 50,
10621 Tallinn, Estonia
gpsr.requests@easproject.com

www.ingramcontent.com/pod-product-compliance
Ingram Content Group UK Ltd.
Pitfield, Milton Keynes, MK11 3LW, UK
UKHW021824140426
5217IPUK00004B/80